In *Elements of Legislation*, Neil Duxbury examines the history of English law through the lens of legal philosophy in an effort to draw out the differences between judge-made and enacted law and to explain what courts do with the laws that legislatures enact. He presents a series of rigorously researched and carefully rehearsed arguments concerning the law-making functions of legislatures and courts, the concepts of legislative supremacy and judicial review, the nature of legislative intent and the core principles of statutory interpretation.

NEIL DUXBURY is Professor of Law at the London School of Economics and Political Science.

D1627850

ELEMENTS OF LEGISLATION

NEIL DUXBURY

London School of Economics and Political Science

CAMBRIDGE UNIVERSITY PRESS
Cambridge, New York, Melbourne, Madrid, Cape Town,
Singapore, São Paulo, Delhi, Mexico City

Cambridge University Press
The Edinburgh Building, Cambridge CB2 8RU, UK

Published in the United States of America by Cambridge University Press, New York

www.cambridge.org
Information on this title: www.cambridge.org/9781107021877

First published 2013

Printed and bound in the United Kingdom by the MPG Books Group

A catalogue record for this publication is available from the British Library

Library of Congress Cataloguing in Publication data
Duxbury, Neil.
Elements of legislation / Neil Duxbury.
p.   cm.
Includes bibliographical references and index.
ISBN 978-1-107-02187-7 (hardback) – ISBN 978-1-107-60608-1 (pbk.)
1. Legislation.   2. Legislation–Great Britain.   I. Title.
K3316.D89 2013
328–dc23
2012023159

ISBN 978-1-107-02187-7 Hardback
ISBN 978-1-107-60608-1 Paperback

For Stella

CONTENTS

vii

PREFACE

There is no shortage of very good studies of statute law and statutory interpretation. These studies fall into two broad types: those which explain the rules, procedures, principles and conventions relating to the enactment, drafting and interpretation of statutes, and those which offer broadly jurisprudential perspectives on, usually, one or the other side of the process: on how legislatures make laws, or on how courts and other decision-making bodies handle the laws that legislatures make. *Elements of Legislation* is a title perhaps best suited to the type of work belonging to the first of these two categories – a treatise on parliamentary procedure, say, or on professional drafting. But while certain treatises belonging to this first category were sometimes close to hand while this book was being written, the book cannot be counted among their number. Rather, it fits squarely within the second category of studies: it sets out a number of arguments concerning what legislatures create and what courts do with those creations.

The account of legislation that I set forth is by no means comprehensive, and I come up with no overarching thesis. My objective in writing the book, rather, has been to explore certain questions about legislation – about the distinction between statute law and case law, about the ideas of parliamentary authority and legislative intent, and about the core principles of statutory interpretation – which I think invite not quite new but certainly significantly revised versions of old answers. My primary interest is in, and my main intended audience is academics and students interested in, English law – albeit English law as part of the law of the United Kingdom. The statute law about which I write is not the product of a single legislature, and while the cases on which I draw for the purpose of developing arguments about legislation are mainly English cases, there are some instances where the arguments depend on case law illustrations from other legal systems. References to 'statutes' are normally to instances of primary legislation; in the sections of the book dealing with statutory interpretation, the word sometimes serves as shorthand for 'statutes and/or statutory provisions'. The term 'parliament' is generally confined to Westminster parliament (none of the arguments in the book specifically concerns the devolved assemblies of Scotland, Wales and Northern Ireland), though 'legislature' is used sometimes to refer to Westminster, sometimes to refer to other specific legislative assemblies and sometimes – most often – to refer to legislative assemblies in general. 'Statutory interpretation' and 'statutory construction' are used interchangeably.

I have found it useful to draw some specific comparisons with legislative practices and conventions in other jurisdictions, and sometimes I engage with theoretical literature concerned either with other legal systems (especially the United States) or with no legal system in particular. The book does not purport to speak to the constitutional and legislative arrangements of other jurisdictions, though it may be that some of the arguments it presents will resonate with common lawyers generally. In Part III, statutory interpretation is presented as an exclusively judicial activity; since courts in the United Kingdom are not accustomed to deferring to administrative agencies on matters of statutory interpretation, questions about the correct interpretive role of agencies, and the balance of interpretive power as between expert agencies and generalist courts, receive no attention.

Early drafts of Chapters 1 and 2 of the book were presented at the University of Virginia School of Law in April 2011, and a late draft of Chapter 1 was presented to the Law Department at the London School of Economics in February 2012. I am grateful to colleagues who provided valuable comments on these occasions, to Grégoire Webber for his detailed observations on the entire manuscript, to Jacco Bomhoff, Conor Gearty, Guy Holborn, Martin Loughlin, Jo Murkens, Thomas Poole, Mike Redmayne and Ted White for their criticisms of particular chapters, and to Richard Ekins for sharing with me his doctoral thesis on legislative intent (the book version of which is forthcoming with Oxford University Press). There is one particular debt I wish to highlight. I appreciate, given that I am only an occasional visitor at Virginia, that the law library staff there would be perfectly within their rights to tell me, on the occasions when I turn up at their desks, that all research-related enquiries ought to be addressed elsewhere. But this has never been their attitude, and in relation to this project there are two members of staff in the UVA law library, Kent Olson and Bryan Kasik, who have been immensely helpful in tracking down and supplying all manner of relevant materials. That they need not have done this did not escape me. That they still took the trouble impressed me no end.

This book examines the idea of legislation. It builds on, and sometimes seeks to correct, certain assumptions that are made about the idea, and in the process of doing so draws on history, on philosophy and – for the purpose of supporting particular arguments – on illustrations from many different areas of the law. The upshot of this is a book which one might think should have the word 'disparate' at the beginning of its title. But variety lies in the sources used and the directions taken, not in the elements of legislation. The book in fact attends to those elements in a fairly straightforward way. Part I (Chapters 1 and 2) begins with an explanation of what legislation is, and how enacted law and judge-made law might be distinguished. To legislate is to make law. 'Legislation' is, nevertheless, a term commonly reserved for enacted law: since, in English law, judicial law making is meant to be confined to the development of the common law – since it is not within the remit of the courts to invent new legal rules – it makes sense not to speak, and indeed English lawyers commonly do not speak, of judge-made law as legislation other than when describing how a court has overextended its law-making function (such as when the judicial construction of a statute yields a meaning which cannot be reconciled with either the enacted text or with the known or reasonably hypothesized intentions of the legislature).

The distinction between enacted and judge-made law has not always been clear, and one of the objectives of the first two chapters is to show how the distinction emerged. That parliament and the courts acquired their own legal functions needs no spelling out. But not all contemporary commentators are agreed as to whether, under the common law, the courts have the power to invalidate statutes which are inconsistent with fundamental constitutional principles. That there should be uncertainty on this matter is not surprising. Anyone with so much as a passing familiarity with the history of the common law knows that English judges have, from time to time, declared themselves capable of treating as void statutes which are contrary to reason. Is this not tantamount to judges claiming

for themselves a common-law capacity to review the legality of what parliament enacts? Not quite. The argument with which Chapter 2 concludes
is that the distinction between declaring a statute void and declaring a
statute invalid is slight but real. One cannot convincingly extrapolate
from English legal history the conclusion that judges are able to strike
down acts of parliament as unconstitutional. What the history reveals is
that judges will sometimes – exceptionally – avoid giving effect to statutory provisions, but that in such instances they still stop short of challenging the authority of parliament.

In Part II (Chapters 3 and 4), the question of the proper scope of judicial review takes on a different form. Legal philosophers, indeed academic
lawyers generally, can often seem less inspired by statute law than they are
by case law. However, reflection on the process by which statutes are typically enacted raises an intriguing jurisprudential question: given that legislative assemblies are, by virtue of their size and diversity, generally better
equipped than are courts to make well-informed, carefully deliberated,
democratically representative decisions, why should judicial review of the
legality of statutes ever be considered permissible? The question is worth
posing in the abstract if only because the case against judicial review
raises a conundrum: if it is argued that courts ought not to be permitted
to review the legality of statutes, and if it is also conceded that the legality of statutes will sometimes need to be reviewed, how – if not by the
courts – is the process of review to be carried out?

Jurisdictions which endorse the principle of legislative supremacy tend
to rely on executive bodies to advise the legislature on the legality of statutes; in some systems, these bodies exercise reviewing functions similar to those of a constitutional court. In the United Kingdom, legislators
certainly take advice on legislative proposals from executive and other
committees, and the courts themselves have the power to declare primary legislation incompatible with human rights norms. But – this is the
argument with which Chapter 3 closes – those who detect a drift towards
'strong' judicial review in the United Kingdom are probably misreading
the signs. It may well be, as judges occasionally speculate, that if parliament were to enact a statute contrary to fundamental democratic commitments then the appropriate judicial reaction would be to declare that
statute inapplicable according to principles of 'higher law'. However, it
seems rash to infer from such speculation that legislatively unauthorized
strong judicial review is a genuine possibility. The principle of parliamentary supremacy remains (which is not to assert that it has to remain) firmly
rooted, and the question why courts might ever be allowed to review the

legality of statutes, although interesting in the abstract, does not resonate in the United Kingdom quite as it does in those jurisdictions where this form of judicial review is part of the constitutional landscape.

Chapter 4 defends the idea of legislative intent. The case against the idea is well known. Intentions attributed to a legislature cannot *be* the intentions of that legislature, for legislatures cannot form intentions in the way that individual agents do. Legislative intentions are not the intentions of the legislature, but of legislators. But which legislators? The text of a statute as enacted might have been amended so that it can no longer be said to reflect the wishes of any particular sponsor or faction. Among the majority who eventually voted in favour of enacting that text there may be members who did not really support it, or whose votes were susceptible to cycling. Not only is it the case that legislators, not legislatures, have intentions, so the argument goes, but all sorts of hazards attach to treating particular legislators' intentions as the intention of the legislature.

It is a mistake, however, to dismiss as unintelligible the notion of agency distinctive to legislatures. A legislature, by legislating, demonstrates the simple general intention to change the law. But a legislature must also be taken to intend to change the law in the particular ways that it does, because the intentions of its members interconnect to form specific shared plans which comply with distinct decision procedures in the form of rules on (among other things) the presentation, scrutiny and amendment of bills. It is by virtue of the operation of these decision procedures that specific law-making proposals can become *acts* of the legislature itself.

It is tempting to claim that statutory interpretation depends upon the attribution of intentions to legislatures. But this claim is best avoided. Part III (Chapters 5 and 6) begins with the distinction between intention and meaning. The meaning that the language of a statute might reasonably be said to yield is unlikely simply to mirror the intention of the legislature in enacting the text. What, then, are courts looking to interpret: the meaning of the text, or the legislature's enacting intentions? The significance of legislative intention can be overestimated. When interpreting statutes, English courts are principally concerned not with the intentions of parliament in enacting the text but with the meanings that the text can be said to bear. Furthermore, judges will sometimes resolve statutory ambiguities by relying on interpretive presumptions – for example, according ambiguous criminal provisions meanings which are the least prejudicial to defendants – which are supposed to ensure fair outcomes rather than that statutes are accorded meanings which parliament can be assumed to have intended them to have.

It would be wrong, however, to conclude that legislative intention is irrelevant to statutory interpretation. When judges find the meaning of statutory language to be plain but absurd, or not plain at all, they often adopt interpretive conventions which take account of enacting intentions that are either identifiable or reasonably presumed. Part III examines the three main interpretive conventions: the so-called plain meaning, golden and mischief rules. One has to chart a fairly tortuous path to understand the history of, and explanations for, these conventions. But the exercise yields some relatively straightforward insights. Various advantages attach to plain-meaning interpretations of statutory language. When judges accord statutory language a plain meaning, it is more likely than not that the law as applied is consistent with what was enacted. Lawyers and their clients can be confident that the meaning of statutes is to be taken at face value. Judges themselves, by adhering to plain meaning, limit the possibility of their reading and applying statutes idiosyncratically. There is, however, no sound basis for thinking that plain-meaning interpretations are fundamentally non-creative, or that judges, when they eschew such interpretations, are somehow seeking to break free of statutes. The core message to emerge from Part III is that statutory interpretation has to be understood as a disciplined activity: when judges either cannot (because the language of a statute is ambiguous) or will not (because the language demands an absurd ruling) abide by plain statutory meaning, their interpretive strategy is usually – though, as intimated already, by no means always – to settle on a principle of interpretation which yields not the legal directive they consider desirable but the one which they believe most closely connects the meaning of the statute to legislative intent (which will not always, as is emphasized at the close of the book, equate with the intention of the legislature in enacting the statute which is being interpreted).

This argument – that statutory interpretation is a disciplined activity – should not be read as a denial of the possibility of judge-made law. That possibility is affirmed in Chapter 1. It is, however, to make a specific claim about how judges prefer to make law. In English law, judges recognize that it is their responsibility to develop the common law but also that they ought not to make law from statutes. The history, certainly the modern history, of English case law shows that judicial creativity is constrained creativity; indeed, the primary forms of decisional constraint – principles of precedent-following and statutory interpretation – have been created mainly by, and partly for the benefit of, judges themselves. Properly creative judges do not approach statutes as a Rabelaisian judge might; they do not simply cast statutes to one side and go with their instincts. Rather, they find within statutes meanings which they consider either always to have been there but previously undetected in the language of the text, or deducible from the legislature's known or reasonably hypothesized intentions (including its intentions in legislating to comply with treaty obligations). When judges are creative with statutes they tend, in short, not to be legislating from them but rather interpreting them so as to bring to the fore what the law already, if perhaps not very clearly, provides.

PART I

Enacted and judge-made law

1

Introduction

To legislate on a matter is to take action which is intended to regulate that matter in some way. This is not to claim that regulation is the only intention behind a legislative initiative. The intention to regulate is, nevertheless, the intention that distinguishes an action as legislative. Other reasons for legislating could be to clarify, consolidate, pronounce authoritatively on or preclude the need for further debate – or possibly (in exceptional instances) even to provoke debate – about a matter. But one could seek to clarify, consolidate, pronounce authoritatively on or preclude or provoke further debate without legislating. Essential to the act of legislation is the intention that it has some kind of controlling or enabling effect – that, from the point at which the legislation takes effect, some aspect of the world should (which is not to say that it will) be treated as governed in a particular way.

In everyday speech, we do not assume legislating to be an exclusively juridical activity: the proposition that poets are the world's unacknowledged legislators,[1] for example, expresses the belief that poetry shapes human thought and conduct, while the claim that there is no legislating for a particular human prejudice or disposition is to assert that this prejudice or disposition is beyond influence. By and large, however, legislating is a juridical activity – law making – and it is on juridical legislation that this book concentrates.[2]

1 Statutes and cases

A law book about legislation might reasonably be assumed to be about statute law – as, indeed, this book is. But should it not be about case law

---

[1] See Samuel Johnson, *The History of Rasselas, Prince of Abissinia*, ed. J. P. Hardy (Oxford University Press, 1968 [1729]), 27; P. B. Shelley, *A Defence of Poetry*, ed. M. W. Shelley (Indianapolis: Bobbs-Merrill, 1904 [1821]), 90.
[2] On legislation as a moral as distinct from a juridical phenomenon, see Conrad D. Johnson, *Moral Legislation: A Legal-Political Model for Indirect Consequentialist Reasoning* (Cambridge University Press, 1991), 7–8, 168–87, 204–6.

as well? Judicial rulings, after all, are regulative determinations. If it is accepted that the juridical meaning of 'legislating' is 'law making', must we not also accept that legislating cannot be the exclusive province of legislatures?

One has to be careful with this proposition. If legislation is the act of making law, and if courts develop the common law by extending the realm of precedent, then judges are indeed legislators. Yet there are reasons to balk at this claim. '[T]he production of authority that this or that is the law,' Brian Simpson has remarked, 'is not the same as the identification of acts of legislation … [Judges'] acts create precedents, but creating a precedent is not the same thing as laying down the law … [T]o express an authoritative opinion is not the same thing as to legislate.'[3] Nigel Simmonds argues that judges' 'interstitial modification of rule-formulations' should not be 'treated … as alterations of the law itself', not least because the judicial modification of an earlier court's formulation of a rule applies 'to the very case that gave rise to the modification': if such modifications are 'construed exclusively in terms of a fundamentally legislative model', we are compelled 'to view a good deal of familiar adjudicative activity as a most serious departure from the rule of law in the form of retrospective rule making'.[4] The term 'legislator' can, John Finnis observes, include 'any judiciary that … enjoys a creative role', but one uses the term thus 'at the expense of some significant differentiations'[5] (such as the one remarked on by Simpson).[6] For courts do not introduce or adopt new rules but rather change settled ones – and, in the case of final courts of appeal, are sometimes not actually changing rules but rather are, as it were, putting the law back on track (by establishing that a rule, though it has 'been at all relevant times legally correct and … authentic', has been obscured because of the way it has been applied in the lower courts, so that the final court of appeal is moved to treat the understanding of the rule that has emerged from its application as 'an error awaiting correction').[7]

There is a fairly obvious and dogmatic way of responding to these assessments. Legislation is typically a process of laying down – which

---

[3] A. W. B. Simpson, 'The Common Law and Legal Theory', in *Oxford Essays in Jurisprudence (Second Series)*, ed. A. W. B. Simpson (Oxford: Clarendon Press, 1973), 77–99 at 85–6.

[4] N. E. Simmonds, *Law as a Moral Idea* (Oxford University Press, 2007), 162, 166.

[5] John Finnis, *Natural Law and Natural Rights*, 2nd edn (Oxford University Press, 2011), 286.

[6] Finnis endorses Simpson's statement regarding the difference between judicial creativity and legislating at ibid. 296 n; see also ibid. 472.

[7] John Finnis, 'Adjudication and Legal Change' (1999), in his *Collected Essays. Volume IV: Philosophy of Law* (Oxford University Press, 2011), 397–403 at 402.

includes measures such as repealing and amending – a law. But this does not exhaust the meaning of 'legislation'. Given that any law-making action is legislative action, legislation must include not only the enactment of rules but also the development of the common law by the courts. Judges' modifications of common-law rule formulations do indeed apply to the cases that occasion the modifications, and so to treat those modifications as legislative is to acknowledge a form of legislation, judicial legislation, which will sometimes retrospectively alter the legal status of acts performed before the legislation came to be. But resistance to this conclusion seems to amount to squeamishness: when a court departs from a precedent (as opposed to when it reaffirms a precedent in the light of its misapplication), it may well attach to an action, at the point when it was taken, a liability which at that point cannot be said to have existed – eschewing the notion of judicial legislation has no bearing on this fact. Certainly it would be a mistake not to regard judicial creativity and the enactment of laws by legislatures as radically different forms of law making. But – here we get to the heart of the response – this is not tantamount to claiming that legislative enactment is legislation whereas judicial creativity is not. The correct conclusion would seem to be, rather, that the enactment of primary legislation by a legislature is a core, perhaps *the* core, instance of legislation, whereas judge-made law is legislation in a relatively qualified or peripheral sense. Finnis, though he resists characterizing judge-made law as legislative, supplies the reasoning for those who would do just that: enacted law might be said to be legislation *simpliciter*, whereas judge-made law is legislation *secundum quid*.[8]

Will this response do? It takes little effort to find judicial and juristic pronouncements to the effect that there is really no other line of response that could do – that judicial legislation is a 'simple and certain fact'.[9] While those who claim as much more often than not refer to judge-made law as a 'special' rather than the standard form of legislation,[10] there are certainly some who appear to draw no significant distinction between the two. Those intent on differentiating the legislative functions of legislatures and courts on anything other than institutional and procedural grounds, Jerome Frank memorably argued, betray a childlike inability

---

[8] See Finnis, *Natural Law and Natural Rights*, 9–11, 365–6, 368, 430–1.

[9] Lord Edmund-Davies, 'Judicial Activism' (1975) 26 *CLP* 1, 2.

[10] See Robert Rantoul, Jr, *An Oration Delivered before the Democrats and Antimasons of the County of Plymouth; at Scituate, on the fourth of July, 1836* (Boston: Beals & Greene, 1836), 38.

to confront legal reality.[11] Lord Diplock spoke of the courts having not only the capacity to develop the common law (a capacity which he both acknowledged and lauded),[12] but also the ability to make new law by interpreting statutes. Through statutory interpretation, the court legislates as much as if it were enacting a fresh legal rule: 'whoever has final authority to explain what Parliament meant by the words it used makes law as much as if the explanation it has given were contained in a new Act of Parliament'.[13] Although the cliché that we are all legal realists now yields more than one meaning, perhaps its most obvious meaning is that we have come to accept judicial legislation as a given.

Yet it is noticeable, certainly if one looks to English case law, that most judges would either qualify or reject the proposition that this particular interpretation of realism has become a commonplace. Judges who consider judicial legislation a reality are quite often coy about the fact, as if they would prefer that the observation were not shouted from the rooftops.[14] Just as often the observation comes with the proviso that while judges legislate, they must not assume parliament's role of forging law out of policy;[15] perhaps this explains why, notwithstanding the occasional judicial proclamation as to the reality of judicial legislation, there appears to be no evidence that English judges have ever treated the proposition that they are *legislators* with anything apart from disdain.[16] The reality is that most English judges frown upon the concept of judicial legislation,

---

[11] See Jerome Frank, *Law and the Modern Mind* (New York: Brentano's, 1930). Frank argued that trial courts in particular have considerable law-making – or rather, law-defeating – power because fact-finding at trial stage will sometimes be carried out in such a way as to make a statute inapplicable to the case to be decided: see Jerome Frank, 'Words and Music: Some Remarks on Statutory Interpretation' (1947) 47 *Columbia L. Rev.* 1259, 1278.

[12] *Home Office* v. *Dorset Yacht Co. Ltd* [1970] AC 1004, 1058 (HL).

[13] Kenneth Diplock, *The Courts as Legislators* (Birmingham: Holdsworth Club, 1965), 6. The essay is the text of Diplock's Holdsworth Club address of March 1965.

[14] See, e.g., Edmund-Davies, 'Judicial Activism', 3 (though a judge is inevitably a legislator 'he risks trouble if he goes about it too blatantly'); Lord Radcliffe, *Not in Feather Beds: Some Collected Papers* (London: Hamish Hamilton, 1968), 273 ('Personally, I think that judges will serve the public interest better if they keep quiet about their legislative function').

[15] See, e.g., *R* v. *Clegg* [1995] 1 AC 482 (HL), 500 (*per* Lord Lloyd); *DPP* v. *Lynch* [1975] AC 653 (HL), 695–6 (*per* Lord Simon).

[16] See, e.g., *Majrowski* v. *Guy's and St Thomas' NHS Trust* [2006] UKHL 34 at [74] (Baroness Hale); *Kamara* v. *DPP* [1973] QB 660 (CA), 667 (*per* Lawton LJ); *Mapp* v. *Oram* [1968] 2 WLR 267 (Ch. D), 272–3 (*per* Ungoed-Thomas J); *IRC* v. *Longford* [1928] AC 252 (HL), 259 (*per* Viscount Sumner).

even judicial quasi-legislation, for they equate it not with the development of the common law but with judges giving effect to their own legal preferences by making statutes mean what they want them to mean.[17] In recent times – particularly since courts became obliged to read down statutes so as to try to ensure their compatibility with human rights norms – the senior judiciary seems to have been more adamant than ever before that there is a line between warranted creativity with a statute and judicial legislation, and that this line should not be crossed.[18]

Where does this leave us? Given that to legislate is to make law, it is a mistake, strictly speaking, to reject the claim that judges legislate. But it is still sensible to eschew the term, 'judicial legislation' – to prefer instead something like 'judge-made law' or 'case law' – because legislating is, typically, a formal process of legal enactment. Legislatures enact laws. Courts, whatever their law-making capacities might be, do not. Recall the

---

[17] See, e.g., *R* v. *PD* [2011] EWCA Crim 2082 at [39] (Thomas LJ); *R (on the application of WL (Congo))* v. *Secretary of State for the Home Department* [2011] UKSC 12 at [87] (Lord Dyson); *Wilkinson* v. *Secretary of State for Work and Pensions* [2009] EWCA Civ 1111 at [19] (Patten LJ); *Inco Europe Ltd* v. *First Choice Distribution* [2000] 1 WLR 586 (HL), 592–3 (*per* Lord Nicholls); *Ropaigealach* v. *Barclays Bank* [2000] QB 263 (CA), 282 (*per* Chadwick LJ); *Murphy* v. *Brentwood DC* [1991] 1 AC 398 (HL), 471 (*per* Lord Keith) and 473 (*per* Lord Bridge); *Western Bank Ltd* v. *Schindler* [1977] Ch. 1 (CA), 18 (*per* Scarman LJ); and *Myers* v. *DPP* [1965] AC 1001 (HL), 1032–4 (*per* Lord Godson). For an endorsement of judicial 'quasi-legislation' when the relevant statutory rules only go to legal procedure and do not affect substantive rights (a distinction which, given that determinations as to procedure can impact on decisions about parties' rights, is far more easily asserted than drawn), see *R* v. *Governor of Brockhill Prison* [2001] 2 AC 19 (HL), 48 (*per* Lord Hobhouse).

[18] See, e.g., *Re S* [2002] UKHL 10 at [39]–[40] (Lord Nicholls) ('Interpretation of statutes is a matter for the courts; the enactment of statutes, and the amendment of statutes, are matters for Parliament ... The area of real difficulty lies in identifying the limits of interpretation in a particular case. This is not a novel problem. If anything, the problem is more acute today than in past times. Nowadays courts are more "liberal" in the interpretation of all manner of documents. The greater the latitude with which courts construe documents, the less readily defined is the boundary. What one person regards as sensible, if robust, interpretation, another regards as impermissibly creative. For present purposes it is sufficient to say that a meaning which departs substantially from a fundamental feature of an Act of Parliament is likely to have crossed the boundary between interpretation and amendment.'); *R (Anderson)* v. *Secretary of State for the Home Department* [2002] UKHL 46 at [30] (Lord Bingham) ('To read section 29 [of the Crime (Sentences) Act 1997] as precluding participation by the Home Secretary, if it were possible to do so, would not be judicial interpretation but judicial vandalism: it would give the section an effect quite different from that which Parliament intended and would go well beyond any interpretative process sanctioned by section 3 of the 1998 [Human Rights] Act ...'); *M* v. *Secretary of State for Work and Pensions* [2004] EWCA Civ 1343 at [90] (Sedley LJ) ('the forbidden frontier'); also *Ghaidan* v. *Godin-Mendoza* [2004] UKHL 30 at [121] (Lord Rodger), about which more in Chapter 6.

proposition postulated earlier in response to Simmonds's contention that it is a mistake to conceive of judicial modifications to rule formulations – 'express formulations of rules in caselaw', that is, as distinct from 'the law itself'[19] – 'exclusively in terms of a fundamentally legislative model': that to resist this conception amounts to squeamishness. That proposition is obviously overblown, certainly if one understands 'fundamentally legislative model' to mean 'fundamentally enacted-law model'.[20]

It might be argued, of course, that the proposition is only overblown if one accepts what is being asserted: that enacted law is fundamentally legislative, but judge-made law is not. We know already that there are those who would reject this assertion. Lord Diplock, it was observed a moment ago, purported to see no significant distinction between parliament's enactment of a text and the judicial interpretation of that text: both, he thought, amount to law making. On this point he had an unlikely ally in the figure of Hans Kelsen, who believed that the very application of a statute to a specific set of facts amounted to an addition to the content of the law beyond what had been added by the statute itself: '[t]he individualization of a general norm by a judicial decision is always a determination of elements which are not yet determined by the general norm … The judge is, therefore, always a legislator … in the sense that the contents of his decision can never be completely determined by the preëxisting norm of substantive law.'[21] When judges settle on an interpretation of a statute, so Diplock and Kelsen would have it, they supplement – make law out of – the statute's meaning.[22]

There is certainly something alluring about this account. Lord Goff's observation that it is one thing to be 'aware of the existence of the boundary' separating warranted and unwarranted judicial creativity and another to be 'sure where to find it'[23] applies no less to the distinction between judges interpreting and amending statutes than it does to the distinction between appropriate judicial development of common-law principles and courts introducing into the law changes which ought to have been decided

[19] Simmonds, *Law as a Moral Idea*, 161.
[20] As Simmonds clearly does: see ibid. 160.
[21] Hans Kelsen, *General Theory of Law and State*, trans. A. Wedberg (Cambridge, Mass.: Harvard University Press, 1946), 146.
[22] Hence Diplock's claim that '[w]henever the Court decides [whether a particular kind of gain is taxable] it legislates about taxation … Do not let us deceive ourselves … that the Court is only ascertaining and giving effect to what Parliament meant.' *The Courts as Legislators*, 6.
[23] *Woolwich Equitable Building Society* v. *IRC* [1993] AC 70 (HL), 173.

on by parliament. To contend, furthermore, that judges aim not to amend and try only to interpret statutes is to risk being accused of approaching statute law with the old-fashioned presumptions of the declaratory theorist who thinks of judges as simply mouthpieces of the common law.[24] But this is a risk worth taking. While it is not impossible for judges to make law out of statutes, to claim that this is what judges normally do when they interpret statutes is wrong. Judges have a responsibility for the development of the common law, but generally seek to avoid departing from the plain meaning of statutory language.[25] Indeed, they negotiate statutes in accordance with a collection of interpretive principles and presumptions which serve to minimize the likelihood of courts making new law from what has been enacted. These principles and presumptions, that is, have been created – mainly by judges themselves – to ensure that interpretations of statutes, even when they modify or shift focus from the text, can be understood as expositions of what the law already is: the court which interprets a statute in light of, say, the remedial intentions of the enacting parliament or overarching treaty obligations is trying to set out contested and unclear yet already existent law rather than to legislate from a statute. To say that those who determine the meaning of statutes are making law as much as if their interpretations were contained in enacted legislation is to fail to see that the point of interpretation is not to establish a new rule which amends or supplants already enacted law but rather to reach a ruling which can, in one way or another, be shown to be in accordance with already enacted law. Part III of this book is intended, in a fairly circuitous way, to bring home this very point.

To detect declaratory sentiments in an explanation of statutory interpretation is to misunderstand the declaratory theory itself. The declaratory theory is a theory of the common law – one which, nowadays, is generally considered to have been discredited.[26] That it became discredited is easily enough explained: the proposition that judges make law – by developing the common law rather than by legislating from statutes – came

---

[24] Charles Louis Montesquieu, *The Spirit of the Laws*, trans. and ed. A. M. Cohler, B. C. Miller and H. S. Stone (Cambridge University Press, 1989 [1748]), 163 ('[T]he judges of the nation are ... only the mouth that pronounces the words of the law, inanimate beings who can moderate neither its force nor its rigor').

[25] 'Judges ... have a responsibility for the common law, but in my opinion they have none for statute law; their duty is simply to interpret and apply it and not to obstruct.' Lord Devlin, 'Judges and Lawmakers' (1976) 39 *MLR* 1, 13–14.

[26] See Jim Harris, 'Retrospective Overruling and the Declaratory Theory in the United Kingdom – Three Recent Decisions' (2002) 26 *Revue de droit de l'Université libre de Bruxelles* 153.

to be regarded as uncontroversial. This study concerns enacted legislation rather than judge-made law, and so there is no need to dwell on the declaratory theory, though there is perhaps no harm in reflecting briefly on whether its status as one of the classic mistakes in common-law thinking is dependent on a somewhat harsh assessment. The stock observation that judges develop the common law should, for two reasons, be treated with caution. First, judicial decision making is not an intrinsically law-changing activity. Many decisions, certainly if we include in our estimation the decisions of lower courts, leave the common law exactly as it stood before the decisions were made. Secondly, the declaratory theorist's conclusion will sometimes be the right one: even when judges do seem to be modifying the common law, they might not be. What appears to be an alteration to precedent will sometimes be a correction of a legal derailment and a reaffirmation of established law – an effort to vindicate the law from past misinterpretation, as Blackstone put it, rather than to make something new.[27] The standard Austinian argument against the declaratory theory of the common law – that it is fantasy to think that judges never develop but only ever recapture the common law[28] – stands in need of no correction: the theory leaves unexplained how the common law came to be, and how it evolves.[29] But to emphasize the Austinian argument is to risk missing the point – which has been subject to various elaborations by those who recoil from the notion of judicial legislation[30] – that what appears to be a judicial alteration of the common law so that a new rule applies with retrospective effect will sometimes in fact be an exposition of law which, though perhaps misread or overlooked, already exists.

It would be foolish, nevertheless, to mount an out-and-out defence of the declaratory theory. There may be good reason to avoid the concept of judicial legislation, but there is no sense at all in arguing that judges do not

---

[27] 1 Bl. Comm. (William Blackstone, *Commentaries on the Laws of England*, 4 vols. (University of Chicago Press, 1979 [1765–9])) 70.

[28] 'There was a time when it was thought almost indecent to suggest that judges make law – they only declare it. Those with a taste for fairy tales seem to have thought that in some Aladdin's cave there is hidden the Common Law in all its splendour and that on a judge's appointment there descends on him knowledge of the magic words Open Sesame. Bad decisions are given when the judge had muddled the pass word and the wrong door opens. But we do not believe in fairy tales any more.' Lord Reid, 'The Judge as Law Maker' (1972) n.s. 12 *JSPTL* 22, 22.

[29] See John Austin, *Lectures on Jurisprudence or the Philosophy of Positive Law*, 2 vols., 5th edn, rev. and ed. R. Campbell (London: Murray, 1885), II, 634.

[30] For two examples, see Finnis, 'Adjudication and Legal Change', 400–3; Simmonds, *Law as a Moral Idea*, 164–8.

change the common law by overruling and distinguishing judicial precedents. When a court of final appeal overrules one of its own precedents,
its reason for doing so is as likely to be that the precedent is simply bad
law as that it is law which has been obscured or overlooked and awaiting
vindication: sometimes, that is, the overruling of precedent is the judicial version of what legislatures do when they expressly repeal statutes.
Distinguishing, on the other hand, is the common-law equivalent of an
amending statute. The court which distinguishes sees, between the precedent and the case at hand, a difference (or differences) which it considers sufficiently significant to justify not following the precedent. But the
ratio decidendi of the precedent case is not overruled or repealed. Instead,
the distinguishing court narrows the *ratio* established in the precedent so
that the new case is beyond its scope: the *ratio* of the new case, that is, contains conditions (though not necessarily all the conditions) that the *ratio*
of the precedent contains, but the *ratio* of the precedent is determined not
to extend to the new case because a condition, or set of conditions, present
in the new case is absent from the precedent. So it is that judicial decisions
do not always, but quite often will, alter or add to the existing common
law. Anyone who insists on describing judge-made law as a form of legislation is not fundamentally mistaken. But the description is misleading,
and so the development of law through judicial negotiation of precedent
does not feature in this study.[31]

2 Differences

Legislatures and courts each have law-making capacities, but there are
significant differences in how they make law and the types of law that they
make. Some of these differences are easily exaggerated: while it is true
that enacted law is normally not retroactive and that courts try to avoid
future-directed rulings, for example, it would be simplistic to assume that
these principles are unassailable.[32] There are, nevertheless, some broad

---

[31] Though there is a companion study: *The Nature and Authority of Precedent* (Cambridge
University Press, 2008).

[32] Although statutes which retroactively alter the legal status of actions or states of affairs
that took place or existed before the statute was enacted are generally considered anti-
thetical to rule-of-law values, it would be a mistake to think that such legislation is always
inherently objectionable. Genuinely retroactive legislation can be used to remedy unfortunate consequences attributable to the operation of a law – for example, to confirm the
validity of marriages which were technically void because it was impossible for the officials
responsible for conducting the ceremonies to comply with a statute setting out the conditions to be met before a marriage certificate could be granted: see Stephen R. Munzer,

distinctions to be identified. Apart from the obvious fact that the two types of law are the products of different organs which abide by their own rules and conventions, and leaving aside that statute law is more likely not to apply with retroactive effect and that judicial rulings are less likely to be directed to the future, statute law is distinguishable from case law on seven primary grounds.

First, legislatures control their law-making function in a way that courts do not. Although a legislature will be subject to various external influences – public opinion, interest group pressure, official reports and so on – when determining the matters on which it might legislate at any particular time, that determination is ultimately its own. But courts, though they have some say in the cases they decide to hear, cannot design their law-making agenda in the same way: the range of matters on which courts can rule is constrained by litigation and the need for clarification of legal principle.[33] Of course, legislatures cannot legislate at whim; they are constrained by time and resources, and completion of the legislative process is usually not possible without the assent – which could be formal (as it is in the United Kingdom) or real (as it is in, for example, the United States) – of the executive. The point, rather, is that the law-making opportunities of a legislature, unlike those of a judicial body, are not dependent on 'an adventitious

'Retroactive Law' (1977) 6 *Jnl Leg. Studs* 373, 387; Lon L. Fuller, *The Morality of Law* (rev. edn, New Haven: Yale University Press, 1969), 53–4. Retroactive legislation perhaps occurs most often in tax law, where the legislature generally wants to stop citizens from stealing a march on new tax rules in the period between the budget and their enactment, and might even legislate *ex post facto* to address tax anomalies which ought to have been rectified by an earlier statute: see, e.g., the Finance Act 2008, s. 58(4–5) and, for the finding that this provision is not, despite its *ex post facto* application, contrary to Article 1 of the First Protocol of the European Convention on Human Rights, *R* v. *HMRC, ex p. Huitson* [2011] EWCA Civ 893. Future-directed court rulings are resisted in English law primarily because of the danger of such rulings unreasonably altering the status of existing vested rights (see, e.g., Lord Mackay, 'Can Judges Change the Law?' (1987) 73 *PBA* 285, 297–9), though the senior judiciary has not been entirely averse to the principle of prospective *over*ruling: see, e.g., *In re Spectrum Plus Ltd* [2005] UKHL 41 at [26]-[38] (Lord Nicholls); *R* v. *Governor of Brockhill Prison, ex p. Evans (No 2)* [1999] QB 1043 (HL), 1058–9 (*per* Lord Woolf); *Prudential Assurance* v. *London Residuary Body* [1992] 3 All ER 504 (HL), 512 (*per* Lord Browne-Wilkinson); *Miliangos* v. *George Frank (Textiles) Ltd* [1976] AC 443 (HL), 490 (*per* Lord Simon); *R* v. *National Insurance Commissioner, ex p. Hudson* [1972] AC 944 (HL), 1015 (*per* Lord Diplock), 1026–7 (*per* Lord Simon).

[33] This statement is too sweeping if applied beyond common-law jurisdictions. The French Conseil d'État, for example, is required to advise the government (on, among other things, draft legislation) as well as operate as a judicial body: see generally John Bell, 'What is the Function of the Conseil d'État in the Preparation of Legislation?' (2000) 49 *ICLQ* 661. English courts may at their own behest issue practice directions. These directions are not uninvited judicial legislation, however, but advice to prospective litigants on courts' expectations and policies.

concatenation of the determined party, the right set of facts, the persuasive lawyer and the perceptive court'.[34] Legislatures have, in a way that courts do not, a capacity to take it upon themselves to change law.

Secondly, even when the implications of a judicial decision are broad ranging, a court will still only have decided on the facts of the case before it, and will have framed its judgment primarily on the basis of the competing claims of the opposing parties.[35] A court, that is, makes a ruling, and it is for later courts (assuming they have the discretion) to determine if the ruling is to be followed as a precedent when materially similar facts are litigated. Legislatures, by contrast, do not issue rulings on specific facts but rather establish abstract rules of general applicability. That enacting rules of general applicability should be the job of legislatures but not courts seems straightforwardly explicable in terms of democratic mandate: the former has one whereas the latter does not. But there is more to it than this. It makes sense that legislatures should have the responsibility for making generally applicable law because, as compared with courts, they are equipped to take into account a wider range of facts, affected parties, competing interests and alternative options. Concern about lack of information, as well as about lack of accountability to the electorate, is at the root of the familiar judicial refrain that changes to the law which raise complex moral or social issues extending beyond the case at hand should be handled by parliament rather than by the courts.[36]

---

[34] Henry J. Friendly, *Benchmarks* (University of Chicago Press, 1967), 46.

[35] It is worth noting, furthermore (though it would be overstating matters to present this as a distinction), that wherever judge-made law is subordinate to statute law, it will usually be the less ambitious form of law. One would expect the principal explanation for this to be that democratically elected legislatures might claim to be making law that reflects majority will. But this is not all that there is to be said. Case law is normally more modest in scope than enacted law because courts are often not in a position to evaluate the extent to which their decisions could disturb existing statutory and common-law rules. In *Hesperides* v. *Muftizade* [1979] AC 508, for example, the House of Lords upheld a rule denying it jurisdiction to hear an action for recovery of damages for trespass on land overseas because, among other things, if the rule were to be revised the court could not know what the consequences would be for English law as it then stood regarding *forum non conveniens*. '[T]he possible entry into and involvement with political questions of some delicacy', Lord Wilberforce remarked, 'does not favour revision … by judicial decision, but rather by legislation.' (That legislation soon came in the form of the Civil Jurisdiction and Judgments Act 1982.) See also *Miliangos* v. *George Frank*, 487 *per* Lord Simon ('a long-established rule of law almost always gathers juridical adhesions, so that its abrogation causes dislocations elsewhere in the legal system. Parliament, on executive or expert advice, can allow for these: the judiciary can rarely do so').

[36] See, e.g., *Shaw* v. *DPP* [1962] AC 220 (HL), 274–5 (*per* Lord Reid); *Lim Poh Choo* v. *Camden and Islington AHA* [1980] AC 174 (HL), 189 (*per* Lord Scarman); *British Leyland Motor*

Thirdly, legislatures typically *pass* the laws they make. Fuller's King Rex quickly realizes that even a legislator unconcerned with democratic pedigree 'cannot escape the need for a published code declaring the rules'[37] so that citizens may discover the laws that bind them. In a democracy those laws, before becoming laws, are put through a public and transparent procedure designed in an effort to ensure that whatever the legislature eventually enacts is carefully drafted, takes into account relevant information and interests, and is representative of democratic will. Case law, though it is likely to be carefully formulated and properly informed, is neither specifically governed by this type of procedure (which is not to deny that courts follow procedures when adjudicating) nor need it be representative of majority will; sometimes, indeed, a court's ruling will modify the law interstitially so as to protect a right which would not be protected if those seeking that right could only rely on the laws which the legislature has passed.[38]

Fourthly, although it would be overstating matters to say that courts never make rulings which read and operate rather like statutory rules,[39] legislation differs from case law in being suited to the task of drawing arbitrary yet clear lines such as eligibility criteria for welfare benefits or limitation periods for bringing legal proceedings.[40] Leaving aside the fact that judges will often not want to draw lines that effectively show them to be policy making, statute law is more appropriate to this task because it tends, as compared with case law, to be less casually written and more carefully structured, and because it never accommodates multiple opinions, dissents and asides.[41] Perhaps there was a time when statute law would have been considered more appropriate to the task because it was

---

    Corporation Ltd v. *Armstrong Patents Co. Ltd* [1986] AC 577 (HL), 623 (*per* Lord Bridge); *Airedale NHS Trust* v. *Bland* [1993] AC 789 (HL), 880 (*per* Lord Browne-Wilkinson), 891 (*per* Lord Mustill).

[37] Fuller, *The Morality of Law*, 35.

[38] See *McLoughlin* v. *O'Brian* [1983] 1 AC 410 (HL), 429–30 (*per* Lord Scarman).

[39] The Court of Appeal sometimes makes this type of ruling, for example, when it sets sentencing ranges which are intended as guidance for judges and magistrates where defendants are found guilty of particular crimes: see, e.g., *Auton* [2011] EWCA Crim. 76 (esp. the statute-like language used at para. [H7]).

[40] See generally Ernst Freund, *Legislative Regulation: A Study of the Ways and Means of Written Law* (New York: Commonwealth Fund, 1932), 5–10.

[41] The point is not that courts always accommodate multiple opinions and dissents, but that, unlike legislatures, they sometimes do. Some courts – the European Court of Justice, for example – do not.

also easier to discover.[42] But nowadays the content of important case law is as publicly available and readily searchable as is the content of statutes. The enduring reason that statute law better accommodates the task of promulgating flat rules which draw sharp distinctions is that it is, unlike case law, always formally drafted and univocal.

Fifthly, statute law, unlike case law, is not precedent-driven. The doctrine of *stare decisis* is unsuited to legislatures because statute law is largely reform-oriented – the motivation for proposing a bill is often specifically to depart from or nullify existing enactments. Certainly a statute may expressly provide that it is to be construed in the light of earlier enacted legislation which is *in pari materia* (on the same subject), and there are occasions when it is reasonable for a court to draw analogies between provisions in different statutes because the statutes can be seen to form part of a comprehensive code;[43] but when courts compare statutes, the point of the comparison is not to follow or distinguish a legal authority but to use a comparator statute as an aid in interpreting the authoritative statute.[44] *Stare decisis* is really only relevant to statute law in so far as a court normally operates on the presumption that an interpretation of a statute already settled on by another court is binding – though, as is generally the case with judicial precedents, this presumption may be rebutted.[45]

---

[42] See P. S. Atiyah and Robert S. Summers, *Form and Substance in Anglo-American Law: A Comparative Study of Legal Reasoning, Legal Theory, and Legal Institutions* (Oxford: Clarendon Press, 1987), 96–7 ('[A]rbitrary lines are more acceptable if they are easily discoverable and known to all, and this is more likely to be achieved if they are embodied in the publicly available textual form of a statute').

[43] See *Pioneer Aggregates (UK) Ltd* v. *Secretary of State for the Environment* [1985] AC 132 (HL), 142 (*per* Lord Scarman).

[44] When 'ascertaining the meaning' of 'the enacting part of a statute', Viscount Simonds observed in 1956, its words 'cannot be read in isolation: their colour and content are derived from their context ... including ... other statutes *in pari materia*'. *A-G* v. *Prince Ernest Augustus of Hanover* [1957] AC 436 (HL), 461 (decided December 1956). See also *R* v. *Secretary of State for the Environment, Transport and the Regions, ex p. Spath Holme* [2001] 2 AC 349 (HL), 389 (*per* Lord Bingham); *Majorstake Ltd* v. *Curtis* [2008] 1 AC 787 (HL), 803 (*per* Lord Carswell).

[45] As when, in *R* v. *Shivpuri* [1987] AC 1, the House of Lords overruled its own interpretation of s. 1 of the Criminal Attempts Act 1981 in *Anderton* v. *Ryan* [1985] AC 560; and, similarly, as when in *Vestey* v. *IRC* [1980] AC 1148 the House observed that s. 412 of the Income Tax Act 1952 and its predecessor provision (s. 28 of the Finance Act 1938) were amenable to two interpretations and that it would now place on s. 412 the interpretation that had not been preferred in *Congreve* v. *IRC* [1948] 1 All ER 948 (HL). Though common-law history shows that courts are not inclined to rebut the presumption lightly: see Henry Campbell Black, *Handbook on the Construction and Interpretation of the Laws,*

Sixthly, statute law is always intentionally made. Jeremy Bentham, according to H. L. A. Hart, thought that all laws are 'but expressions of the human will', that '[l]aw is something men add to the world, not find within it'.[46] But case law, conceived as a human addition to the world, is distinguishable from statute law.[47] Law produced by legislatures is produced deliberately – which is not to deny that the notion of legislative deliberateness is (as we will see in Chapter 4) far from easy to pin down. Judge-made law, by contrast, sometimes will and sometimes will not be law that is intentionally made. It is not unknown for judges to insist that they have no intention to modify the common law but only to honour an obligation to declare what that law is. A 'course of decisions on the construction of an Act of Parliament may be binding on a Judge even though his own opinion may be the other way', Sir George Jessell, MR, observed in *In re Bethlem Hospital*.[48] In that case, he added, since 'a series of authorities [wa]s produced' which '[we]re on the exact point ... raised', and which all reached the same conclusion as to the 'true meaning' of the relevant statutory provision, he was 'precluded from considering whether' he 'should be of the same opinion' as those authorities. 'I simply follow the decisions, and make the order.'[49]

Judges may well sometimes intend, as Jessell did, to do no more than apply a relevant line of judicial authority without seeking to add to it. And

2nd edn (St Paul, Minn.: West Publishing Co., 1911), 616–8. The main reason for this disinclination is that abiding by *stare decisis* when interpreting statutes has the advantage of minimizing the risk of interference with vested rights: if courts depart from an established interpretation of a statute, citizens who have relied on that statute as initially interpreted may turn out to have taken actions which they would have avoided taking had they understood what their obligations under the statute – as revealed by the new interpretation – in fact were.

[46] H. L. A. Hart, *Essays on Bentham: Studies in Jurisprudence and Political Theory* (Oxford: Clarendon Press, 1982), 26.

[47] Though Bentham famously resisted including the common law within the realm of law: see, e.g., Jeremy Bentham, 'To the Citizens of the Several American United States' (1817), in *The Works of Jeremy Bentham*, 11 vols., ed. J. Bowring (Edinburgh: Tait, 1843), IV, 478–507 at 485 (on common-law judgments as rules but not rules *of law*); Bentham, *Truth versus Ashhurst; or Law as it is, contrasted with what it is said to be* (London: Moses, 1823 [1792]), 11–12 ('It is the Judges ... that make the common law: Do you know how they make it? Just as a man makes laws for his dog. When your dog does any thing you want to break him of, you wait till he does it, and then beat him for it ... What way then has any man of coming at this dog-law? Only by watching [Judges'] proceedings: by observing in what *cases* they have hanged a man, in what *cases* they have sent him to jail, in what *cases* they have seized his goods, and so forth').

[48] *In re Bethlem Hospital* (1875) LR 19 Eq. 457, 460.

[49] Ibid. 460–61.

it has been observed already that it is not impossible for judicial decisions simply to replicate or reiterate what courts have already established. But judges who purport to do nothing other than reaffirm established authority will sometimes embellish that authority despite themselves; indeed, it would be unusual for an appeal court's negotiation of precedent not to introduce – though not necessarily intentionally to introduce – something new to the common law. Even the judge who 'commend[s] himself to the most rigid principle of adherence to precedent', Lord Radcliffe observed, will find that, 'when he repeats' what 'his predecessors ... decided before him[,] ... their words ... mean something materially different in his mouth ... The context is different; the range of reference is different; and, whatever his intention, the hallowed words of authority themselves are a fresh coinage newly minted in his speech.'[50] A judge might inadvertently change the common law while intending to apply it, and keep it, exactly as it stands.[51]

Finally, statutes are formulated with the intention that they be interpreted. In 1908, Roscoe Pound ventured that American law was evolving so that, eventually, statutes would be 'reasoned from by analogy the same as any other rule of law', and that the only lingering uncertainty would be whether they were 'of superior authority to' or 'of equal or co-ordinate authority ... with judge-made rules upon the same general subject'.[52] In the mid-1930s, a United States Supreme Court Justice went so far as to lend some substance to Pound's observation, professing that he could see 'no adequate reason for our failure to treat a statute much more as we treat a judicial precedent' – not only as 'a declaration and a source of law', that is, but also 'as a premise for legal reasoning' which might 'be extended to apply to situations analogous to those embraced within [its] terms'.[53] The reason statutes are, in fact, not treated like precedents has to do with

---

[50] Radcliffe, *Not in Feather Beds*, 271.
[51] One might argue, as some judges have, that legislatures are doing the same when they introduce consolidating legislation: see, e.g., Reid, 'The Judge as Law Maker', 27; Diplock, *The Courts as Legislators*, 12. But consolidating legislation is supposed to be more than reiterative. The legislature intends, through consolidation, not merely to restate existing law but to alter it (by putting a collection of common-law principles in one statute, by harmonizing inconsistent enactments, by substituting modern for antiquated legal language, and so on) – otherwise, there would be no point in consolidation. See W. M. Graham-Harrison, 'An Examination of the Main Criticisms of the Statute Book and the Possibility of Improvement' [1935] *JSPTL* 9, 22.
[52] Roscoe Pound, 'Common Law and Legislation' (1908) 21 *Harvard L. Rev.* 383, 385–6.
[53] Harlan F. Stone, 'The Common Law in the United States' (1936) 50 *Harvard L. Rev.* 4, 13–14.

the manner in which statutes are formulated and enacted. Casual use of language serves the process of statutory enactment badly, for meaningful legislative debate – and the guarantee that legislators are ultimately voting on the same matter – depends upon there being before an assembly a precise motion or resolution for discussion (any amendment to which must itself be precisely formulated).[54] The enactment process is, therefore, normally institutionalized so as to avoid or eradicate casual language and verbal errors, and to emphasize that the words that the drafters of bills use are not to be read as dictum.[55] The upshot of this is that statutes differ from case law in that they yield rules in a fixed verbal form which judges – apart from in exceptional instances when it is necessary to modify statutes to avoid outcomes which the legislature could never have intended, or to ensure treaty compliance – cannot abandon in favour of their own choice of words.[56] Judge-made law, by contrast, is not typically intended as a strict verbal formulation of legal principle.[57] Judges do not draft rulings as legislators draft rules – they do not expect their articulations of legal principle to be accepted (notwithstanding that, occasionally, they will be accepted) as an authentic form of words[58] – and courts customarily follow, distinguish or overrule precedents rather than interpret them as they would a statute.[59]

---

[54] See Jeremy Waldron, *Law and Disagreement* (Oxford: Clarendon Press, 1999), 80–2.

[55] See Edward H. Levi, *An Introduction to Legal Reasoning* (University of Chicago Press, 1949), 6, 28.

[56] See Neil MacCormick, *Legal Reasoning and Legal Theory*, rev. edn (Oxford: Clarendon Press, 1994), 58; Richard A. Posner, 'Legal Formalism, Legal Realism, and the Interpretation of Statutes and the Constitution' (1986) 37 *Case Western Reserve L. Rev.* 179, 187.

[57] See, e.g., *Cassell & Co. Ltd* v. *Broome* [1972] AC 1027 (HL), 1085 *per* Lord Reid ('it is not the function of … judges to frame definitions or to lay down hard and fast rules. It is their function to enunciate principles and much that they say is intended to be illustrative or explanatory and not to be definitive'). Though if a court had in an earlier case made an unequivocal ruling to compensate for the vagueness or obscurity of a particular statutory provision, subsequent courts might well treat the ruling as if it were itself a hard and fast rule. A court, furthermore, might occasionally be specifically entrusted with the task of clarifying the law, as, for example, when an Attorney-General's reference is passed on to it by the Court of Appeal under the Criminal Justice Act 1972, s. 36(3).

[58] See Frederick Pollock, *A First Book of Jurisprudence for Students of the Common Law* (London: Macmillan, 1896), 239; also Diplock, *The Courts as Legislators*, 14; and John Laws, 'Is the High Court the Guardian of Fundamental Constitutional Rights?' (1993) *Public Law* 59, 66–7.

[59] '[I]n dealing with precedents the most dangerous pitfall is to treat the words of eminent judges as if they were provisions in an Act of Parliament.' Reid, 'The Judge as Law Maker', 26; and see also *Jones* v. *Kernott* [2011] UKSC 53 at [59] (Lord Collins). It would be

It might be objected that there is a fundamental distinction between case law and statute law which, so far, has been overlooked: that one is law while the other is not. Whereas 'judge-made law' is 'lawyer's law', Lord Radcliffe claimed, '[l]awyers tend to regard statute law as not quite the equivalent of real law'.[60] Why ever might anyone believe this? Radcliffe was of the view that statute law, absent judicial interpretation, is not quite the equivalent of real law because it is essentially an expression of political will.[61] Only through the courts could that will become real law. His claim echoes that of the eighteenth-century cleric, Benjamin Hoadly, who argued that 'He, who is truly the Law-giver' is 'not the person who first wrote, or spoke' the law but 'whoever hath an absolute authority to interpret' what was written or spoken[62] – a claim which inspired John Chipman Gray to pronounce that 'all the Law is judge-made law', and that statutes are 'not … part of the law itself' but merely the 'sources of Law' which the courts invest with legal meaning.[63]

That general position is rejected here, though not only for the reason commonly offered against it. The standard criticism of Gray's argument in particular is that many statutes are never subjected to judicial interpretation and yet are still understood to be law.[64] This is true. Indeed, a statute which has never been subjected to judicial interpretation might not only be understood to be law but also relied upon and applied as law (by businesses, local authorities, magistrates, police officers and so on). But the point of Gray's argument is that such a criticism rests on a misunderstanding as to what law is. This observation hardly dispenses with the criticism – the claim that statute law is not genuine law founders because it rests on the evidently erroneous assumption that law cannot have been made until it has been judicially pronounced – but it does take us to the heart of the problem. Any answer to the question of whether judicial precedents and statutes are both genuine forms of law depends

---

equally foolish for the drafter of a bill to treat earlier statute law as precedent: see Geoffrey Bowman, 'The Art of Legislative Drafting' (2006) 64 *Amicus Curiae* 2, 2.

[60] Lord Radcliffe, 'The Place of Law Courts in Society', *The Listener*, 20 August 1953, 289–99 at 298.

[61] See Lord Radcliffe, *Law and the Democratic State* (Birmingham: Holdsworth Club, 1955), 9.

[62] Benjamin Hoadly, *A Sermon Preach'd before the King at the Royal Chapel at St. James's on Sunday March 31, 1717*, 3rd edn (London: printed for James Knapton, 1717), 12.

[63] John Chipman Gray, *The Nature and Sources of the Law*, 2nd edn (New York: Macmillan, 1921), 125.

[64] See, e.g., Carleton Kemp Allen, *Law in the Making*, 3rd edn (Oxford: Clarendon Press, 1939), 412; Rupert Cross and J. W. Harris, *Precedent in English Law*, 4th edn (Oxford: Clarendon Press, 1991), 170.

on what is intended by the word 'law'. One could counter the proposition that case law is law and statutes but sources of law with the proposition that it is, in fact, statutes that are law and that case law is but an elaboration of law. Each proposition is as spurious as the other. Enactments of legislatures and rulings of courts are legally authoritative directives: both are law, that is, albeit different forms of law. Statute law differs from case law because it 'is paradigmatically law' – because legislatures make law *de novo* rather than out of legal authorities that already exist.[65] Judges develop the common law rather than make it their business to introduce new legal rules; they make law, but it risks confusion to describe the law that they make as 'legislation' – even though they do, in the literal sense, legislate.

3   Early English legislation

This argument, that courts and legislatures make law albeit in very different ways, needs to be approached with care, for in English legal history it is only really from the sixteenth century onwards that we can distinguish the law-making initiatives of each on the basis that one enacts law whereas the other does not. How did things stand before then? The answer is complicated. It makes sense to outline it, none the less, for, without some understanding of how statutes were created before the sixteenth century, we can have no proper grasp of how case law and enacted law came to be the distinct entities that they are today.

So far as can be ascertained from the evidence that exists, what passed for legislation between the Anglo-Saxon and the Norman periods – the various articles, dooms, *leges*, assizes, ordinances, charters and constitutions which feature in the histories of the old English kingdoms – did not generally alter or add to the law but rather sought to declare or clarify customs which were in some way ambiguous (customs, for example, which were treated differently from one locality to another). Before the second half of the thirteenth century, furthermore, almost every legislative initiative – the only obvious exception being the Magna Carta of 1215 – was on a small scale and concerned with no more than one topic.[66] Although, in the twelfth century, declarations and clarifications of customs were

---

[65] See John Gardner, 'Some Types of Law', in *Common Law Theory*, ed. D. E. Edlin (Cambridge University Press, 2007), 51 at 55, 67.

[66] See Paul Brand, *Kings, Barons and Justices: The Making and Enforcement of Legislation in Thirteenth-Century England* (Cambridge University Press, 2003), 409.

occasionally designated by the word 'statuta',[67] neither *Glanvill* nor *Bracton*, the principal English legal treatises of the High Middle Ages, provide any indication that 'statute' formed part of the familiar speech of lawyers at that time.[68] Not until late in the thirteenth century does the word come to be commonly understood as denoting a form of law distinct from the common law.[69]

Once the word had acquired this meaning, the concept of 'statute' remained somewhat vague – primarily because not all statutes were enacted through the same process. The king was, theoretically, the fountain of all law, and statutes were, technically speaking, the king's acts.[70] But a statute could be created by the king in person, in council, in parliament or in the company of some ad hoc advisory assembly.[71] '[O]ur statutes, to an observer in the year 1300, would have appeared as novelties sprung from very different origins and exhibiting considerable diversity of form.'[72] Before 1299 there was no official procedure for enrolling statutes, which meant that the medieval courts had no authentic statutory texts available to them and that arguments rarely turned on how a statute was worded. Judges would quite often avoid applying statutory provisions, especially if they were unconvinced that those provisions were the result of direct royal command.[73]

Even when early fourteenth-century judges did apply statutes, they did not interpret them as they would today, for no real distinction was made between enactment and adjudication. The king's justices were not mere officers of the law but important members of his council with responsibility

---

[67] See H. G. Richardson and G. O. Sayles, *Law and Legislation from Æthelberht to Magna Carta* (Edinburgh University Press, 1966), 34; F. M. Stenton, *The First Century of English Feudalism, 1066–1166*, 2nd edn (Oxford: Clarendon Press, 1961), 39–40.

[68] See H. G. Richardson and George Sayles, 'The Early Statutes' (1934) 50 *LQR* 201, 540 at 202–4.

[69] See Paul Brand, 'English Thirteenth-Century Legislation', in *Colendi iustitiam et iura condendo. Federico II legislatore del Regno di Sicilia nell'Europa del Duecento: Per una storia comparata delle codificazione europee*, ed. A. Romano (Rome: Edizioni De Luca, 1997), 325–44.

[70] A proposition regularly emphasized in both *Glanvill* and *Bracton*: see Jean Dunbabin, 'Government', in *The Cambridge History of Medieval Political Thought c. 350–1450*, ed. J. H. Burns (Cambridge University Press, 1988), 477–519 at 486–8.

[71] See J. H. Baker, *An Introduction to English Legal History*, 4th edn (London: Butterworths, 2002), 205.

[72] Theodore F. T. Plucknett, *Statutes & Their Interpretation in the First Half of the Fourteenth Century* (Cambridge University Press, 1922), 12.

[73] See ibid., 57–61.

for drafting, or at least assisting with the drafting of, statutes.[74] When, in 1305, a serjeant endeavoured to explain to the Court of Common Pleas the meaning of the second Statute of Westminster, Hengham CJ cut him short: 'Ne glozes point le statut: nous le savons meiuz de vous, quar nous le feimes' ('Do not gloss the statute: we know it better than you, for we made it').[75] The Statute of Westminster was passed in 1285, when Hengham was Chief Justice of the King's Bench; he would no doubt have been consulted on it.[76] His reasoning is hardly unassailable – makers are not necessarily the best equipped, or to be trusted, to explain their products – but it illustrates the absence, around this time, of a conscious differentiation of power as between the legislature and the judiciary. Problems of legislative intent and statutory interpretation were as yet in the distance, as too was logomachy over 'legislation', because in the early fourteenth century statutes could be both interpreted and made by judges.[77]

In the second half of the fourteenth century, judges appear to have been less ready to speak for the drafters of statutes where the intentions of those drafters were ambiguous.[78] While the practice did not become established until the fifteenth century, furthermore, we witness around this time the start of the gradual movement towards the requirement that statutes have the separate consent of king, lords and commons.[79] From 1414, when it was established that lords' amendments to commons' petitions had to be

---

[74] See Richardson and Sayles, 'The Early Statutes', 545; G. Barraclough, 'Law and Legislation in Medieval England' (1940) 56 *LQR* 75, 79; Pollock, *A First Book of Jurisprudence*, 330–1; Baker, *An Introduction to English Legal History*, 204; John F. Manning, 'Textualism and the Equity of the Statute' (2001) 101 *Columbia L. Rev.* 1, 40–1; though cf. Morris S. Arnold, 'Statutes as Judgments: The Natural Law Theory of Parliamentary Activity in Medieval England' (1977) 126 *Univ. Pennsylvania L. Rev.* 329, who, on the basis of limited evidence, argues that at the end of the fourteenth century statutes and judgments were distinguishable in terms of both their promulgators and their respective effects on the world.

[75] *Aumeye's Case* (1305) YB 33–5 Edw. I, 78 at 82; repr. in Plucknett, *Statutes & Their Interpretation*, 183–4.

[76] Though this is perhaps immaterial – even judges without any personal involvement in the drafting of a statute would sometimes claim to know what the legislators had intended but had omitted to say: see *Belyng v. Anon.* (1312) B & M 52, 53 *per* Bereford CJ ('He that made the statute [*De donis* of 1285] meant to bind the issue in fee tail as well as the feoffees until the tail had reached the fourth degree; and it was only through negligence that he omitted to insert express words to that effect in the statute; and therefore we shall not abate this writ').

[77] 'In its early stages it seems to have been the practice if not the theory of English law that the maker of a statute should also be its interpreter if need be.' Plucknett, *Statutes & Their Interpretation*, 21.

[78] See ibid. 55–6; S. E. Thorne, 'The Equity of a Statute and Heydon's Case' (1936) 31 *Illinois L. Rev.* 202, 207–8.

[79] See Baker, *An Introduction to English Legal History*, 205; C. P. Ilbert, *Parliament: Its History, Constitution and Practice*, 3rd edn (Oxford University Press, 1950), 13–14;

resubmitted to the House of Commons for approval, the control of the House of Commons over the enactment process was enhanced significantly. By the second half of the fifteenth century, the House of Commons had begun to settle on what would become its standard practice of putting into the texts of bills the exact wording of the statutes being proposed.[80] This particular development marked an important break with the past: statutes were beginning to resemble canonical texts which were not to be rewritten or ignored by judges at their discretion.[81]

Though only to resemble such texts. There was certainly, at this point, no reliable way of discovering the contents or even the existence of a statute. Even though it was judicially decreed as early as the 1360s that 'the law presumes that every person has cognizance of' what is done in parliament,[82] ascertaining what parliament had enacted would be immensely difficult for centuries to come. '[N]one can have knowledge of [Acts of Parliament] but the Members of the Houses of Parliament', Thomas Hobbes remarked in 1681. 'I know that most of the Statutes are Printed, but it does not appear that every Man is bound to Buy the Book of Statutes, nor to search for them at *Westminster* or at the *Tower*, nor to understand the language wherein they are for the most part Written.'[83] Not that there was a definitive book of statutes that anyone in Hobbes's day could have bought. Unofficial collections of statutes had been in circulation for a good two centuries before he offered his lament, but barely any of them provided identical content, none of them was comprehensive, and many misrepresented as statutes various ordinances, procedural directives, writs and even passages from *Glanvill* and *Bracton*.[84] No systematic attempt to promulgate statutes was undertaken until the end of the eighteenth century; and when eventually, in the early decades of the following century, the Record Commission published the first official

---

Barraclough, 'Law and Legislation in Medieval England', 89–90. Even before this time, there was an expectation that parliament would be consulted on matters of fundamental constitutional importance: see Plucknett, *Statutes & Their Interpretation*, 20–1.

[80] See Baker, *An Introduction to English Legal History*, 206; Ilbert, *Parliament*, 14.

[81] See Allen, *Law in the Making*, 366 ('gradually ... the Judges feel themselves to be bound strictly by the precise terms of an enactment and compelled to apply them without recourse to their own discretion').

[82] *R* v. *Bishop of Chichester* (1364) YB 39 Edw. III, 7 (summarized at 4 Co. Inst. 26) *per* Thorpe CJ.

[83] Thomas Hobbes, *A Dialogue between a Philosopher and a Student of the Common Laws of England*, ed. J. Cropsey (University of Chicago Press, 1971 [1681]), 71–2.

[84] A similar story can be told in relation to civilian legal systems of the period: see Ian Maclean, *Interpretation and Meaning in the Renaissance: The Case of Law* (Cambridge University Press, 1992), 32–3.

collection of statutes, the Statutes of the Realm, they were incomplete and contained substantial inaccuracies.[85]

The effort systematically to compile parliamentary enactments might not have reached fruition until the nineteenth century, but parliament itself had started to come into its own as a distinct source of law as early as Tudor times.[86] At least four factors explain why this should have happened. There was, first of all, the introduction in the mid fifteenth century of movable type printing. From the beginning of the reign of Henry VII, all acts of parliament were printed as soon as they were passed; with the ascension of Henry VIII, it became the convention to publish them under the authoritative imprint of the king's printer.[87] Secondly, during the reign of Henry VIII in particular there was a prodigious outpouring of statute law, much of it – most memorably the achievements of the Reformation Parliament – of considerable political and religious significance.[88] Thirdly, during Henry VIII's reign there was not only a dramatic increase in parliamentary activity but also a significant change in parliament's function – primarily owing to the fact that he used the instrumentality of parliament to its fullest, so that statute law became the effective controlling force in not only the temporal but also the spiritual sphere (as in the case of the Act of Appeals 1533, which negated the pope's claim to act as ultimate court in church affairs).[89] The use of legislation for instrumental rather than merely declarative purposes became the norm from the Henrician Reformation onwards. When Mary I, as a Catholic queen, sought to abolish the religious laws of the Reformation and revalidate the canon law of the universal church, her method – unlike her objective – was much the same as was her father's and her half-brother's (Edward VI's) before her: to invalidate all laws contrary to the laws of God by enacting parliamentary legislation.[90]

---

[85] See W. S. Holdsworth, *A History of English Law*, 3rd edn, vol. 2 (London: Methuen, 1923), 427; Baker, *An Introduction to English Legal History*, 206–7.

[86] See generally Charles Howard McIlwain, *The High Court of Parliament and its Supremacy: An Historical Essay on the Boundaries between Legislation and Adjudication in England* (New Haven: Yale University Press, 1910), 109–256.

[87] See Joseph H. Beale, 'The Early English Statutes' (1922) 35 *Harvard L. Rev.* 519, 522–5.

[88] See Baker, *An Introduction to English Legal History*, 207.

[89] See generally G. R. Elton, '*Lex Terrae Victrix:* The Triumph of Parliamentary Law in the Sixteenth Century', in his *Studies in Tudor and Stuart Government and Politics. Volume IV: Papers and Reviews 1982–1990* (Cambridge University Press, 1992), 37–57.

[90] i.e., the Statute of Repeal 1553. See Elton, '*Lex Terrae Victrix*', 53; Martin Loughlin, *Foundations of Public Law* (Oxford University Press, 2010), 253.

Finally, because of the tendency of government officers, from the mid fifteenth century onwards, to insert into bills the exact wording of proposed statutes, parliament was increasingly inclined to adopt the *ipsissima verba* of the bill rather than the general policy embodied in it. 'The lawyers in the Commons, the judges in the Lords, and the council … were all dealing with specific and carefully drafted texts. Under this improved and businesslike procedure … [l]egislation … was no longer the Government's vague reply to vaguely worded complaints, but rather the deliberate adoption of specific proposals … emanating from the Crown or its officers.'[91] Although the language of a statute from this period would – certainly in comparison with the language of most modern statutes – have been broadly rather than precisely formulated, judges of the time, when they came to apply statutes, were more likely than they had been in the past to take the view that the text was the result of careful thought and that, if its import was clear and not contrary to reason, they should decide according to what it said. So it is that statutory enactment became something distinct from what judges do. And as it became ever more common for legislative drafting to be treated as the skilful, professionalized activity of Crown lawyers, it became increasingly less acceptable for judges to be creative with statutes in the way that their medieval forebears had often been.

---

[91] T. F. T. Plucknett, 'Ellesmere on Statutes' (1944) 60 *LQR* 242, 248.

2

The supremacy problem

Statutory interpretation – a topic to be examined in Part III of this book – only came into its own as a judicial exercise once judges no longer played a dominant role in the preparation of statutes. But it would be a very long time before their role in this process disappeared altogether. Certainly in the first half of the seventeenth century, judges – no doubt because many of them gained experience in drafting statutes before taking office – were still at the service of both commons and lords. 'In parliament they assisted committees for bills, drafted enactments, explicated points of law and defended them in conferences with the House of Commons.'[1] Even in the eighteenth century, judges continued to advise the lords on matters pertaining to pending legislation.[2] 'On the slightest view of the British constitution, we must perceive', Madison observed in 1788, 'that the legislative, executive and judiciary departments are by no means totally separate and distinct from each other', not least because '[t]he judges ... are so far connected with the legislative department, as often to attend and participate in its deliberations, though not admitted to a legislative vote'.[3] 'The supreme court of the English people ought to be a great conspicuous tribunal', Bagehot remarked in 1867, which 'ought not to be hidden beneath the robes of a legislative assembly'.[4] Yet it was not until the inauguration of the United Kingdom Supreme Court in October 2009 that the appellate top tier was removed from the legislature and that Law Lords (or rather, as they became at that point, justices of the Supreme Court) were actually disqualified from speaking on legislation before the House

---

[1] Elizabeth Read Foster, *The House of Lords, 1603–1649: Structure, Procedure, and the Nature of its Business* (Chapel Hill: University of North Carolina Press, 1983), 82.

[2] See Stewart Jay, 'Servants of Monarchs and Lords: The Advisory Role of Early English Judges' (1994) 38 *Am. J. Leg. Hist.* 117, 126–7.

[3] *Federalist 47* [James Madison], in Alexander Hamilton, James Madison and John Jay, *The Federalist* (New York: Barnes & Noble, 2006 [1787–8]), 269.

[4] Walter Bagehot, *The English Constitution*, ed. P. Smith (Cambridge University Press, 2001 [1867]), 91.

of Lords and its committees.[5] Before then, the rights of Law Lords to participate in the business of the House of Lords were the same as those of any other life peer, and some twentieth-century Law Lords – sometimes encouraged by lay peers – contributed significantly to legislative debates.[6] The complete separation of judicial and parliamentary functions was a long time coming.

1 Legislative versus judicial supremacy

It is perhaps to be expected that only gradually did statutory enactment become a function that was distinctively not one performed by judges. And there is certainly nothing surprising about the fact that, once judges were divested of significant input into the enactment process, they were anything but quick to concede that it was now their duty to give effect to whatever parliament laid down. In the fifteenth century, English judges would occasionally formulate an argument which, judging by the Year Books, had never been lost on them but which – until statutory enactment and statutory interpretation began to disentangle from one another – they had never had much cause to rely upon: the Aristotelian argument (which medieval English lawyers appear to have found in Roman and civil law)[7] that 'it is right, where the legislator fails us and has erred by over-simplicity, to correct the omission – to say what the legislator himself would have said had he been present, and would have put into his law if he had known'.[8] A proper examination of where this Aristotelian argument fits within the

---

[5] Constitutional Reform Act 2005, s. 137(3).

[6] Examples would be Lord Sumner on the Law of Libel Amendment Bill in 1927, Lord Reid on the Murder (Abolition of the Death Penalty) Bill in 1964, Lord Wilberforce on the State Immunity Bill in 1978 and Lord Hoffmann on the Defamation Bill in 1996. In June 2000, responding to the Report of a Royal Commission on the Reform of the House of Lords chaired by Lord Wakeham, the Law Lords asserted their right to participate in the business of the House, but accepted that they would not engage in matters of party-political controversy (as some of them had in the mid-1990s, for example, when they criticized proposals for new sentencing legislation): see HL Debs, 5th ser., vol. 614, cols. 418–20 (22 June 2000); Martin Loughlin, *Sword and Scales: An Examination of the Relationship between Law and Politics* (Oxford: Hart, 2000), 46–9 (sentencing proposals); and, generally, David Hope, 'Voices from the Past – The Law Lords' Contribution to the Legislative Process' (2007) 123 *LQR* 547.

[7] See Frederick J. de Sloovère, 'The Equity and Reason of a Statute' (1936) 21 *Cornell L. Q.* 591 at 593, 604; W. H. Loyd, 'The Equity of a Statute' (1909) 58 *Univ. Pennsylvania L. Rev.* 76, 77–9; John F. Manning, 'Textualism and the Equity of the Statute' (2001) 101 *Columbia L. Rev.* 1, 29–30.

[8] *Nicomachean Ethics*, V. 10. 1137[b]. See also *Rhetoric*, I. 13. 1374[a] – [b]. For instances and discussion, see Loyd, 'The Equity of a Statute', 77–8; James McCauley Landis, 'Statutes

history and philosophy of statutory construction in common-law courts is best left until Chapter 6. But it should be immediately obvious that the argument is open to more than one interpretation.

It would be 'right', on this argument, for a court to 'correct' the language of a statute where it omits to deal with an exception which the legislator would have had the statute address had he contemplated it. It would, presumably, also be right for the court to intervene where a statute does deal with a particular problem but the inordinate breadth or narrowness of, or some other 'over-simplicity' in, the statute's wording suggests that the legislator failed to recognize the true complexity of that problem (reasonably assuming also that, had the legislator not failed thus, he would have worded the statute differently). In the first instance, the statute is supplemented so that it now addresses a matter about which it was previously silent. In the second instance, the statute is rewritten so that it addresses a matter it already addressed, but differently. Given how the procedure for drafting bills became increasingly businesslike from the mid fifteenth century onwards, neither of these interpretations of the Aristotelian argument fared especially well in the courts during the Tudor period. But a third, yet more radical reading of the argument – that a statute which yields an outcome contrary to justice ought to be not supplemented or revised, but disregarded in favour of something else – provoked lasting controversy.

In the 1530s, the Church of England lost its legislative supremacy in spiritual matters once the Reformation Parliament had transferred authority from the pope to the king. But to whom did the Church cede this supremacy? Royalists maintained that it was ceded to the king, who acted with divinely ordained authority when he legislated with the consent of his subjects in parliament. Parliamentarians maintained that it was ceded to the king, lords and commons in parliament, and that it was parliament – as representative and chief protector of the rights of the people – that held supreme legislative authority. Though royalists and parliamentarians disputed whether parliament could exercise this authority without the assent of the king, both agreed that when this authority was exercised and laws were enacted, judges had no power to challenge the validity of those laws. Presumably any

---

and the Sources of Law', in *Harvard Legal Essays Written in Honor of and Presented to Joseph Henry Beale and Samuel Williston* (Cambridge, Mass.: Harvard University Press, 1934), 213–46 at 215–16, 235 nn. 6–8; J. H. Baker, *An Introduction to English Legal History*, 4th edn (London: Butterworths, 2002), 106; though cf. S. E. Thorne, 'The Equity of a Statute and Heydon's Case' (1936) 31 *Illinois L. Rev.* 202, 204–5, who doubts that anything resembling a doctrine of equitable statutory interpretation emerged until early in the fifteenth century.

citizen could disobey a statute which was manifestly contrary to the laws of God. But judges could not declare such a statute invalid.[9]

'But what', asked Thomas Egerton in the mid sixteenth century, 'yf the wordes of an estatute be contraryant', requiring two actions that are mutually inconsistent or an action which is impossible to perform, or if in some other way 'yt can not be avoided but that a repugnancie must nedes be' in the event that the statute is applied – 'what is there then to be saide?'[10] If the king, or king in parliament, had erred, could the only earthly remedy be repeal by a subsequent statute? When judges were occasionally confronted with statutes demanding something absurd or repugnant, would they be obliged to apply them? In the second half of the 1520s the then Solicitor-General, Christopher Hales (echoing words written around the same time by St German),[11] observed that any statute which 'is absurd' or 'is so obscure that the intention thereof cannot be understood by law or reason ... is void'.[12] The best-known formulation of this argument comes almost a century later in *Bonham's Case* (1610), when Sir Edward Coke declared that:

> it appears in our books, that in many cases, the common law will controul Acts of Parliament, and sometimes adjudge them to be utterly void: for when an Act of Parliament is against common right and reason, or repugnant, or impossible to be performed, the common law will controul it, and adjudge such Act to be void.[13]

Many a gloss has been put on this clumsy, repetitious statement. Although no other judge in the case decided it on the basis of Coke's reasoning, Coke himself seemed to consider his argument significant – he

---

[9] See Jeffrey Goldsworthy, *The Sovereignty of Parliament: History and Philosophy* (Oxford: Clarendon Press, 1999), 122, 230–1.

[10] *A Discourse upon the Exposicion & Understanding of Statutes, With Sir Thomas Egerton's Additions*, ed. S. E. Thorne (San Marino, Calif.: Huntington Library, 1942 [c. 1565]), 132–3. Thorne resists identifying Egerton as the author, though it now seems settled that he was: see Louis A. Knafla, *Law and Politics in Jacobean England: The Tracts of Lord Chancellor Ellesmere* (Cambridge University Press, 1977), 45–7.

[11] Christopher St German, *Doctor and Student*, ed. W. Muchall (Cincinnati: Clarke, 1874 [1530]), 15 ('... if any general custom were directly against the law of God, or if any statute were made directly against it ... the custom and statute were void').

[12] The observation is to be found in a Gray's Inn moot from around 1526–29 (British Library Add. MS 35939, f. 269) – translated from the law French by John Baker, and reproduced as Appendix I of his 'Human Rights and the Rule of Law in Renaissance England' (2004) 2 *Northwestern Univ. Jnl of International Human Rights* i, xviii–xixi at xviii – and is complemented by a remark by one of Hales' fellow mooters, Wroth: 'Parliament may not do something which is against law and reason, any more than a party may' (ibid.).

[13] *Dr Bonham's Case* (1610) 8 Co. Rep. 107a, 118a.

wrote the passage out on other occasions[14] – and his assertion that it was supported by authorities was certainly not unwarranted, though those authorities are not as convincing as Coke would have us believe.[15] There is evidence stretching to the time of the civil war, furthermore, of judges and lawyers treating the passage as authority for the proposition that courts can sometimes invalidate statutes.[16] Yet within two years of *Bonham's Case* being decided, Coke himself appeared to retreat from his argument,[17] and in the *Fourth Institute* he would famously endorse parliamentary supremacy.[18] In America, the argument in *Bonham's Case* was relied upon until the late eighteenth century to support the possibility of a court determining the validity of a statute,[19] though it inevitably became less relevant once the states adopted the practice of drafting their own constitutions embodying the principle of judicial review of legislative enactments.[20] But in England the argument had, by the time of the American Revolution, been unequivocally rejected. 'I know it is generally laid down', Blackstone observed in 1765, 'that acts of parliament contrary to reason are void. But if the parliament will positively enact a thing to be

---

[14] See Baker, 'Human Rights and the Rule of Law', xv.

[15] See Theodore F. T. Plucknett, 'Bonham's Case and Judicial Review' (1926) 40 *Harvard L. Rev.* 30, 36–45.

[16] See, e.g., ibid. 49–50, 52; Charles M. Gray, 'Bonham's Case Reviewed' (1972) 116 *Proc. Am. Philosophical Soc.* 35, 51–5; Goldsworthy, *The Sovereignty of Parliament*, 231–2. Reported dicta of Holt CJ in *City of London* v. *Wood* (1701) 12 Mod 669, 687–8 suggest that the evidence extends to the early eighteenth century, but the report of this case is seriously inaccurate: Holt was in fact arguing that judges *do not* have the capacity to invalidate statutes. In his own manuscript report of his opinion (British Library Add. MS 34125, f. 68r), Holt writes that 'an act of Parliament … binds absolutely without any dispute to be made of its justice or equity'. See Philip A. Hamburger, 'Revolution and Judicial Review: Chief Justice Holt's Opinion in *City of London* v. *Wood*' (1994) 94 *Columbia L. Rev.* 2091, 2139.

[17] See *Rowles* v. *Mason* (1612) 2 Brownl. 198; S. E. Thorne, 'Dr. Bonham's Case' (1938) 54 *LQR* 543, 544–5.

[18] See 4 Co. Rep. 36 ('the power and jurisdiction of the Parliament for making laws in proceeding by Bill … is … transcendent and absolute … it cannot be confined either for causes or persons within any bounds').

[19] See Plucknett, 'Bonham's Case and Judicial Review', 61–7; William Michael Treanor, 'Judicial Review Before *Marbury*' (2005) 58 *Stanford L. Rev.* 455, 468–73.

[20] See Plucknett, 'Bonham's Case and Judicial Review', 68; also *Seminole Tribe of Florida* v. *Florida*, 517 US 44, 162 n. 56 (1996) (Souter J, dissenting) (observing that 'although Coke's dictum was to have a somewhat greater influence in America [than in England], that influence took the form of providing an early foundation for the idea that courts might invalidate legislation that they found inconsistent with a *written* constitution' rather than 'the idea that legislation may be struck down based on principles of common law or natural justice not located within the constitutional text'). (Emphasis in original.)

done which is unreasonable, I know of no power that can control it … for … to set the judicial power above that of the legislature … would be subversive of all government.'[21]

This observation hardly came out of the blue. In 1616, James I had taken Coke's argument in *Bonham's Case* into account when he suspended Coke from his position as Chief Justice of the King's Bench.[22] In the previous year Egerton, now Lord Chancellor Ellesmere, had written of how it is far preferable 'that Acts of parliament should be corrected by the same penn that drew theym, thayn to be dasht in peeces by the opinion of a few Judges'.[23] Halfway between the time of Ellesmere's rebuke and the time of Blackstone's is the most decisive moment of all in this story: with the limitations on the power of the king following the Revolution of 1688, and the replacement of James II by William and Mary, the legislative authority of parliament became settled. The judiciary – which had generally supported parliament in its opposition to the royal claims[24] – could do little but accept that they must apply what is contained in a statute and that parliament alone can change what a statute contains.[25] With so few supporters and so many detractors, the idea of judicial review of the validity of statutes was, in England, always fated to abandonment.

Whether Coke was, in fact, arguing for judicial review of the validity of statutes is a long-standing topic of debate. On one account, his contention that statutes 'against common right and reason' are 'utterly void' cannot be taken as 'mere assertion of a power to interpret statutes in light of equitable principles' but rather must be read to imply 'judicial review in the full sense over Parliament in … [its] *legislative* capacity'.[26]

---

[21] 1 Bl. Comm. 91.

[22] See Plucknett, 'Bonham's Case and Judicial Review', 50; Goldsworthy, *The Sovereignty of Parliament*, 126.

[23] Lord Ellesmere, 'The Lord Chancellor Egertons Observacions Upon ye Lord Cookes Reportes' (1615) in Knafla, *Law and Politics in Jacobean England*, 297–318 at 307. Ellesmere was echoing the then Solicitor-General, Henry Yelverton: see ibid. 149.

[24] Though not always: see, e.g., *Godden* v. *Hales* (1686) 2 Shower 475.

[25] See Carleton Kemp Allen, *Law in the Making*, 3rd edn (Oxford: Clarendon Press, 1939), 371; Plucknett, 'Bonham's Case and Judicial Review', 53, 69; Peter Stein, *Legal Institutions: The Development of Dispute Settlement* (London: Butterworths, 1984), 90.

[26] Thomas C. Grey, 'Origins of the Unwritten Constitution: Fundamental Law in American Revolutionary Thought' (1978) 30 *Stanford L. Rev.* 843, 856. See also Mark D. Walters, 'Common Law, Reason, and Sovereign Will' (2003) 23 *UTLJ* 65 (arguing that Coke's argument is inspired by St German, who, when observing that statutes contrary to the law of nature are void, would not have been using 'void' in any sense 'different … from that of the other uses of the term in *Doctor and Student* in which it clearly referred to *legal* invalidity' (ibid. 80)).

Legal historians, however, have tended to conclude that Coke's notion of a court controlling an Act of parliament and adjudging it to be void embodies a principle of statutory interpretation rather than full-scale judicial review: that controlling an Act and adjudging it void means not invalidating it but interpreting it and – if, through interpretation, the statute cannot be saved[27] – finding it to be, while technically valid, 'of no effect'.[28] This conclusion is certainly supported by Year Book reports stretching back to the early fifteenth century, which provide considerable evidence that judges and lawyers would often take the view that a statute contrary to reason, though it ought not to be used, remains legally valid until repealed or amended.[29] The famous dictum in *Bonham's Case* – the high water mark of lingering judicial resistance to parliamentary supremacy once judges no longer played a significant part in the enactment process – was probably not the assertion of judicial supremacy that it is sometimes taken to be.

2   Parliamentary sovereignty

Whatever the argument in *Bonham's Case* might have meant for Coke, it is clear that with the entrenchment of parliamentary sovereignty in the late seventeenth and eighteenth centuries it became well-nigh impossible to take the idea of judicial review of statutory validity seriously. By the second half of the eighteenth century, 'almost all politicians, lawyers, and political theorists agreed that Parliament possessed a legally unlimited

---

[27] See Gray, 'Bonham's Case Reviewed', 41–2.

[28] Ian Williams, '*Dr Bonham's Case* and "Void" Statutes' (2006) 27 *J. Leg. Hist.* 111, 125; see also Henry Finch, *Law: or, a Discourse thereof, in foure books* (London: printed for John Moore, 1636), 74–5 ('Lawes positive, which are directly contrary to the former [*sc.*, '[t]he Law of nature and of reason'], lose their force, and are no Lawes at all'); Thomas Hobbes, *A Dialogue between a Philosopher and a Student of the Common Laws of England*, ed. J. Cropsey (Chicago: University of Chicago Press, 1971 [1681]), 20 ('are ... Void and of no Effect, and ought to be recalled'); Philip Allott, 'The Courts and Parliament: Who Whom?' (1979) 38 *CLJ* 79, 82–6; Thorne, 'Dr. Bonham's Case', 549 ('the argument is derived from the ordinary common law rules of statutory interpretation'); J. W. Tubbs, *The Common Law Mind: Medieval and Early Modern Conceptions* (Baltimore: Johns Hopkins University Press, 2000), 154–67, 183–6; John Finnis, *Natural Law and Natural Rights*, 2nd edn (Oxford University Press, 2011), 353.

[29] See Norman Doe, *Fundamental Authority in Late Medieval English Law* (Cambridge University Press, 1990), 57–8, 74, 78; though cf. the 'unusual' case of 1506 set out at ibid. 142–3 in which 'the judges relax[ed] the strict prohibitions of the statute in favour of custom rooted in reason and conscience'.

legislative authority within Britain'.[30] Even though reported judgments from this period 'provide frequent instances of fulsome judicial attacks on ill-drafted and misconceived acts of parliament ... none of the most dedicated defenders of judicial creativity was prepared, any more than Blackstone, to claim that the courts might control parliament's legislative will'.[31] The apparent comment of Holt CJ in 1701 that 'an act of Parliament can do no wrong, though it may do several things that look pretty odd' is, even if misreported, an accurate summary of what many eighteenth-century judges and treatise-writers thought.[32]

By the early nineteenth century, not only was parliamentary sovereignty taken for granted in Britain, but – because parliament had, since 1688, left the common law largely untouched – the courts had seen little reason to try to challenge this state of affairs. With the efforts (beginning around the time of the Reform Bill of 1831) to make parliament more representative came an outpouring of statute law, much of which was intended to eradicate some of the more antiquated common-law principles.[33] This statute law was often the outcome of enquiries by government departments which had gathered and drawn on information formally unavailable to the courts. The English judiciary of the nineteenth century was, in so far as it cared at all about its own remoteness from social affairs, less concerned about its rulings occasionally representing, as Dicey put it, 'the opinion of the day before yesterday'[34] as it was about its capacity to develop certain areas of law in the informed way that parliament could. And so 'when issues of major public concern arose for decision in the Courts after 1830, the judges' – considering themselves 'less informed than Parliament' – 'began to be reluctant to tread in political fields' and 'to show a greater deference to Parliament than they had

---

[30] Goldsworthy, *The Sovereignty of Parliament*, 233. (Britain, not England, because of the Acts of Union 1707.)

[31] David Lieberman, *The Province of Legislation Determined: Legal Theory in Eighteenth-Century Britain* (Cambridge University Press, 1989), 71–2.

[32] *City of London* v. *Wood* (1701) 12 Mod 669, 687. See generally Goldsworthy, *The Sovereignty of Parliament*, 197–204.

[33] As was the case, for example, with much of the Whig legislation altering punishments for forgery, larceny, rape and other criminal offences: see Leon Radzinowicz, *A History of English Criminal Law and its Administration from 1750. Volume IV: Grappling for Control* (London: Stevens, 1968), 303–26, 590–5.

[34] A. V. Dicey, *Lectures on the Relation between Law & Public Opinion in England*, 2nd edn (London: Macmillan, 1926), 33, 369 (contending that '[l]egislative opinion ... is ... the opinion of yesterday' – a representation of arguments which 'exerted their influence long before the change in the law took place' – whereas 'judge-made law occasionally represents the opinion of the day before yesterday').

shown before'.[35] Denman CJ, in the case of *Hitchcock* v. *Coker* in 1837, remarked that it is impossible to establish if a contract should be held valid when it is for adequate consideration but in restraint of trade without applying a test which the courts, unlike parliament, are simply not equipped to apply: a test to determine not only if the consideration is at least equal in value to the degree of restraint acceptable to the defendant, but also if the restraint interferes too much with the public interest. 'It may indeed be said that all such agreements [in restraint of trade] interfere in some degree with the public interest; and great difficulty may attend the application of that test,' owing to 'the variety of opinions that may exist on the question of interference with the public interest which the law ought to permit'.[36] The move to achieve reforms through parliamentary enactment, typified in the 1830s by the initiatives of social reformers such as Henry Brougham, Edwin Chadwick and James Kay, not only resulted in significant parts of the common law being replaced by statute law, but also seemed to convince many among the judiciary that this was no bad thing, that many legal rules – particularly outside the realms of traditional criminal and private law – are best laid down by a legislative assembly.

There is no need to dwell on this tale. The point for emphasis is simple: occasional instances of judicial resistance notwithstanding, the common law came to be subordinate to statute law. After the Glorious Revolution, it became orthodoxy – accepted as logic – that courts cannot overrule what parliament enacts, that judges are bound to apply a statute whether or not they approve of what the statute says, and that, while parliament cannot pass statutes which are incapable of being abrogated, it is not the job of the courts to alter statute law when that law calls out for amendment or repeal. Although '[i]t is often said that it would be unconstitutional for … Parliament to do certain things, meaning that the moral, political and other reasons against doing them are so strong that most people would regard it as highly improper if Parliament did' do them, Lord Reid declared in *Madzimbamuto* v. *Lardner-Burke* (1968), 'that does not mean that' doing these things 'is beyond the power of Parliament … If Parliament chose to do any of them the courts could not hold the Act of Parliament invalid.'[37] For, as Dicey famously remarked, it 'is a legal fact,

---

[35] P. S. Atiyah, *The Rise and Fall of Freedom of Contract* (Oxford: Clarendon Press, 1979), 384.

[36] *Hitchcock* v. *Coker* (1837) 6 Ad. & E. 438, 445.

[37] *Madzimbamuto* v. *Lardner-Burke* [1969] 1 AC 645 (PC), 723. (Decided July 1968.)

fully recognized by the law of England', that while 'Parliament … has the right to make or unmake any law whatever … no person or body' can 'set aside [its] legislation'.[38]

This is, of course, a straightforward rejection of the most radical version of the Aristotelian argument regarding the judicial negotiation of statutes. In the middle of the twentieth century, Denning LJ sought to revive one of the less radical readings of that argument: that it is only right that judges fill the holes in legislation. '[I]f the draftsmen have not provided for this or that … a judge cannot simply fold his hands and blame the[m] … [H]e must supplement the written word so as to give "force and life" to the intention of the legislature.'[39] Even this was a step too far. Denning's claim was soon castigated in the House of Lords as tantamount to encouraging 'a naked usurpation of the legislative function under the thin disguise of interpretation'.[40] Not until after the United Kingdom's accession to the European Community in 1973 would there be any significant alteration to the statute-negotiating role of the courts, and even then the most notable alteration would be at the behest of parliament itself: the Human Rights Act 1998 not only obliges judges, so far as is possible, to interpret primary and subordinate legislation in ways compatible with the European Convention on Human Rights but also confers on them the power to declare particular statutes incompatible with the UK's Convention obligations. Though the capacity of the courts to control statutes looks to be all the greater in light of this last power, parliament, in granting

---

[38]   A. V. Dicey, *Introduction to the Study of the Law of the Constitution*, 8th edn (London: Macmillan, 1927; 1st edn publ. 1885), 37–8.

[39]   *Seaford Court Estates Ltd* v. *Asher* [1949] 2 KB 481 (CA), 499; and see also *Magor & St Mellons RDC* v. *Newport Corporation* [1950] 2 All ER 1226 (CA), 1236 *per* Denning LJ ('We sit here to find out the intention of Parliament and of Ministers and carry it out, and we do this better by filling in the gaps and making sense of the enactment than by opening it up to destructive analysis'). In the 1970s, Denning even went so far as to suggest that a court is constitutionally entitled to decline to apply a statutory provision where its application would violate a fundamental right (such as the right not to be detained unlawfully): see *Birdi* v. *Secretary of State for Home Affairs* (1975) 119 Sol. Jo. 322.

[40]   *Magor and St. Mellons RDC* v. *Newport Corporation* [1952] AC 189 (HL), 191 *per* Lord Simon ('the general proposition that it is the duty of the court to find out the intention of Parliament – and not only of Parliament but of Ministers also – cannot by any means be supported. The duty of the court is to interpret the words that the legislature has used; those words may be ambiguous, but, even if they are, the power and duty of the court to travel outside them on a voyage of discovery are strictly limited … This proposition [*sc.*, 'What the legislature has not written, the court must write'] … appears to me to be a naked usurpation of the legislative function under the thin disguise of interpretation. And it is the less justifiable when it is guesswork with what material the legislature would, if it had discovered the gap, have filled it in. If a gap is disclosed, the remedy lies in an amending Act').

it, very clearly did not cede legislative supremacy. For a judicial declaration of incompatibility does not invalidate an impugned statute: in the event of such a declaration, it remains the task of parliament to determine if and how the law is to be changed.

3   Three notes of caution

While it is all very well to claim that legislatures are superior law-making bodies as compared with courts, it should be borne in mind that courts often have the last word in the law-making process because the meaning of a statutory provision will be settled by judicial construction. Statutory interpretation will, as has been intimated already, be dealt with as a discrete topic in Part III of this study. There is no need to deal with the topic at this juncture, apart from to reiterate that when a court deliberately or inadvertently breaches the sometimes fuzzy border between interpretation and judicial legislation – by, say, reading words into a statute so as to vest it with a meaning which parliament never intended, and never would have intended, it to have – it offends against the principle of parliamentary supremacy. What does deserve a little more attention at this point is this very principle, for there are at least three important reasons for treating the story of the rise and consolidation of parliamentary supremacy with some caution.

(a)   The presumption against alteration

In the mid nineteenth century, we have observed, not only was there enacted a significant amount of statute law which altered common-law doctrine, but the courts were noticeably deferential towards these statutory interventions precisely because the alterations were by and large the product of a parliament reformed to become a well-informed and more representative institution. There is something about this observation that calls for clarification. Just how deferential were the courts willing to be? It defies plausibility that judges would, in effect, just step aside and watch while legislators put paid to common-law principles. Surely there would have been *some* judicial resistance to what the legislature was doing.

Indeed there was, though it would be wrong to think that the method of resistance was devised in response to the growth and reach of statute law in the nineteenth century. According to Maitland, not only were most statutes of the previous century characterized by 'extreme and verbose particularity' – parliament seemed 'rarely to rise to the dignity of a general proposition' – but the common law was protected 'by a niggardly exposition of every legislating word'.[41] One consequence of judges taking a strict approach to the construction of statutes – and here we come to our first note of caution – was that there operated in the courts a general presumption which served as a significant check on the doctrine of parliamentary supremacy: the presumption that statutes derogating from common-law principles mean what they say and nothing else, and that a statute therefore only ever alters the common law to the extent that its words make absolutely clear.[42] 'The general rule in exposition of all Acts of Parliament', Trevor CJ is reported to have remarked in 1707, 'is ... that in all doubtful matters, and where the expression is in general terms, they are ... not presumed to make any alteration in the common law ... for if the Parliament had had that design, they would have expressed it in the Act.'[43]

Judges can be found endorsing this sentiment well into the twentieth century.[44] Lord Wright, a judge who rarely accepted orthodoxies without

---

[41] F. W. M[aitland], 'English Law', in *Encyclopædia Britannica*, 11th edn (New York: Cambridge University Press, 1910), IX, 600–7 at 605.

[42] See Roderick Munday, 'The Common Lawyer's Philosophy of Legislation' (1983) 14 *Rechtstheorie* 191, 195 ('This principle, which comes close to questioning Parliamentary supremacy ...'); Hans W. Baade, 'The *Casus Omissus*: A Pre-history of Statutory Analogy' (1994) 20 *Syracuse Jnl of International Law & Commerce* 45, 90 ('The "sovereignty" of Parliament was therefore more apparent than real ...').

[43] *Arthur* v. *Bokenham* [1707] 11 Mod 148, 150.

[44] See, e.g., *Rendall* v. *Blair* [1890] LR 45 Ch. D. 139 (CA), 155 *per* Bowen LJ ('I think we ought not to assume without the clearest language that Parliament intended to destroy common law rights of Her Majesty's subjects'); *R* v. *Bishop of Salisbury* [1901] 2 KB 225 (CA), 227–8 (*per* A. L. Smith MR); *Leach* v. *R* [1912] AC 305 (HL), 311 *per* Lord Halsbury ('... to suggest that that is to be dealt with by inference, and that you should introduce a new system of law without any specific enactment of it, seems to me to be perfectly monstrous'); and consider also Browne-Wilkinson LJ in his Court of Appeal dissent in *Wheeler* v. *Leicester City Council* [1985] AC 1054, 1065 ('Basic constitutional rights in this country such as freedom of the person and freedom of speech are based not on any express provision conferring such a right but on freedom of an individual to do what he will save to the extent that he is prevented from so doing by the law ... These fundamental freedoms ... are not positive rights but an immunity from interference by others ... I do not consider that general words in an act of Parliament can be taken as authorising interference with these basic immunities which are the foundation of our freedom. Parliament (being sovereign) can legislate so as to do so; but it cannot be taken to have conferred such a right on others save by express words'). Note that in Australia, where it is misleading to speak of an unqualified doctrine of parliamentary sovereignty given that the powers of parliamentarians are subject to the written Constitution and ultimately determinable by courts of law, subtly different presumptions appear to have emerged: see

question, declared in 1944 that the principle that statutes in derogation of the common law must be strictly construed – which he considered an 'attenuated form' of Coke's argument in *Bonham's Case* – was 'now ... discredited'.[45] Judges, he argued, are not only obliged to respect what the legislature enacts – '[t]he days are long past when a judge could say that he was not bound to enforce an Act of Parliament which he thought contrary to the common law' – but in any event usually do best when they respect what the legislature enacts: in a lecture to the Harvard Law School in September 1938 he observed, echoing Denman a century earlier, that judges 'neither desire nor are qualified' to 'introduce into law the principles of state policy, or to depart from the common law in order to invent doctrines of what is good for the common weal'; it is better, he insisted, that this be 'the work of the legislature, which in a democratic state represents the common will of the people after full public discussion and which can revise and alter what it has done if that does not work'.[46]

There will still, nevertheless, be occasions when the legislature's intervention strikes a judge as unwelcome; and when this is the case a judge might mount a legitimate if limited resistance by resorting to the principle which, in 1944, Wright proclaimed discredited. Wright resorted to the principle himself not five months before his Harvard lecture, when, eschewing an expansive interpretation of section 21 of the Indian Securities Act 1920, he asserted that the 'statute is, *prima facie*, to be

---

Paul Finn, 'Statutes and the Common Law' (1992) 22 *Univ. Western Australia L. Rev.* 7, 23–4.

[45] Lord Wright, 'Liberty and the Common Law' (1945–7) 9 *CLJ* 2, 3. See also John Willis, 'Statute Interpretation in a Nutshell' (1938) 16 *Can. Bar Rev.* 1, 20 ('What then is the present status of this presumption [against taking away a common-law right]? It still appears in the textbooks, of course; otherwise it seems to be falling into disuse. When the courts do make use of it, they tend to emblazon it with rhetorical glorification of the rights of Englishmen').

[46] Lord Wright, 'Public Policy' (1938), in his *Legal Essays and Addresses* (Cambridge University Press, 1939), 66–95 at 68, 71, 70. In the same year, Roscoe Pound offered much the same observation in the form of a lament: 'The common law has never been at its best in administering justice from written texts ... [I]ts traditional attitude toward statutes stands in the way of making them a basis of creative development ... [T]he common-law lawyer ... assumes that the statute is not meant to change the common law, or at least is meant to change it as little as possible, and so is prone to hold it declaratory if he can and at any rate to construe it strictly when it seeks to effect a change ... [A]n attitude which has a long-taught tradition behind it and will not readily yield ... make[s] the path of the legislative lawmaker a rough one.' Roscoe Pound, 'The Formative Era of American Law' (1938), in *The Life of the Law: Readings on the Growth of Legal Institutions*, ed. J. Honnold (New York: Free Press, 1964), 52–78 at 60–1.

construed as changing the law to no greater extent than its words or necessary intendment require'.[47] Even after Wright's retirement in 1947, many among the senior judiciary continued to work to this principle.[48] There is no doubt that the significance of the presumption against implicit alteration of the common law is easily overstated; some areas of modern law are almost entirely statute-based, after all, and offer up no distinctive common-law principles for preservation. But it seems equally beyond doubt that the presumption has sometimes proved to be a handy device for English judges disinclined to concede any more than the bare minimum to the will of parliament.

(b) From parliament to government

It was observed in the final section of the last chapter that there was a time when no distinction was drawn between the law-making functions of the legislature and the courts. The distinction started to emerge during the Tudor period, though it would be some way into the seventeenth century before the modern notion that parliamentary law making is legislation proper became fully accepted. Our second note of caution has to do with the idea that legislation proper – statute law – is straightforwardly the work of parliament.

To explain statute law as the work of parliament is an oversimplification. The removal of judges from the process of enacting statutes was, as we have seen, slow. While judges were gradually disinvested of their part in the process, moreover, others steadily acquired influence over it. 'When Parliament is called the Legislature', John Griffith wrote in 1951, 'what is meant is that no body or person can issue an order, rule, regulation, scheme or enactment having the force of law without Parliamentary authority. But it does not follow that Parliament is responsible for the whole of the legislative process or that an enactment which Parliament has not

---

[47] *Secretary of State for India in Council* v. *Bank of India Ltd* [1938] LR 65 Ind. App. 286 (PC), 298.

[48] See, e.g., *National Assistance Board* v. *Wilkinson* [1952] 2 QB 648 (Div. Ct.), 661 (*per* Devlin J); *Murugiah* v. *Jainudeen* [1955] AC 145 (PC), 152–3 (*per* Lord Morton); *George Wimpey & Co. Ltd* v. *BOAC* [1955] AC 169 (HL), 191 *per* Lord Reid ('where [statutory] language not calculated to deal with an unforeseen case must nevertheless be so interpreted as to apply to it … it is, I think, right to hold that, if the arguments are fairly evenly balanced, that interpretation should be chosen which involves the least alteration of the existing law'); *Mixnam's Properties Ltd* v. *Chertsey UDC* [1964] 1 QB 214 (CA), 233–4 (*per* Danckwerts LJ); *Black-Clawson International Ltd* v. *Papierwerke Waldhof-Aschaffenburg AG* [1975] AC 591 (HL), 613 (*per* Lord Reid).

specifically examined is invalid.'[49] One consequence of the mid nineteenth century reform initiatives was that legislation became ever more reliant on informed opinion. At the point of drafting bills, the views of advisory bodies and those likely to be directly affected by a proposed new law were increasingly regarded as significant; the culmination of this tendency is the modern expectation that the concerns and recommendations of relevant special interest groups, investigative bodies, law reform agencies and even the general public be taken into account when any notable change through statute law is being proposed.[50]

The most significant transformation of all since the mid nineteenth century has been government's role in the legislative process. While, particularly after the Reform Act of 1832, parliament started to legislate 'with remarkable vigour', setting down 'general rules' about 'what commons shall be enclosed, what roads should be widened, ... and so forth', it seemed to govern less as it increasingly entrusted the 'working' of those rules to the executive.[51] During the twentieth century, and particularly with the expansion of the welfare state, this trend intensified as parliaments with neither the time nor the capacity to attend to administrative detail increasingly delegated legislative powers to government departments. 'No amount of Montesquieu and Dicey could blind students of practical government to the obvious fact', John Willis wrote in 1932, 'that the government departments have long been permitted by statute to exercise powers of legislation and judicial decision delegated to them by Parliament.'[52]

---

[49] J. A. G. Griffith, 'The Place of Parliament in the Legislative Process' (1951) 14 *MLR* 279, 425 at 291.

[50] See David R. Miers and Alan C. Page, *Legislation*, 2nd edn (London: Sweet & Maxwell, 1990), 18–31. The UK Coalition Government which was elected in 2010 set about broadening the consultation process by introducing a public reading stage for all bills. In February 2011, the Protection of Freedoms Bill was used to pilot the initiative.

[51] See F. W. Maitland, *The Constitutional History of England* (Cambridge University Press, 1908), 383–4. It is perhaps worth spelling out – for the benefit of any readers unfamiliar with parliamentary systems – that the terms 'government' and 'executive' are being used interchangeably (and that the legislature is understood to be separate from government).

[52] John Willis, 'The Delegation of Legislative and Judicial Powers to Administrative Bodies: A Study of the Report of the Committee on Ministers' Powers' (1932) 18 *Iowa L. Rev.* 150, 151. Many lamented this trend – nobody complained more vociferously than did Lord Hewart in *The New Despotism* (London: Benn, 1929) – but Willis was among those who considered subordinate legislation a 'pressing necessity' which was constitutionally unobjectionable so long as its use was subject to safeguards reconciling it with the requirements of parliamentary sovereignty: see, e.g., John Willis, *The Parliamentary Powers of English Government Departments* (Cambridge, Mass.: Harvard University Press, 1933), 4. In a similar vein, see William A. Robson, *Justice and Administrative*

The modern redistribution of legislative power from parliament to government is attributable to more than just the growth of subordinate legislation. During the twentieth century, not only did the putting into effect of primary legislation increasingly become the task of the executive, but the executive was becoming ever more responsible for proposing primary legislation itself and indeed – because the government controls both the voting of the majority of the commons and, to a considerable extent, the legislative programme for a parliamentary session – for determining which legislative proposals were most likely to be enacted.[53] The officials who draft legislation, furthermore, are agents of the executive, under the control not of parliament but of the government of the day. A government, even one backed by a strong majority, by no means has complete control over the legislative process: real or anticipated backbench revolt, or voter mobilization, can quickly stymie a legislative proposal, and the government's legislative endeavours still cannot pass into law without parliament's approval. Most modern legislation is, nevertheless, government legislation, and only formally is parliament a law-making body[54] (a point which some observers considered reinforced when the House of Lords resolved in its judicial capacity to relax the rule prohibiting courts from using ministerial explanations of bills in parliament as aids to statutory construction).[55]

Law (London: Macmillan, 1928), 32; J. A. G. Griffith, 'Delegated Legislation – Some Recent Developments' (1949) 12 *MLR* 297, 305; Griffith, 'The Place of Parliament in the Legislative Process', 288–94; though cf. the more cautious note sounded by their principal French counterpart, Leon Duguit, in *Law in the Modern State*, trans. F. & H. Laski (London: Allen & Unwin, 1921), 125.

[53] And also – through the use of Henry VIII clauses (named after the Statute of Proclamations 1539, which gave Henry VIII legislative power by proclamation) – for determining whether primary legislation might be repealed or amended by subordinate legislation (and therefore without parliamentary scrutiny): see Lord Rippon, 'Henry VIII Clauses' (1989) 10 *Statute L. Rev.* 205; Lord Judge, Mansion House Speech, Lord Mayor's Dinner for the Judiciary, 13 July 2010, at www.guardian.co.uk/law/2010/jul/14/lord-igor-judge-henry (visited 3 February 2012). Judge (ibid. 6) reports that, so far as it is possible to tell from information provided by the Ministry of Justice, 120 Henry VIII clauses were passed in the 2008–9 parliamentary session alone. Some of the repealing and modifying powers conferred by such clauses can be remarkably wide-ranging (recent examples are the far-reaching powers granted to the Treasury under the Banking (Special Provisions) Act 2008 and to all ministers under the Constitutional Reform and Governance Act 2010, s. 51): see ibid. 5.

[54] See Henry Parris, *Constitutional Bureaucracy: The Development of British Central Administration since the Eighteenth Century* (London: Allen & Unwin, 1969), 184.

[55] *Pepper* v. *Hart* [1993] AC 593 (HL). The argument being that the relaxation of this rule created the possibility of statements of government policy being treated as indicative of parliamentary intentions. See, e.g., Johan Steyn, '*Pepper* v *Hart*; A Re-examination'

(c)   Common-law constitutionalism

Is it a problem that government, rather than parliament, tends to pull the legislative strings? In 1993 a then High Court judge, Sir John Laws, set out some extra-judicial observations on why we should be concerned. Legislative supremacy and parliamentary sovereignty, he noted, are truisms. 'In a democracy, the rule and the power of the elected legislature must command a unique authority, to which other public bodies, such as unelected judges, must pay unequivocal respect: they cannot share it, nor should they think of doing so.'[56] It 'is a received nostrum', furthermore, 'that Parliament is entirely free to legislate as it chooses'.[57] But if the government of the day controls an effective majority in the House of Commons, parliament is 'more often than not ... bent to the will of the Executive'.[58] It is all very well to say that 'the doctrine of Parliamentary sovereignty is an absolute rule', but where is 'the protection of the Queen's subjects against encroachments on what should be regarded as their fundamental freedoms by measures which the Government of the day may persuade the Legislature to adopt'?[59] 'I am not much impressed', Laws confessed, if 'the freedoms of the people are in the end protected only by the expectation, however confident, that the Government will behave decently'.[60]

The most obvious potential source of this protection – a 'Fundamental Rights Act'[61] – was clearly visible on the horizon at the time when Laws offered these remarks. But he was making more than just 'a plea for

---

(2001) 21 *OJLS* 59, 68 ('To give the executive, which promotes a Bill, the right to put its own gloss on the Bill is a substantial inroad on a constitutional principle, shifting legislative power from Parliament to the executive. Given that the ministerial explanation is *ex hypothesi* clear on the very point of construction, *Pepper* v *Hart* treats qualifying ministerial policy statements as canonical ... It is in constitutional terms a retrograde step: it enables the executive to make law'). The argument seems to overstate the case. Making legislative history admissible does not mean that it has to be treated as canonical: see Stefan Vogenauer, 'A Retreat from *Pepper* v *Hart*? A Reply to Lord Steyn' (2005) 25 *OJLS* 629, 657–65.

[56] John Laws, 'Judicial Remedies and the Constitution' (1994) 57 *MLR* 213, 223. (A version of the article was delivered as a lecture at Lincoln's Inn in May 1993.)

[57] Ibid.

[58] Ibid. See also John Laws, 'Law and Democracy' [1995] *Public Law* 72, 90–1 ('[T]he fact that Parliament often, perhaps generally, lacks sufficient systematic control over the Executive government has become a melancholy truism of our day ... [I]n the end, for most of the time, the Executive can bend Parliament to its will').

[59] Laws, 'Judicial Remedies and the Constitution', 223.

[60] Ibid. 224.   [61] Ibid. 227.

incorporation' of the European Convention on Human Rights into the law of the United Kingdom.[62] '[F]undamental freedoms', such as freedoms 'of speech, religion, political opinion and access to an impartial judiciary' are, he insisted, 'logically prior to ... democratic government', and are not to be 'left ... in the hands of a Legislature with unlimited power, however respectable its democratic credentials'.[63] Rather, it is the task of the courts to identify the nature of our fundamental rights and to articulate them as 'norms' or our 'constitutional fabric; ... however desirable may be the incorporation of the European Convention', he argued in 1993, 'this process may continue apace without that being done'.[64]

Laws's argument is illustrative of what nowadays goes under the name of *common-law constitutionalism*. The basic common-law constitutionalist thesis is that the common law already protects, or can certainly be developed by the courts so that it will protect, fundamental rights against legislative violation. The intricacies of this jurisprudence – a modern-constitutional variant on the so-called Radbruch formula[65] – need not be explored here. But the basic thesis warrants examination, for it has some support among senior judiciary, and sounds our third and final note of caution, which is that the spirit of *Bonham's Case* lives on[66] – that, to this day, judges in the United Kingdom can seem uncomfortable with the idea of unqualified parliamentary supremacy, and will even occasionally assert that there must be exceptional[67] instances where it is their task not merely to interpret a statute, or even to declare its incompatibility with human rights norms, but to determine whether it should be applied, and perhaps even (though this is not a proposition that any judge appears to be ready to advance in court) whether it should be recognized as legally valid.

---

[62] Ibid. 225.   [63] Ibid. 225–6.   [64] Ibid. 227.

[65] See Gustav Radbruch, 'Statutory Lawlessness and Supra-Statutory Law (1946)' (2006) 26 *OJLS* 1, 7 (Eng. trans. B. L. & S. L. Paulson) ('Where there is not even an attempt at justice, where equality, the core of justice, is deliberately betrayed in the issuance of positive law, then the statute is not merely "flawed law", it lacks completely the very nature of law').

[66] An observation which common-law constitutionalists themselves make now and again: see, e.g., T. R. S. Allan, *Constitutional Justice: A Liberal Theory of the Rule of Law* (Oxford University Press, 2001), 204–5; Allan, *Law, Liberty, and Justice: Legal Foundations of British Constitutionalism* (Oxford: Clarendon Press, 1993), 267–9; and, from a critical angle, Thomas Poole, 'Back to the Future? Unearthing the Theory of Common Law Constitutionalism' (2003) 23 *OJLS* 435, 444–7.

[67] See T. R. S. Allan, 'Deference, Defiance, and Doctrine: Defining the Limits of Judicial Review' (2010) 60 *UTLJ* 41, 54–5 ('[C]ourts should seek to avoid ... [t]he ... error ... [of] repudiat[ing], strik[ing] down, or hold[ing] incompatible with constitutional standards, a statute that is capable of a more benign construction ... it is only rarely in the Western liberal democracies that statutes are wholly incapable of such construction').

Consider, for example, how Laws developed his argument in subsequent essays. Not long after having declared that the authority of the elected legislature is something to which unelected judges must pay unequivocal respect, he offered a more nuanced claim: while 'it is for the courts to police the statute', they 'do not act under the statute. Their power is not derived from it; nor, ultimately, from any Act of Parliament.'[68] This is not to deny that 'the courts have been at pains to respect what they regard as Parliament's rights', including 'the freedom of members of either House ... to say whatever they choose during a Bill's passage'.[69] Not only, however, is there 'not a great deal ... to be said about' the fact 'that Parliament can enact whatever it chooses',[70] but the fact that parliament has this right 'says nothing' to detract from the very real 'power in the courts to strike down' statutes 'as inconsistent with' either fundamental freedoms or 'democracy itself'.[71]

Note Laws's language: courts have the power to *strike down* statutes because of their inconsistency with what would, in due course, be termed a 'constitutional fundamental'.[72] The assertion lends itself to a fairly obvious interpretation: that the courts can, exceptionally, review the legality of statutes. But if one accepts Laws's other main assertion – that parliament commands a unique authority to which judges must pay unequivocal respect – it is difficult to see how the courts could ever have so extensive a power of review. Judges could, none the less, logically claim to respect all legislative enactments as valid legal rules while assuming the power to control ('police') those rules so as to try to ensure that they are not given effect when their application would necessarily generate a ruling inconsistent with some constitutional fundamental. The court which exercised this power would not be striking down a statute in the sense of declaring it legally invalid, but would be determining it to be without effect in the immediate instance and leaving its fate – most likely invalidation through repeal, replacement or amendment – to parliament. Just what Laws understands the extent of the courts' power to be is not entirely clear: it seems most likely that he is making a case for – though he is not necessarily making a case for – judicial review in its strongest sense.

---

68   Laws, 'Law and Democracy', 77.

69   Ibid. 87.

70   John Laws, 'Public Law and Employment Law: Abuse of Power' [1997] *Public Law* 455, 455.

71   Laws, 'Law and Democracy', 87.

72   *R (Jackson and others)* v. *A-G* [2005] UKHL 56 at [102] (Lord Steyn).

The core of Laws's argument is that the courts derive this power (leaving aside the question of just what the power might be) from a category of 'higher-order law'.[73] Unlike 'ordinary laws',[74] this form of law is 'nowhere to be found'[75] set down. It is essential, nevertheless, to 'the survival and flourishing of a democracy',[76] and is incapable of being 'abrogated ... by the passage of a statute'.[77] The key to understanding higher-order law is the sovereignty or 'autonomy of every individual ... the ideal ... expressed in the well-known Kantian perception that the individual is an end in himself, never a means'.[78] It is a condition of an 'open society' where this ideal is accepted that there be a 'bias for freedom' which 'cannot be legitimately overridden by any government'.[79] In such a society, it 'must be a legal fact' that parliament 'holds power in trust for the people', that its power should be exercised at the service of and never against the principle of human autonomy; only 'on pain of self-contradiction' could one say otherwise.[80] On the basis of this higher-order law, the courts ensure – primarily by creating and applying 'substantive principles of judicial review'[81] – that 'basic rights ... are not only respected but enshrined',[82] and that 'those who exercise democratic, political power must have limits set to what they may do: limits which they are not allowed to overstep'.[83] So it is that the power of parliament can never 'in the last resort be absolute', for the courts can always rely on 'higher-order law ... for the entrenchment of constitutional rights and the protection of democracy itself'.[84]

---

[73] Laws, 'Law and Democracy', 84.

[74] Ibid. 87.   [75] Ibid. 90.   [76] Ibid. 81.

[77] Ibid. 84. Not only cannot higher-order law be abrogated by statute, Laws argues, but statutes implementing higher-order law – what he terms 'constitutional statutes' – are protected against implied repeal: see *Thoburn* v. *Sunderland CC* [2002] EWHC 195 (Admin) at [62]–[63].

[78] John Laws, 'The Constitution: Morals and Rights' [1996] *Public Law* 622, 623.

[79] Ibid. 635; also John Laws, 'Is the High Court the Guardian of Fundamental Constitutional Rights?' [1993] *Public Law* 59, 60 ('in the community of developed democracies, we have reached the stage where it can be said that rights of this kind [i.e., 'which broadly find their place in the principal substantive provisions of ... the ECHR'] have become an axiom').

[80] Laws, 'The Constitution: Morals and Rights', 635.

[81] Laws, 'Law and Democracy', 80.

[82] Ibid. 81.   [83] Ibid.

[84] Ibid. 92. Cf. F. A. Hayek, *Law, Legislation and Liberty: A New Statement of the Liberal Principles of Justice and Political Economy* (London: Routledge and Kegan Paul, 1982), III, 3–4 ('[W]ith the precious institutions of representative government Britain gave to the world also the pernicious principle of parliamentary sovereignty, according to which the representative assembly is not only the highest but also an unlimited authority. The latter is sometimes thought to be a necessary consequence of the former, but this is not so.'

There exists plenty of commentary and analysis supporting this sentiment.[85] There are also many critics – asking, among other things, how, in the United Kingdom, judicial review could ever operate so as to *ensure* the protection of fundamental rights,[86] why the protection of democracy should be entrusted to an unelected judiciary in any event,[87] whether the common-law constitutionalist argument rests on a wrongheaded conception of higher-order law,[88] and whether in fact it is not higher-law authority but something akin to self-confidence or audacity that

Its power may be limited, not by another superior "will" but by the consent of the people on which all power and the coherence of the state rest. If that consent approves only of the laying down and enforcement of general rules of just conduct, and nobody is given power to coerce except for the enforcement of these rules ... even the highest constituted power may be limited').

[85] See, e.g., Owen Dixon, 'The Common Law as an Ultimate Constitutional Foundation' (1957) 31 *Australian L. J.* 240; Dixon, 'The Law and the Constitution' (1935) 51 *LQR* 590, 596 ('... it is of the essence of the supremacy of the law that the Courts shall disregard as unauthorized and void the acts of any organ of Government, whether legislative or administrative, which exceed the limits of the power that organ derives from the law'); H. W. R. Wade, 'The Basis of Legal Sovereignty' [1950] *CLJ* 172, 189; Jeffrey Jowell, 'Beyond the Rule of Law: Towards Constitutional Judicial Review' [2000] *Public Law* 671, 675 ('Without the aid of the Human Rights Act ... our courts have begun ... explicitly endorsing a higher order of rights inherent in our constitutional democracy. These rights emanate not from any implied Parliamentary intent but from the framework of modern democracy within which Parliament legislates'); T. R. S. Allan, 'The Constitutional Foundations of Judicial Review: Conceptual Conundrum or Interpretative Inquiry?' (2002) 61 *CLJ* 87, 102 ('... Parliament's power to determine the outcome of particular cases is confined by the judges' duty to make sense of the law as a whole. Each person's rights and duties are those that relevant statutes confer or impose, when fairly construed in the light of general principles of justice deriving their constitutional status (at least primarily) from the common law'); and Tom Hickman, *Public Law after the Human Rights Act* (Oxford: Hart, 2010), 76–81.

[86] See, e.g., Thomas Poole, 'Dogmatic Liberalism? T. R. S. Allan and the Common Law Constitution' (2002) 65 *MLR* 463, 472–4; 'Questioning Common Law Constitutionalism' (2005) 25 *Legal Studies* 142, 155–7.

[87] 'The trouble with the higher-order law is that it must be given substance, be interpreted, and be applied. It claims superiority over democratically elected institutions; it prefers philosopher-kings to human politicians; it puts faith in judges whom I would trust no more than I trust princes.' J. A. G. Griffith, 'The Brave New World of Sir John Laws' (2000) 63 *MLR* 159, 165.

[88] See Martin Loughlin, *Foundations of Public Law* (Oxford University Press, 2010), 1–6. Note that in the United States, 'common-law constitutionalism' is generally understood to be the application of standard common-law philosophy (i.e., that the common law is a steady accretion of latent wisdom) to constitutional adjudication rather than the thesis that there is a realm of a priori principles or higher-order law to which courts can resort in order to protect fundamental rights. For a (modern Benthamite) critique of US-style common-law constitutionalism, see Adrian Vermeule, 'Common Law Constitutionalism and the Limits of Reason' (2007) 107 *Columbia L. Rev.* 1482.

motivates a court when it nullifies a statute.[89] None of this particularly concerns us here. What is of interest is the fact that the sentiment remains alive on the bench. Various extra-judicial hints to this effect were made in the 1990s,[90] though it is only quite recently that any senior judge has said anything in court that comes close to an endorsement of common-law constitutionalism. 'As a judge I am very conscious of the proper reluctance of the courts to intervene in issues of the validity of Acts of Parliament', Lord Carswell observed in *Jackson* v. *Attorney-General* in 2005. 'I do not', he continued,

> have any wish to expand the role of the judiciary at the expense of any other organ of the state or to seek to frustrate the properly expressed wish of Parliament as contained in legislation. The attribution in certain quarters of such a wish to the judiciary is misconceived and appears to be the product of lack of understanding of the judicial function and the sources of law which the courts are bound to apply.[91]

But other Law Lords in *Jackson* seemed to take a different position. One matter which was 'not directly in issue'[92] in the case, but which none the less had 'drastic [constitutional] implications',[93] was the scope of the Parliament Act 1949. In *Jackson*, the Act – which restricts the legislation-blocking powers of the House of Lords, but which was itself passed by the House of Commons without the lords' assent – was considered compatible with the principle of parliamentary sovereignty and upheld as valid. But could the Act be used, as the Attorney-General surmised it could, 'to bring about constitutional changes such as altering the composition of the House of Lords'[94] or 'introduc[ing] oppressive and wholly undemocratic legislation' (such as a statute which 'abolish[ed] judicial review' of administrative action)?[95] 'We ... in the United Kingdom have ... a legal order ... which ... assumes obligations to protect fundamental rights' of 'all individuals within [the] jurisdiction', Lord Steyn answered (elaborating an argument

---

[89] See Goldsworthy, *The Sovereignty of Parliament*, 240–2. The argument is (as Goldsworthy acknowledges) Hartian: see H. L. A. Hart, *The Concept of Law*, 2nd edn (Oxford: Clarendon Press, 1994), 153–4.

[90] Along with Laws's essays see, e.g., Lord Woolf, 'Droit Public – English Style' (1995), in his *The Pursuit of Justice*, ed. C. Campbell-Holt (Oxford University Press, 2008), 69–87 at 82–4; Stephen Sedley, 'The Common Law and the Constitution' (1997) 19 *London Review of Books* 8; 'The Sound of Silence: Constitutional Law without a Constitution' (1994) 110 *LQR* 270; 'Human Rights: A Twenty-First Century Agenda' [1995] *Public Law* 386, 389.

[91] *R (Jackson and others)* v. *A-G*, at [168].

[92] Ibid. at [73] (Lord Steyn).   [93] Ibid. at [100] (Lord Steyn).

[94] Ibid. at [101] (Lord Steyn).   [95] Ibid. at [102] (Lord Steyn).

which he had already hinted at extra-judicially);[96] and so, while parliamentary supremacy remains 'the *general* principle of our constitution', it 'is not unthinkable' that judges – who, after all, 'created this principle' – might '[i]n exceptional circumstances' have to determine the constitutional propriety of upholding parliamentary sovereignty itself.[97] 'Step by step, gradually but surely,' Lord Hope added, 'the English principle of the absolute legislative sovereignty of Parliament ... is being qualified'.[98] This is not, he insisted, an unwarranted usurpation of power by the judiciary. 'The principle ... has been created by the common law' and 'is built upon the assumption that Parliament represents the people whom it exists to serve'.[99] It stands to reason that '[t]he rule of law enforced by the courts' should be 'the ultimate controlling factor on which our constitution is based'.[100]

There are at least four general observations to be made about these *obiter dicta* in *Jackson*. If it is argued, first of all, that the capacity of judges exceptionally to determine the constitutional propriety of upholding parliamentary sovereignty can be attributed to the fact that the principle of sovereignty is itself a creation of the common law, it would seem to follow that this judicial capacity could be altered or abrogated by parliamentary

---

[96] See Johan Steyn, 'The Intractable Problem of the Interpretation of Legal Texts' (2003) 25 *Sydney L. Rev.* 5, 18–19; 'Dynamic Interpretation Amidst an Orgy of Statutes' (2004) 3 *European Human Rights L. Rev.* 245, 251–2.

[97] *R (Jackson and others)* v. *A-G*, at [102]. See also Lord Steyn, 'Democracy, the Rule of Law and the Role of Judges' (2006) 3 *European Human Rights L. Rev.* 243, 253 ('For my part the dicta in *Jackson* are likely to prevail if the government tried to tamper with the fundamental principles of our constitutional democracy, such as five-year Parliaments, the role of the ordinary courts, the rule of law, and other such fundamentals. In such exceptional cases the rule of law may trump parliamentary supremacy').

[98] *R (Jackson and others)* v. *A-G*, at [104]. See also his observations in *AXA Insurance* v. *Lord Advocate* [2011] UKSC 46 at [50]–[51].

[99] *R (Jackson and others)* v. *A-G*, at [126]. There are 'cases which turn on common law principles of judicial review', and 'where Parliamentary authority is at best implicit and at worst non-existent', another Supreme Court Justice has argued, but '[t]he problem in cases governed by common law principles of judicial review is that the [courts] do not do it [*sc.*, assess the limits beyond which law cannot be expected to carry moral authority] on a sufficiently principled or consistent basis'. Jonathan Sumption, 'Judicial and Political Decision-Making: The Uncertain Boundary' [2011] *Judicial Review* 301, 314–15. Cf. Stephen Sedley, 'Judicial Politics', *London Review of Books*, 23 February 2012, 15 ('The courts go to considerable lengths to respect the constitutional supremacy of Parliament; Sumption gives no serious instances to the contrary').

[100] *R (Jackson and others)* v. *A-G*, at [107]. See also ibid. at [159] (Baroness Hale): 'The courts will treat with particular suspicion (and might even reject) any attempt to subvert the rule of law by removing governmental action affecting the rights of the individual from all judicial scrutiny.'

enactment, 'since the prime characteristic of any common law rule is that it yields to a contrary provision of statute'.[101] Common-law constitutionalism – constitutionalism grounded in the common law – would seem by definition to be at the mercy of parliamentary sovereignty. Secondly, neither Lords Steyn nor Carswell explains the basis for their supposition that legislative supremacy is open to question. Both would appear to assume, yet it does not logically follow, that the principle of parliamentary sovereignty must be under the ultimate control of the courts because the courts created it. Thirdly, the representative nature of parliament is glided over too easily: the enactment of statutes is a formal, bicameral process involving multiple stages of deliberation and voting, careful scrutiny of bills in chamber and consultation with likely affected parties. (Aristotle considered 'the claims of justice and expediency' better served by statutes because they 'are made after long consideration, whereas decisions in the courts are given at short notice'.)[102] Recent history certainly offers examples of governments controversially forcing through commons and lords legislation curtailing civil liberties, and genuinely anti-democratic legislation – ousting the possibility of judicial review of administrative action, for example – cannot be dismissed as an impossibility. But – a point to be considered at length in the next chapter – courts do not make law according to the same public, transparent and highly-formalized procedures that apply to the legislature,[103] and the imperfections of the process by which parliament enacts statutes do not in themselves offer sufficient reason to conclude that an unelected judiciary might be, even if only exceptionally, warranted to assume for itself the power to review the legality of statutes.

Assuming that this is what is being assumed. The fourth, and the most important, general observation to make about the remarks in *Jackson* is that we should be wary of taking them too seriously. Is it really correct to claim that '[t]he dicta in *Jackson* go further than any judicial pronouncements to date to suggest that the absolute sovereign authority of Parliament

---

[101] Tom Bingham, *The Rule of Law* (London: Allen Lane, 2010), 167; and see also Mark Elliott, 'The Sovereignty of Parliament, the Hunting Ban, and the Parliament Acts' (2006) 65 *CLJ* 1, 4 ('It is simplistic to suggest that parliamentary sovereignty was straightforwardly judicially created in the same way as regular common law rules').

[102] *Rhetoric*, I. 1. 1354[b]. These would not have been unconsidered words: on the rigours and cumbrousness of the enactment procedure in Athens of the fourth and fifth centuries BC, see K. M. T. Atkinson, 'Athenian Legislative Procedure and Revision of Laws' (1939) 23 *Bulletin of the John Rylands Library* 107.

[103] See Jeremy Waldron, 'Legislation and the Rule of Law' (2008) 1 *Legisprudence* 91, 99–100.

is no longer acceptable as our prime constitutional principle', and that we now have 'compelling evidence that there are changed understandings and expectations ... which ... reject the notion of the unfettered authority of a legislature'?[104] We are, after all, dealing only with fairly meagre – and confined – dicta: in *Jackson*, the House of Lords was reviewing legislation with the aim of interpreting it rather than determining whether it should be struck down. Possibly the dicta are part of a broader process of judicial self-assessment, an early indication of a new emerging dynamic between courts and legislature.[105] But more likely they are simply a reminder of a long-established fact: that judicial awkwardness in the face of parliamentary supremacy is a hydra head. No generation of judges seems entirely comfortable with the proposition that a court can never query what parliament enacts. And, very occasionally, judges will assert it to be not beyond the bounds of legitimacy for a court, in the most exceptional circumstances, to stymie parliamentary will.

[104] Jeffrey Jowell, 'Parliamentary Sovereignty under the New Constitutional Hypothesis' [2006] *Public Law* 562 at 571, 563; and see also Aileen Kavanagh, *Constitutional Review under the UK Human Rights Act* (Cambridge University Press, 2009), 328 ('The dicta in *Jackson* are a dramatic expression of ... the new [*sc.*, post-HRA 1998] sense of legitimacy attached to the courts' ability to engage in constitutional review'); though cf. Richard Ekins, 'Acts of Parliament and the Parliament Acts' (2007) 123 *LQR* 91, 103 ('It is possible that *Jackson* will be remembered primarily for these assertions [by Lords Steyn and Hope]. This would be unfortunate for, with respect, the dicta in question are unargued and unsound, as well as less interesting than the live issues in the case'). '[N]ot only', according to Adam Tucker, do the 'conclusions [of Lords Steyn and Hope and Baroness Hale] ... cast doubt on the orthodox doctrine. Each of these three judges is deriving their stance on the scope of parliamentary power from their conception of the appropriate role of the courts in a democracy, and this resort to evaluative reasoning is entirely alien to the dogmatic approach that has dominated constitutional discourse for so long.' Adam Tucker, 'Uncertainty in the Rule of Recognition and in the Doctrine of Parliamentary Sovereignty' (2011) 31 *OJLS* 61, 87. This could be correct. But the conclusion for which he uses this proposition as support – 'the requirements of the rule of recognition in ... novel situations [such as *Jackson*] are indeterminate and, in line with all social rules, the concretization of an indeterminate social rule depends on an evaluative judgment by those trying to conform to it' (ibid. 88) – is questionable. The relevant dicta in Jackson acknowledge a determinate rule of recognition – legislative supremacy as a general constitutional principle – but can be read as suggesting that there may be exceptions to the principle which would, if constitutionally accepted as genuine exceptions, thereby revise the rule of recognition. That a rule of recognition can be qualified or revised does not mean that its current requirements must be indeterminate.

[105] '[T]he British constitution can be described as being in an historically unstable moment, one which may well be looked back on as a period of transition from parliamentary sovereignty to constitutional democracy.' Kate Malleson, 'The Evolving Role of the UK Supreme Court' [2011] *Public Law* 754, 762. Or may well not be. Malleson concedes that '[i]t is impossible to predict whether ... the Supreme Court' will 'find its *Marbury* v.

If a court stymies parliamentary will, however, must it be determining that an enactment is legally invalid? Might it not instead be interpreting the legislation and judging it to be ineffective? To be committed to the notion that parliamentary supremacy may have to yield to the rule of law when a statute offends against some constitutional fundamental does not necessarily entail commitment to the proposition that courts are entitled to strike down acts of parliament, for it is possible for a court to put a limit on parliamentary supremacy by resisting but not actually repudiating legislative will. This is not to suggest that it must be beyond the bounds of possibility for a court to declare a statute invalid: 'with or without a written constitution the courts may one day find themselves emboldened or provoked to strike down primary legislation', Stephen Sedley has observed.[106] But it is not clear that any modern judge genuinely does anticipate, much less favour, acquiring the power to review the legality of acts of parliament; only Laws, writing extra-judicially, appears to have taken something akin to this position.

If asked how British judges ought to deal with statutes depriving Jews of their citizenship or dissolving marriages between people of different races, F. A. Mann once warned, do not evade the issue by declaring oneself confident that parliament would never pass such laws.[107] The fact is that the courts are, sometimes, confronted with statutes laying down the fundamentally objectionable. But what do judges do in these instances? While some judges have hypothesized about how they might have to uphold the rule of law by challenging the propriety of parliamentary supremacy should a statute undermine a constitutional fundamental, striking down statutes as illegal has not been part of their actual repertoire. It is not unheard of, however, for courts to resolve not to apply an egregious statute. The old English common-law rule decreeing marital rape impossible found statutory support in section 1(1)(a) of the Sexual Offences (Amendment) Act 1976, which, in defining 'unlawful

---

Madison moment and cross the constitutional Rubicon by striking down legislation on the basis that it has breached a "constitutional fundamental"' (ibid. 763), that '[i]t is early days in the life of the new Supreme Court and [that] any assessment of its future role is inevitably speculative' (771).

[106] Stephen Sedley, *Ashes and Sparks: Essays on Law and Justice* (Cambridge University Press, 2011), 253. Though he is careful to add that he is 'not ... among those judges who have suggested that a point may come at which it became a judicial duty to override or annul laws passed by Parliament' (ibid. xiv), and that the possibility of judges acquiring this duty is 'not something' he 'either anticipate[s] or favour[s]' (246). See also ibid. 129–30, 352.

[107] See F. A. Mann, 'Britain's Bill of Rights' (1978) 94 *LQR* 512, 513.

sexual intercourse', provided that 'unlawful' must refer to intercourse outside marriage. When, in the early 1990s, a husband sought to rely on section 1(1)(a), the House of Lords held that marital rape was unlawful despite the statutory provision: the old common-law proposition that 'by marriage a wife gives her irrevocable consent to sexual intercourse under all circumstances' was, as Lord Keith put it, 'quite unacceptable', and it did not become acceptable because parliament had endorsed it.[108] But in refusing to give effect to the statutory provision, the House of Lords was not striking it down – that step in the nullification process was left, as indeed it had to be left, to parliament (which eventually aligned the statutory position with that of the House of Lords by enacting section 142 of the Criminal Justice and Public Order Act 1994). In an era when the judiciary is entrusted by parliament with the task of determining when parliament itself has passed legislation incompatible with the European Convention on Human Rights, the approach that the House of Lords took to the statutory provision on marital rape seems less radical than it did at the time. But the lesson to be taken from the House of Lords' ruling is as simple as it is important: a court need not strike down a statute if it is to restrict parliament's supremacy. The spirit of *Bonham's Case* does indeed live on, but primarily in the sense that we are as unclear today as Coke seemed unclear as to whether judges minded to resist parliament's will understand their power in upholding the rule of law to be confined to controlling a statute by declaring it to be of no effect, or whether some of them might genuinely believe – and, if ever faced with a constitutionally repugnant statute, would act on their belief – that they have the power to review legislation so as to determine whether it is legally valid or invalid.

It will be suggested, in the closing pages of the next chapter, that even if it is the case that there are judges today who do not consider the possibility of striking down legislation absolutely unthinkable, this does not sustain the conclusion that the United Kingdom must be moving towards a US-style system of judicial review. Nor, however, would it be correct to conclude – something that should be plain from this chapter – that judges always consider it their responsibility to give effect to parliament's laws, no matter how repugnant those laws might be. Recall that common-law constitutionalism was introduced into this discussion to sound a note of caution: when speaking of legislative supremacy, it is important to keep in mind that there appear always to have been judges who are intent on questioning parliament's wisdom. This hydra head ought not to be scorned.

---

[108] *R* v. *R* [1991] 4 All ER 481, 484.

Judges can, and do, significantly rein in statutes – sometimes to the point of rendering them ineffective. The mistake, it has been emphasized, is to deduce from this that the courts are able to derive from the common law the power to pronounce on the actual legality of legislation.

It is perhaps worth noting, finally, that when courts do stymie statutes, there may be a strong suspicion that they are seeking to replace parliament's law with legislation of their own. The fact, however, that a court refuses to abide by a statute which makes an unreasonable imposition does not mean that it must be replacing enacted legislation with a new law of its own making. A court which declines to give effect to an Act of parliament, and which does not find the justification for its action in statute law itself, may well be trying not to make new law but to uphold the customary part of the common law, or something akin to what Laws terms higher-order law. Courts engage in appropriate law making – by establishing, for example, principles of judicial review – so as to preserve or enshrine this higher-order law. But this is not to create the higher-order law itself; that law is, rather, the *status quo ante* which courts occasionally seek to reassert. The objective of a court which declines to give effect to an unreasonable statute might be not to replace the statute with judge-made law, but rather to make a decision on the basis of common-law constitutionalism in its authentic form – on the basis, that is, of a principle which the court considers to be long, perhaps immemorially, enshrined in the customary norms and practices of the community.

PART II

The jurisprudence of statutes

3

The quest to intellectualize statute law

It can often seem that while legal philosophers have much to say about judicial decision making, statute law has stirred their imaginations comparably little. Yet two important themes in modern jurisprudence, legal interpretation and the relevance of intentions in law, invariably – which is not to say always explicitly – inform analyses of statute law.[1] The first of these themes is central to Part III of this book, while the next chapter will address – and will take a position on – the question of whether intentions can be ascribed to legislatures. This chapter shows that it overstates matters to claim that jurisprudence has been inattentive to statute law. In modern legal philosophy, the authority of statutes has been subjected to considerable analysis, and the democratic superiority of enacted over judge-made law robustly defended. Generally speaking, none the less, the common-law jurist's preoccupation with statute law has been sporadic at best. What explains this?

1   Block-heads' law

The beginnings of an answer can be found, oddly enough, in an assessment of statute law offered by one of the most renowned critics of judge-made law, Jeremy Bentham. Bentham's assessment was hardly romantic. Eighteenth-century English statute drafters, he asserted, 'understand' – and are 'better paid' when they practise – 'the art of poisoning language', and so they tend to produce statutes which are blighted by 'repetitions and words' which 'are of no use',[2] and which are beyond the ken of ordinary

---

[1] There is also an important jurisprudential argument which, though not specifically about statute law, is often illustrated by reference to statute law: the argument that the idea of the rule of law is grounded in specific values of legality. The classic text is Lon L. Fuller, *The Morality of Law*, rev. edn (New Haven: Yale University Press, 1969).

[2] Jeremy Bentham, *Truth* versus *Ashhurst; or Law as it is, contrasted with what it is said to be* (London: Moses, 1823 [1792]), 15.

citizens.[3] It need not be this way, he insisted. Statutes could be written 'with no more words than necessary ... not only more intelligibly, but surer, in short sentences'.[4] They could be 'put into one great book, (it need not be a very great one) and what is particular to this and that class of persons ... into so many little books, so that every man should have what belongs to him apart, without being loaded with what does not belong to him'.[5] Bentham saw, in the discipline of statute drafting, an opportunity for the advancement of 'the art of legislation' – legislation, that is, conforming to the principle of utility.[6] Although the legislative initiatives of nineteenth-century English law reformers may have borne Bentham's influence, however, they were, by his own standards (and estimation), piecemeal and insufficiently ambitious.[7] His vision of a properly codified, utilitarian system of law was never – it never could be – realized.

Bentham's proposed remedy for the communicative deficiencies of statute law might have been a counsel of perfection, but there was nothing controversial about the diagnosis. Statutes, even when drafted with care, are often difficult to read. The primary reason for this is that the precise purview and objective of a statute may be complicated, technical or settled on after compromise, so that the determination of satisfactory statutory wording is likely to be borne of a drafter's anxieties as to whether the text captures everything that it is supposed to capture, and, if it does, whether it captures too much. It is not surprising that when a statute is described as 'utilitarian', the implication may be not philosophical but pejorative: 'utilitarian' in the sense of prosaic or functional as opposed to underpinned by the greatest happiness principle or some other articulation of utilitarian doctrine. Perhaps it is no accident, furthermore, that

---

[3] See ibid. 14.   [4] Ibid. 15.   [5] Ibid 14.

[6] '[T]he art of legislation ... teaches how a multitude of men ... may be disposed to pursue that course which upon the whole is the most conducive to the happiness of the whole community, by means of motives to be applied by the legislator.' Jeremy Bentham, *An Introduction to the Principles of Morals and Legislation*, ed. J. H. Burns and H. L. A. Hart (Oxford University Press, 1970 [1780]), 293.

[7] See Philip Schofield, *Utility and Democracy: The Political Thought of Jeremy Bentham* (Oxford University Press, 2006), 304–36; also Michael Oakeshott, 'The New Bentham' (1932) 1 *Scrutiny* 95, 123 ('It is all very well to see Bentham's influence everywhere in the legislation of the nineteenth century, but when we consider how extreme his views about English law actually were, what must be noticed is, not the number of his isolated suggestions which have been put into practice, but the total rejection which his fundamental principles have suffered'). Only in Portugal were Bentham's proposals for codification pursued in earnest, and even there the project was eventually abandoned: see Juan Pablo Couyoumdjian, 'An Expert at Work: Revisiting Jeremy Bentham's Proposals on Codification' (2008) 61 *Kyklos* 503.

statutes are normally spoken of as being not written but drafted – 'drafting' having the connotation of drawing technical plans. One cannot imagine many lawyers, certainly many common lawyers, interpreting as anything other than sardonic Stendhal's claim that, while working on *La Chartreuse de Parme*, he read two or three pages of the *Code civil* each morning in the hope that he might 'acquire the tone'.[8]

Nor should it seem surprising that jurists have struggled to conceive of statutes as something to be studied as case law is studied. Statutes 'are particularly fit for academic treatment',[9] P. J. Fitzgerald concluded in the 1970s, but his reasoning in support of this conclusion suggested that statute law makes for an interesting academic topic only if one focuses on something other than the statutes themselves – on the culture and the dynamics of the legislature, say, or on drafting techniques, or on the enactment process, or on statutory interpretation, or on legislative history, all of which, Fitzgerald believed, enable us 'to deepen our understanding and appreciation of what statutes are, how they came to be written and how they work'.[10] Nothing in his argument served to rebut his instinctive presumption that 'academics prefer cases to statutes as a subject of study … because cases are interesting and statutes dull'.[11]

While it seems an oversimplification to presume that in common-law teaching and scholarship there is a tendency to pay less attention to statute law than to case law because the former is leaden whereas the latter is not, there are certainly reasons for thinking that cases are generally more engaging than are statutes. Cases tend to concern protagonists in actual conflict, whereas statutes usually offer abstract solutions to potential conflicts. Case law usually sets out reasons for the solution of a problem in a particular way, while statutory provisions tend to stipulate how a problem is to be negotiated in general terms. In specific areas of law, some cases will tend to form a chain whereas the enacted law is more likely to take the form of discrete initiatives making no reference to, and usually requiring that the interpreter make no reference to, other statutes.[12]

---

[8] 'En composant *La Chartreuse*, pour prendre le ton, je lisais chaque matin deux ou trois pages du code civil, afin d'être toujours naturel; je ne veux pas, par des moyens factices, fasciner l'âme du lecteur.' Stendhal to Honoré de Balzac, 20 Oct. 1840, in Paul Arbelet, 'La véritable lettre de Stendhal à Balzac' (1917) 24 *Revue d'Histoire littéraire de la France* 537, 552.

[9] P. J. Fitzgerald, 'Are Statutes Fit for Academic Treatment?' (1970) n.s. 11 *JSPTL* 142, 148.

[10] Ibid. 146.   [11] Ibid. 144.

[12] Though the interpretation of a statute in context might sometimes require that it be read in the light of other statutes dealing with the same subject: see Rupert Cross, *Statutory Interpretation*, 3rd edn J. Bell and G. Engle (Oxford University Press, 2005), 56.

Judicial opinions, even when delivered extempore, tend to be literary; they exhibit an authorial voice, sometimes a very distinctive authorial voice, whereas statute law more often than not reads as if composed by committee. Unlike statute law, case law tends to flatter juristic intelligence by challenging the reader to follow and assess reasoned arguments, and to distinguish the reasoning in the case which is incidental to the ruling (the *obiter dicta*) from that which is necessary to it (the *ratio decidendi*). '[T]he formulary and statutory part of the law' is something at which even 'a plodding block-head may excel', Dr Johnson rather harshly concluded, precisely because statutes do not require that the reader be able to exercise this special capacity for distinguishing the wheat from the chaff.[13]

That cases tend to 'yield up their kernel slowly and painfully' rather than 'for the asking'[14] might be expected to be a cause for concern among common lawyers. As often as not, however, the difficulty is packaged as somehow indicative of the superiority of case law over statute law, the gist of the argument being that within the common law there rests a discernible – though not always easily discernible – collection of core principles the discovery of which makes immersion in cases, and the analysis of the arguments they set out, the most important undertaking on which a prospective lawyer could ever embark.[15] Lord Radcliffe seemed to be offering up a romanticized version of Bagehot when he remarked on how the prosaic nature of statute law might be likened to 'the ugly modern highway with its roaring traffic and its straight harsh lines', whereas the circuitousness of the common law resembles 'the by-ways that lead so pleasantly to park and manorhouse and old world cottages and the village green'.[16]

---

[13] James Boswell, *Life of Johnson*, ed. R. W. Chapman (Oxford University Press, 1980 [1791]), 358.

[14] Benjamin N. Cardozo, *The Nature of the Judicial Process* (New Haven: Yale University Press, 1921), 29.

[15] The classic statement along these lines being Coke's in his account of his colloquy between himself and James I: *Prohibitions del Roy* (1607) 12 Co. Rep. 63, 65 ('... causes which concern the life, or inheritance, or goods, or fortunes of [the King's] subjects, are not to be decided by natural reason but by the artificial reason and judgment of law, which law is an act which requires long study and experience, before that a man can attain to the cognizance of it').

[16] Lord Radcliffe, *Law and the Democratic State* (Birmingham: Holdsworth Club, 1955), 1. Cf. Walter Bagehot, *The English Constitution*, ed. P. Smith (Cambridge University Press, 2001 [1867]), 182–3 ('Our law very often reminds one of those outskirts of cities where you cannot for a long time tell how the streets come to wind about in so capricious and serpent-like a manner. At last it strikes you that they grew up, house by house, on the devious tracks of the old green lanes; and if you follow on to the existing fields, you may often find the change half complete').

Though Radcliffe suspected that we might sometimes underestimate the value of the highway, Lord Reid was convinced that the scenic route is always the better route. 'If you think in months, want an instant solution for your problems and don't mind that it won't wear well, then go for legislation. If you think in decades, prefer orderly growth and believe in the old proverb more haste less speed, then stick to the common law.'[17]

This association of statute law with directness and the quick fix seems almost ironic given that the history of English law is strewn with complaints about otiose and obsolete legislation and about the stultifying mysticism of badly drafted acts. Private international law, G. C. Cheshire observed in the first edition of his treatise on the subject, has been 'only lightly touched by the paralysing hand of the Parliamentary draftsman', and so it provides 'a golden opportunity, perhaps the last opportunity, for the judiciary to show that a homogeneous and scientifically constructed body of law, suitable to the changing needs of society, can be evolved without the aid of the legislature'.[18] Section 21 of the Finance Act 1922 is 'perfectly unintelligible to any layman or any lawyer who has not made a prolonged study with all his law books at his elbow', Rowlatt J objected in 1928, 'and it is a crying scandal that legislation by which the subject is taxed should appear in the Statute Book in that utterly unintelligible form'.[19] The Town and Country Planning Act 1959 provided nothing like an instant solution, the Court of Appeal concluded in 1964, to the question of how levels of compensation for the compulsory purchase of land are to be set. '[R]arely have I come across such a mass of obscurity, even in a statute', Lord Denning complained. 'I cannot conceive how any ordinary person can be expected to understand it.'[20] Harman LJ was no less damning: the Act is 'a monstrous legislative morass', he concluded, 'a slough of despond through which the court would never drag its feet'.[21]

In the common-law tradition, this lament has many variants. In his *Discourse on the Reformation of Abuses* (1551), a fourteen-year-old Edward VI complained of how too much statute law is 'superflous and

---

[17] Lord Reid, 'The Judge as Law Maker' (1972) n.s. 12 *JSPTL* 22, 28. See also *Morris* v. *C. W. Martin & Sons Ltd* [1966] 1 QB 716 (CA), 730 *per* Diplock LJ ('[T]hat is the beauty of the common law; it is a maze and not a motorway').

[18] *Cheshire, North & Fawcett: Private International Law*, 14th edn J. J. Fawcett, J. M. Carruthers and P. North (Oxford University Press, 2008), vii (preface to first edition [1935]).

[19] *Lionel Sutcliffe Ltd* v. *Commissioners of Inland Revenue* (1928) 14 TC 171, 187.

[20] *Davy* v. *Leeds Corporation* [1964] 1 WLR 1218, 1222.

[21] Ibid. 1224.

tediouse'[22] (though his contribution to the Reformation – especially the reform of liturgical rituals and communion service under the Acts of Uniformity of 1549 and 1552 – makes it abundantly clear that he had no objection to statute law in principle). Blackstone was convinced that if 'ill-judging and unlearned legislators' became 'proportionably better informed ... in the knowledge of the common law' before they set about legislating on a matter, they would discover that much legislation is surplus to requirement and that there is no need for the current 'statute book' to be 'swelled to ten times a larger bulk'.[23] Approximately a decade after Blackstone offered this advice, Thomas Jefferson disparaged 'the style of the later British statutes' and emphasized how important it was that the Virginia legislature did not seek to mimic 'their verbosity, their endless tautologies, their involutions of case within case, and parenthesis within parenthesis, and their multiplied efforts at certainty by saids and aforesaids, by ors and by ands'.[24] Statutes 'are a kind of hieroglyphics to the ordinary Englishman', Frederick Pollock wrote in his late thirties; it seemed to him impossible to avoid the conclusion 'that Parliament generally changes the law for the worse, and that the business of judges is to keep the mischief of its interference within the narrowest possible bounds'.[25] His view was unaltered by the time he reached his late sixties. 'It rather pleases me', he remarked in 1911, 'to dream of some planet where ... judicial discretion ... is not hampered at every turn by the meddling of partisan statutes with their crude remedies of contrary excess'.[26]

During Pollock's era, efforts were made – particularly through the Statute Law Revision Acts (the first of which was enacted in 1861) – to remove obsolete legislation from the statute book. But the rise of

---

[22] Edward VI, *On the Supremacy, with his Discourse on the Reformation of Abuses; and a Few Brief Notices of His Life, Education, and Death*, ed. R. Potts (Cambridge: Metcalfe, 1874), 8.

[23] 1 Bl. Comm. 10–11. See also Francis Bacon, 'Example of a Treatise on Universal Justice or the Fountains of Equity, by Aphorisms: one Title of it' (1623), in *The Works of Francis Bacon*, 14 vols. ed. J. Spedding, R. L. Ellis and D. D. Heath, (London: Longmans, 1861–79), V, 88–110 at 100 ('let those laws which are found to be wordy and too prolix be more compressed and abridged'), 104 ('The loquacity and prolixity used in the drawing up of laws I do not approve').

[24] *The Autobiography of Thomas Jefferson, 1743–1790*, ed. P. L. Ford (Philadelphia: University of Pennsylvania Press, 2005), 70.

[25] Frederick Pollock, *Essays in Jurisprudence and Ethics* (London: Macmillan & Co., 1882), 85.

[26] Frederick Pollock, *The Genius of the Common Law* (New York: Columbia University Press, 1912), 66. (Lectures delivered 1911.)

subordinate legislation in the late-nineteenth and twentieth centuries more than cancelled out the effects of this initiative, and from the 1940s the body of statute law expanded prodigiously decade upon decade.[27] While many would join with Bentham and Jefferson in calling for laconic, simply worded statutes,[28] furthermore, it is not particularly surprising that exhortation should have proved much easier than realization. Legislators, after all, cannot always treat the short, straightforward statute as a realistic option. Drafters may consider themselves obliged to use language consistent with that employed in related statutory provisions. Sometimes, they will have to tackle novel or complex subjects which leave them with no choice but to use esoteric words and phrases which have precise legal meanings. Quite often, they will be constrained from preferring the simple statement precisely because their task is to formulate nuanced, qualified, technical provisions in order to capture legislative compromises or to ensure that powers and obligations conferred on addressees neither fall short nor go too far.

Although, from time to time, academics bemoan the Cinderella status of statutes as compared with cases,[29] it is entirely understandable that the study of legislation should never have been at the heart of the law school curriculum. Students tend to assume that, as compared with case law, statute law is not only the most austere and technical (and least memorable)[30] part of the primary reading assignment, but also – since reported judicial opinions often excerpt, and build up from, relevant statutory

---

[27] See A. F. Wilcox, 'Too Many Laws' (1975) 125 *New LJ* 1082. For relevant figures, see *The Preparation of Legislation: Report of a Committee Appointed by the Lord President of the Council*, Cmnd 6053. (Chair: Sir David Renton, MP) (London: HMSO, 1975), para. 7.2. In recent decades the number of statutes enacted per session has plateaued, but the average length of statutes has increased considerably: see Michael Zander, *The Law-Making Process*, 6th edn (Cambridge University Press, 2004), 1–2. If one takes into account delegated as well as primary legislation, the decade-on-decade trend as regards both number and length appears to be one of growth: see Carol Harlow and Richard Rawlings, *Law and Administration*, 3rd edn (Cambridge University Press, 2009), 163–7.

[28] This was a popular hobby-horse among late nineteenth- and early twentieth-century parliamentary counsel: see, e.g., Courtenay Ilbert, *Legislative Methods and Forms* (Oxford: Clarendon Press, 1901); Henry Thring, *Practical Legislation* (London: Murray, 1902).

[29] See, e.g., William A. Robson, 'Legislative Draftsmanship' (1946) 17 *Political Quarterly* 330, 342; Julius Cohen, 'On the Teaching of "Legislation"' (1947) 47 *Columbia L. Rev.* 1301, 1306.

[30] An assumption somewhat validated by the fact that it is still quite common within the British university examination system for directors of undergraduate law courses to stipulate that no materials other than statutory materials may be brought into an exam. Whereas students are expected to remember case law, there seems often to be an assumption that they cannot be expected to remember statute law.

provisions – the least important. As for their teachers, the aspects of academic law that they value highest – explaining (and correcting mis-perceptions of) particular rules, principles, doctrines and premises, justifying their own theories and assessing the theories of others – are strongly reflected in judicial opinion writing. Statutory language, by con-trast, is more likely to put them in mind of what they tend to like the least about their jobs: the formulation and interpretation of memoranda, com-mittee minutes, rules, criteria, procedures and the like. The enthusiasm for studying judicial decisions in preference to enacted legislation is evi-dent from the English law journals, in which there is discernible a distinct tradition of case-note writing but relatively little commentary dedicated to statutes. Generally speaking, statute law has been regarded as a dusty and uninviting academic topic – in so far as it has been considered an aca-demic topic at all.

2   Statutes and statute making

While there are reasons for statutes receiving a raw deal in the history of the study of English law, it would be a mistake to deduce from these reasons that statutes are best understood as a humdrum subspecies of real law. English lawyers are wont to claim that many of the significant devel-opments in the principal areas of private law are essentially attributable to the courts. But such claims rarely withstand close scrutiny: negligence, contract and land are but three major areas of private law which, in the twentieth century, were significantly altered as much by parliament as by the courts. Some law-making initiatives – such as the establishment of the courts themselves, of certain types of legal procedure and of regula-tory agencies – have to be undertaken by legislatures; were they not, many tribunals and legal officials would be conferring powers on themselves or acting as judges in their own cause. Other initiatives, such as the creation of rules determining taxation and the distribution of benefits, entail pol-itical choices which are not only unsuited to courts and other bodies lack-ing democratic accountability but also, if they are to have the force of law, need to be approved by parliament in nothing short of statutory form.[31] Within some legal systems, legislation performs a particularly important role in specifying (though with the attendant danger of overspecifying) the scope and limitations of rights and principles which are articulated in

---

[31] See *Bowles* v. *Bank of England* [1913] 1 Ch. 59 (HL).

an underdetermined form in the constitution.[32] Statutes may have had a lowly place on the curriculum, but this bears no relationship to their place in the world.

It is, none the less, what might be termed the law-school conception of statutes that is central to this book. Statutes, viewed through this lens, are not normally understood to be discrete entities. Intellectual curiosity about a statute is usually curiosity not about the statute itself, as a (proposition of) law, but about the process of enactment, or how the statute is drafted, or how it is received by and interpreted in the courts, or the unintended consequences of enacting new law. Most of the interesting jurisprudential questions about statutes have to do not with the enacted law, but with matters such as how statutes come into being, the nature of legislative intent, the forms of 'law' that a statute can take (from the minor technical amendment to the ambitious codifying initiative), the types of legal intervention to which statutes are best suited and the differences between and comparative merits of statute and judge-made law.

But it would be a mistake, for at least three reasons, to think that statutory texts have no jurisprudential significance whatsoever. First, questions about how best to interpret statutory texts, the distinction between textual interpretation and interpolation, and the authority of the text vis-à-vis the authority of the interpreter are, as we will see in Part III, constants throughout jurisprudential history. Secondly, the culture and values of a legal system will be exhibited in part by the size and content of its statute book, the degree to which statutory texts are clear, intelligible, prospective and demand only actions which it is possible for addressees to perform, and the range of topics that statutes address and the types of rules they contain (whether, for example, the legislation of a particular period or in a particular area of law shows the legislature to be more disposed to enacting incentivizing rather than command-and-control legislation, say, or to enacting general standards instead of precise directives). Finally, although critical commentary on statutory texts sometimes trades on the simplistic, hortatory argument that the law would be so much better if only the language of statutes was always simple and unambiguous – an American legal realist once proposed that much that is wrong about the law could be put right if only every statute were drafted 'as clearly ... as ... a cook-book or an almanac or a column of classified

---

[32] See Grégoire Webber, *The Negotiable Constitution: On the Limitation of Rights* (Cambridge University Press, 2009), 147–80. On the danger of legislative overspecification, see ibid. 75.

advertisements'[33] – more serious scholarship on statute drafting acknowledges that clarity is a double-edged sword. For not only is it a mistake to
think that simplifying the language of the law is tantamount to simplifying the problems – often very complicated problems – that the relevant
law is supposed to address, but the consequence of laconic drafting may
be that a significant amount of interstitial law making has then to be done
by the courts.[34]

So it would be rash to deny that the statute, *qua* text, has intellectual
significance. Yet, if we leave statutory interpretation aside, what we find
is that the thorniest and most intriguing questions about statute law arise
when we turn our attention from the text to the general legislative process
culminating in the text. Many of the most valuable accounts of this process are essentially technical and explain matters such as the composition
of the legislative chamber, the steps involved in drafting a bill, consultation requirements, the legislative timetable, the hurdles that have to be
cleared before a bill can be submitted for assent, and the procedure and
conventions governing the legislative drafting agency. This chapter and
the next one deal with none of these matters. Instead, they address two
jurisprudential arguments concerning the enactment process.

The first of these arguments can be read as an attempt to vindicate a
little-celebrated body of legal theory known as 'legisprudence'. The argument culminates with the claim that there are compelling reasons against
empowering courts to declare invalid statutory provisions which infringe
against constitutional norms – against courts undertaking, to use the
common shorthand, 'strong' judicial review. It is the reasoning building up to this claim, rather than the claim itself, which is central to this
chapter. The reasoning might be summarized thus: judicial panels are
usually small, fairly homogeneous bodies composed of narrowly trained
legal experts who tend not to be appointed, and who can almost never be
removed, through a process of democratic election, whereas legislatures
are nearly always large, diverse assemblies which have the backing of
the electorate, pay considerable attention to law-making procedure and,

---

[33] Fred Rodell, *Woe Unto You, Lawyers!* 2nd edn (New York: Berkeley, 1980 [1957]), 123.
[34] 'Where a statute has been in force for some time, any gain in apparent clarity and sim-
      plicity in the statute itself may be found merely to have shifted the complex task of ascer-
      taining its precise effect, in a particular case, further into the area of case-law. Where the
      statute is a new one, there may be a period of greater uncertainty while the lines on which
      the principles stated in the statute should be applied are being settled by the courts, often
      at considerable expense to individual litigants.' *The Preparation of Legislation*, para.
      10.10.

owing to their size, tend to make better informed and more intelligent decisions than do courts. Since judicial decisions do not emerge out of a rigorous and electorally accountable law-making process – and since most courts will, by virtue of the size of their panels, be denied the benefit of considerable collective wisdom – judicial invalidation of legislation, so the argument goes, is very difficult to justify in a democracy. The question of how egregious enactments are to be handled absent this power to invalidate is a jurisdictional and empirical one. In the United Kingdom, as we have seen, courts do not consider themselves at liberty to invalidate what parliament enacts and must interpret or make declarations on such enactments according to the terms that parliament itself legislated in the form of the Human Rights Act 1998. The argument against strong judicial review can, in relation to the UK, only serve as a note of warning. This chapter will conclude with some reflections on whether there is much point to this warning, though the bulk of the chapter concerns the more abstract question of how legislative enactments can be said to be legally authoritative.

The next chapter concerns legislative intent. The concept is much scorned by legal and political theorists, not least because to ascribe the capacity for intention formation to a body which lacks a mind is to assume the impossible. Yet the notion of legislative intent is not unintelligible. Legislatures exhibit the most rudimentary of intentions simply by deliberately changing the law. More than this, they exhibit intentions by forming and carrying out plans distinctive to the legislature itself, plans which – because legislatures operate according to robust decision procedures relating to debate, amendment, voting and so on – the legislature ratifies as its own (rather than particular members' or a majority's) unique acts. Although an argument will be set out very much in support of the concept of legislative intent, the point of the next chapter is not to claim that legislatures' intentions must always have a bearing on how judges interpret statutes. The identification of a general legislative intention – the intention simply to change the law – is of no real help for the purposes of statutory interpretation. And even when a legislature's specific intention in enacting a statutory provision seems clear, a court might have strong reasons for declining to abide by that intention. Not the least of these reasons is that judges are guided, first and foremost, by the plain meaning of the statutory text: this meaning might, but will not necessarily, mirror the identifiable or reasonably inferred specific intentions of the enacting legislature. To make the case for the intelligibility of legislative intention does not by itself entail a commitment to what American lawyers would term an intentionalist over a textualist approach to statutory interpretation; indeed, this study, though it abstains from elaborating a position on intentionalism versus textualism, builds from the presumption that only exceptionally will there be compelling reasons to look to sources extraneous to the statutory text to try to determine legislative intent.

3   An agenda for legisprudence?

In *Taking Rights Seriously*, Ronald Dworkin sets out an argument which is commonly summarized by the proposition that principles are moral standards which courts invoke in order to protect individual rights, whereas policies are standards which legislatures enact in order to pursue some general (social, economic or political) goal.[35] Discussions of this aspect of Dworkin's jurisprudence have tended to focus on the claim that judicial decisions are implicitly or explicitly based on arguments of principle. Since Dworkin was elaborating a rights thesis – that courts are the fora of principle and protectors of rights – this particular bias is only to be expected. But what of the proposition that the legislature is the primary arena for the advancement of policy? In explaining the rights thesis, Dworkin does not explicitly identify policy advancement as a task best performed by legislatures.[36] His acceptance of the proposition is, nevertheless, easily inferred – though it is perhaps more accurate to say that his acceptance of it requires no explanation given that the rights thesis concerns not the effort to bring policies to fruition through the enactment of statutes, but the work of the courts (including the work that courts do when they interpret statutes).

In *Law's Empire*, Dworkin does draw attention to the connection between legislatures and policy advancement. Legislators, like judges, ought to aspire to the ideal of integrity. 'A judge who accepts integrity will think that the law it defines sets out genuine rights litigants have to a

---

[35] See, e.g., David Dyzenhaus, 'The Rule of Law as the Rule of Liberal Principle', in *Ronald Dworkin*, ed. A. Ripstein (Cambridge University Press, 2007), 56–81 at 60 ('In the "Introduction" [to *Taking Rights Seriously*], Dworkin outlined the distinction … between policy and principle, according to which the role of judges is to be the guardians of the moral "principles" immanent in the law, whereas legislatures make decisions about policy or collective welfare …'); T. R. S. Allan, 'Dworkin and Dicey: The Rule of Law as Integrity' (1988) 8 *OJLS* 266, 270 ('[T]he court's function is to determine the legal rights of the parties and not to adopt a particular view of the general welfare. The latter is a function properly left in a democracy to the legislature').

[36] See Ronald Dworkin, *Taking Rights Seriously* (London: Duckworth, 1977), 22–3, 90–100.

decision before him. They are entitled, in principle, to have their acts and affairs judged in accordance with the best view of what the legal standards of the community required or permitted at the time they acted, and integrity demands that these standards be seen as coherent, as the state speaking with a single voice.'[37] Judicial decisions reached in accordance with this ideal do not simply treat like cases alike but rather try 'to find, in some coherent set of principles about people's rights and duties, the best constructive interpretation of the political structure and legal doctrine of their community'.[38] Legislative integrity likewise 'asks those who create law by legislation to keep that law coherent in principle'[39] (an ambition which legislatures motivated by principles of justice and fairness will not always pursue successfully).[40] But the demands of legislative integrity can only realistically be pitched at the level of general welfare, and so, as compared with the demands of adjudicative integrity, they are less exacting: given, that is, that the legislative process would be 'paralyzed' if legislators tried to do anything more than 'pursue general strategies that promote the overall good as defined roughly and statistically',[41] integrity in decisions on policy necessarily 'commend[s] a general collective goal that respects equality of concern overall … rather than … supposing that each individual statute … must award each citizen something he is entitled to have'.[42] In *Law's Empire*, the jurisprudence of legislation does make it onto the stage, though the jurisprudence of judicial decision making is still the star of the show.

Should it be this way? This is not a loaded question. It is all very well to imply that there must be something amiss when one of the most

---

[37] Ronald Dworkin, *Law's Empire* (London: Fontana, 1986), 218.

[38] Ibid. 255.

[39] Ibid. 167, also 176 ('… asks lawmakers to try to make the total set of laws morally coherent').

[40] See ibid. 178–84.   [41] Ibid. 222.

[42] Ibid. 311. See also Ronald Dworkin, *Freedom's Law: The Moral Reading of the American Constitution* (Oxford University Press, 1996), 344 ('It is true, of course, that when political controversies are decided by legislatures … the decision is likely to be governed by what most people want. That is desirable when an issue turns on what is in the best interests of the community as a whole, and the gains to some groups are balanced by losses to others. In such matters, numbers should count. But they need not count, at least not for that reason, in matters of fundamental principle … In such cases, it is important that the public participate in the decision not because the community should reach the decision most people favor, but for the … reason that … self-respect requires that people participate, as partners in a joint venture, in the moral argument over the rules under which they live … [T]hat citizen's *role* as a moral agent participating in his own governance … is sometimes better protected if the mechanisms of decision are not ultimately majoritarian').

carefully developed jurisprudential projects of the past four decades is dedicated principally to the matter of what makes for good judicial decision making and devotes comparatively slight attention to the question of what makes for good statute making. But the fact is that the project has made a significant impression on academic lawyers (and not only legal philosophers) in the common-law world and beyond, while scholarship dedicated to the path not taken – scholarship sometimes filed under the heading of 'legisprudence' – has never moved in very far from the margins of legal philosophy. Oliver Wendell Holmes famously declared that what he meant by 'the law' was simply '[t]he prophecies of what the courts will do in fact'.[43] While neither Holmes nor the jurists who followed in his wake seemed particularly committed to this narrow definition,[44] it is hardly controversial to describe the American legal realist tradition as predominantly concerned with what goes on in the courtroom. Even though not every branch of modern jurisprudence has been as court-oriented as was realism, none – with the exception of public choice-inspired research in the field of law and economics – has focused primarily on the law-making function of legislative assemblies. In 1950, Julius Cohen, a law professor and former adviser to the West Virginia state legislature, wondered aloud why the legal realists had taken so little interest in statute law. 'Assuming much of judicial law to be nothing more than policy-making, is there anything inherently unique in its make-up or in its impact upon human relations to justify the realists in singling out this area of policy-making as the major target of their attacks? Is one to assume that policy-making on the legislative level is not in need of a good dose of the same kind of "realism"? How explain [sic] so bold an attack on so narrow a front?'[45]

By 1983, Cohen's message was essentially unchanged: '[l]egisprudence' had for the most part 'been left to languish' and '[t]he inquiries of jurisprudence' remained 'focused mainly on the judicial side of the legal

---

[43] O. W. Holmes, Jr, 'The Path of the Law' (1897) 10 *Harvard L. Rev.* 457, 461.

[44] Cf., e.g., Karl Llewellyn, *The Bramble Bush: On Our Law and Its Study* (New York: Oceana, 1951), 2–3: 'law ... is about the fact that our society is honeycombed with disputes ... Actual disputes call for somebody to do something about them ... This ... is the business of the law. And the people who have the doing in charge, whether they be judges or sheriffs or clerks or jailers or lawyers, are officials of the law. *What these officials do about disputes is, to my mind, the law itself*' (emphasis in original). Holmes himself seemed merely to be emphasizing that what ultimately matters for the parties to a dispute is what a court orders.

[45] Julius Cohen, 'Towards Realism in Legisprudence' (1950) 59 *Yale L. J.* 886, 887.

order'.[46] But on what, exactly, was legisprudence supposed to focus? After over three decades campaigning for the topic, Cohen was still unsure. '[L]egisprudence has suffered an identity problem'; any 'proposed agenda … is suggestive' and cannot 'pretend to be exhaustive' – it could concern the statutory text, the process leading to the creation of that text, principles of good statute making, approaches to statutory interpretation and much more besides.[47]

It would be a mistake to assume Cohen to be wholly without jurisprudential allies. There are votaries for legisprudence around to this day, and, over the past decade or so, there has emerged a significant body of literature concerning legisprudence as a theory of rational legislation.[48] Much of this literature assesses particular concepts, conventions, procedures and proposals – such as legislative deliberation, democratic legitimacy, drafting techniques and digitization – which reveal obstacles to, or which might be elaborated so as to facilitate, the improved use of legislation as a rational means to achieve particular social and political ends.[49] Some theorists working within this modern legisprudential tradition have pursued a more ambitious objective: that of developing models of legislative rationality.[50] The efforts at modelling which have emerged to date have tended to be schematic, abstract and oriented towards civilian juristic preoccupations and cultures. Not only do most of these efforts seem, in substance and in form, to relate more immediately to civil law than to common-law legal theory and legislative arrangements, but they sometimes build on

---

[46] Julius Cohen, 'Legisprudence: Problems and Agenda' (1983) 11 *Hofstra L. Rev.* 1163, 1163–4.

[47] Ibid. 1165, 1182.

[48] See, e.g., *Legisprudence: A New Theoretical Approach to Legislation*, ed. L. J. Wintgens (Oxford: Hart, 2002); *The Theory and Practice of Legislation: Essays in Legisprudence*, ed. L. J. Wintgens (Aldershot: Ashgate, 2005); *Legislation in Context: Essays in Legisprudence*, ed. L. J. Wintgens and P. Thion (Aldershot: Ashgate, 2007). In 2007, *Legisprudence: International Journal for the Study of Legislation* was founded. The journal publishes – in the words of its own advertisement – studies of 'the rational creation of legislation' which make 'use of the theoretical insights and tools of current legal theory', and which look beyond the 'problems of the *application* of law by the *judge*' to 'the possibilities of the enlargement of the field of [jurisprudential] study [so] as to include the *creation* of law by the *legislator*' (emphases in original).

[49] For evidence of the teleological orientation of this literature, see, e.g., Manuel Atienza, 'Practical Reason and Legislation' (1992) 5 *Ratio Juris* 269; Kaarlo Tuori, *Critical Legal Positivism* (Aldershot: Ashgate, 2002), 134–7.

[50] See, e.g., A. Daniel Oliver-Lalana, 'Legitimacy Through Rationality: Parliamentary Argumentation as Rational Justification of Laws', in Wintgens (ed.), *The Theory and Practice of Legislation*, 239–58; Manuel Atienza, 'Reasoning and Legislation', in Wintgens (ed.), *The Theory and Practice of Legislation*, 297–317.

conceptions of statutory rules which common lawyers are likely to consider inordinately mechanistic or limiting.[51] Both initiatives – the elaboration of particular legislative concepts and the development of general legislative models – seem to be regarded by common-law legal theorists as not so much uninteresting as at the periphery of their own enquiries. The lowly status of legisprudence as a type of jurisprudence is perhaps also attributable to the fact that the abiding concerns of legisprudents – legislative deliberation, democratic representation, political compromise and so on – make it look less like legal philosophy and more akin to a theory of democratic decision making, a cousin of polyarchy and public choice rather than positivism and natural law. In modern times, furthermore, legal philosophers have tended to regard citizens' deference to the enactments of legislatures essentially as an empirical matter, explained by the fact that statutes have democratic legitimacy. Perhaps the main reason legisprudence has resonated little among legal philosophers is that some of the most interesting legisprudential questions – what judges might be entitled to do with statutory rules, whether those rules are genuine law, whether legislatures can meaningfully be said to have intentions and whether there exist general principles distinguishing good from bad legislation[52] – have never been absent from their agenda. Whatever explains the status of legisprudence, the fact of the matter is that a dedicated jurisprudence of statute law has seemed hardly more enticing to modern legal theorists – certainly common-law legal theorists – than has the study of statutes themselves.

Not everybody has accepted this state of affairs lying down. 'I know of no safe depository of the ultimate powers of the society but the people themselves', Thomas Jefferson wrote to William Jarvis in 1820.[53] Jefferson took issue with Jarvis's apparent faith in 'the judges as the ultimate arbiters

---

[51] Cf., e.g., Luc J. Wintgens, 'Legisprudence as a New Theory of Legislation' (2006) 19 *Ratio Juris* 1 with Vlad Perju, 'A Comment on "Legisprudence"' (2009) 89 *Boston Univ. L. Rev.* 427 – Perju's principal criticism of Wintgens's account of legislation being that Wintgens pays insufficient attention to the capacity of legislation to be freedom-enabling as well as freedom-constraining.

[52] This last question is one which most common-law legal philosophers will identify with Fuller's eight precepts of legality: see Fuller, *The Morality of Law*, 33–94; though see also Edward L. Rubin, 'Law and Administration in the Administrative State' (1989) 89 *Columbia L. Rev.* 369. For similar civilian attempts at identifying and elaborating principles of sound statute law making, see e.g. Norberto Bobbio, 'Le bon législateur' (1971) 14 *Logique et Analyse* 243; Manuel Atienza, *Contribución a una teoría de la legislación* (Madrid: Civitas, 1997), 27–40.

[53] Thomas Jefferson to William C. Jarvis, 28 September 1820, in *The Writings of Thomas Jefferson*, ed. P. L. Ford (New York: Putman's, 1899), X, 161.

of all constitutional questions; a very dangerous doctrine indeed, and one which would place us under the despotism of an oligarchy'.[54] This way of thinking, if not quite this conclusion, is echoed in a series of writings produced over the past two decades by the legal and political philosopher, Jeremy Waldron. In these writings, legisprudence – Waldron's preferred term would probably be 'democratic jurisprudence'[55] – at last finds a clear agenda.[56] Waldron makes a powerful case for legislation by legislatures as the quintessentially democratic form of law making, while calling into question the democratic acceptability of subjecting such legislation to strong judicial review. While his case against judicial review has attracted considerable comment,[57] and while the following discussion elaborates on some of the elements of that case, it is his explanation of the authority of legislation by assembly rather than his position on judicial review that focuses our attention.

---

[54] Ibid. 160.

[55] See Jeremy Waldron, 'Can there be a Democratic Jurisprudence?' (2009) 58 *Emory L. J.* 675.

[56] Modern positivists, he asserts, have generally neglected the structural features of legislatures: see Jeremy Waldron, *Law and Disagreement* (Oxford: Clarendon Press, 1999), 27, 44–5. (Hereafter *LD*.) Generalizations about modern positivists are always risky given that one of the most well known among their number, Hans Kelsen, was so prolific and eclectic. In the early 1940s, Kelsen observed that Austrian constitutional arrangements for the review of legislation were markedly different from those which exist in the United States because responsibility for review was vested not only in the Austrian Supreme Court but also in a separate administrative court (*Verwaltungsgerichtshof*) staffed not by regular judges but by jurists, politicians with legal experience, and other legally qualified (but politically appointed) officials from outside the court system: see Hans Kelsen, 'Judicial Review of Legislation: A Comparative Study of the Austrian and the American Constitution' (1942) 4 *Jnl of Politics* 183, 188–97. The gradual erosion of democracy in Austria during the 1930s, Kelsen recognized, meant that the administrative court became an instrument of Austrofascism. But he believed that by 1934, the year in which 'the semi-fascist Austrian Constitution' was enacted, the court system as a whole was succumbing to the same fate in any event: see ibid. 187–8. Under a democratic system, he thought, it is better that judicial review not simply be entrusted to an ordinary judiciary (a position which many other European lawyers would come to share: see David Robertson, *The Judge as Political Theorist: Contemporary Constitutional Review* (Princeton University Press, 2010), 11–13, 193).

[57] See, e.g., Dimitrios Kyritsis, 'Representation and Waldron's Objection to Judicial Review' (2006) 26 *OJLS* 733; Dean Machin, 'Democracy, Judicial Review and Disagreements about Justice' (2009) 3 *Legisprudence* 43; Richard Stacey, 'Democratic Jurisprudence and Judicial Review: Waldron's Contribution to Political Positivism' (2010) 30 *OJLS* 749; Annabel Lever, 'Is Judicial Review Undemocratic?' (2007) *Public Law* 280; Aileen Kavanagh, 'Participation and Judicial Review: A Reply to Jeremy Waldron' (2003) 22 *Law and Philosophy* 451; Richard H. Fallon, Jr, 'The Core of an Uneasy Case for Judicial Review' (2008) 121 *Harvard L. Rev.* 1693.

4   The many versus the few

Waldron presents his case against judicial review of legislation as a contribution to constitutional debate in the United Kingdom.[58] The case is intended, one assumes, as a warning against following a path taken by other jurisdictions, for, as has been observed already, judicial review in this strong sense – as opposed to judicial review of administrative action, or judicial declarations that particular statutes are incompatible with human rights norms – is not an option which UK courts have at their disposal. In the United States, by contrast, there does exist in the courts the power to review the constitutionality of statutes. The counter-majoritarian dilemma that the existence of this power poses has, in the US, long been recognized.[59] A standard response to the dilemma, certainly in the second half of the twentieth century, has been to contend that so long as the courts undertake constitutional adjudication in accordance with some general principle of adequate neutrality or prudence, judicial review of legislation will amount not to the imposition of the arbitrary will of the minority over the majority, but to a responsible and politically impartial (and also, theorists within this tradition came to argue, a democracy-enhancing) method of checking that the legislature does not abuse the immense power that citizens grant it by virtue of elections.[60]

It is not surprising, however, that US constitutional lawyers have occasionally wondered if the potential dangers of law making by the elected representatives of the people are overstated, and whether the counter-majoritarian conclusion entailed by judicial review of legislation is really justifiable.[61] Waldron is among the unconvinced. 'The concern most commonly expressed about legislation', he observes, 'is that legislative procedures may give expression to the tyranny of the majority'; as a result of this concern, we take the 'need for constitutional constraints

---

[58] *LD* 16.

[59] For an account of the dilemma (conceived in philosophical and constitutional terms), see Michael Walzer, 'Philosophy and Democracy' (1981) 9 *Political Theory* 379.

[60] See, e.g., Herbert Wechsler, 'Toward Neutral Principles of Constitutional Law' (1959) 73 *Harvard L. Rev.* 1; Alexander M. Bickel, *The Least Dangerous Branch: The Supreme Court at the Bar of Politics* (New Haven: Yale University Press, 1962); John Hart Ely, *Democracy and Distrust: A Theory of Judicial Review* (Cambridge, Mass.: Harvard University Press, 1980).

[61] See, e.g., Mark Tushnet, *Taking the Constitution Away from the Courts* (Princeton University Press, 1999), 154–76. The question is not unique to the US constitutional context: see, e.g., Allan C. Hutchinson, *The Province of Jurisprudence Democratized* (Oxford University Press, 2008), 167–96.

on legislative decisions' to be 'more or less axiomatic'.[62] There is relatively little concern, however, about the power of a small group of 'black-robed celebrities'[63] to impose these constraints. Why not? The answer cannot be that courts are better placed to reach correct conclusions about justice, rights and the common good, for judges disagree with one another no less than do members of legislatures regarding the rights that citizens should have. '[I]t seems something of an insult' to citizens, Waldron suggests, to assign the resolution of disagreements over what rights we have to the judiciary on the basis that such disagreements ought not to be resolved 'by majoritarian processes', only for it then to transpire that 'the judges disagree among themselves along exactly the same lines as the citizens and representatives do'.[64]

Not only are courts as likely as legislatures to be beset by internal disagreement, but legislatures are, compared with courts, better structured to handle such disagreement. For not only do legislatures 'incorporate disagreement into their proceedings'[65] – as do courts – but they operate according to rules and procedures governing (among other things) representation, hearings, debate, voting and proposals for amendment.[66] Statute law 'deserves respect',[67] indeed, because it is an achievement secured through a process which puts a premium on not only majority decision and giving each person's view the greatest possible weight in relation to others,[68] but also on formal procedures, civility, toleration of dissent and workable solutions to large-scale disagreements.[69]

---

[62] *LD* 11.   [63] *LD* 291.

[64] *LD* 15; see also Jeremy Waldron, 'Rights and Majorities: Rousseau Revisited', in his *Liberal Rights: Collected Papers 1981–1991* (Cambridge University Press, 1993), 392–421 at 416–8; and Adrian Vermeule, *Judging under Uncertainty: An Institutional Theory of Legal Interpretation* (Cambridge, Mass.: Harvard University Press, 2006), 20, 242–3.

[65] *LD* 24.

[66] See *LD* 40, 70, 76; and cf. Roscoe Pound, 'Common Law and Legislation' (1908) 21 *Harvard L. Rev.* 383, 384 ('[M]odern statutes are not to be disposed of lightly as off-hand products of a crude desire to do something, but represent long and patient study by experts ... [W]hile bench and bar are never weary of pointing out the deficiencies of legislation, to others the deficiencies of judge-made law are no less apparent').

[67] *LD* 108.   [68] *LD* 114.

[69] See *LD* 102, 106. Of course, majority decision is the preferred method of adjudicative bodies as well as legislatures. 'In the Supreme Court of the United States, for example, decisions are taken by voting; and five votes prevail over four, whatever the merits of the individual decisions ... The difference, when an issue is shifted from legislature to court ... is a difference of constituency, not a difference of decision method. We stick to the principle of majority rule; only now [i.e., in the case of the US Supreme Court] it is applied to a decision-making body of nine individuals, rather than a body of hundreds'. Jeremy Waldron, 'Deliberation, Disagreement, and Voting', in *Deliberative Democracy*

Perhaps the strongest reason for questioning why courts should be assumed to be better guardians of individual rights than legislatures has to do with the relative size of each body, and the fact that legislatures tend to be composed of large numbers of people representing diverse and often conflicting views. Many a reservation has been expressed about vesting legal decision-making capacities in large bodies. 'How', Rousseau asked (rhetorically) in 1762, 'can a blind multitude, which ... rarely knows what is good for it, carry out for itself so great and difficult an enterprise as a system of legislation?'[70] Blackstone spelled out the implication behind this question only a few years after Rousseau had posed it: 'When laws are to be framed by popular assemblies, even of the representative kind, it is too Herculean a task to ... extract a new system from the discordant opinions of more than five hundred counsellors.'[71] For James Madison, the difficulty with inordinately large representative assemblies is not that they do not easily yield a decision but that the decisions they do yield tend to be emotive, confused, even cabalistic: 'the more numerous any assembly may be ... the greater is known to be the ascendancy of passion over reason ... The countenance of the government may become more democratic; but the soul that animates it, will be more oligarchic. The machine will be enlarged, but the fewer, and often the more secret, will be the springs by which its motions are directed.'[72] Madison's perspective is echoed in modern studies demonstrating how groups deliberating on a matter about which its members are essentially like-minded tend, after deliberation, to take a more extreme position on that matter than was taken by its median member before deliberation began.[73]

However, large *diverse* groups of people, possessing varying degrees of knowledge, are likely to make more intelligent decisions than individuals (even very intelligent individuals) or smaller groups; their errors tend to cancel one another out, and their average solution will often be at least as

---

and Human Rights, ed. H. Hongju Koh and R. C. Slye (New Haven: Yale University Press, 1999), 210–26 at 215.

[70] Rousseau, *The Social Contract*, II. 6.

[71] 3 Bl. Comm. 267.

[72] *Federalist 58* [James Madison], in Alexander Hamilton, James Madison and John Jay, *The Federalist* (New York: Barnes & Noble, 2006 [1787–8]), 326.

[73] See, e.g., Amiram Vinokur and Eugene Burnstein, 'Novel Argumentation and Attitude Change: The Case of Polarization Following Group Discussion' (1978) 8 *European Jnl of Social Psychology* 335; Cass R. Sunstein, *Why Societies Need Dissent* (Cambridge, Mass.: Harvard University Press, 2003), 111–44.

good as that suggested by their smartest member.[74] The legislative assembly, Waldron argues, exemplifies the large, diverse group (although one would never guess as much, he claims, from reading the works of modern legal philosophers, who invariably seem 'most comfortable'[75] treating the legislature as 'a single author'[76]), and individuals generally do well to defer to its wisdom: as a 'large and polyphonous'[77] assemblage of 'many people … with quite radically varying states of mind',[78] intent on combining 'their diverse views into something singular',[79] the legislature has 'available a broader range of experience and insight than I can accumulate on my own' and so 'is likely to come up with better answers than I can'.[80]

---

[74] See James Surowiecki, *The Wisdom of Crowds* (London: Little, Brown, 2004), 4–7, 9–11, 29–39, and (on democratic decision making) 269–71.

[75] *LD* 42.

[76] *LD* 45. Waldron repeatedly claims that one of the failings of traditional positivist jurisprudence is its conceptualization of the legislature according to the single author model (see, e.g., *LD* 42–3, 121; also Jeremy Waldron, *The Dignity of Legislation* (Cambridge University Press, 1999), 25–31). This claim invites at least four brief responses. The first is that neither Austin nor Bentham, both of whom expressed strong views on parliamentary reform, were ignorant of the intricacies of parliamentary procedure and the composition of the legislative assembly. The second is that Bentham, precisely because he did understand that the legislature is an elected assembly and not a single author, was as disapproving of judicial review of legislation as is Waldron: '[t]he people', Bentham wrote, 'have had, at least, some share in chusing [Parliament]. Give to the Judges a power of annulling its acts; and you transfer a portion of the supreme power from an assembly which the people have had *some* share, at least, in chusing, to a set of men in the choice of whom they have not the least imaginable share; to a set of men appointed solely by the Crown: appointed solely, and avowedly and constantly, by that very magistrate whose partial and occasional influence is the very grievance you seek to remedy.' Jeremy Bentham, *A Comment on the Commentaries and a Fragment on Government*, ed. J. H. Burns and H. L. A. Hart (Oxford University Press, 1977 [1774–6]), 488. Thirdly, as Waldron himself concedes, both Bentham and Austin acknowledge in their accounts of legal authority that sovereignty might rest either in one person or an assembly or body of persons (*LD* 43). Given that both are theorizing about authority, and therefore deliberately writing in fairly abstract terms, their descriptions of legislatures might better be described as written in a form of shorthand rather than premised on a single author model. Finally, in directing his critique at Hart's version of positivist jurisprudence as set out in *The Concept of Law*, Waldron laments 'Hart's failure to consider the deeper jurisprudential significance of legislative structure and its relation to rules of recognition' (*LD* 41–2). Possibly. But what Waldron seems not to account for in his discussion of *The Concept of Law* is that Hart was writing not a detailed, technical work of jurisprudence but a 'short monograph[] unencumbered by detailed footnotes and designed to introduce students' – primarily, undergraduate students – to a general legal topic 'in an interesting and thought-provoking way'. Nicola Lacey, *A Life of H. L. A. Hart: The Nightmare and the Noble Dream* (Oxford University Press, 2004), 172.

[77] *LD* 10.   [78] *LD* 43.

[79] *LD* 45.   [80] *LD* 85.

While the positions taken by Rousseau, Blackstone and Madison are not lost on Waldron, there are, he thinks, persuasive probabilistic and philosophical arguments in favour of trusting the wisdom of large, diverse legislatures. There is, first of all, the basic insight behind Condorcet's jury theorem: if the likelihood (in the case of an either–or decision) of any individual vote after deliberation being correct is greater than if an individual were to toss a coin, the probability that the decision opted for by a simple majority of voters is greater than 0.5 – and rises as the size of the voting group increases. Certainly the assumptions behind this theorem – particularly that votes are cast independently,[81] that there are only two possible outcomes and that each voter has a better than even chance of being correct – restrict the range of real decision-making scenarios to which it might apply. Nevertheless, in those scenarios where the premises are satisfied, the theorem, Waldron believes, supports the conclusion that '[i]f a large number of legislators address themselves scrupulously to some objective issue and if they each have a better than even chance of being right, then the ordinary citizen would be wise to trust the decision generated by a majoritarian machine out of their individual votes'.[82]

It matters little that these scenarios will not materialize very often, for there is no need to commit to the assumptions of Condorcet's jury theorem to reach the conclusion that large, diverse legislatures are likely to make particularly intelligent decisions. '[J]ust as a feast to which many contribute is better' – larger and more varied – 'than a dinner provided out of a single purse', Aristotle observed, 'so too with regard to … character and thought'.[83] The Aristotelian case for having faith in the wisdom of crowds deserves, Waldron thinks, especially serious consideration. On the Aristotelian account, when a multitude converges in order to make decisions, it is able – because members pool their knowledge, experience, insight and perspectives – to make judgments which are likely to be better than any reached by the individuals within it.[84] '[A]ny member of the assembly, taken separately, is certainly inferior to the wise man. But the

---

[81] On the ambiguity of this notion in Condorcetian analyses – it is impossible, in many voting scenarios, for voters to *form* their voting preferences independently of other voters – see David M. Estlund, Jeremy Waldron, Bernard Grofman and Scott L. Feld, 'Democratic Theory and the Public Interest: Condorcet and Rousseau Revisited' (1989) 83 *Am. Pol. Sci. Rev.* 1317 at 1326–8, 1338.

[82] *LD* 135–6.

[83] *Politics*, III. 11. 1281[b].

[84] See Jeremy Waldron, 'The Wisdom of the Multitude: Some Reflections on Book 3, Chapter 11 of Aristotle's *Politics*' (1995) 23 *Political Theory* 563, 568–9.

state is made up of many individuals. And as a feast to which all the guests contribute is better than a banquet furnished by an individual man, so a multitude is a better judge of many things than any individual.'[85] Large groups of people with diverse views 'are capable of pooling ... perspectives to' demonstrate 'a practical intelligence that outstrips the intelligence of which any one of them is capable' and thereby 'come up with better decisions than any one of them could make on his own'.[86]

5   The authority of statute law

From this premise – that the wisdom of the many tends to be superior to the wisdom of the few – Waldron develops two lines of argument, one about the authority of statute law and the other about judicial review. The argument about judicial review deserves no special attention in a study of legislation. Let us, then, focus not on the question, 'why judicial review?' but on the question, 'why not majority decision instead?'

An argument in favour of deferring to majority decision might be constructed from one of the core theses of modern analytical jurisprudence. According to the relevant thesis, legitimate authoritative directives provide exclusionary reasons for action: our recognizing a directive as authoritative, in other words, means that as a matter of rational choice we treat our own personal thinking regarding how to act in a particular situation as excluded from the judgment process, and that we instead defer to the authority's judgment as to what is right on the balance of reasons.[87] We can infer from this, Waldron claims, that a legislature can only issue directives which satisfy this formula for authoritativeness if it is able to synthesize 'the diverse experiences and knowledge of the various legislators' so 'that their interaction will produce standards that are superior to those that any individual citizen could work out for himself'.[88] Statute law only meets this criterion of authority, that is, if there 'is something about [its] provenance or procedure ... that gives us greater confidence in our trying to follow [it] than in our trying to figure out for ourselves what is to be done about the matter that [it] addresses'.[89] Are the enactments of legislatures authoritative in this sense?

---

[85] *Politics*, III. 15. 1286ᵃ.
[86] LD 72; also ibid. 137 and Jeremy Waldron, 'Legislation by Assembly', in *Judicial Power, Democracy and Legal Positivism*, ed. T. Campbell and J. Goldsworthy (Aldershot: Dartmouth, 2000), 251–77 at 251–7.
[87] See Joseph Raz, *The Morality of Freedom* (Oxford: Clarendon Press, 1986), 57–69.
[88] LD 85.   [89] LD 96.

Part of the reason we should answer affirmatively is that large, diverse assemblies generally produce more intelligent answers than individuals.[90] But this, for Waldron, is not the end of the matter. Statute law has, as it were, earned its stripes: it emerges out of a formal procedure whereby parties with diverse interests deliberate on a precise text and in accordance with formal rules. '[T]he best reason a court or a citizen can have for deferring to [a legislature's] decisions' is that the process of 'law-making … matches the plurality of the represented with a plurality of representatives'.[91] Through the process leading to enactment, statute law acquires 'democratic legitimacy':[92] it 'is an *Act of Parliament*, not an act of the majority party … made in the name, and for the sake, of the entire community'.[93] Deference to an enactment of the legislature, as exhibited by ordinary citizens and by legal officials (including citizens and officials who were not in favour of the particular enactment), is attributable to the principle, *e pluribus unum*: to the fact that the legislature battles with plurality, disagreement, factionalism, self-interest, political deal making and more – factors which Waldron bundles together as 'the circumstances of politics'[94] – in order to produce its own all-things-considered position.[95] The authority of a statute is attributable, in other words, to 'its emergence, under specified procedures, as an *"unum"* out of a plurality of ideas, in circumstances where we recognize a need for one decision made together'[96] by the citizenry represented 'as a political community' rather than as 'simply the aggregate of its individual members'.[97]

There are two general questions raised by this argument. First, is the authority of enacted legislation always ascribable to its democratic legitimacy, even within a democratic system? Waldron presents a confident case in the affirmative. Majority decision 'allow[s] a voice and a vote in

---

[90] See *LD* 135–6.   [91] *LD* 54.

[92] *LD* 53. The term as used here connotes democratic decision making on legislative proposals before a legislative assembly. It has another, no less straightforward connotation: the democratic election of those who constitute the assembly.

[93] *LD* 144 (emphasis in original); and see also Jeremy Waldron, 'Legislating with Integrity' (2003) 72 *Fordham L. Rev.* 373, 389–92.

[94] *LD* 102, 106, 144, 159–60.

[95] 'A piece of legislation deserves respect because of the achievement it represents in the circumstances of politics: action-in-concert in the face of disagreement.' *LD* 108. See also Waldron, *The Dignity of Legislation*, 156–7.

[96] *LD* 144; and see also Waldron, *The Dignity of Legislation*, 91.

[97] *LD* 272; and see also Jeremy Waldron, 'Legislation by Assembly' (2000) 46 *Loyola L. Rev.* 507, 526–31.

a final decision-procedure to every citizen of the society'.[98] It enables 'rights-bearers ... to resolve disagreements about what rights they have among themselves and on roughly equal terms',[99] and accords them equal concern 'by respecting the fact of their differences of opinion' and by 'not requir[ing] anyone's view to be played down or hushed up'.[100] The realization of majority decision – the enactment of statute law – 'has the characteristic that it gives ordinary people a stake in the rule of law, by involving them directly or indirectly in [a statute's] enactment, and by doing so on terms of fair political equality ... [It] is a means by which the members of the society can take control of the basic structure of their society'.[101]

It might be argued that such observations do not always synchronize with political reality. The strength and the discipline of the British party system, for example, along with the fact that a considerable proportion of members of parliament hold safe seats, ensures that British politicians are not accountable to the people in quite the same way as are elected representatives in the United States; indeed, British politicians are often free to support and vote for legislative proposals which most of the 'rights-bearers' in their constituencies, and possibly countrywide, would prefer to reject – the vote for the abolition of the death penalty in 1965 is an obvious example. A significant portion of the legislation that is enacted looks to be not so much contrary to democratic will as disconnected from it. Furthermore, even if one confines one's attention to primary legislation (and also leaves aside laws resulting from private members' bills), it quickly becomes clear, on perusing the statute book, how most enacted legislation is non-political and esoteric; much of this legislation generates little in the way of parliamentary debate. To describe such legislation as having democratic legitimacy might seem inordinately grandiose.

Neither of these arguments need be taken particularly seriously, however. Waldron's depiction of majority decision making is better read as an effort to represent not political reality (he certainly appreciates that real democratic-legislative processes are often far from exemplary)[102] but something like a paradigmatic or central case of legislative law making

---

[98] *LD* 299.   [99] *LD* 254.   [100] *LD* 111.

[101] Jeremy Waldron, 'Legislation and the Rule of Law' (2008) 1 *Legisprudence* 91, 100.

[102] See, in particular, his candid assessment of New Zealand's parliament in Jeremy Waldron, *Parliamentary Recklessness: Why We Need to Legislate More Carefully* (Auckland: Maxim Institute, 2008), 14–33.

in a democracy.[103] Although many instances of majority decision will be 'more or less peripheral' or 'watered-down versions of the central cases',[104] and although these cases should not be ignored, they do not invalidate the argument that we might obtain a better understanding of the nature of legislative authority if we treat central cases of majority decision seriously. Furthermore, even a central case of law making by majority decision will entail some arbitrariness and compromise – as when a political system requires the electorate to vote along party lines. Concessions and shortcomings in such a system are defensible, Waldron argues, if they are 'reasonable in the circumstances of politics'[105] – reasonable, that is, in the sense that the resulting legislation can be understood as an acceptable (though imperfect) effort at 'action-in-concert in the face of disagreement'.[106] Statute law, however modest or ambitious its aims, has democratic legitimacy in the sense that it must be subject to norms of due process (a canonical text, the opportunity for clause-by-clause scrutiny and so on), there must be the opportunity for formal deliberation on the legislative proposal – even if there is little expectation that the opportunity will be taken up with any enthusiasm – and, perhaps most importantly of all, any citizen has a case for crying foul if a bill were to become law without regard for established principles of statutory enactment.[107]

The second general question arising out of Waldron's argument that the authority of enacted legislation is ascribable to its democratic legitimacy is essentially about quality control. What if the decision of the political community, as represented in a statute, turns out to be a very bad decision? Waldron offers two answers to this question. First, if a bill is enacted and becomes authoritative law but it turns out to be 'the wrong decision about what democracy requires, then although there is a loss to democracy in the substance of the [statute], it is not silly for citizens to comfort themselves with the thought that at least they made their *own*

---

[103] Recently, he has come close to this reading himself: see Jeremy Waldron, 'Thoughtfulness and the Rule of Law' (Summer 2011) 18 *Brit. Acad. Rev.* 1, 1 ('often it represents a paradigmatic exercise …').

[104] John Finnis, *Natural Law and Natural Rights*, 2nd edn (Oxford University Press, 2011), 11. On watering down, see also ibid. 431–2.

[105] *LD* 116.   [106] *LD* 108.

[107] In modern times, instances of crying foul are as often as not attributable to the applicability of subordinate legislation, which is typically drafted by officials acting alone or as members of administrative agencies. It would be misleading, however, to characterize these officials and agencies as acting in disregard of legislative due process, since their authority to produce subordinate legislation will usually have been granted by the legislature.

mistake about democracy rather than having someone else's mistake'[108] – the mistake, say, of 'a nine man junta clad in black robes'[109] – 'foisted upon them'.[110] Secondly, when legislators trample on human rights they 'forfeit their authority'.[111] This does not mean that there is a 'need for an *additional* institution' to determine what should happen next; on the contrary, 'if there are controversies ... about natural law, it is important that a *representative* assembly resolve them' – '[t]he institution which comprises our representatives and the institution which resolves our ultimate differences in moral principle should be one and the same'.[112] Review of legislation should be the job of the legislature itself.

The first of these answers is not only fatalistic, but it also relies on a false assumption. To claim that we could, in the event that a legislature enacted a statute contravening a constitutional fundamental, at least console ourselves with the knowledge that it was *our* legislature that did the deed, is to commit to the fallacy of thinking that there is a distinctive *we* – the (majority of the) people – who wanted a particular instantiation of the legislature and got it by voting for it.[113] Most if not all of those who voted in the UK elections of February 1974 and May 2010 no doubt wanted a clear majority for their preferred party rather than the hung parliaments that they got. Furthermore, although in modern times there has been in the United Kingdom something of a redistribution of legislative power from parliament to the executive (as was observed in Chapter 2), it is still the case that an elected government cannot actually determine what does and does not become law – that even a government voted in by a clear majority may find itself in the minority on many legislative proposals. In short, it clarifies matters not at all to conceive of democracy-stymieing legislation as being a mistake which is somehow owned by the people.

The second answer invites the obvious objection that the legislature becomes a judge in its own cause.[114] But then might we not say that members in the majority on *any* decision-making body of last resort must judge in their own cause – that the body, 'since it has the last word', is '*ipso facto* ruling on the acceptability of [the majority's] own view'?[115] The analogy

---

[108] *LD* 293–4.   [109] *LD* 309.   [110] *LD* 294.

[111] *LD* 307.   [112] *LD* 309.

[113] See John Finnis, 'Human Rights and their Enforcement' (1985), in his *Collected Essays. Volume III: Human Rights and Common Good* (Oxford University Press, 2011), 19–46 at 22.

[114] See *LD* 296–7.

[115] *LD* 297; also Jeremy Waldron, 'Legislatures Judging in Their Own Cause' (2009) 3 *Legisprudence* 125 at 137, 144–5.

is a little too simple. A legislature which reviews old statutes of bygone incarnations of the assembly may be having the last word on those statutes, but it is not in any real sense judging in its 'own' cause. Similarly, the members of a modern constitutional court empowered to review legislation might have the final say on the legality of that legislation, but they can be assumed to have no political investment in the legislation itself (or in its removal).[116] If a legislature were to review the validity of a statute which was enacted after being proposed and supported by some of its current members, by contrast, it would most likely – particularly in instances where it reached the conclusion that the legislation ought to remain exactly or substantially as it stands – be suspected of performing a manoeuvre tantamount to judging in its own cause.

Does this mean, then, that the idea of legislation being reviewed by the legislature is indefensible? Not at all. One could be unconvinced by Waldron's arguments about the superior decision-making capacities of legislatures as compared with courts and yet still reasonably reject the proposition that it is better if judges rather than legislators review the legality of statutes, for incommensurability considerations make it impossible to demonstrate that a system of parliamentary supremacy is preferable to a system of strong judicial review, or vice versa: '[t]rue, the English-speaking North Atlantic courts which invalidate legislation under bills of rights have a record disfigured with unjust or malign and ill-reasoned decisions ... But legislatures, too, fail in justice, or promote injustice ... [I]t is absurd to seek

---

[116] Though it would be overstating matters to claim that judges (leaving aside the matter of whether they are judges on a constitutional court) never have any stake in enacted legislation. As we have seen already in this study, there was a time when Law Lords could – and sometimes would – contribute to legislative debates. Only in very recent times has there been a concerted attempt to ensure a clearer separation of powers (see Chapter 2). One aspect of this endeavour is the disqualification of justices of the Supreme Court from speaking and voting on legislation before the House of Lords and its committees in an effort to minimize the possibility of credible claims being made to the effect that Justice A can be shown to have taken a definite position on the enactment of statute Y, which is being challenged as incompatible with Convention rights in case P – presided over by, among others, Justice A. It is also worth noting that in Strasbourg jurisprudence the principle that tribunal members must not act in both an advisory and a judicial function with respect to the same matter has been cited as the main reason for requiring changes to the composition of bodies such as the Conseil d'État in Luxembourg and the Raad van State in The Netherlands (which advise on legislation but also adjudicate administrative law disputes in the final instance) so as to ensure their compliance with the independence and impartiality requirement under Article 6.1 of the European Convention on Human Rights: see *Procola* v. *Luxembourg* (1995) 22 EHRR 193; *Kleyn* v. *Netherlands* (2004) 38 EHRR 14.

an "overall balance" sheet, identifying possible worlds with and without judicial review of legislation as better and worse states of affairs all things considered."[117] Perhaps the principal worry about leaving the decision to abrogate a statute in the hands of the body responsible for enacting it is that it invites the tyranny of the majority. But this worry trades on an over-simplification of the democratic law-making process. Legislators know that their choice to enact, and their failure to repeal or amend, contro-versial statutes can rebound on them in the courts and, perhaps more sig-nificantly, in elections: the costs of egregious legislation, as Lord Hoffman once observed, are ultimately political rather than legal.[118] In recent years, furthermore, parliamentary systems founded on the Westminster model have sometimes appeared to mimic some of the characteristics associated with strong judicial review by establishing executive committees to advise their legislatures on the constitutionality of statutes. So it is that there exist in Canada, New Zealand and the United Kingdom vetting bodies which consider proposed legislation and changes to legislation in order to advise on the consistency of the proposals with human rights norms.[119] A legisla-ture's decision to change the law might be prompted by such advice, or by a judicial declaration.[120] Mimicry, nevertheless, is all that this can be. The

---

[117] Finnis, 'Human Rights and their Enforcement', 21.

[118] 'Parliamentary sovereignty means that Parliament can, if it chooses, legislate contrary to fundamental principles of human rights. The Human Rights Act 1998 will not detract from this power. The constraints upon its exercise by Parliament are ultimately polit-ical, not legal. But the principle of legality means that Parliament must squarely con-front what it is doing and accept the political cost.' *R* v. *Secretary of State for the Home Department, ex p. Simms* [2000] 2 AC 115 (HL), 131.

[119] See Janet L. Hiebert, 'Parliament and the Human Rights Act: Can the JCHR Help Facilitate a Culture of Rights?' (2006) 4 *Int. J. Const. Law* 1, 17–27; David Feldman, 'Parliamentary Scrutiny of Legislation and Human Rights' [2002] *Public Law* 323; and, on the draft legislation scrutiny processes in New Zealand and Canada, Richard Clarke *et al.*, *Legislation Advisory Committee Guidelines: Guidelines on Process and Content of Legislation* (Wellington: Legislation Advisory Committee, 2001); James B. Kelly, 'Bureaucratic Activism and the Charter of Rights and Freedoms: The Department of Justice and its Entry into the Centre of Government' (1999) 42 *Can. Pub. Admin.* 476, 486–503.

[120] As when, for example, ministers use the fast-track procedure established under s. 10 of the Human Rights Act 1998 to amend a statute in the event of a judicial declaration of its incompatibility with the European Convention on Human Rights. On the availabil-ity and use of this particular procedure, see Stephen Gardbaum, 'Reassessing the New Commonwealth Model of Constitutionalism' (2010) 8 *Int. Jnl Const. Law* 167, 200; Jack Beatson *et al.*, *Human Rights: Judicial Protection in the United Kingdom* (London: Sweet & Maxwell, 2008), 36–7, 709–16. The original proposed power was considerably stronger than that contained in s.10, but it was reined in at committee stage in the commons: See

principle of legislative supremacy has it that it is ultimately for the legislature to determine the fate of the law. Advisory panels and the courts might persuade the legislature of the need for change, but it is not for them to make the changes; they cannot guarantee that fundamentally objectionable laws will never be passed, moreover, even though they provide an estimable safeguard against this happening.

One might argue that this is all fine and well, but that it obscures the central question: if, in a jurisdiction which accepts the principle of legislative supremacy, only the legislature can review the legality of legislation, what is the point of making a case for the courts undertaking this form of review? In recent years, Waldron has directed his argument primarily at those jurisdictions which permit strong judicial review.[121] But he is clear that the argument is also intended as a warning: jurisdictions which enable courts and committees to urge legislatures to reconsider statutes ought to stick to that practice, and to resist allowing courts to strike down statutes as unlawful. 'To the extent … that there is a political edge to my comments on judicial review', he remarked in 1999, 'I intend them to be heard in the British debate', since 'in the United Kingdom … constitutional reform is now firmly on the political agenda and the institution of a Bill of Rights … together with something akin to American-style judicial review is a distinct possibility'.[122] This is not intended as an argument against judicial review of administrative action.[123] 'My target', he states, 'is strong judicial review',[124] and his message as regards the United Kingdom is that there should be resistance to anything akin to 'an American-style mechanism of judicial review of legislation'[125] whereby the Supreme Court – pronouncing in terms of general principle, and paying little attention to the circumstances of the litigants who initiated a case – is entrusted with making final decisions regarding the suitability of particular statutes for the protection of rights.

To end this chapter by asserting that there is simply no need to sound this warning in relation to the United Kingdom would be to invite the obvious charge of complacency. Those minded to make this charge could point to numerous developments – that it is no longer the judicial heresy it once

---

K. D. Ewing, 'The Human Rights Act and Parliamentary Democracy' (1999) 62 *MLR* 79, 92–3.

[121] See, e.g., Jeremy Waldron, 'The Core of the Case Against Judicial Review' (2006) 115 *Yale L. J.* 1346; 'Judges as Moral Reasoners' (2009) 1 *I-CON* 2.

[122] *LD* 16.

[123] See Jeremy Waldron, 'Refining the Question about Judges' Moral Capacity' (2009) 7 *Int. Jnl Const. Law* 69, 77.

[124] Waldron, 'The Core of the Case Against Judicial Review', 1354.

[125] *LD* 257.

was to speak of there being limits on what parliament might lawfully enact, for example, or that declarations of incompatibility under section 4 of the Human Rights Act 1998 are invariably a spur to legislative amendment – which might be read as indicative of a move towards strong judicial review. The fact of the matter is that there is little that can be said on this subject at present that is not speculative. Even the future of the Human Rights Act has been cast in doubt. Certainly, as was indicated in the last chapter, some senior judges have referred to the possibility of their taking untoward action in the event of parliament legislating contrary to some fundamental constitutional principle – '[i]f parliament did the inconceivable', the president of the Supreme Court has remarked, 'we might do the inconceivable as well'[126] – but this sentiment has not been put to the test, and it is difficult to know how to interpret it. To assume that it must be a veiled threat that the Supreme Court might strike down legislation as invalid seems rash, especially since – as, again, was made clear in the last chapter – judges need not make quite so radical a manoeuvre in order to stymie parliament's will.

Yet those inclined to argue that judges in the United Kingdom might just make such a manoeuvre will observe that the case-load of the Supreme Court is becoming ever less distinguishable from that of a court with the power to review the constitutionality of legislation: that questions about how to interpret and uphold human rights, and about the relationship between the political and judicial branches of government, are no longer marginal to the Court's business, and that it would be surprising if this development were not a sign of drift – perhaps part of a more general jurisdictional drift – towards accepting strong judicial review. Those attracted to this line of argument might also point out that the history of other jurisdictions has shown that advisory bodies sometimes develop so as to acquire the review functions of a constitutional court: such was the case in the 1970s with the French *Conseil Constitutionnel*.[127] Certainly some scholars purport to detect, within a variety of legal orders, a transition in power from

---

[126] BBC interview (*Today* programme, 2 August 2010), reported by Clive Coleman, 'A Power Supreme?' http://news.bbc.co.uk/today/hi/today/newsid_8875000/8875944. stm (accessed 4 February 2012). The underlying worry runs in both directions. While some politicians are concerned that the courts risk engaging in a form of judicial review which undermines parliamentary sovereignty, some judges object that parliamentary privilege as established in the 1689 Bill of Rights has been abused by politicians who undermine judicial decisions by, for example, naming in parliament individuals who have obtained court orders forbidding their identification.

[127] Though it would be simplistic to claim that its reviewing function is similar to that of the US Supreme Court (see Olivier Beaud, 'Reframing a Debate among Americans: Contextualizing a Moral Philosophy of Law' (2009) 1 *I-CON* 53, 60–3), just as it would be simplistic to think that 'judicial review' carries the same connotations for French as it does for Anglo-American

representative institutions to judiciaries which could be read as indicative of a general jurisdictional trend in the direction of US-style judicial review.[128] One argument to be derived from a contemporary American defence of judicial review is that this manner of development ought to be endorsed on the basis that it is better to be safe than sorry: if it is considered appropriate for a legislature to take advice from governmental committees on the constitutionality of proposed statutes, so goes the claim, it is unclear why there should be any harm in allowing the judicial branch – which has 'neither force nor will, but merely judgment'[129] – a vital part in the screening process.[130] An even more straightforward argument for judicial review is that those who successfully challenge the law are rewarded for their endeavour – the law is reviewed in their favour – whereas those whose cases prompt declarations of incompatibility might (since the court still must decide according to the impugned legislation) consider their victories hollow.

Speculation that the United Kingdom is heading in the direction of strong judicial review is difficult to assess. The roles of legislators and judges in the UK with respect to the resolution of disagreements over fundamental rights are traditionally very different from those of legislators and judges in, say, the United States. In the UK, parliament has readily legislated in core areas of human rights – the death penalty, suicide, abortion, racial and sexual discrimination, police misconduct and so on – which in the United States have been constructed by the courts on the basis of general statements of principle in the Bill of Rights.[131] The balance of power between the legislature(s) and the courts in the United Kingdom may well have started to alter significantly,[132] but it is important to distinguish a

---

lawyers (see L. Neville Brown and John S. Bell, *French Administrative Law*, 5th edn (Oxford: Clarendon Press, 1998), 6: 'English lawyers speak ... of "judicial review" ... but this refers *ex hypothesi* to review or control of the administration by the "ordinary" courts of law, whereas in France ... the Conseil d'État is by no means an ordinary court but the head of a separate hierarchy of special administrative courts. Moreover, "judicial review" carries a very different connotation in the USA and certain other parts of the English-speaking world, where it refers to the power of the courts to declare legislation to be unconstitutional – a task reserved in France to the Constitutional Council, albeit in limited form').

[128] For example, the tendency is detected (and lamented) in Ran Hirschl, *Towards Juristocracy: The Origins and Consequences of the New Constitutionalism* (Cambridge, Mass.: Harvard University Press, 2004).

[129] *Federalist 78* [Alexander Hamilton], in Alexander Hamilton, James Madison and John Jay, *The Federalist*, 428.

[130] See Fallon, 'The Core of an Uneasy Case *for* Judicial Review', 1708–9.

[131] See Lord Hoffmann, 'Human Rights and the House of Lords' (1999) 62 *MLR* 159, 160.

[132] See Thomas Poole and Sangeeta Shah, 'The Law Lords and Human Rights' (2011) 74 *MLR* 79; also Alan Paterson, *Lawyers and the Public Good: Democracy in Action?* (Cambridge University Press, 2012), 129–37.

general shift in power from a specific judicial determination to engage in strong judicial review – between courts acquiring (along with other stakeholders) an ever greater capacity to offer pointed advice to legislatures on how to improve their product and courts being able to decide on the legality of that product. Were the Supreme Court to review the legality of primary legislation, not only would its decision to do so meet with political outcry – as can be inferred from parliamentary reactions to rulings by the European Court of Human Rights blocking the deportation of terrorist suspects to home countries where they might be tortured[133] and, no less controversially, requiring that parliament revisit the question of extending voting rights to prisoners[134] – but it would be establishing that it has a rights-determining capacity extending significantly beyond that which the UK's court of last resort has exercised to date.

Perhaps the best way to conclude this chapter is not by speculating on where we might be heading, but by recalling where we stand. Courts in the United Kingdom are required to hear and decide any problem that is validly brought before them and to justify their decisions publicly. Judicial assessment of legislation is a necessary incident of this process, much as is statutory interpretation or judicial review of the legality of administrative action. But the capacity of judges to assess legislation cannot, owing to legislative supremacy, equate to a judicial right to challenge the validity of legislation. '[T]he function of independent judges charged to interpret and apply the law is universally recognised as a cardinal feature of the modern democratic state, a cornerstone of the rule of law itself', Lord Bingham observed in *A* v. *Secretary of State for the Home Department*. A court might conclude that the law cannot be applied because it is necessarily incompatible with the European Convention on Human Rights. To conclude thus 'is not', however, 'to override the sovereign legislative authority of the Queen in Parliament, since if primary legislation is declared to be incompatible [with the terms of the European Convention under the Human Rights Act, s. 4] the validity of the legislation is unaffected ... and the remedy lies with the appropriate

---

[133] See *Babar Ahmad* v. *United Kingdom* (2010) 51 EHRR SE6; *Othman (Abu Qatada)* v. *United Kingdom* [2012] ECHR 56.

[134] *Hirst* v. *United Kingdom (No. 2)* (2006) 42 EHRR 41. These and other rulings suggest that the most significant judicial test of parliamentary supremacy is located outside the national jurisdiction. The UK courts must give effect to the rules and principles laid down in Strasbourg jurisprudence. But the correct question to ask is not whether the UK's courts will adopt an American approach to judicial review, but whether a legislature of one of the member states of the Council of Europe could ever be entitled to thwart a decision of the Strasbourg court regarding treaty obligations.

minister ... who is answerable to Parliament'.[135] Lord Scott expressed the point yet more forcefully:

> It has not been suggested, nor could it be suggested, that the 2001 [Anti-terrorism, Crime and Security] Act is otherwise than an effective enactment made by a sovereign legislature. It was passed by both Houses of Parliament and received the Royal Assent. Whether the terms of the 2001 Act are consistent with the terms of the European Convention on Human Rights ... is, so far as the courts of this country are concerned, relevant only to the question whether a declaration of incompatibility under section 4 of the Human Rights Act 1998 should be made. The making of such a declaration will not, however, affect in the least the validity under domestic law of the impugned statutory provision.[136]

In this particular case, the government respected the House of Lords' decision and its declaration of incompatibility, and parliament repealed the offending legislation. But when the case went to the European Court of Human Rights it was conceded that, as a matter of principle, when a declaration of incompatibility is issued the UK government should be entitled to defend its legislation, 'even if that involve[s] calling into question the conclusions of the state's highest court'.[137] The principle of parliamentary sovereignty is not to be treated lightly. If parliament did the inconceivable, it is not clear how the judiciary could do the inconceivable as well, unless one understands the inconceivable to be something that courts have, exceptionally, already done: uphold the rule of law by declining to apply a statute.[138] Lord Reid's observation in *Madzimbamuto* v. *Lardner-Burke*, quoted in Chapter 2, resonates to this day. If parliament were to legislate in a way that most citizens found improper, a court might nullify the statute's effect. But the UK does not have a constitutional court

---

[135] *A v. Secretary of State for the Home Department* [2004] UKHL 56 at [42]. See also Philip Sales, 'Judges and Legislature: Values into Law' (2012) 71 *CLJ* 287, 294.

[136] *A v. Secretary of State for the Home Department*, at [142].

[137] *A v. United Kingdom* (2009) 49 EHRR 625, 630.

[138] What a court can do, judges have regularly observed, is presume that a generally or ambiguously worded statute is not to be interpreted as offending against the rule of law: see, e.g., *R v. Secretary of State for the Home Department, ex p. Pierson* [1998] AC 539 (HL), 591 (*per* Lord Steyn); *AXA Insurance* v. *Lord Advocate* [2011] UKSC 46 at [151]–[152] (Lord Reed). But this presumption does not run counter to the principle of parliamentary sovereignty: 'we should never forget that, however we develop or apply the law', one senior judge has observed, 'we cannot go against Parliament's will when it is expressed' – *sc.*, clearly expressed – 'through a statute'. Lord Neuberger, 'Who are the Masters Now?' (Weedon lecture, Brick Court Chambers, February 2012), excerpted at http://ukscblog.com/who-are-the-masters-now (visited 3 February 2012), para. 73.

vested with the power to strike down statutes; judges cannot remove laws from the statute book. Absent the conferral of that power on judges by parliament itself, it is difficult to see how a court might ever legislate – using that term in its paradigmatic sense (see Chapter 1) – so that a ruling could be accepted as rendering a statute legally invalid.

4

Legislatures and intentions

Legisprudence, once cast as an argument in favour of majority decision and against judicial review of the constitutionality of legislation, looks to be a more provocative project than it has ever appeared hitherto. But it would be uncharitable to suggest that legisprudence offers only one argument of note; it has on its agenda certainly one other topic of long-standing concern to jurists and political theorists, a topic which ranks as one of the core conundrums of legal philosophy. This is the problem of legislative intent. If intentions can reasonably be ascribed to legislatures, then courts and other interpretive agencies – if they are to abide by the separation of powers doctrine, and if they are to treat legislatures as vested with a mandate to enact laws for the citizenry – have a prima facie obligation to strive to respect those intentions. But how, if at all, could it ever make sense to speak of 'legislative intent', given that legislatures, as corporate bodies, cannot form and act on intentions as individual agents do?

One response to this question delivers it short shrift. If we accept that 'one cannot look at the marks on a page and understand those marks to be a text (i.e., a meaningful writing) without assuming that an author made those marks intending to convey a meaning by them',[1] then it matters not whether the text is ascribed to an individual or corporate author. The text was intended. Interpreting a statute simply means working out (and, if we are to avoid interpolation, not going beyond) the intention of the statute's author in the same way that we work out a speaker's intention in everyday life – by taking into account not only the words used but also what we know about the author and the context of the author's pronouncement.[2] If there appear to be inconsistent intentions embodied in a legislature's rules, the interpreter should take it that 'the meanings of the rules are ... what binding effects the rule maker would declare the rules to have

---

[1] Larry Alexander and Emily Sherwin, *Demystifying Legal Reasoning* (Cambridge University Press, 2008), 197.
[2] See ibid. 132–4, 140–1.

when confronted with such conflicts and inconsistencies'.[3] The fact that intentions may be difficult to discern – because of such inconsistencies, or because legislators sometimes use words which express more or less than what they meant to say, or because a legislature may have more than one intention when enacting a statute – does not mean that no legislative intention exists. It has to exist. There cannot be a statute without it.

1 Contesting legislative intent

Many academic lawyers and political scientists treat this line of argument sceptically. To cite the existence of the statute as proof of the legislature's intent, these sceptics argue, is to evade the question of how this intent might ever be located. Within political science, perhaps the best-known illustration of the difficulty of locating legislative intent is the classic insight of social choice theory regarding the problem of rational preference ordering given the possibility of cycling among discrete options.[4] A condition for a rational system of preferences is that if one prefers C to V and V to S then one must prefer C to S. But of course preference ordering need not be rational in this sense: one can prefer chocolate to vanilla and vanilla to strawberry but strawberry to chocolate (so that an attempt to rank one's preferences ends up cycling around the options). Groups operating by majority decision may, likewise, sometimes find it impossible to aggregate individual preferences to construct a coherent group preference: the majority vote may reveal a preference for C over V and V and S but S over C. On this account, where the preferences of the members of a legislature display at least a modicum of diversity, all we can say for certain about the intention behind a statute is that the legislature preferred its enactment to the retention of the status quo. The relationship between the content of the statute and the preference of the legislature is taken to be indemonstrable, because the likelihood of cycling makes it impossible to state with confidence that a particular preference was the legislature's favourite.[5]

---

[3] Ibid. 153.

[4] See Kenneth J. Arrow, 'A Difficulty in the Concept of Social Welfare' (1950) 58 *Jnl Pol. Econ.* 328.

[5] See Kenneth A. Shepsle, 'Congress is a "They", Not an "It": Legislative Intent as Oxymoron' (1992) 12 *Int. Rev. L. & Econ.* 239, 241 ('Arrow's famous impossibility theorem ... [i]n the context of majority rule voting ... implies that it is not possible to guarantee that a majority rule process will yield coherent choices. Put differently, if the preferences of the members of a voting body display a modicum of diversity, then majority voting need not generate a transitive ordering of the alternatives available for choice; the alternatives

The sceptical tack commonly taken by jurists is rather more rudimentary than the social choice perspective, though the conclusion – that there is a world of difference between finding intentions *within* the legislature and attributing any such intention *to* the legislature – is essentially the same. The straightforward advice to be found in Blackstone's *Commentaries* – that '[t]he fairest and most rational method to interpret the will of the legislator, is by exploring his intentions at the time when the law was made'[6] – is patently unsatisfactory. Legislatures are not amenable to being anthropomorphized, not only because the assembly itself lacks the capacity to form intentions but also because it will be composed, as Thomas Egerton put it, of 'so manie heades … so many wittes; so manie statute makers, so many myndes'[7] that it is impossible to identify within it any particular intention that can safely be treated as decisive. The concept of intention can be used in relation to legislatures to draw an analogy with individual agency, but, if this analogy is drawn, there remains the difficulty of specifying whose intention counts. 'So long as we think legislative intention is a matter of what someone has in mind and means to communicate' – rather as we normally think the statement of an individual speaker 'describes something about his state of mind when he spoke, some idea he meant to communicate to us in speaking as he did' – 'we must take as primary the mental states of particular people … and then we must worry about how to consolidate individual intentions into a collective, fictitious group intention'.[8] Are we concerned only with the aggregate intention of the members of the legislature who debate and vote on

cycle, even though individual preferences are quite coherent. Indeed, incoherence will often take the form of the nonexistence of a collectively "best" alternative …'). Shepsle explores the implications of this insight for voting strategies and sequence. Since this part of his discussion takes us beyond the issue of legislative intent, and since it relates specifically to the US legislative process, it is not examined here. Note also that although the policy preferences of a legislature's members may cycle, it does not follow that those members could not (though it is highly unlikely that they would) all share the same understanding of what the statute that they eventually enact means: see Caleb Nelson, 'A Response to Professor Manning' (2005) 91 *Virginia L. Rev.* 451, 458.

[6] 1 Bl. Comm. 59.

[7] [Thomas Egerton] *A Discourse upon the Exposicion & Understanding of Statutes, With Sir Thomas Egerton's Additions*, ed. S. E. Thorne (San Marino, Calif.: Huntington Library, 1942 [*c*. 1565]), 151.

[8] Ronald Dworkin, *Law's Empire* (London: Fontana, 1986), 335–6, 315, 336. Dworkin's work after *Law's Empire* shows him to have become markedly less sceptical about the possibility of analogizing legislative intention to speaker's meaning: see the quotations collected together and discussed by Jeffrey Goldsworthy, 'Dworkin as an Originalist' (2000) 17 *Constitutional Commentary* 49, 65–7.

a statute? What significance, if any, should we accord to the intentions of those members of the legislature who vote against the bill? Are we concerned with the intentions of the person or team who drafted the statute? What about the intentions of members of agencies and interest groups consulted on the legislative proposal? Even if we assume that legislative intention rests only with the members of the legislature, the fact is that those members may have radically unclear intentions regarding a proposed statute: their intentions may waver (one's intention to vote for an amendment to a bill might depend, for example, on how the amendment is worded or whether it is introduced at an early or late stage in the legislative process);[9] some members might not have been present when assent to the statute was given; some will have voted for it because they were told to do so; different members are likely to have been involved in the various stages of the bill's passage; and amendments to the bill may mean that the eventual statute no longer reflects, or no longer reflects only, the intentions of its original promoters. How are we to determine – even if we confine our attention to the intentions of those within the legislature – which parties' mental dispositions are relevant, what these dispositions are and how they might be said to constitute legislative intent?[10]

Some of these questions inform reservations about an exercise which will occupy us in Chapter 6: that of trying to determine legislative intent by looking at what was said in the legislature before a statute was enacted. The exercise meets with a variety of objections. Particular statements and exchanges in legislative debates should not be assumed to reflect the legislature's intention, and one of the dangers of looking to them to deduce such intention is that no individual member of the legislature is in a position to say what that intention is. If, as is the case in systems with bicameral legislatures, two chambers have a role (even if it is an unequal role) in determining what is enacted as law,[11] there is an obvious peril in

---

[9] See also Frank H. Michelman, 'Statutes' Domains' (1983) 50 *Univ. Chicago L. Rev.* 533, 548 ('The [voting system] used by [US] legislatures is particularly dependent on the order in which decisions are made. Legislatures customarily consider proposals one at a time and then vote them up or down. This method disregards third or fourth options and the intensity with which legislators prefer one option over another. Additional options can be considered only in sequence, and this makes the order of decision vital. It is fairly easy to show that someone with control of the agenda can manipulate the choice so that the legislature adopts proposals that only a minority support').

[10] See Dworkin, *Law's Empire*, 315–6; also Ronald Dworkin, *Justice for Hedgehogs* (Cambridge, Mass.: Belknap Press, 2011), 129–30.

[11] In the United Kingdom, neither commons nor lords alone, but only the Crown in both houses, has the capacity to enact statutes: *Stockdale* v. *Hansard* (1839) 9 Ad. & El. 1; *Bowles* v. *Bank of England* (1913) 1 Ch. 57. Until the early twentieth century, the legislative

treating statements and exchanges made in only one chamber as evidence of legislative intention.[12] Remarks in one chamber might not register in the other.[13] Given that the floor of a chamber might be almost empty, they will sometimes barely register where they are delivered. In the United Kingdom, a minister introducing a bill before parliament really speaks for the government rather than parliament, and in any event will often be articulating the government's desire on a matter of policy rather than making an authoritative statement about the meaning of a clause in a bill.[14] The thrust and parry of parliamentary debate, moreover, is 'not always conducive to a clear and unbiased explanation of the meaning of statutory language';[15] indeed, '[i]n the case of an Act dealing with a controversial subject ambiguous phrases are often used designedly, each side hoping to have thereby expressed its own view'.[16] Many, sometimes the majority of, members of parliament will not contribute to particular debates. Not only will there be abstentions from the vote, and members whipped into voting for motions they are privately inclined to oppose, but there will be those who register assent to a bill yet – though parliamentary procedure does not normally acknowledge this nuance – dissent from some, possibly all, of the reasons given by other legislators who support it.[17] Legislatures are,

---

powers of lords and commons were (leaving aside ancient commons' privileges regarding bills of supply) treated as equal: see *The Prince's Case* (1606) 8 Co. Rep. 1a. The Parliament Act 1911, s. 2, conferred power on the commons, under certain specified conditions and subject to royal assent, to legislate without the lords' consent. This power was the beginning of the problem, as it were, in *R (Jackson and others)* v. *A-G* [2005] UKHL 56 (see Chapter 2).

[12] See Hersch Lauterpacht, 'Some Observations on Preparatory Work in the Interpretation of Treaties' (1935) 48 *Harvard L. Rev.* 549, 559.

[13] *Millar* v. *Taylor* (1769) 4 Burr 2303 (KB), 2332 (*per* Willes J).

[14] Lord Haldane's further objection, in *Viscountess Rhondda's Claim* [1922] 2 AC 339 (HL), 383 – that '[t]he history of previous changes made or discussed cannot be taken to have been known or to have been in view when the Royal assent was given' – is far less compelling in modern times as compared with during the seventeenth and eighteenth centuries, when there were strict prohibitions on the reporting of parliamentary debates and proceedings.

[15] *Davis* v. *Johnson* [1979] AC 264 (HL), 350 (*per* Lord Scarman).

[16] *R* v. *West Riding of Yorkshire CC* [1906] 2 KB 676 (CA), 716 (*per* Farwell LJ).

[17] Imagine, for example, a bill being read in parliament which, if passed as law, will allow abortions only within the first twelve weeks of pregnancy. It seems fair to assume that most legislators who support the bill will not be categorically opposed to abortion; broadly speaking, their reason for supporting the bill is likely to be that they believe abortion should be permitted but regulated differently than it is under the current law. But it is also possible that a legislator might vote for the bill without accepting this reason: a particular member of parliament who believes abortion to be a sin, who would not vote to keep the law as it currently stands, and who is disinclined to abstain in case the vote

in a literal sense, equivocal, and so it is hazardous to fix on any remark or exchange, however pertinent it might appear to be, as if it were evidence of the legislature's collective intention.[18]

It is, accordingly, not surprising that the idea of legislatures having intentions should often be met with resistance. Early twentieth-century American jurists showed a particular talent for stating the case sharply. Though 'a judge, starting from the words of a statute, is often led to results which he applies as if they had been the thought of the legislature', John Chipman Gray claimed, he in fact 'does not believe, and has no reason to believe, that his present thought is the same as any thought which the legislature really had', for 'the Legislature has ... no meaning at all'; and so when judges 'determine what the Legislature did mean on a point ... they are in truth, themselves legislating to fill up *casus omissi*'.[19] Max Radin, writing apropos of those instances in which the words used in a statute yield no clear meaning, was even more forthright:

> A legislature ... has no intention whatever in connection with words which some two or three men drafted, which a considerable number rejected, and in regard to which many of the approving majority might have had, and often demonstrably did have, different ideas and beliefs ... The chances that of several hundred men each will have exactly the same determinate situations in mind ... are infinitesimally small ... Even if the contents of the minds of the legislature were uniform, we have no means of knowing that content except by the external utterances or behavior of these hundreds of men, and in almost every case the only external act is the extremely ambiguous one of acquiescence, which may be motivated in literally hundreds of ways.[20]

One might think that the case against legislative intent has been thoroughly made and that there is nothing more that can usefully be said on the matter. Jeremy Waldron, in setting out his jurisprudence of legislation,

---

turns out to be close, might support the bill – and support it in good conscience – because its enactment should reduce the occurrence of something he believes ought to be impermissible. See John Finnis, 'Just Votes for Unjust Laws' (2004), in his *Collected Essays. Volume IV: Philosophy of Law* (Oxford University Press, 2011), 436–66.

[18] See J. H. Baker, 'Statutory Interpretation and Parliamentary Intention' (1993) 52 *CLJ* 353, 354–5; Johan Steyn, '*Pepper v Hart*; A Re-examination' (2001) 21 *OJLS* 59, 64–5.

[19] John Chipman Gray, *The Nature and Sources of the Law*, 2nd edn (New York: Macmillan, 1921), 171, 173. See also Roscoe Pound, 'Courts and Legislation' (1913) 77 *Central L. J.* 219, 230.

[20] Max Radin, 'Statutory Interpretation' (1930) 43 *Harvard L. Rev.* 863, 870–1; see also Frank E. Horak, Jr, 'In the Name of Legislative Intention' (1932) 38 *W. Virginia L. Q.* 119, 125 ('The accuracy of this observation cannot be questioned').

makes it clear that he thinks otherwise. Statute law, he observes, is typically the product not of 'single expert authors' but of 'large multi-member assemblies', the members of which issue nothing specific that 'amount[s] to a legislative act' but rather 'integrate a diversity of purposes, interests, and aims among their members into the text of a legislative product'.[21] To understand the authority of statute law, we do well to focus on this general integration of purposes rather than on 'the intentions of particular legislators'.[22] Above all, we must avoid the error of trying to deduce from the statute 'a particular intention'.[23]

The absence of such intention is, Waldron believes, no barrier to a statute having authority. In accepting that we do better to comply with the directives in a statute rather than acting on our own reasons, we do not have to accept or pretend that the statute has an individual author.[24] Waldron draws an analogy between statutory directives and computer-generated information: while the computer is intentionally programmed to produce general outputs, it is 'not ... for me, an intentional system' because I know – when, for example, I telephone an automated system to find out my credit card balance – that no individual agent 'is intentionally conveying to me the message' communicated.[25] All the same, I treat the information as authoritative. If citizens were to feed their votes on matters of policy into a machine which aggregated individual inputs, furthermore, the outcome would not be the product of an identifiable intention, yet it could again be argued that citizens – because the machine will aggregate individual inputs so as to maximize welfare, or because outcomes based on majority preference are more likely to be correct than those which are not – have good reasons to treat the machine-generated outcome as an authoritative directive. Similarly, a statute is authoritative – in the sense that individuals have reason to forsake reliance on their own reasons for action and instead act in accordance with the statute's provisions – even though statutes 'are never produced exactly as the product of one person's coherent intention'[26] and 'there is no ... reason for according authority to the particular views of any individual participant' in the legislative process.[27] What matters, for the purpose of establishing statutory authority, is not the intentions of individual members of the legislature, but 'the formal specification of the act [the legislature] has performed'[28] – i.e., 'the

[21] Jeremy Waldron, Law and Disagreement (Oxford: Clarendon Press, 1999), 121. (Hereafter *LD*.)
[22] *LD* 122.   [23] *LD* 127, also 129.
[24] *LD* 131.   [25] *LD* 132.   [26] *LD* 127.
[27] *LD* 138.   [28] *LD* 142.

text that has been voted on'[29] and that is ratified not merely as the product of 'the majority' but, more significantly, 'of a legislature' acting as one 'in the name, and for the sake, of the entire community'.[30]

It seems odd, given Waldron's insistence 'on the authoritativeness of the text and nothing but the text',[31] that he should consider his argument to be compatible with the proposition that courts should be entitled to determine legislative intent by looking to 'statements on the legislative record'.[32] Jurisdictions which permit resort to such statements have adapted their rule of recognition, he asserts, so that it embodies an expansive judicial conception of 'what counts as *the text* of [the] statute'.[33] This assertion might be questioned. Extrinsic materials are always subordinate to the statutory text itself: even in legal systems where statements on the legislative record are entertained and accorded weight by courts, the presumption is not that those statements form part of the statute, but that they may be relied on as probative evidence for the purpose of deciding how ambiguous statutory language is to be construed.[34]

Equally puzzling is Waldron's argument that the notion of legislative intention undermines the possibility of statute law being authoritative. The argument proceeds thus: (1) if we understand authority in the sense that people recognize, as a matter of rational choice, that they do better to follow the directives of a statute rather than acting on their own assessments of what is right or wrong in the situations that the statute covers; (2) if statutes are taken to be attributable to the particular views of participants in the legislative process; and (3) if we accept that 'legislators themselves should be bound by the laws they enact',[35] then it is 'impossible that a law could have *authority vis-à-vis* a legislator, for it makes no sense to say that X has better reason to trust the directives of X than he has to trust his own reasoning on the matter that X is addressing'.[36] This argument only has a chance of succeeding if one ignores two important points. The first

---

[29] *LD* 141.   [30] *LD* 144.   [31] *LD* 145.

[32] *LD* 145.   [33] *LD* 146.

[34] '[T]he function in construing a statute is to ascertain the meaning of the words used by the legislature', Felix Frankfurter observed, and while 'nothing that is logically relevant [to this exercise] should be excluded' from its performance, exchanges in debates and the like must not be accorded so much significance as to make resonant 'the quip that only when legislative history is doubtful do you go to the statute'. Felix Frankfurter, 'Some Reflections on the Reading of Statutes' (1947) 47 *Columbia L. Rev.* 527 at 533, 541, 543; see also *Greenwood* v. *United States*, 350 US 366, 374 (1956) (Frankfurter J).

[35] *LD* 138.

[36] *LD* 139. (Emphasis in original.)

is that even if one takes legislation to be the product of intention, one is still ultimately claiming that statutes represent the will of the legislature rather than the will of the individual members who voted for them. The bill which has received assent is – as Waldron acknowledges – something more than just the directive of those who supported it, and the legislator who abides by that bill once it becomes law cannot accurately be described as simply respecting his own edict. The second point is that, just as an ordinary citizen may encounter 'dissonance between what [he] takes to be the right choice and what [he] takes to be the authoritative choice in political decision-making' (to the extent, indeed, that he 'may find himself committed to the view that the wrong decision ought to prevail'),[37] so too the legislator *qua* legislator may reason differently, and on particular statutes may take a different position, from the legislator *qua* private citizen. In accepting the authority of a statute, a member of a legislature may well be complying with reasons other than his own – notwithstanding that he may have voted for the statute's enactment.

Neither of these criticisms goes to the heart of Waldron's argument regarding legislative intent. Legislation is best described, he thinks, as 'unintentional'.[38] Yet his argument is really directed only at efforts to demonstrate the existence of specific rather than general legislative intentions. Explanations of the authority of statute law should not, he claims, appeal to the intentions of particular legislators. But the fact that the outputs of a system – of law enactment, data generation or whatever – cannot be ascribed to a particular intention does not mean that the system must be unintentional. The existence and operation of the system will depend on general intentions – to enact laws which will be binding within a jurisdiction, to generate data relevant to accounts held among a network of banks and so on. This much is evident from the language that Waldron himself uses to describe the enactment process: '[w]hat the decision [*sc.*, the legislature's enactment] is – what *we* [*sc.*, 'the entire community'] have done – is the text of the statute as determined by the institution's procedures. Those procedures make us *one* in action … the authors of a deed'.[39] This decision or deed – our doing, our action – is not unintentional. To limit intentionality to intentions which are particular, and to conclude,

---

[37] *LD* 246.   [38] *LD* 119, 124.

[39] *LD* 144–5. (Emphases in original.) Likewise, when Waldron supports the Aristotelian case for collective decision making he reasons from the presumption that a legislative assembly possesses something analogous to an individual's mental capacity for directing knowledge, experience, judgment and insight to problems – hence the (applied) wisdom specific to the multitude. See, e.g., Jeremy Waldron, *The Dignity of Legislation* (Cambridge University Press, 1999), 93.

on the basis of this limitation, that legislation 'can be conceived to emerge non-intentionally'[40] is to found one's argument about legislative intent on an inordinately narrow conception of intention.

It should be evident by now that what is unfolding in this chapter is a defence of intentionalist legisprudence. This defence, it will become clear, extends to the concept of specific as well as to that of general legislative intention. But note, before we consider it in detail, that the defence comes with a significant proviso attached. Arguments against the notion of legislative intent tend to fall into two broad types: the first is that there is no meaningful way to conceive of an existent legislative intent, whereas the second is that such intent, whether or not it exists, is forever elusive. Even if an account of legislative intent successfully negotiates these objections, the victory may be Pyrrhic, either because the form or level of intention ultimately identified as ascribable to the enacting legislature might be of no practical use to anyone seeking to resolve how to interpret a statute, or because questions about legislative intent turn out to be beside the point given that the language of the statute yields a meaning which – no matter that it might not mirror the intentions of the legislature – is plain to any reasonable interpreter. To state the proviso in accordance with the argument which is developed in the remainder of this chapter: although an institution such as a legislature is capable of having not only general (law-changing) intentions but also specific – which is not to say always readily identifiable – intentions in the form of distinct proposals and plans, those specific legislative intentions, even when discernible, do not have to guide statutory interpretation.

2 Mapping intention

When Egerton wrote of legislatures being composed of 'many myndes', he was obviously emphasizing the difficulty of locating legislative intent. But he did not consider this difficulty insurmountable. Most statutes never come before courts for interpretation because the wording chosen by the drafter, 'taken straightelie according to the naked & bare letter', yields a meaning so uncontroversial that there is no need to delve deeper into what the legislature might have intended.[41] Where this is not the case ('where a statute shall be taken by equytie'), anyone seeking to determine legislative intent might still be aided by 'certen notes' in the statute 'by which a man

---

[40] LD 138.
[41] Egerton, *A Discourse upon the Exposicion & Understanding of Statutes,* 151.

maie knowe what it was', or even, where a statute is of recent provenance, by the 'livinge voice' of 'the penners & devisors'.[42]

There is, of course, the difficulty of determining just whose living voice one is supposed to seek out. Even if one were to locate it, moreover, there may be doubts as to its authoritativeness. Given the fact of periodic elections, Egerton's contemporary, Christopher Hatton observed, the devisors of a statute may, by the time the matter of its interpretation arises, be '*Functi sunt officio* [finished in their duty]', so that, even if the parliament to whom the devisors belonged was 'altogether assembled again for interpretation by a voluntary meeting', it could no longer offer interpretive advice in an official capacity ('*Eorum non esset interpretari*').[43] Hatton was not convinced, however, that this was a real problem. 'For the Sages of the Law' – the king's judges – 'whose wits are exercised in such matters, have the interpretation in their hands, and their Authority no man taketh in hand to control.'[44] Much the same argument, addressing the absence of a single parliamentary mind rather than the limitations on a parliament's life, was offered by a serjeant arguing before the court of common pleas in 1552: 'the life of the statute rests in the minds of the expositors of the words, that is, the makers of the statutes. And if they are dispersed, so that their minds cannot be known, then those who may approach nearest to their minds shall construe the words, and these are the … sages of the law whose talents are exercised in the study of such matters.'[45]

It might be objected that this simply takes us back to square one, that to treat interpretation as a matter for judges is to gloss over the essential problem: what, if the language of the statute is unclear as to meaning, are judges interpreting? But these mid sixteenth-century lawyers were, in fact, trying to answer this very question. When judges are unable or unwilling to accord statutory language a plain meaning, they are likely to be drawn to certain sources of information bearing upon but not part of the enacted text – annotations to statutes, for example, or what members of the legislature said in debate – to see if they stand as reliable evidence of what the legislature's enacting intentions were. There are always risks accompanying this strategy. Indeed, in the mid sixteenth century, when parliament met infrequently and judges were rarely able to resort

---

[42] Ibid.

[43] Christopher Hatton, *A Treatise Concerning Statutes, or Acts of Parliament: And the Exposition thereof* (London: printed for Richard Tonson, 1677 [*c.* 1570]), 29–30. Hatton (1540–1591) was appointed Lord Chancellor in 1587.

[44] Ibid. 30.

[45] *Partridge* v. *Strange and Croker* (1553) 1 Plowd. 77, 82 *per* Saunders (*arguendo*).

to reliable legislative history, the risks were perhaps greater than they are today. That judges could not always confidently discern the legislature's enacting intentions did not mean, however, that efforts to discern those intentions were likely to be arbitrary. During the sixteenth century – this argument dominates much of Chapter 6 – the courts formulated principles of statutory construction which enabled judges, when faced with statutes which were not to be interpreted on their plain meaning, to adopt a disciplined (if by no means foolproof) approach to unmasking legislative intent.[46]

We have encountered already the types of objection that an intent-oriented approach to statutory construction invites. Of all the intentions of all the participants in the legislative process, which ones stand as the legislature's 'intent'? What about the fact that some participants' intentions will not be revealed? Even if we can say whose intentions count, and even if their intentions happen to be transparent, how can we aggregate the particular intentions of legislators to reveal a coherent intention of the legislature? These are not trivial questions. Nor is it trivial, however, to point out that the idea of the legislature exercising collective agency cannot simply be shrugged off as mystical nonsense. Our reliance on the idea, though often unreflective and unarticulated, comes naturally. Consider, for example, the concepts of regulatory failure and purposive construction: both build from the premise that through the process of enactment the legislature intends (and can fail in its intention) to regulate some state of affairs or remedy an existing legal deficiency in a particular way.[47] It should become clear as Part III of this study unfolds – though it is impossible to do anything other than assert the point now – that a proper account of statutory interpretation is inconceivable absent the presupposition that intentions can be ascribed to legislatures. The question still to be answered in this chapter is obvious enough: how might we speak meaningfully of a legislature having intentions?

---

[46] See, e.g., *Stradling* v. *Morgan* (1559) 1 Plowd. 199, 205 ('... the intent of the Legislature ... collected sometimes by considering the cause and necessity of making the Act, sometimes by comparing one part of the Act with another, and sometimes by foreign circumstances'); *Heydon's Case* (1584) 3 Co. Rep. 7a, 7b.

[47] Consider also how the presumption of legislative intent informs Savigny's distaste for statute law (specifically, Anton Thibaut's codification proposals): legislation, Savigny insisted, is to be distrusted precisely because it is intentional rather than organic law, because it owes its existence to the successful imposition of a particular will rather than to acceptance among the people. See Friedrich Carl von Savigny, *De la vocation de notre temps pour la législation et la science du droit*, Fr. trans. A. Dufour (Paris: PUF, 2006 [1814]), 53–62.

(a)   Minimal legislative intent

Any defence of the idea of legislative intent counts for nothing, it might be objected, unless it first deals with the problem of intention formation. How is the concept of intention being applied, given that groups can never have intentions in the literal (mental) sense? Consider three standard modern answers to this question. The first is that certain officials within the legislative process – particularly the drafters of legislation and those who chair committees – are, in effect, agents of the legislature's intent by virtue of the fact that the legislature delegates to them certain responsibilities regarding the aims and the content of statutes.[48] There is certainly evidence that members of some legislatures conceive of legislative intention in this way.[49] That members of legislatures might sometimes think this way, however, is not a sufficient reason to conclude that they do in fact delegate to (say) legislative drafters the power to determine what they intended in voting for a bill. More importantly, the proposition that the legislature itself acts as a principal, delegating authority to speak on its behalf to certain agents, simply relocates the problem of legislative intent, since it demands an explanation as to how the legislature forms the intention to communicate its wishes to its agents.[50]

The second answer to the question of how legislatures may be said to have intentions is premised on the idea that a bill's passage through the legislature can be understood as the emergence of legislative intent in the form of a bargain or compromise among the members of the assembly. 'All bills', it has been argued in relation to the US legislative process,

> are bargains among the members of some winning coalition … By understanding the legislative path of a bill – including who the decisionmakers were at key stages in the legislative process and what demands they made on the bill – an outside observer can begin to identify the elements of the agreement that the coalition thought it was making that are not explicit in the language of the statute. Because the coalition's agreements represent a compromise among its members, the ascertainment of an implied agreement rests on understanding what interests were compromised.[51]

[48] See Gerald C. MacCallum, Jr, 'Legislative Intent' (1966) 75 *Yale L. J.* 754, 781–4.
[49] See Lawrence M. Solan, 'Private Language, Public Laws: The Central Role of Legislative Intent in Statutory Interpretation' (2005) 93 *Georgetown L. J.* 427, 442–9.
[50] See Heidi M. Hurd, 'Sovereignty in Silence' (1990) 99 *Yale L. J.* 945, 974–5; also MacCallum, 'Legislative Intent', 782.
[51] McNollgast [*sc.*, Mathew D. McCubbins, Roger G. Noll and Barry R. Weingast], 'Legislative Intent: The Use of Positive Political Theory in Statutory Interpretation' (1994) 57 *Law & Contemporary Problems* 3, 16.

Although legislators may 'all have different intentions', there is no reason to think 'that they do not or cannot strike bargains in order to construct a common understanding of the intention of a particular statute',[52] for the statements and actions of the primary agents of this coalition – those who are pivotal in shaping the content of statutes (chairs of committees, majority party leaders)[53] – 'provide information about legislative intent'.[54] This approach, which relies heavily on legislative history, identifies not an intention of the legislature but an intention of a winning coalition within the legislature. For a bargain to stand as legislative intent, the pivotal legislators would have to persuade the entire legislature, not merely the members of the coalition, to accept the bargain. Something like this bargain would have to form part of any coherent account of legislative intent, but such intent cannot properly be equated with the agreement reached by the winning coalition.

A third answer to the question of how legislatures could be said to have intentions – one which is not convincing, but which for our purposes proves interesting because of what it overlooks – is that group intention can be explained as summative: the intention of the group is revealed in the beliefs of the majority of its members.[55] A basic difficulty with seeking to ascertain legislative intent by this method is, as we have already seen, that the beliefs of each of those who compose the majority may be difficult to determine: not every member of the legislature will say what he or she really thinks, or necessarily say anything at all, about the content of a bill. It might be argued that this difficulty is easily handled by treating one's vote as evidence of one's intention, so that the intention of the group is therefore captured by the majority vote. But even if we attribute no significance to the fact that not everyone in the majority will have had the same reasons for voting as they did, there might still be good cause – because, for example, the dissenting votes and abstentions outnumbered the assents – to question why the majority vote should be treated as indicative of legislative intent.[56]

A more fundamental objection to the summative account is that the individual intentions of the members of a group – even when the group members all have the same intention – do not necessarily constitute a group intention. If several people sitting on a lawn all suddenly run for

---

[52] Ibid. 19.   [53] See ibid. 18–19.   [54] Ibid. 20.

[55] See MacCallum, 'Legislative Intent', 777–80.

[56] See Ronald Dworkin, *A Matter of Principle* (Oxford: Clarendon Press, 1986), 45–8, though, as should become clear in due course, this difficulty can be exaggerated.

shelter because it has started to rain, they all have the same intention, but they do not have a group intention. There would be a group intention, however, if those people were together performing outdoor theatre, and their running for shelter was part of a scene in a play.[57] The group intention is identifiable as such not by the summation of corresponding individual intentions but by virtue of the fact that the individuals are understood to be co-ordinating their actions in order to achieve a particular end. Collective intentionality, understood thus, means not adding up a collection of coinciding individual intentions but recognizing that those intentions interlock and that the individuals who compose the group are in fact co-operating in carrying out a plan.

Note that this claim concerns both agency and teleology: legislatures are capable of forming intentions and have objectives that they intend to pursue. The intention of a legislature exists in much the same way as does the intention of a theatre group, sports team or orchestra.[58] The performance of the collective derives, but is also distinct, from the individual performances of its members. Only the legislature itself can legislate, while the individual member, not the legislature, has the capacity to scrutinize bills, table amendments and cast votes.[59] To conceive of the legislature as therefore having an intention is to use the concept of intention analogously – to draw a comparison between group and individual agency – rather than literally. But this does not mean that the concept is being used unintelligibly or inappropriately.[60] Statutes are the product of legislative intent in the sense that statutes derive from concerted action by the members of the legislature.

Concerted action as to what? A legislature must, by the very act of legislating, have had a general intention to change the law.[61] Even those

---

[57] See John Searle, 'Collective Intentions and Actions', in *Intentions in Communication*, ed. P. R. Cohen, J. Morgan and M. E. Pollack (Cambridge, Mass.: MIT Press, 1990), 401–16 at 403.

[58] See Jeffrey Goldsworthy, *The Sovereignty of Parliament: History and Philosophy* (Oxford: Clarendon Press, 1999), 251.

[59] See John Gardner, 'Some Types of Law', in *Common Law Theory*, ed. D. E. Edlin (Cambridge University Press, 2007), 51–77 at 57. Gardner also makes the point that the concerted action of the legislature entails a combination of natural concerted agency (each member working co-operatively so as to contribute to that which is the distinctive product of the legislature) and artificial or vicarious concerted agency (certain members' actions being treated as representative of the legislature). Ibid. 58–9.

[60] See Brian Bix, *Law, Language, and Legal Determinacy* (Oxford: Clarendon Press, 1993), 189.

[61] See Gardner, 'Some Types of Law', 56. Note that the relevant law-making intention is in the act of legislating, but not necessarily in the act of making the legislative proposal. The

members of a legislature who vote against a particular legislative initiative share this general intention. Their participation in the legislative process demonstrates that they accept its legitimacy – that they intend, as a matter of general principle, that through the process of legislative enactment the law on particular matters should change (even if they would prefer it did not change) precisely because it is the task of the legislative assembly to determine whether the content of the relevant law should be altered.

We can go further than this, and state not only that the legislature, when it legislates, has a general intention to change the law, but that the particular laws that the legislature makes when it legislates must be the laws it intended to make. To assume the contrary would be to assume that the legislature does not know what laws will be made as a result of its actions. If members of the legislature could not anticipate how the law will change owing to their collective action, it would be of no consequence were they (say) immature, bigoted, mentally incompetent, not democratically elected or in some other way unsuited to their roles: the laws they would end up making would not represent their intentions, and so the likelihood of their intentions being foolish, malign or self-serving would be irrelevant.[62]

One might not dispute the argument set out so far regarding legislative intent – that legislatures are appropriately described as having intentions (notwithstanding that these are not literal intentions) and that the laws which a legislature enacts are, certainly in broad outline, laws it intended to make – and yet, for at least two reasons, still find it unsatisfactory. The first is that to make a case for the existence of legislative intent is not to make a case for resorting to legislative intent when interpreting statute law. Statutes are not like the directives of testators or military commanders, where there is a clear expectation that the addressee follows the wishes of the addressor because the addressor's intentions are integral to the very exercise of satisfying those directives.[63] This insight is perhaps

intention in proposing new legislation might not be to secure a change in the law, even though a government may foresee that this is a possible consequence of its proposal, and would no doubt have to take responsibility for what it had knowingly brought about were the proposal to make it onto the statute book. When, in February 2010, the then Labour Government introduced a bill to scrap the UK's 'first past the post' voting system – a bill which stood little if any chance of passing into law at that point – this was generally interpreted as a signal not of Labour's intention to change the law but of the party's desperation to hold onto political power.

[62] See Joseph Raz, *Between Authority and Interpretation: On the Theory of Law and Practical Reason* (Oxford University Press, 2009), 275.

[63] See Frederick Schauer, *Playing by the Rules: A Philosophical Examination of Rule-Based Decision-Making in Law and in Life* (Oxford: Clarendon Press, 1991), 219–20.

part of the explanation for a long line of English judicial pronouncements to the effect that the interpretive task of a court is to work out what the language used in a statute means rather than what parliament intended by using that language.[64] Since the meaning of statutory language may be unclear, judges will sometimes seek to discern the legislature's intention *faute de mieux*. But – and this is the second reason for being dissatisfied with the argument presented so far – discerning legislative intention is essentially pointless if the revealed intention is so anodyne as to provide no guidance for the purpose of statutory interpretation. The claim that legislatures intend to create laws in their general outline but cannot, given their size and the diverse views of their members, be taken to endorse the specific content of the laws they create seems to establish nothing other than that legislatures have the minimal intent that is necessary for their acts to count as law making.[65] For anyone struggling to interpret a statute, there is little if any enlightenment in the revelation that the legislature intended to change the law in the general way that it did.

Interpreters of statutes attribute no real significance to the fact that there exists minimal legislative intent. Rather, they normally try to ascertain the meaning of a statute from its text and its structure. The interpretive conventions of some jurisdictions permit courts to look to committee reports, *travaux préparatoires*, statements made in the legislature and other sources orthogonal to a statute so as to try to draw conclusions about the legislature's enacting intentions when text and structure leave questions about proper construction unresolved. But reliance on such sources is, as we have observed already, a perilous business, not least because it incurs the risk of mistaking the intentions of particular legislators and advisers for the intention of the legislature itself. Furthermore, even if it is, by one means or another, reasonable to draw inferences about legislative intent beyond the mere fact that the legislature intended to change the law by enacting a statute corresponding, in general outline, with the one which it enacted, it does not follow that this more fine-grained conception of legislative intent should bear on how a particular statute is to be interpreted.

---

[64] See, e.g., *IRC v. Hinchy* [1960] AC 748 (HL), 767 (*per* Lord Reid); *Stock v. Frank Jones (Tipton) Ltd* [1978] 1 WLR 231 (HL), 234–5 (*per* Viscount Dilhorne); *Black-Clawson International Ltd* v. *Papierwerke Waldhof-Aschaffenburg AG* [1975] AC 591 (HL), 613 (*per* Lord Reid) and 629 (*per* Lord Wilberforce). The argument uniting these pronouncements is considered in Chapter 5.

[65] See Raz, *Between Authority and Interpretation*, 279–85.

If specific legislative intentions can be ascertained, why might we resist prioritizing them when interpreting statutes? There are two reasons that might explain our resistance. The first is that interpreters of statutes will sometimes consider it reasonable, and may even feel compelled, to depart from an enacting legislature's specific intention. A bygone legislature's intention when it used a particular word or phrase in a statute may be clear enough, yet contemporary judges may balk at giving effect to that intention, preferring instead to interpret the word or phrase in a manner which renders it more congenial to modern values or – what usually amounts to the same thing – compliant with treaty obligations. The second reason has to do with the fact that applying a statute and giving effect to the specific intentions of the enacting legislature will not always amount to the same thing. Since interpretation is the interpretation of meaning, and since, so far as we can tell, there is only meaning in the world in so far as the world has been invested with meaning by human beings, we tend to assume that a good interpretation must retrieve what a human agent meant (i.e., intended). But sometimes the meaning of what we do is not exhausted by what we intend our actions to mean: some of our actions create – without our necessarily knowing this – more than what we intended to create.[66] An interpretation of a statute is not to be declared illegitimate on the basis that it does not conform with what are known to be the specific intentions of the legislature in enacting that statute, for it is the promulgated text, not the motivation behind that text, which is to be interpreted. Judges are perfectly within their rights, as it were, to place upon a statute an interpretation at odds with the specific law-changing intentions of the enacting legislature if the meaning of the statutory language supports that interpretation.

Supports that interpretation how? An interpretation of a statute which defies the intentions of the enacting legislature is only justifiable, one might think, if the plain meaning of the text floats free of those intentions – if the interpretation accords, that is, with the ordinary meaning of the relevant statutory language as employed in context. The proposition that an interpretation must be grounded in the plain meaning of statutory language if it is to trump legislative intention seems, however, a little too strict. A judge who strives to take a creative approach to statutes without undermining the principle of legislative supremacy will appreciate that if the words of a statute do not yield a clear meaning, the most appropriate interpretive strategy may be to try to apply the statute in a way

---

[66] See ibid. 230.

which nobody involved in the legislative process appears to have entertained, but which nobody involved would have considered outside the remit of the statute had it been entertained. As we will see in Chapter 6, this approach to statutory interpretation is typically understood to be an exercise in conjecture about the legislature's intent, as if the interpretive trick is to land on some intention that an enacting legislature cannot be shown to have had but which it is reasonable to think it would align itself with were it possible to bring that instantiation of the legislature back to life and ask it. Sometimes that will, indeed, be the interpretive trick that judges are playing. But there is another possibility: an interpretation of an ambiguously worded statute might occasionally uncover not real or hypothesized legislative intent, but a previously unearthed dimension to the actual statutory language – something hidden from its framers as well as from everyone else – which was present all along.[67]

(b) Intentions, plans, purposes

The answer set out so far to the question, 'Can we meaningfully speak of legislatures having intentions?' is 'Yes, but …' – with an emphasis on the 'but'. It makes sense to set about answering the question in this way because it is important not to underestimate the very real difficulties and limitations that attach to arguments from legislative intent. These difficulties and limitations do not, however, preclude the possibility of developing a theoretical argument showing that statutes can be said to derive from specific intentions.

The basic difficulty with the notion of legislative intention, James Landis once argued, is that 'intention' denotes both 'the teleological concept of purpose and the more immediate concept of meaning'.[68] So far, our reflections on legislative intent have been mainly to do with the idea that the legislature, when it enacts a statute, intends – as Landis would have it, means – to change the law in accordance with the enacted text. But we can pose the problem of legislative intent in another way. Instead of asking after the legislature's specific intentions in enacting a statute, we might ask: what was, and indeed what was the nature of, the enacting

---

[67] Something resembling (though not identical to) this interpretive approach is attempted by Baroness Hale in *Yemshaw* v. *London Borough of Hounslow* [2011] UKSC 3. The case is considered in Chapter 6.

[68] James M. Landis, 'A Note on "Statutory Interpretation"' (1930) 43 *Harvard L. Rev.* 886, 888.

legislature's plan?[69] It might be objected that altering the question does not, in any real sense, alter the answer: the legislature planned to change the law. It becomes clear on close analysis, however, that an enquiry into the concept of legislative intent which emphasizes the idea of legislatures forming and acting on plans yields an explanation of the concept which is somewhat richer than one built on the more common (which is not to say incorrect) observation that when legislatures enact a statute they are realizing a specific intention to change the content of the law.

Consider, first of all, the assertion that legislatures have intentions much as do sports teams and orchestras. The intentional actions of those that compose the group combine to form a collective act that is more than the inputs of the individuals: everybody plays their part, but only the group performs the entirety. However, the concerted action of the members of a sports team or an orchestra looks to be directed towards a more specific end than is the concerted action of the legislature. We do not say of orchestras or football teams that their intention is simply to play music or football. Their intentions, rather, are particular: to play in a particular style, to win matches, and so on. The team members are on-message, as it were, but the message is quite specific: their intention is to do more than just play. A large legislature, composed of members representing a diversity of views, will have a general intention to change the law, and will take concerted action to achieve that end, but it is difficult to move beyond this proposition and ascribe to a legislature a more specific intention, other than (perhaps) the intention that the legislature intends to change the law for the better.

This contrast between the intentions of legislatures and those of groups such as sports teams and orchestras turns out, however, to be unpersuasive on closer inspection. The example of the people in the rainy park was used earlier to try to show that group intentionality depends not on multiple people sharing the same intention but on the intentions of those individual people interlocking to form a shared aim: 'a group ... whether team, club, society, enterprise, corporation, or community, is to be said to exist wherever there is, over an appreciable span of time, a co-ordination of activity by a number of persons, in the form of interactions, and with a view to a shared objective'.[70] We recognize that for many groups these

---

[69] See Bix, *Law, Language, and Legal Determinacy*, 187.

[70] John Finnis, *Natural Law and Natural Rights*, 2nd edn (Oxford: Clarendon Press, 2011), 153 (for the full argument, of which the quotation is part of a summary, one should start at 150). See also ibid. 458–9 and, on the limited significance of legislative intent in the context of Finnis's own theorizing, 335–6 and 338–42.

aims or objectives can be quite specific. But the contrast drawn above – between legislatures and, for example, orchestras – hinges on the notion that legislatures are a type of group that is incapable of having anything other than the most general of objectives. The reason for thinking of legislatures in this way seems to be that they are usually composed of large numbers of people holding diverse views on a variety of matters, and have memberships which can change not only from one election to the next but from one bill, even from one stage of a bill's consideration, to the next. Even if orchestras and sports teams share some of the compositional attributes of legislatures, so the argument goes, it seems to be irrelevant to what they do: size, diversity and flux preclude the formation of specific intentions in a decision-making body such as a legislature, whereas these features are of little or no consequence as regards the formation of specific intentions by groups such as sports teams and orchestras.

A basic shortcoming of this argument is that it takes no account of the fact that legislatures invariably have built into them processes which enable the assembly to deal with the problem of intention formation given the size and diversity of its membership. It is sometimes observed, in response to social choice-based critiques of legislative decision making, that legislatures seem to make remarkably stable collective choices.[71] One explanation for this appears to be that legislators themselves recognize that the cycling of preferences is irrational and costly, and so they seek to ensure that the institutional design of the legislature is such that it operates according to procedures which reduce the possibility of its choices being unstable or incoherent. A legislature, that is, besides having a general intention to make law, typically implements decision procedures – majority voting and deliberation on a specifically worded text being the most obvious examples – which enable it to determine what, in the absence of unanimity among its members, will count as its particular law-making intentions (as opposed to what would count as, say, the results of opinion polls conducted among the legislature's members).[72] The operation of a

---

[71] See, e.g., Kenneth A. Shepsle and Barry R. Weingast, 'Structure-Induced Equilibrium and Legislative Choice' (1981) 37 *Public Choice* 503. Stability in legislative choice will be attributable to various exogenous factors as well as to institutional design: see Arthur Luppia and Mathew McCubbins, 'Lost in Transation: Social Choice Theory is Misapplied against Legislative Intent' (2005) 14 *Jnl of Contemporary Legal Issues* 585. More generally, see Gerry Mackie, *Democracy Defended* (Cambridge University Press, 2005).

[72] See Richard Ekins, 'The Nature of Legislative Intent' (D. Phil. thesis, Oxford University, 2009), 62–3; also Christian List and Philip Pettit, *Group Agency: The Possibility, Design, and Status of Corporate Agents* (Oxford University Press, 2011), 31–5; Finnis, *Natural Law and Natural Rights*, 232–3 and (quoting Yves Simon) 253; and Frank H. Easterbrook, 'The

legislature's decision procedures enables its members to form, and act on, distinct plans.

This attempt to defend the notion of legislatures forming specific intentions meets with a fairly obvious objection. A majority of a legislature, we have observed already, may have voted for a particular bill, but we should be wary of declaring that vote to represent the specific intention of the legislature, or even the specific intention of those who compose the majority of the voters. Even a defender of the summative approach to legislative intention – of the idea, that is, that the legislature's intention is captured by what its majority voted for – might hesitate to endorse the straightforward proposition that votes capture specific legislative intentions. It is 'sometimes embarrassingly difficult to answer the question of just whose intentions count', Andrei Marmor observes, and the correct conclusion on occasions might well 'be that the legislature had no particular intention with respect to the issues bearing on a case before the court'. Nevertheless, he continues,

> it would be a great distortion to maintain that this is always the case. Suggesting that there are never, or almost never, cases where the majority of legislators share a certain intention *vis-à-vis* a law they have enacted would render the phenomenon of legislation a rather mysterious achievement. After all, legislation is a complex political action which strives to bring about a certain change in the normative fabric of the law. It is the kind of action that is done with a purpose in sight, striving to achieve something. The fact that legislation in legislative assemblies is a complex and concerted action involving elaborate procedures does not undermine this simple fact. On the contrary: unless we assume that the legislators have a pretty good sense of what it is that they strive to achieve by enacting a law, it would be very difficult to understand how they manage to achieve the fact of legislation at all. A group of people who do not sufficiently share certain intentions would normally find it very difficult to achieve the kind of concerted action which is required in passing a law.[73]

Role of Original Intent in Statutory Construction' (1988) 11 *Harvard J. Law & Pub. Pol.* 59, 64–5 ('[T]here is a question of legitimacy … If we took an opinion poll of Congress today on a raft of issues and found out its views, would those views become the law? Certainly not. They must run the gamut of the process – and process is the essence of legislation. That means committees, fighting for time on the floor, compromise because other members want some unrelated objective, passage, exposure to veto, and so on … Imagine how we would react to a bill that said, "From today forward, the result of any opinion poll among members of Congress shall have the effect of law." We would think the law a joke at best, unconstitutional at worst').

[73] Andrei Marmor, *Interpretation and Legal Theory*, 2nd edn (Oxford: Hart, 2005), 125–6.

Marmor is right to defend the possibility of specific legislative intentions. But the central claim against those who would resist such a defence is not, as he suggests, that difficulties with the summative approach can be exaggerated. Arguments for and against the summative approach are neither here nor there, for the approach is irrelevant for the purpose of ascertaining legislative intent. It is not majorities within legislatures, but legislatures using majority voting (and other decision procedures), that enact legislation. The majority vote determines what the legislature legislates, but this does not mean that the majority legislates for the legislature. The assembly, not the majority, has legislative authority.[74] Contrary to what Marmor claims, it could sometimes be the case that a majority of legislators do not share a certain intention, or that many members of the legislature have not carefully studied or do not really understand a particular bill. But this is of no consequence, for majority intent is not legislative intent. Those who vote for a bill intend it to become law, even though they may have different reasons for voting and even though some of those who vote may prefer that only some parts of the bill were enacted. Those who vote against the bill hold the same intention in the event that they should find themselves in the minority: they participate in the process on the understanding that the legislature enacts what is supported by the majority vote. Each member participates in the legislative process intending not that he or she or the majority, but that the legislature, enacts legislation.[75]

Furthermore, if all that legislatures intended to do in enacting legislation were to change the law – change for the sake of change and nothing else, as it were – then we would have no reason to treat legislative enactments as authoritative. The legitimacy of legislative enactments is attributable to the fact that a legislature – not a selection of its officers or the majority of its members – intends not simply to change the law but to change some of the specific content of the law as a result of having deliberated and voted on (and possibly amended) what are usually carefully reasoned, precisely formulated proposals.[76] (One of the reasons that statutes

---

[74] See Ekins, 'The Nature of Legislative Intent', 283.

[75] See further *Wilson* v. *First County Trust Ltd (No. 2)* [2003] UKHL 40 at [139]–[140] (Lord Hobhouse).

[76] See Richard Ekins, 'The Intention of Parliament' [2010] *Public Law* 709 ('The intention of the group is the plan of action that its members adopt, and hold in common, to structure how they are to act in order to achieve some end. When the members play their part in the plan, and carry it out to completion, the group has acted on its intention' [714]. '[T]he content of [a legislative] proposal is the particular plan on which the legislator acts, and … is the primary intention of the legislature' [715–6]. '[T]he legislators act by reference to this proposal, which must be set out to be as open and accessible to the legislators as

tend to be drafted carefully is that legislatures do not want courts and litigants radically to misunderstand their specific law-making intentions.)
Besides having a general intention to change the law, a legislature also,
after due deliberation and opportunities for amendment, assents to particular plans of action which thereby become its own; its specific intentions are revealed in its choice to alter the law in the particular ways, and
for the particular reasons, set out in the texts which survive the process
of determining which plans should be adopted, as those not of the legislators who sponsored and supported favoured bills, but of the legislature
itself.[77]

3 Existence and identification

There is nothing unintelligible about the proposition that legislatures
have not only a general intention to change law but specific intentions
in the form of purposes or plans of action which are properly ascribable
to the legislature rather than to its members. The assembly engages in
co-ordinated interaction to achieve its general law-making function and
to determine which specific law-making proposals should be ratified as
the intentional acts of the legislature *sui generis*. Even though one can
identify general legislative intention, it was argued earlier, the very fact
that an intention is general means that identifying it is of little if any help
to those seeking to interpret particular statutes and statutory provisions.
But what is to be said about specific legislative intentions? What is their
interpretive value?

If it is accepted that specific legislative intentions can be identified,
then it seems reasonable to argue that, prima facie, statutes ought not to
be interpreted by courts so as deliberately to contravene those intentions.
This argument, though defensible, moves a little too quickly. Making the
case for the existence of specific legislative intentions and locating such
intentions, it might be objected, are different exercises. Assuming that
specific legislative intentions must exist (and, of course, there are those
who deny even this proposition), how are they to be identified? The obvious answer is: by looking to the enacted text. But we know already that
this answer meets with objections. Often, statutory language will be over-
rather than under-inclusive: drafters, mindful of the fact that 'in laws all

---

is possible' [718]. 'The proposal is a detailed, reasoned choice of how the law shall be
changed ... communicated to the community at large in ... statutory language' [726]).

[77] See Ekins, 'The Nature of Legislative Intent', 321, 329.

cases cannot be foreseen or expressed',[78] will sometimes employ porous words and phrases – 'vehicle', for example, rather than particular types of vehicle, to be operated not above 'a reasonable speed' as opposed to a specified speed limit – which invite interpretations that may attribute to an enacting legislature an intention which was never specifically formed or even contemplated but which, given the choice to enact open-textured language, cannot be said to have been ruled out. Even when the wording of a statutory provision is relatively determinate, it will not necessarily capture the legislature's intentions in full, for the semantic content of a precise directive does not always completely express what the issuer of the directive meant.[79] Whether a statutory provision reads as a general standard or as a specific rule, furthermore, the notion that it can be traced to a singular enacting intention might be contested on the basis that there is always a range of specific and general reasons for making any change to the law – to impose liability in specific circumstances, to protect a particular category of claimant, to deter wrongdoing, to promote well-being, to govern appropriately and so on. The 'obvious purpose' of a statute declaring gambling contracts void, Max Radin observed, appears to be 'to discourage gambling'.

> But ... can we be quite sure about it? There are purposes and purposes ... [N]early every end is a means to another end ... [C]an we say simply that [the] purpose [of the gambling statute] is to discourage gambling? That is obviously a remoter purpose, but the immediate purpose is something less. It is to make it impossible to sue on gambling contracts, or at any rate to make their gambling character a defense ... It may be said that its better and larger purpose is that its immediate one may never be effectuated.[80]

Even defenders of intentionalism tend to concede that there is a world of difference between ascertaining that legislative intent exists and demonstrating what the specific point of enacting a law was.[81] Perhaps the simplest way to draw out the difference between hidden and non-existent legislative intent is to consider the case of the statute enacted by a long-gone legislature. Intellectual historians tend to abide by the principle that the only intentions which may legitimately be ascribed to a text of the distant past are those which might plausibly have been ascribed

---

[78] 1 Bl. Comm. 61.

[79] See Ekins, 'The Nature of Legislative Intent', 237–8; Alexander and Sherwin, *Demystifying Legal Reasoning*, 150.

[80] Radin, 'Statutory Interpretation', 876.

[81] See Alexander and Sherwin, *Demystifying Legal Reasoning*, 150–1.

to it by the text's contemporaries.[82] This principle does not always govern the judicial interpretation of statutes. Sometimes, instead of trying to hypothesize convincingly about the actual intentions of past legislatures, courts will impute to the enacting assembly an intention that it cannot be shown to have had. If, for example, a statute reveals the legislature's intention that jurors be selected from citizens eligible to vote, but the statute was passed at a time when women were ineligible to do so (leave aside, in this instance, the issue of compliance with subsequent treaty obligations) then a court, assuming there is no evidence as to what the legislature would have wanted were women's suffrage introduced, might decide that the statute should be interpreted today as granting women the right to serve as jurors.[83] The legislature's actual intention regarding women as jurors may be elusive, and a court might suspect the truth about that intention to be inconvenient. But this is a problem to do with the discovery of, rather than a question about the existence of, legislative intent: it points to the fact not that bygone legislatures never had intentions, but that courts will sometimes be susceptible to ascribing to those legislatures intentions which cannot necessarily be upheld as corresponding with the intentions they had when they legislated.

Just as it makes sense to mark the difference between hidden and non-existent legislative intentions, so too it is important not to be inordinately sceptical about the capacity of courts to distinguish between the specific intentions for, and the background purposes motivating, the enactment of a statute. Where statutes yield a plain meaning, courts are unlikely to draw the distinction in any event – although judges will sometimes draw it when to apply a statute on its plain meaning risks an injustice which might be avoided by giving effect to what appears to have been the legislature's general, mischief-remedying objective in enacting new law.[84] When the distinction is entertained, some of the larger purposes for enacting a statute are easily discounted because they reveal nothing specific – or nothing apart from the blindingly obvious – regarding how the

---

[82] See Quentin Skinner, 'Meaning and Understanding in the History of Ideas' (1969) 8 *History and Theory* 3.

[83] See, e.g., *Edwards* v. *A-G for Canada* [1930] AC 124 (PC), where the words 'qualified persons' in the British North America Act 1867, s. 24, were construed to include women – notwithstanding that, at the time the Act was passed, 'persons' (and, thereby, citizens eligible to sit in the Canadian Senate) would have meant only men – primarily on the basis that such a legislative provision has to be treated as adaptive and organic, 'like a living tree capable of growth and expansion' (*per* Lord Sankey at 136).

[84] See *Maunsell* v. *Olins* [1975] AC 373 (HL), 391 (*per* Lord Simon); *Duport Steels Ltd* v. *Sirs* [1980] 1 WLR 142 (HL), 168 (*per* Lord Scarman).

statute ought to be interpreted. Just which intentions should not be discounted might be evident from some of the features of the statute itself – such as the long title or the preamble – or from extraneous materials such as reports of advisory committees and the legislative record. Furthermore, common-law courts tend to employ various conventions – for instance, the convention that some possible statutory meanings will not be presumed to have been intended by the legislature unless they have been stated with special clarity – which assist them in determining when it will be appropriate to treat certain types of background law-making desideratum (such as giving the accused the benefit of the doubt when the applicable criminal law is ambiguous) as relevant to statutory construction.[85]

We have begun to stray close to the terrain covered in the final Part of this book. By way of conclusion to this Part, consider two possible objections to the defence of legislative intention that has been advanced. The first objection concerns the proposition that legislatures have a general intention to change the law. Is it not possible that certain bills will signal a different intent? It may be that, on a particular matter, the government does not expect or even want the law to change, and that the introduction of a bill is nothing more than political strategy: the intention to appear controlling, say, or to be committed to real action. Leaving aside the fact that legislatures have no reason to countenance legislative proposals if the proposals are not driven by a genuine commitment to legislate, the objection suffers from two flaws. The first is that the point of introducing a bill is to change the law, no matter that the likelihood of that bill receiving assent may be remote. The second is that while a government may be motivated by political strategy in proposing particular legislation, that strategy is distinct from the intentions of the legislature. The principal reason that the bill will probably not become law is precisely that the legislature is not the government – that the intention behind the introduction of the bill is distinguishable from the intention of the legislature in debating, voting on and accepting or (more likely) rejecting it.

The second objection is that even if a legislature can have specific intentions, its specific intention might sometimes be to avoid revealing an intention. Imprecision in statutory language might be purposive, that is, in the sense that the legislature may be deliberately transferring to the

---

[85] See The Law Commission and the Scottish Law Commission, *The Interpretation of Statutes*, Law Com. No. 21; Scot. Law Com. No. 11 (London: HMSO, 1969), para. 34; also Stefan Vogenauer, 'What is the Proper Role of Legislative Intention in Statutory Interpretation?' (1997) 18 *Statute L. Rev.* 235, 238–9.

courts the capacity to determine the content of the rules that it enacts.[86] But if most statutes are neither determinate nor indeterminate – if '[m]ost … fall somewhere in between these two extremes'[87] – one would expect that judges cannot often be confident that they are being invited to take on this law-making function. How might they ever know that this was the legislature's intention? To answer that a legislature, because it 'always has an option of choosing between precision and imprecision in language', makes a choice which 'must be thought to be deliberate and, thus … purposive'[88] is simplistic. The wording of some statutes will be, and sometimes will even be known to be, deliberately ambiguous.[89] Normally, however, the use of ambiguous statutory language is not deliberate, and so not purposive. But it would be difficult to state with certainty when a legislature has consciously opted for ambiguity, and when the ambiguity is accidental. After all, the possible explanations for statutory ambiguity are many and diverse: drafters of bills might choose language which is capable of supporting two or more meanings in an effort to accommodate a legislative compromise, or they might receive inadequate instructions from the bill's promoters, or the ambiguities might be attributable to amendments at committee stage, or someone responsible for writing, amending or vetting the text might have had a bad day at the office. When statutory language is ambiguous, courts will take the initiative – by producing a strained interpretation based on a plausible secondary meaning that can be given to that language, say, or by interpreting the statute on the basis of legislative intent. But a court cannot always be certain that the text of the statute is, as it were, studiedly ambiguous – that a legislature, by enacting an ambiguous text, was seeking to hand over the legislative reins.

---

[86] See Arthur S. Miller, 'Statutory Language and the Purposive Use of Ambiguity' (1956) 42 *Virginia L. Rev.* 23.

[87] Ibid. 39. [88] Ibid. 34.

[89] See W. M. Graham-Harrison, 'An Examination of the Main Criticisms of the Statute Book and the Possibility of Improvement' [1935] *JSPTL* 9, 31–2.

PART III

The interpretation of statutes

5

Fidelity to text

When we interpret something, we find meaning in it. This is not to claim that all cognition is interpretive, for we can react to something without detecting meaning. Nor would it be correct to say that when we interpret we must be seeking to explain, for we can draw inferences about matters within our awareness without trying to provide an explanation of them (even an explanation to ourselves).[1] It does seem right, however, to say that interpretation and explanation are close cousins in the sense that, often, the point of interpretation is to make a case regarding how something might be understood, or how it is best understood.

The meaning we find in something may be that which we put there, as when we attribute significance to omens or certain types of memento. But often interpretation is a matter of purporting to find in something a meaning which is in some way attributable to someone else, as when a musician interprets a composer's score. Meaning, understood in this attributive sense, is sometimes used as a synonym: what the interpreter took the author to have meant is what he took the author to have intended. But – this point surfaced in the last chapter, and is worth keeping in mind when thinking about statutory interpretation – meaning and intention are distinguishable concepts. The meaning of a text does not have to connect to the intentions of the person who produced or endorsed it. If I randomly plagiarise from a variety of sources, without even bothering to read the passages that I cut and paste, the resultant text may still be interpreted as having meaning, even though I had no intentions as to what the text ought to be taken to mean. Even when communicative intention is discernible, it might still be possible to distinguish intention and meaning. The language we use when addressing others, for example, may contain

---

[1] Cf. Joseph Raz, *Between Authority and Interpretation: On the Theory of Law and Practical Reason* (Oxford University Press, 2009), 299 ('[A]ll interpretations purport to explain or display the meaning of an object'), also 50 n 9. Though Raz does point out that when we explain we do not necessarily offer an interpretation: ibid. 258–9.

meanings which our addressees infer but which we never intended. While these inferences might not always be reasonable – when I ask my class if everybody can hear me, only a wag would answer that they will be straining to catch my words in downtown Albuquerque – it will nevertheless sometimes be the case that the inferences drawn in interpreting the words that the addressor used are understandable and legitimate because the addressor's language, taken in context, accommodates the addressee's interpretation of what he meant as well as, and possibly even over and above, what the addressor intended his words to mean. Interpretation is better understood as the derivation rather than the retrieval of meaning, for the meaning that an interpreter reasonably attributes to an addressor's communication is not necessarily limited to the meaning that the addressor intended to communicate.

1   The hazards of statutory interpretation

Statutory interpretation is the interpretation of attributive meaning, and English judges implicitly accept that the attributive meaning of statutes is to be derived rather than retrieved. The starting principle of statutory interpretation is that the language of a provision should be taken to mean what reasonable people would have meant by using the statutory language as written in its context.[2] A court might be confident that parliament took the language of the statute to bear a meaning different from that which it seems reasonable to ascribe to it (or to treat as its primary meaning).

[2] See, e.g., *Maunsell* v. *Olins* [1975] AC 373 (HL), 391 (*per* Lord Simon); Lord Oliver, 'A Judicial View of Modern Legislation' (1993) 14 *Statute L. Rev.* 1, 3 ('[T]he judge who is called upon to construe statutory language should ask himself whether the meaning that is urged upon him is one which can fairly be drawn by a person of reasonable intelligence ordinarily conversant with the English language'). One drafter-turned-judge once observed that it would be inordinately optimistic to draft statutes on the assumption that citizens will always interpret them reasonably: 'I have had … to draft Acts of Parliament' not only with 'a degree of [linguistic] precision which a person reading in good faith can understand' but also with 'a degree of precision which a person reading in bad faith cannot misunderstand', James Fitzjames Stephen lamented in 1891, given that 'people continually try to misunderstand' what parliament enacts: *Re Castioni* [1891] 1 QB 149, 167. He did not extend the lament to include judges: see James Fitzjames Stephen, 'The Criminal Code (1879)' (January 1880) 7 *The Nineteenth Century* 136, 141 ('Difficulties of interpretation which, before an Act passes, are pronounced to be insuperable, are overcome when they arise in actual practice. The reason is that the minds of the critic and the judge are, and indeed ought to be, in attitudes essentially different. The critic is trying to detect faults. The judge is trying to do justice. The one, in other words, is intent on showing that this or that expression is incomplete, or capable of being misunderstood. The other is trying in good faith to ascertain the real meaning of the words before him').

But this is of no consequence. 'That … the Parliament that passed it may have thought the words bore a different meaning cannot affect the matter. Parliament, under our constitution, is sovereign only in respect of what it expresses by the words used in the legislation it has passed.'[3] Legislative intent, even if we grant that it can be established, will not necessarily determine how a statute is to be interpreted, for it will sometimes be possible reasonably to ascribe to statutory language meanings which do not correspond with the ascertainable intentions of parliament in enacting the statute. 'We often say that we are looking for the intention of Parliament,' Lord Reid observed in 1975,

> but that is not quite accurate. We are seeking the meaning of the words which Parliament used. We are seeking not what Parliament meant but the true meaning of what they said. In the comparatively few cases where the words of a statutory provision are only capable of having one meaning, that is an end of the matter and no further inquiry is permissible.[4]

This statement has to be approached with caution since the passing of the Human Rights Act 1998, section 3 of which requires courts, '[s]o far as it is possible', to 'read and give[] effect' to statutory language, even unambiguous statutory language, 'in a way which is compatible with' the European Convention on Human Rights. If we leave cases concerning human rights compatibility to one side, however, the point that statutes ought to be interpreted in accordance with reasonable understandings holds good: where it is possible to form such an understanding of a statutory provision, then, for at least two reasons, a court ought to abide by that understanding. First, a court which does otherwise risks corroding public confidence in the law, since citizens might fairly protest that, absent a line of precedent revealing an established judicial interpretation, there will be no way of knowing how to organize one's affairs – and, perhaps more importantly, legal advisers will have no way of knowing how to advise their clients on organizing their affairs – in the light of what a statute provides.[5] Secondly, statutory provisions should not be accorded meanings

---

[3] *Black-Clawson International Ltd* v. *Papierwerke Waldhof-Aschaffenburg AG* [1975] AC 591 (HL), 638 (*per* Lord Diplock). See also Frank H. Easterbrook, 'The Role of Original Intent in Statutory Construction' (1988) 11 *Harvard Jnl of Law & Public Policy* 59, 61 ('What any member of Congress thought his words would do is irrelevant. We do not care about his mental processes. Meaning comes from the ring the words would have had to a skilled user of words at the time, thinking about the same problem').

[4] *Black-Clawson International* v. *Papierwerke Waldhof-Aschaffenburg*, 613.

[5] See ibid. 638, *per* Lord Diplock ('The acceptance of the rule of law as a constitutional principle requires that a citizen, before committing himself to any course of action, should be able to know in advance what are the legal consequences that will flow from it. Where

other than those which can reasonably be ascribed to them because a statute is not a casually produced text but rather the outcome of a rigorous drafting and reasoning process.[6] Indeed, even if it is the statutory language as reasonably understood, rather than the legislature's enacting intention, that should govern the interpretation of a statute, it is normally fair to presume – given the nature of the enactment process – that the meaning of the text and the enacting intention will not be radically dissimilar; so it is that English judges have in the past (though not so much in recent times)[7] occasionally explained their interpretive task to be that of giving effect to the legislature's intention as revealed by the text of the statute, as if legislative intention and the meaning of the text are necessarily indistinguishable.[8]

The mantra that statutory language ought to be given its ordinary or natural meaning only takes us so far, however. Judges certainly cannot rewrite statutes simply because they do not like what they know them to mean. Yet they will still sometimes seek to avoid giving statutory language its obvious meaning. It may be that a statute which is applicable,

those consequences are regulated by a statute the source of that knowledge is what the statute says. In construing it the court must give effect to what the words of the statute would be reasonably understood to mean by those whose conduct it regulates'); also F. A. Hayek, *The Road to Serfdom* (London: Routledge and Kegan Paul, 1944), 54–6; and cf. Joseph Raz, *The Authority of Law: Essays on Law and Morality* (Oxford: Clarendon Press, 1979), 213–5, 220.

[6] Hence the advice, in a classic US legal treatise, that interpreters consider the statute as the product of 'reasonable persons pursuing reasonable purposes reasonably': see Henry M. Hart, Jr and Albert M. Sacks, *The Legal Process: Basic Problems in the Making and Application of Law*, ed. W. N. Eskridge and P. P. Frickey (Westbury, N.Y.: Foundation Press, 1994), 1378.

[7] Presumably because the judicial interpretation of statutes has altered somewhat since the enactment of the Human Rights Act 1998, s. 3, and because the decision of the House of Lords in *Pepper* v. *Hart* [1993] AC 593 relaxed the rule prohibiting courts from considering ministerial explanations of bills in parliament (though this is a decision which applies specifically to the interpretation of ambiguous statutory provisions). Both of these developments are considered in the next chapter.

[8] See, e.g., *Cockburn* v. *Harvey* (1831) 2 B. & Ad. 797, 801 *per* Lord Tenterden CJ ('The Court … can know the intention of the Legislature only from the language of a statute'); *Gorham* v. *Bishop of Exeter* (1850) 15 QB 52 (PC), 74 *per* Lord Campbell CJ ('Sitting here, we can only interpret the law, and try to discover the intention of the Legislature from the language of the Statute Book'); *R* v. *Commissioners of the Port of Southampton* (1869–70) LR 4 HL 449, 470 *per* Blackburn J ('[W]e must collect the intention of the Legislature from the language of the enactment'); *DPP* v. *Shannon* [1975] AC 717 (HL), 757 *per* Viscount Dilhorne ('We are only entitled to infer what was the intention of Parliament from the language used in the enactment'); *Worthing Rugby Football Club Trustees* v. *IRC* [1985] 1 WLR 409 (Ch. D), 414 *per* Peter Gibson J ('one must look for Parliament's intention in the statutory language itself').

and therefore cannot be dismissed as irrelevant, to a case requires the unreasonable or the impossible, or contains contradictory directives, so that a court's interpretive task is to make sense out of (literal or figurative) nonsense. In this situation, a judge who resolves to be unremittingly faithful to enacted texts would decree that nonsense should prevail. This judge is not necessarily fictitious: our body of enacted law 'is sure to contain … blemishes … which a philosopher or a nomothete would have contrived to avoid', one of them once reasoned, but '[i]t cannot be helped. It is too late for the law courts to improve or explain them away. That is for the Legislature'.[9]

But even judges who endeavour to accord statutory language its ordinary meaning tend to recognize that uncompromising fidelity to the text can prove unwise, if only because statutes will sometimes contain patent errors – such as where a drafter has mistakenly used 'and' instead of 'or'[10] – which lend themselves to obvious correction. The more difficult cases are those where the point of an interpretation is not to render a statutory provision intelligible, workable or reconcilable with the rest of the statute, but to support a determination that a particular meaning yielded by the provision is preferable to other possible meanings, or to justify interference with statutory language because the only meaning that can be attributed to that language puts the law at odds with justice. If the language of a provision is ambiguous – if, even when considered in the context of the statute as a whole, more than one meaning might reasonably be attributed to it[11] – a court will not be able to ascribe to it a plain meaning and so

[9] *Rodriguez* v. *Speyer Bros.* [1919] AC 59 (HL), 133 (*per* Lord Sumner).

[10] See, e.g., *Sutherland Publishing Co. Ltd* v. *Caxton Publishing Co. Ltd* [1938] Ch. 174 (CA), 201 (*per* MacKinnon LJ); *R* v. *Oakes* [1959] 2 QB 350 (CCA), 354 (*per* Lord Parker CJ); *Federal Steam Navigation Co. Ltd* v. *Department of Trade and Industry* [1974] 1 WLR 505 (HL), 522 *per* Lord Wilberforce ('To substitute "and" for "or" is a strong and exceptional interference with a legislative text, and in a penal statute one must be even more convinced of its necessity. It is surgery rather than therapeutics. But there are sound precedents for so doing'). On latent complications attaching to the notion of 'drafting error', see Caleb Nelson, 'What is Textualism?' (2005) 91 *Virginia L. Rev.* 347, 379 n 99.

[11] Note that ambiguity should be distinguished from vagueness (and vagueness from open texture). A concept is ambiguous when it can be understood in two or more distinct senses, whereas a concept is vague when there are borderline cases for its application. An instruction to 'collect the light books from the reading room' is ambiguous in that 'light' could refer to the colour or the weight of the books. If the instruction were known unambiguously to refer to weight, it would be vague without any specification as to how to distinguish light weight from other possible ranges of weight. See Timothy A. O. Endicott, *Vagueness in Law* (Oxford University Press, 2000), 31–41, 54; Willard Van Orman Quine, *Word and Object* (Cambridge, Mass.: MIT Press, 1960), 129–32; and, on open texture (i.e., the possibility of vagueness), see Frederick Schauer, *Playing by the*

might try to draw reasonable inferences as to what the enacting legislature would have intended had it contemplated the specific problem at bar,
or try to discover actual legislative intent by looking to sources beyond the
statute. If the meaning of the statutory language is unambiguous but can
only facilitate unfairness, a court might decide to modify the language
on the basis that the legislature could never have intended the outcome
that the unmodified language compels. In each of these instances, judges
are relying on something other than what, a moment ago, was termed the
starting principle of statutory interpretation.

There is a temptation to assert that when courts modify statutory language they cross the boundary separating judicial interpretation and
judicial legislation. Most, in fact nearly all, judicial alterations to statutes
are properly described in exactly this way. Yet the boundary between
interpretation and legislation is not straightforwardly marked. A court's
objective in modifying statutory language is not necessarily to supplant
the intention of the enacting legislature. The court might conclude that
although a particular statute is meant to be applied to the dispute at hand,
the enacted text gives no clues as to how the legislature intended such a
dispute to be resolved and that it is impossible to say if the modification of
the text would have met with the legislature's approval. Or the point of the
modification may be to try to give effect to legislative intention: one might
interpolate by altering, and thereby changing the meaning of, a text, and
yet – since the reason for the alteration is to seek to capture what one is
confident was the author's intention – act with the motives of a faithful
interpreter. The possibility of interpolative interpretation Jacques Derrida
explained as *supplementation*. Interpretation, he claimed, supplements a
text much as a text can supplement speech. Supplementation can enrich
a text or replace it (Derrida believed that it is never clear if a supplement

Rules: A Philosophical Examination of Rule-Based Decision-Making in Law and in Life
(Oxford: Clarendon Press, 1991), 35–7. In this chapter and the next, far less is made of
vagueness than of ambiguity. One study of statutory interpretation offers the argument
that '[a]mbiguity is a disease of language, whereas vagueness, which is sometimes a disease, is often a positive benefit' (Reed Dickerson, *The Interpretation and Application of
Statutes* (Boston: Little Brown & Co., 1975), 48). This is correct, though the observation
perhaps benefits from elaboration. A legislature will quite often deliberately enact vague
statutory language, and judges will be settling not so much on the meaning of the language as on the particular circumstances to which the language applies. But ambiguities
in statutory language are not normally intended; the interpretive task of judges faced
with statutory ambiguity is likely to be that of dealing with a legislative oversight rather
than exercising a deliberately conferred discretion. See further Caleb Nelson, *Statutory
Interpretation* (New York: Foundation Press, 2011), 77–80.

adds to or takes the place of the original);[12] whatever the effect, its occurrence demonstrates only that the text is in some way incomplete.[13] A more prosaic acknowledgment of the possibility of interpolative interpretation can be found in Austin's *Lectures on Jurisprudence*. Enacted legislation, according to Austin, is 'proper legislation' whereas judicial legislation is, generally speaking, 'improper'.[14] When we see 'the judge ... depart from the manifest sense of a statute ... he is not a *judge* properly interpreting the law, but a ... *legislator*' who '*substitutes* for the clear expressions which the lawgiver has actually used' expressions which he '*would* have used ... or ... supposes ... the lawgiver *would* have made ... This ... is not *interpretation*, but a process of legislative amendment, or a process of legislative correction'.[15] But not every interstitial correction of a statute should be deemed improper, Austin thought, for genuinely garbled statutory communications may have to be judicially resolved.[16] 'Proper' judicial legislation – the modification of statutory language to dispel an inconsistency to which there is an obvious solution, for example, or the remedying of a patent drafting error – serves not to replace existing law with new law, but to make existing law intelligible.

We know that statutory interpretation, certainly in English law, has traditionally been understood to be an exercise in establishing what statutory language means rather than what the legislature intended the language to mean. But from this it does not follow that judges will be indifferent whether the meanings they attribute to statutes correspond with legislative intentions. Judges may want to ensure correspondence between the two if only to avoid being accused – even falsely accused – of law making beyond their constitutional limits. Principles of statutory interpretation, most of which have been developed through the common law, serve them well in this regard: many such principles connect statutory meaning to legislative intention (though not necessarily to the intention of the legislature which enacted the statute). Not that they guarantee this connection. Interpretive principles will not always enable – indeed, are not always devised to enable – interpreters to distinguish what was

---

[12] See Jacques Derrida, *Of Grammatology*, trans. G. C. Spivak (Baltimore: Johns Hopkins University Press, 1976), 144–5.

[13] See ibid. 280–1; also Jacques Derrida, *Writing and Difference*, trans. A. Bass (London: Routledge and Kegan Paul, 1978), 178–9.

[14] John Austin, *Lectures on Jurisprudence or the Philosophy of Positive Law*, 2 vols., 5th edn, rev. and ed. R. Campbell (London: Murray, 1885), II, 620.

[15] Ibid. 629. (Emphases in original.)

[16] See ibid. 641–7, 660–1.

the legislature's intent from what was not, and, even when they do help with this distinction, the interpreter will not necessarily use the available principles to support a ruling consistent with the intentions of the legislature.[17] Karl Llewellyn famously wrote of how any principle of statutory construction nearly always has an equal opposite, and so can be manipulated by those with a will and the skill: 'there are two opposing canons on almost every point' of construction, and so if counsel wants 'any canon to take hold in a particular instance [before a court], the construction contended for must' – given that opposing counsel can very likely rely on an applicable counter-canon – 'be sold, essentially, by means other than the use of the canon'.[18]

Llewellyn's claim has been subjected to regular – and sometimes painstaking[19] – criticism, the primary objection being that opposing canons rarely stand in formal contradiction to one another but rather operate as rebuttable presumptions which are subject to exceptions.[20] Occasionally, however, canons do stand in formal contradiction to one another: for example, the presumption that statutes which list some items within a category thereby exclude items belonging to but not listed among that category straightforwardly conflicts with the presumption that a statute which lists certain items within a category thereby includes analogous

[17] See Antonin Scalia, 'Assorted Canards of Contemporary Legal Analysis' (1990) 40 *Case Western Reserve L. Rev.* 581, 582; Richard A. Posner, 'Legal Formalism, Legal Realism, and the Interpretation of Statutes and the Constitution' (1986) 37 *Case Western Reserve L. Rev.* 179, 196.

[18] Karl N. Llewellyn, 'Remarks on the Theory of Appellate Decision and the Rules or Canons about How Statutes are to be Construed' (1950) 3 *Vanderbilt L. Rev.* 395, 401.

[19] See Michael Sinclair, '"Only a Sith Thinks Like That": Llewellyn's "Dueling Canons," One to Seven' (2005–6) 50 *New York Law School L. Rev.* 919; '"Only a Sith Thinks Like That": Llewellyn's "Dueling Canons," Eight to Twelve' (2006–7) 51 *New York Law School L. Rev.* 1003; '"Only a Sith Thinks Like That": Llewellyn's "Dueling Canons," Thirteen to Sixteen' (2008–9) 53 *New York Law School L. Rev.* 953; '"Only a Sith Thinks Like That": Llewellyn's "Dueling Canons," Seventeen to Twenty', *New York Law School Legal Studies Research Paper* (April 2009), no. 08/09–27, at http://ssrn.com/abstract=1387503 (visited 18 July 2011); Adam Schlusselberg and Michael Sinclair, '"Only a Sith Thinks Like That": Llewellyn's "Dueling Canons," Twenty-One to Twenty-Four', *New York Law School Legal Studies Research Paper* (February 2010), no. 09/10–22, at http://papers.ssrn.com/abstract_id=1557831 (visited 18 July 2011).

[20] See, e.g., Antonin Scalia, 'Common-Law Courts in a Civil-Law System: The Role of United States Federal Courts in Interpreting the Constitution and Laws', in *A Matter of Interpretation: Federal Courts and the Law*, ed. A. Gutmann (Princeton University Press, 1997), 3–47 at 26–7; Richard Ekins, 'The Nature of Legislative Intent' (D. Phil. thesis, Oxford University, 2009), 273–4; Cass R. Sunstein, 'Interpreting Statutes in the Regulatory State' (1989) 103 *Harvard L. Rev.* 405, 451–4.

unlisted items belonging to that category.[21] Llewellyn was not entirely wrong. It is important, indeed inevitable, that judges make use of principles of statutory interpretation, but it would be naïve to think that reliance, even judicious reliance, on these principles precludes the possibility of some statutory ambiguities being arbitrarily resolved in favour of a judge's preferred construction. One can expect too much of interpretive principles, just as one can expect too little.

In this chapter and the next, we will focus on the three main principles of statutory interpretation. The first of these principles emphasizes the importance of the text. The second does the same, but urges avoidance of textual interpretations that lead to patently unjust or absurd rulings. The third – which, since it takes a number of distinct forms, has the next chapter all to itself – is premised on the notion that what matters most in the process of statutory interpretation, certainly though not only when the language of a statute is ambiguous, is not the text but the purpose behind it (purpose meaning, normally, the purpose of enactment). But before we start to consider these principles, there are two further points that ought briefly to be made regarding interpretive hazard.

First, it is sometimes argued that the interpretive hazard which so troubled Austin, improper judicial law making, is checked by the doctrine of precedent. The 'tendency to follow precedents in statutory interpretation', so the argument goes, means that common-law judges often consider themselves constrained from, say, reading anything new into statutory language if a previous court – particularly a previous higher court – has already placed an interpretation on that language.[22] There is nothing contentious about this point. But, as anyone who makes the point would no doubt concede, it is important to keep in mind that precedents, in this context as elsewhere, have only limited constraining force. Although courts with the power to overrule a precedent will tend to respect a previous decision on the interpretation of a statute – not least because departure from the decision may risk disadvantaging citizens whose long-term plans and activities have been arranged on the basis of the prior construction – there is, given that precedents will sometimes support egregious interpretations, only a rebuttable presumption (albeit, as was noted in

---

[21] See Einer Elhauge, 'Preference Eliciting Statutory Default Rules' (2002) 102 *Columbia L. Rev.* 2162, 2212; John Willis, 'Statute Interpretation in a Nutshell' (1938) 16 *Can. Bar Rev.* 1, 19–20.

[22] Max Radin, 'Statutory Interpretation' (1930) 43 *Harvard L. Rev.* 863, 881–2. See also H. C. Gutteridge, 'A Comparative View of the Interpretation of Statute Law' (1933) 8 *Tulane L. Rev.* 1, 16.

Chapter 1, usually a strong rebuttable presumption) that an established interpretation will be followed.[23] Even when judges do consider themselves constrained to follow the construction placed on a statute by an earlier court, moreover, their decision to do so will reinforce rather than militate against improper law making if the earlier court's reading of the statute deliberately subordinated legislative to judicial will.

Secondly, it is worth noting the possibility of interpretive hazard in the form of what might be termed legislative symbiosis. It was observed in Chapter 3 that the drafting of a statute may influence the interpretive role of a court. The more open-ended or 'standard-like' a statute's wording ('drive safely'), the greater the likelihood that judges will seek to supplement the enacted text; the more precise or 'directive-like' the statutory wording ('always wear a seat belt'), the more likely judges will abide by the plain meaning of that text.[24] This process could, of course, cut in the opposite direction as well. The nineteenth-century German-American jurist, Francis Lieber, drew attention not to the drafter's but to the judge's way with words, and lamented in particular what he perceived to be the tendency of the English judiciary to interpret statutes according to their plain meaning. 'This ... induced the law-makers to be, in their phraseology, as explicit and minute as possible, which causes ... tautology and endless repetition ... [L]ittle or nothing is gained by attempting to speak with absolute clearness, and endless specifications.'[25]

If drafters and interpreters do influence one another in this way, the process could be iterative – whereby, for example, a preferred legislative drafting style leads most judges to opt for a particular approach to statutory interpretation, which then leads drafters to revise their drafting style, which in turn leads most judges to settle on a different interpretive

---

[23] See also Rupert Cross, *Statutory Interpretation*, 3rd edn J. Bell and G. Engle (Oxford University Press, 2005), 148. It might be expected that the longer and more established the line of decisions, the less likely it is that the presumption as to binding precedent will be rebutted. But when judges decline to rebut the presumption it seems more likely that their principal motivation is not straightforwardly the strength of the precedent but the fact that legislative conditions have not changed: i.e., that the interpretation of the statute by the precedent-setting court is considered to capture the enacting legislature's intention and that the intention of today's legislature appears not to have, or not to have significantly, altered. See Einer Elhauge, *Statutory Default Rules: How to Interpret Unclear Legislation* (Cambridge, Mass.: Harvard University Press, 2008), 211–23.

[24] See Quintin Johnstone, 'An Evaluation of the Rules of Statutory Interpretation' (1954) 3 *Kansas L. Rev.* 1, 18; Nelson, 'What is Textualism?', 399.

[25] Francis Lieber, *Legal and Political Hermeneutics, or Principles of Interpretation and Construction in Law and Politics, with Remarks on Precedents and Authorities* (Boston: Little & Brown, 1839), 30.

approach, which causes drafters to revise their style again, and so on – though extensive empirical research would be required to determine whether, in the United Kingdom, anything like this feedback loop has ever existed between the Office of the Parliamentary Counsel and the courts.[26] One indication – although not an especially strong indication – that it might sometimes exist is to be found in the approaches of parliament and the courts to reverse burdens of proof in the criminal law. Reverse burdens, whereby defendants must prove on the balance of probabilities (rather than the prosecution disprove beyond reasonable doubt) that they benefit from a defence to the crime, are, in every case apart from the common-law defence of insanity, established by statute. Where a reverse burden is imposed by express words rather than necessary implication, parliament has tended to indicate its intention to place the onus of proof on the defendant by using the expression, 'It shall be a defence to prove x.'[27] But statutory reverse burdens do not sit comfortably with article 6(2) of the European Convention on Human Rights, which provides that every-one charged with a criminal offence shall be presumed innocent until proved guilty according to law. After the enactment of the Human Rights Act 1998, the UK courts began to read the words, 'It shall be a defence to prove ...', not as automatically imposing a statutory reverse burden but rather as an invitation to judges to consider, first, whether the burden was imposed in pursuance of a legitimate aim, and secondly, whether it is pro-portionate to the achievement of that aim.[28] There exists, however, at least one post-HRA statutory provision, section 118(2) of the Terrorism Act 2000, which could be interpreted as indicating parliament's clear inten-tion to reverse the burden of proof. This provision identifies certain other provisions in the Terrorism Act as imposing only an evidential burden on a defendant, so that the defendant need only adduce 'evidence which

---

[26] For a preliminary exploration of the thesis in relation to statutes and statutory inter-pretation in the United States, see Adrian Vermeule, 'Cycles of Statutory Interpretation' (2001) 68 *Univ. Chicago L. Rev.* 149; also Nelson, 'What is Textualism?', 391; and Elhauge, 'Preference Eliciting Statutory Default Rules', 2173–7. The process might also influence which cases get litigated, in so far as lawyers are likely to come to understand which interpretive conventions will probably, and which will probably not, be sympathetically entertained by the courts: see Caleb Nelson, 'A Response to Professor Manning' (2005) 91 *Virginia L. Rev.* 451, 459.

[27] See, e.g, the Misuse of Drugs Act 1971, s. 28(2) ('[I]t shall be a defence for the accused to prove that he neither knew of nor suspected nor had reason to suspect the existence of some fact alleged by the prosecution which it is necessary for the prosecution to prove if he is to be convicted of the offence charged').

[28] See *R* v. *Lambert* [2002] 2 AC 545 (HL); *Brown* v. *Stott* [2003] 1 AC 681 (PC).

is sufficient to raise an issue with respect to the matter' (whereupon 'the court or jury shall assume that the defence is satisfied unless the prosecution proves beyond reasonable doubt that it is not'). The clear implication is that sections of the Act not listed in section 118(2) reverse the burden of proof, requiring the defendant to establish the matter on the balance of probabilities. Yet in the *Attorney-General's Reference (No. 4 of 2002)* the House of Lords held otherwise, reading down section 11(2) of the Terrorism Act as if section 118(2) applied to it (even though it is not one of the sections listed there).[29] If parliament were to legislate today to reverse a burden of proof, it would have to devise a new method for doing so: it could not be sure to achieve the desired result, that is, either by using the expression, 'It shall be a defence to prove ...', or by omitting a section from a list of statutory provisions as it did under section 118(2).

Senior judges have certainly accepted that there is some evidence of simple or non-iterated symbiosis as between parliament and the courts. 'The canons of construction', Lord Simon ventured in 1975,

> constitute a code of communication between the draftsman and the court of construction. Observing the code on his side, the draftsman will use language in such a way that its meaning represents what Parliament means to say; and it is only by observance of the code by the court on its own side that a divergence can be avoided between its interpretation of what the words mean from what Parliament meant to say.[30]

Some judges have been uncomfortable with this code of communication – not out of concern over the drafting abilities of parliamentary counsel, but out of fear that the quality of legislative drafting could be diminished if judges opt for the wrong interpretive principles. An obvious case in point is the relaxation of the principle – to which English courts adhered between the late 1760s and the early 1990s – that statutory

---

[29] See *Attorney-General's Reference (No. 4 of 2002)* [2005] 1 AC 264, esp. at 314 (*per* Lord Bingham).

[30] *Maunsell* v. *Olins*, 391. See also *Quazi* v. *Quazi* [1980] AC 744 (HL), 824 *per* Lord Scarman (on *ejusdem generis*); Kenneth Diplock, *The Courts as Legislators* (Birmingham: Holdsworth Club, 1965), 11 ('a vicious circle ...'); The Law Commission and the Scottish Law Commission *The Interpretation of Statutes*, Law Com. No. 21; Scot. Law Com. No. 11 (London: HMSO, 1969), para. 5 ('If defects in drafting complicate the rules of interpretation, it is also true that unsatisfactory rules of interpretation may lead the draftsman to an over-refinement in drafting at the cost of the general intelligibility of the law'); *The Preparation of Legislation: Report of a Committee Appointed by the Lord President of the Council* (Chair: Sir David Renton, MP) (Cmnd 6053, London: HMSO, 1975), para. 19.1; Louis L. Jaffe, *English and American Judges as Lawmakers* (Oxford: Clarendon Press, 1969), 76; and Roderick Munday, 'The Common Lawyer's Philosophy of Legislation' (1983) 14 *Rechtstheorie* 191, 198–9.

interpretation on the basis of legislative history is to be prohibited. One of the many arguments that judges over the centuries have advanced against relaxing this principle (which is examined in the next chapter) is that drafters might not feel obligated to draft precisely if they perceive that the courts will readily try to determine statutory meaning by relying on ministerial statements of intention and the like.[31]

2 Against interpretation

These introductory observations flag up a simple point: that statutory interpretation is a potentially tricky and contentious business. The obvious question this point invites – how, then, is statutory interpretation handled? – cannot be satisfactorily met with a simple response. The very general answer to the question seems to be that statutory interpretation is steered by tradition. Within a particular legal, cultural, religious or other tradition, we learn how to interpret by becoming familiar with and inculcating general understandings as to what are considered reliable and legitimate sources of information and what constitutes permissible innovation when negotiating those sources. In the domain of statute law, these understandings commonly take the form of interpretive principles and presumptions. About the main examples of these principles and presumptions, and the reasons for their existence, we will have more to say in a moment. But consider, first of all, what must be the most uncompromising principle of legal interpretation ever to have been devised. In the introduction to Justinian's *Digest*, it is decreed that

> no one, of those who are skilled in the law at the present day or shall be hereafter, may dare to compose any commentary on these laws [*nemo neque eorum, qui in praesenti iuris peritiam habent, nec qui postea fuerint audeat commentarios isdem legibus adnectere*], except in so far as he may wish to translate them into the Greek language in the same order and sequence as those in which the Roman words are written (known to the Greeks as κατά πόδα [word for word]), or to annotate titles to explain any fine points, or to compose what are called παράτιτλα [explanatory notes]. We do not permit them [*sc.*, jurists] to put forward other interpretations, or rather perversions, of the laws [*Alias autem legum interpretationes, immo magis perversiones eos iactare non concedimus*], lest

---

[31] See Johan Steyn, 'The Intractable Problem of The Interpretation of Legal Texts' (2003) 25 *Sydney L. Rev.* 5, 15. For the same argument advanced by an American judge, see Felix Frankfurter, 'Some Reflections on the Reading of Statutes' (1947) 47 *Columbia L. Rev.* 527, 545; 'A Symposium on Statutory Construction: Foreword' (1950) 3 *Vanderbilt L. Rev.* 365, 368.

their verbosity may cause such confusion in our legislation as to bring
discredit upon it.[32]

This bizarre prohibition on nearly all interpretations of the *Digest* –
the passage brings to mind Nietzsche's injunction that one beware
interpretation, for it is 'in truth' always someone's 'means of becoming
master of something'[33] – was regularly ridiculed during the Renaissance.
It is 'facetious' to think that such a decree could be enforced, one
sixteenth-century Romanist is reported to have remarked, for 'if a dog
has pissed somewhere, there is no mongrel ... that will not come to raise
his leg and do likewise ... [I]f ... some legal pettifogger [*protenotaire
du droit*] discusses a point in some passage, no matter how long or how
irrelevant, the entire pack of doctors [of the law] will come to befoul the
same passage with conclusions, conditions, reasons pro and con ... and
other apparatus'.[34] Justinian's edict drew an equally robust response from
Montaigne, who emphasized that law has to involve interpretation. Since
no legal problem is likely to seem 'any less vast when examining the meanings of others than when formulating [a meaning of] our own', he argued,
'there is as much freedom and scope in interpreting laws as in making
them'.[35] For legislators to try 'to rein in the authority of the judges' by
drafting statutes which seek to deal with every likely instantiation of a
particular legal problem is futile, moreover, because '[t]he multiplicity of
our human inventions will never attain to the diversity of our cases'.[36] Not
that Montaigne's conclusion was that we should regard the inevitability of
legal interpretation as a matter for celebration: 'interpretations dissipate
the truth and break it up ... By steeping our material we macerate and
stretch it'.[37] It is understandable why the authors of legal texts might wish
to control the interpretation of those texts, he thought, even if it is foolish
to believe that such control might be established – for now and forever –
by issuing a decree.[38]

---

[32] *De confirmatione Digestorum (Tanta)* § 21.

[33] 'In Wahrheit ist Interpretation ein Mittel selbst, um Herr über etwas zu werden.' Friedrich
Nietzsche, *Nachlaß 1885–1887*, ed. G. Colli and M. Montinari (Berlin: de Gruyter/DTV,
1999), XII, 14.

[34] Noël du Fail, *Contes et discours d'Eutrapel*, in his *Oeuvres facétieuses*, 2 vols. (Paris: Dafis,
1874 [1585]), I, 263 (du Fail attributes the remark to Eguinaire Baron, a sixteenth-century
law professor at the University of Bourges).

[35] Michel de Montaigne, *The Complete Essays*, rev. edn trans. M. A. Screech (London:
Penguin, 2003 [1580–95]), 1208.

[36] Ibid.   [37] Ibid. 1210.

[38] Though, in the history of French law, decrees to control the judicial interpretation of statutes are not unknown. Consider, for example, the late eighteenth-century proclamation

Anyone seeking to understand the distinction between proper and improper interpretations of the *Digest* must risk interpreting Justinian's proclamation in a manner which he most likely would have considered improper. The wording of the provision suggests an absolute ban on any interpretation of the *Digest* except for literal translations into Greek,[39] brief explanatory notes and – possibly – insertions drawing attention to cognate passages. Some Renaissance scholars approached the provision differently, arguing that its purpose was to outlaw efforts to legislate under the name of interpretation, and that any interpretation which served to clarify the codified law rather than make it afresh could not be regarded as a perversion.[40] Modern Roman law scholarship, furthermore, generally suggests that in the fifth century BC a broader range of interpretations than those specified in the provision would have been deemed permissible: the dominant line of reasoning in support of this conclusion is that when the *Digest* became law in 533, Justinian considered the entire text to be crystal clear as it stood, and would have introduced the prohibition for the purpose of outlawing only those interpretations which deliberately aimed to expose textual contradictions or raise other exegetical doubts.[41] But these last two readings of Justinian's edict require that one

that courts must not take any direct or indirect part in the exercise of legislative power and, should they wish to interpret any law, must apply to the legislature for permission to do so: see *La loi sur l'organisation judiciaire des 16–24 août 1790*, title II, arts. 10–11 ('Les tribunaux ne pourront prendre directement ou indirectement aucune part à l'exercice du pouvoir legislative ... Ils seront tenus de faire transcrire purement et simplement dans un registre particulier, et de publier dans la huitaine, les lois qui leur seront envoyées').

[39] The implication of κατά πόδα being to follow closely in a leader's footsteps so that they remain in one's sight: see Claire-Hélène Lavigne, 'Droit, traduction, langue et idéologie: *Kata poda* ou la traduction pas à pas selon Justinien 1er' (2005) 18 *Traduction, terminologie, rédaction* 183, 189–90.

[40] See Ian Maclean, *Interpretation and Meaning in the Renaissance: The Case of Law* (Cambridge University Press, 1992), 56, also 118, 157–8.

[41] See Fritz Pringsheim, 'Justinian's Prohibition of Commentaries to the Digest' (1950) 5 *Revue internationale des droits de l'antiquité* 383, 387–90; Adolf Berger, 'The Emperor Justinian's Ban upon Commentaries to the Digest' (1945) 3 *Quarterly Bulletin of the Polish Institute of Arts and Sciences in America* 656, esp. at 672–4 (arguing that the prevalent but mistaken assumption that Justinian sought a complete ban on interpretation stems from an inordinately narrow reading of κατά πόδα); Georg S. Mandarikis, 'Justinians Verbot der Gesetzeskommentierung' (1956) 78 *Zeitschrift der Savigny-Stiftung für Rechtsgeschichte: Romanistische Abteilung* 369, 375 ('Justinian wanted to exclude not the interpretation of the law, but that method of interpretation which, through recourse to the old laws and comparison of them with the current law, explored what the new norms were'); Eberhard Klingenberg, 'Justinians Verbot der Digestenkommentierung', in *Text und Kommentar. Archäologie der literarischen Kommunikation IV*, ed. J. Assmann and B. Gladigow (Munich: Fink, 1995), 407–22 at 416–8.

look beyond its wording and instead interpret according to what is presumed to have been the motivation for it. Are these not exactly the types of 'commentary' that Justinian sought to outlaw? Anyone answering in the affirmative might reasonably observe that the language of near-absolute prohibition which characterizes Justinian's decree is, considered in context, hardly incongruous – that there are other provisions in the *Digest*, such as the *poena falsi*,[42] which are no less uncompromisingly worded. Yet anyone answering to the contrary might note (though it seems at least generally agreed that Justinian would not have wanted them to note!) that the *Digest* also contains statements about legal interpretation which do not square easily with the prohibition.[43] Justinian's decree could be read as an invitation to work out one's own stance on interpretation.[44]

Conventional principles of statutory interpretation differ from Justinian's in that they are intended to help rather than discourage would-be interpreters. But explaining just how these principles are supposed to assist in the task of interpretation is not easy. It has been observed already that they do not all serve the same objective. More often than not, a principle operates so as to narrow the gap between what the language of a statute means and what the legislature evidently or presumably intended in enacting that statute. But, as will become clear in the next chapter, not all interpretive principles function in this way. It is obvious, furthermore, that different legal systems value particular interpretive principles differently: system *A* might require its courts to interpret domestic statutes in accordance with international treaty obligations, and its judges might be generally wary of allowing legislative debates to be used as aids to statutory interpretation, whereas system *B* might resist the possibility of statutes being interpreted so as to accord its citizens rights extending beyond

---

[42] i.e., D 48. 10. 1. 13 ('The penalty for forgery or its equivalent is deportation and confiscation of all property …').

[43] e.g., D 1. 3. 18 ('Statutes ought to be given the more favourable interpretation'); also D 1. 3. 37 ('… custom is the best interpreter of statutes'); D 1. 3. 17 ('To know the law is not to stick to its words, but to grasp its force and power'); and (on the law of succession) D 32. 69 ('One should only depart from the sense of words when it is clear that the testator meant something else'). See also Maclean, *Interpretation and Meaning in the Renaissance*, 143–6, 172–3.

[44] See also ibid. 204 ('What emerges clearly as a feature of the [Renaissance] texts which grapple with this prohibition is the claim to authority in matters of language and meaning which jurists, as judges, interpreters and pedagogues, are constrained to make. This bears upon interpretation in so far as the legal interpreter takes the place of the authorities to which he should be subservient; in fulfilling his functions, he becomes the voice of the legislator in declaring his intention, and the embodiment of right reason in declaring equity').

those conferred by its own constitution, and its judges might generally take a relaxed position on the use of legislative history. This study does not purport to rationalize, or even to take account of, the many different principles – and valuations of principles – of statutory construction. Rather it attempts, primarily in the context of English law, to trace the development of what are commonly considered to be the main principles with a view to showing how judges have understood and relied upon them. During the twentieth century, senior judges would occasionally express bewilderment as to why statutory interpretation should be deemed a topic fit for juristic scrutiny: all we are doing, so went the refrain, is applying common sense.[45] But this is hardly the half of it. Judges recognize and make use of a fairly sophisticated repertoire of interpretive principles – such as that statutory language should normally be given its ordinary meaning, that strained interpretations (and sometimes even minor amendments) of statutes may be warranted to avoid absurd legal outcomes, that an ambiguously worded statute should be interpreted by reference to the defect parliament intended it to remedy, that ambiguous penal statutes should be interpreted to give defendants the benefit of the doubt and that statutes should be presumed not to interfere with vested rights. Quite often, judges differ in their understandings of particular principles, have formulated and refined some of the principles with considerable precision and take different views on where, and whether, certain principles might appropriately be relied on. To study the main principles of interpretation is to examine not mere reliance on common sense, but a set of different perspectives – sometimes quite elaborate perspectives – on the negotiation of statutes, particularly statutes which are worded ambiguously or which, if given their obvious meaning, support an objectively unjust outcome.

One question which this chapter passes over completely is why principles of statutory interpretation ever evolved in English law. This study has already sought to attend to that mystery. Books and commentaries expounding principles of statutory interpretation started to appear in

---

[45] See, e.g., HL Debs, 5th ser., vol. 277, col. 1294 (16 November 1966, Lord Wilberforce) ('[Statutory interpretation] is what is nowadays popularly called a non-subject. I do not think that law reform can really grapple with it'); ibid. col. 1278 (Lord Reid) ('We are always told that construing Acts of Parliament is a mystery, and books have been written about the subject. I always advise young men "Don't read them", because the rules are extremely simple'); HL Debs, 5th ser., vol. 418, col. 73 (9 March 1981, Lord Wilberforce) ('I still think that the interpretation of legislation is just part of being a good lawyer; a multi-faceted thing, calling for many talents; not a subject that can be confined in rules').

England in the second half of the sixteenth century.[46] It would be startling were it otherwise, because, as was explained in the closing section of
Chapter 1, only from the sixteenth century onwards can we meaningfully
speak of the courts being distinguishable from the legislature on the basis
that the legislature alone enacts statutes. Principles of statutory interpretation began to emerge, that is, once judges gradually became removed
from the enactment process and could no longer claim that they knew
what a statute meant because they, or their colleagues on the bench, had
been involved in devising it.

3   Plain meaning

The interesting questions about statutory interpretation concern the
principles that did emerge once the courts and the legislature began to
disentangle. Perhaps the most obvious – though, as we will see, historically not the first – of these principles has it that interpretation should
begin with the words of the statute, and that those words should be taken
to mean what they would ordinarily mean for reasonable people (which
is not to discount the fact that technical words will have technical meanings) using them in the context of the statute. This principle is sometimes
referred to as the 'literal' rule – 'rule' signifying, in this context, 'convention' – of statutory interpretation, though it is more accurately described
as the 'plain-meaning' rule, for, as has been observed already, what is literally said is not necessarily what is plainly meant.[47]

It might be thought that the safest way to establish the plain meanings
of statutory terms is to look them up in a dictionary. Sometimes, indeed,
commentators refer to plain meaning and dictionary meaning as if they

---

[46] See Maclean, *Interpretation and Meaning in the Renaissance*, 182–6, 202.

[47] Lawrence Solan distinguishes plain-meaning and ordinary-meaning interpretations
on the basis that a plain meaning is that which a word unequivocally yields whereas
an ordinary meaning is that which is ordinarily preferred, assuming that any is ordinarily preferred, when a word has more than one meaning. See Lawrence M. Solan, *The
Language of Statutes: Laws and their Interpretation* (Princeton University Press, 2010),
11, 66. Solan concedes that the two approaches often coincide (ibid. 62). But it is not clear
that they amount to different approaches. Whereas the plain-meaning approach, which
Solan thinks is the approach most commonly adopted by American judges, is essentially 'definitional', the ordinary meaning approach is, he argues, 'prototypical' (ibid.
65). According to the ordinary meaning account, categorization by prototype allows
for a degree of shading or nuance that definitional categorization sometimes misses:
so it is that psychologists report that certain types of bird, say, or items of furniture

were all of a piece.[48] But judges, even judges who subscribe to the plain-meaning rule, tend to consider dictionaries and the like to be occasionally valuable but generally very limited aids to statutory construction.[49] One explanation for this attitude is that interpretation with the assistance of a dictionary may prove historically or culturally insensitive. Diplock LJ observed in 1965 that Webster's *Third New International Dictionary*, an American publication of 1961, lists pheasants as an example of 'poultry'. But it would be inappropriate to use this dictionary definition to interpret the word 'poultry' as it appears in section 2 of the Fertilisers and Feeding Stuffs Act, Diplock insisted, not only because no 'ordinary educated Englishman would call pheasants "poultry"', but also because pheasants were not included in the definitions of poultry to be found in English

---

are considered by their respondents to be prototypical whereas others are not (robins are more 'bird-like' than ostriches, tables more 'furniture-like' than lamps, and so on: see ibid. 63–4). But this observation does not, *pace* Solan, invite a distinction 'between definitional and ordinary meaning' (ibid. 65), for definitions do not exclude – indeed, they often take account of – the possibility of objects having prototypical instances and attributes. What Solan in fact wants to draw attention to is the case where a definition technically applies, but the non-prototypical nature of the case suggests that we should not accord the definition much, if any, weight. So: '"bachelor" is a category better described by ordinary usage than by definitions' because 'we are uncomfortable calling some people bachelors, such as the pope', notwithstanding that they fall within the definition ('unmarried adult males') (ibid. 63); Bill Clinton '[n]o doubt ... lied' in denying that he ever had sexual relations with Monica Lewinsky, but 'his doing so to avoid disclosure of sexual misconduct ... was not the worst kind of lie' (ibid. 65). Whatever else one makes of these propositions, they do not distinguish what Solan presents as the ordinary and the plain-meaning approaches; rather, they indicate that what some people might consider non-standard illustrations of a concept nevertheless fall within the concept's definition. It might be objected that without Solan's distinction we cannot, when interpreting statutory language, make the sorts of gradations that he sees as important. Statute law often accommodates such gradations (different degrees of murder, different grades of title to land and so on). But so too do the rulings of courts: for what statutory language is interpreted to mean does not determine how it is applied. Sentences of different lengths could be imposed on two people charged with the same statutory offence, for example, precisely because a court recognizes the actions of both offenders to be materially different while falling within the plain meaning of the statutory provision.

[48] See, e.g., Sunstein, 'Interpreting Statutes in the Regulatory State', 416 ('the "plain meaning" or dictionary definition of statutory terms ...').

[49] For examples of dictionaries being used for the purpose of establishing the plain meaning of statutory terms, see *Mandla* v. *Lee* [1983] QB 1 (though note that the Court of Appeal was careful to stipulate that dictionaries were being used to assist in, rather than as authorities for, determining statutory meaning); *United States* v. *LaBonte*, 520 US 751, 757 (1997) (Thomas J on 'maximum'); *Allentown Mack Sales & Service, Inc.* v. *NLRB* 522 US 359, 367 (1998) (Scalia J on 'doubt').

dictionaries available in 1926, when the statute was passed.[50] Another explanation for the tendency of judges to approach dictionaries cautiously is that dictionaries often simply confirm rather than resolve interpretive difficulties. 'It is highly dangerous, if not impossible, to attempt to place an accurate definition upon a word in common use', Lord Upjohn once observed; 'you can look up examples of its many uses if you want to in the Oxford Dictionary but that does not help on definition'.[51] For example, the *Oxford English Dictionary* defines the word 'obtained' in a variety of senses, including both the active sense of having come into possession by one's own effort and the passive sense of having received without request. In *Attorney-General's Reference (No. 1 of 1988)*, the House of Lords, seeking to determine the meaning of 'obtained' in the context of section 1 of the Company Securities (Insider Dealing) Act 1985, took the view that – as Lord Lowry put it – there is 'no point' in looking to the *Oxford English Dictionary*, or 'shopping around among a variety of dictionaries', for the meaning of the word.[52] The House of Lords' explanation of its position was straightforward: while a dictionary may establish that 'obtained' has active and passive meanings, the question to be answered – and which a dictionary does not answer – is whether the word should be taken to accommodate one or both of these meanings in the context of the Company Securities (Insider Dealing) Act 1985. We can answer that question, Lord Templeman remarked, 'without troubling any dictionary':[53] the word 'obtained' clearly accommodates both the active and the passive meanings, but in this instance must be given only its active meaning by virtue of the principle that ambiguous provisions in penal statutes ought to be construed narrowly.

The main reason judges tend to be wary of relying on dictionaries as interpretive aids is that a dictionary is essentially an archive which offers synonyms for words, explanations of their core meanings and samples of their exemplary use, rather than a sense of the meanings that words might be taken to bear in the context of a particular statute. It is appropriate, of

---

[50] *Hardwick Game Farm* v. *Suffolk Agricultural and Poultry Producers Association* [1966] 1 WLR 287 (CA), 324. The House of Lords, while conceding that pheasants did not fall within the dictionary definition of poultry, nevertheless took the view that parliament intended that pheasants be treated as poultry: *Henry Kendall & Sons* v. *William Lillico & Sons Ltd* [1969] 2 AC 31, 126–7 (*per* Lord Wilberforce).

[51] *Customs and Excise Commissioners* v. *Top Ten Promotions Ltd* [1969] 1 WLR 1163 (HL), 1171.

[52] *Attorney-General's Reference (No. 1 of 1988)* [1989] AC 971, 991.

[53] Ibid. 988.

course, that interpretations of statutes will sometimes depend on dictionary definitions: dictionaries, after all, enable us to understand words which are new to us, or which bear meanings beyond or other than those which we currently ascribe to them.[54] But plain-meaning interpretations rarely simply repeat or endorse definitions of words. The objective of such an interpretation, rather, will usually be to settle on a meaning that a particular application of statutory *language* can reasonably be said to support.[55]

This last point – that judges are usually trying to establish the plain meaning of statutory language rather than statutory words – deserves emphasis. '[P]roblems of interpretation', Joseph Raz has observed, 'are more often than not questions of the interpretation of sentences, or of articles' rather than 'of the meaning of one term or phrase'.[56] The question, as regards statutory interpretation, is conceivably broader still: in order to ascertain the plain meaning of a specific portion of a statute, judges may feel compelled to try to make sense of the statute in its entirety.[57] Although the principle that 'no one should profess to understand any part of a statute … before he had read the whole of it'[58] is, in the case

---

[54] For an example of a dictionary definition satisfactorily answering a court's interpretive dilemma, see *R* v. *Fulling* [1987] 2 WLR 923 (on the meaning of 'oppression' in the Police and Criminal Evidence Act 1984, s. 76).

[55] See *Cabell* v. *Markham*, 148 F.2d 737, 739 (2nd Cir. 1945) (Hand J) ('[I]t is one of the surest indexes of a mature developed jurisprudence not to make a fortress out of the dictionary'); Frank H. Easterbrook, 'Text, History, and Structure in Statutory Interpretation' (1994) 17 *Harvard Jnl of Law & Public Policy* 61, 67 ('a dictionary … is a museum of words, an historical catalog rather than a means to decode the work of legislatures'); Lord Steyn, 'Dynamic Interpretation Amidst an Orgy of Statutes' (2004) 3 *European Human Rights L. Rev.* 245, 249.

[56] Raz, *Between Authority and Interpretation*, 356. Judges tend, understandably, to be especially wary of resorting to dictionaries when they are called upon to interpret phrases and passages rather than words in statutes. See, e.g., *Lee* v. *Showmen's Guild of Great Britain* [1952] 2 QB 329 (CA), 339 *per* Somervell LJ ('I do not think that if the words "unfair competition" stood alone they are apt to describe what happened here. It is often fallacious in considering the meaning of a phrase consisting of two words to find a meaning which each has separately and then infer that the two together cover the combination so arrived at. The two together may, as here, have acquired a special meaning of their own').

[57] Which statute has itself to be understood in the context of the general (statutory and common-law) legal framework: see Roger J. Traynor, 'Statutes Revolving in Common-Law Orbits' (1968) 17 *Catholic Univ. L. Rev.* 401; P. S. Atiyah, 'Common Law and Statute Law' (1985) 48 *MLR* 1; Jack Beatson, 'The Role of Statute in the Development of Common Law Doctrine' (2001) 117 *LQR* 247; Paul Finn, 'Statutes and the Common Law: The Continuing Story', in *Interpreting Statutes*, ed. S. Corcoran and S. Bottomley (Sydney: Federation Press, 2005), 52–63.

[58] *A-G* v. *Prince Ernest Augustus of Hanover* [1957] AC 436 (HL), 463 (*per* Viscount Simonds). See also Francis Bennion, 'The Need for Training in Statute Law' (1982) 79 *Law Soc. Gaz.* 219, 219.

of some very lengthy statutes, much easier stated than followed, efforts to establish the plain meaning of statutory language cannot be inattentive to other enacting provisions in the same Act, or to its interpretation sections, schedules, the long title, headings, saving clauses (i.e., 'Nothing in this section shall be construed as …') and the like.[59] As at least one modern monograph on statutory interpretation makes clear, plain meaning and purposive approaches to statutory interpretation are one and the same thing to the extent that both take account of meanings discernible from the entirety of the text.[60]

It is sometimes assumed that the plain-meaning purist is a caricature – that no judge accepts the proposition that where the meaning of statutory language is plain, this meaning should prevail come what may.[61] Oliver Wendell Holmes played the arch-purist in a letter to Harold Laski in 1920, when he observed that the Sherman Antitrust Act 1890, though 'a foolish law', is one 'that the country likes … [A]nd I always say … that if my fellow citizens want to go to Hell I will help them. It's my job'.[62] But play is probably all this was. Holmes thought that '[d]elusive exactness is a source of fallacy throughout the law'[63] and that a 'word generally has several meanings, even in the dictionary'.[64] He was not averse, moreover, to discounting the plain meaning of statutory language and instead interpreting legislation on the basis of the general purpose for which it had been enacted.[65]

---

[59] *Brett* v. *Brett* (1826) 3 Add. 210, 216 *per* Sir John Nicholl ('[T]o arrive at the true meaning of any particular phrase in a statute, that particular phrase is not to be viewed detached from its context in the statute: it is to be viewed in connexion with its whole context – meaning by this as well the title and preamble as the purview or enacting part of the statute').

[60] See Cross, *Statutory Interpretation*, 57–8.

[61] See, e.g., 'The Case of the Speluncean Explorers Revisited' (1999) 112 *Harvard L. Rev.* 1876, 1913 (Easterbrook J).

[62] O. W. Holmes, Jr to Harold J. Laski, 4 March 1920, in *Holmes–Laski Letters: The Correspondence of Mr. Justice Holmes and Harold J. Laski 1916–1935*, 2 vols., ed. M. DeWolfe Howe (Cambridge, Mass.: Harvard University Press, 1953), I, 249.

[63] *Truax* v. *Corrigan*, 257 US 312, 343 (1921) (Holmes J, dissenting).

[64] O. W. Holmes, Jr, 'The Theory of Legal Interpretation' (1899) 12 *Harvard L. Rev.* 417, 417; also *Towne* v. *Eisner*, 245 US 418, 425 (1918) ('A word is not a crystal, transparent and unchanged, it is the skin of a living thought and may vary greatly in color and content according to the circumstances and the time in which it is used').

[65] See, e.g., *In re House Bill No. 1,291*, 178 Mass. 605, 60 NE 129, 130 (1901) (Holmes finding that a statutory requirement of 'written votes' permitted the use of paperless voting machines because the general purpose of the statute was to prevent oral voting and voting by hand); also, more generally, Richard A. Posner, *The Problems of Jurisprudence* (Cambridge, Mass.: Harvard University Press, 1990), 267–9.

Yet cases decided in accordance with the strict plain-meaning approach to statutory interpretation are by no means undiscoverable. The Game Act 1670 provides that 'every person not having ... some ... estate ... in his own ... right ... (other than the son and heir apparent of an esquire, or other person of higher degree ...) is ... not allowed to have ... any guns ... for the taking and killing of game'. *Jones* v. *Smart* concerned a doctor who, remarkably (this was the late eighteenth century), held no land in his own right and who was therefore not permitted to own a gun for the purpose of killing game. But his son – being 'the son ... of an ... other person of higher degree' – was allowed to own a gun for this purpose. Buller J was in 'no doubt but that the Legislature took it for granted' that if the son of a doctor should be permitted to own a gun for gaming, the doctor would be as well.[66] He recognized the peculiarity of reading the words on their plain meaning. 'Be that as it may', he concluded, 'we are bound to take the Act of Parliament, as they have made it: a *casus omissus* can in no case be supplied by a Court of Law, for that would be to make laws.'[67] Lord Mansfield took the same view: '[t]o be sure, absurd consequences may seem to follow from giving a privilege to the son, which the father has not: but the question is, has the statute done it or not?'[68]

Jones v. *Smart* is not unique. On a 'plain and literal construction', when a legislature uses the word 'year' it must be taken 'to have meant, one entire consecutive period of 365 days', Abbot CJ declared in *R* v. *Turvey*, and so a servant who took a month's break midway through a year's labour and then made up that time by working for a month after the end of the 365-day period could not be said to have worked for a year and therefore was not entitled to a settlement.[69] Cases of this kind, whereby courts dealt harsh blows (usually to vulnerable plaintiffs) by sticking to a statute's plain meaning, appear with some frequency in law reports from the end of the eighteenth century onwards.[70] Throughout the nineteenth century,

---

[66] *Jones* v. *Smart* (1785) 1 Term Rep. 44, 52.

[67] Ibid.

[68] Ibid. 48. But Willes J dissented: 'nothing can be more oppressive than the present system of the game laws ... And wherever a law is productive of tyranny, I shall ever give my consent to narrow the construction' (ibid. 49).

[69] *R* v. *Turvey* (1819) 2 B. & Ald. 520, 521.

[70] See, e.g., *R* v. *Hodnett* (1786) 1 Term Rep. 96, 101 (*per* Buller J); *R* v. *Newark-upon-Trent* (1824) 3 B. & C. 59, 63–4 (*per* Littledale J); *Brandling* v. *Barrington* (1827) 6 B. & C. 467, 475 *per* Lord Tenterden CJ ('Speaking for myself alone, I cannot forbear observing, that I think there is always danger in giving effect to what is called the equity of a statute, and that it is much safer and better to rely on and abide by the plain words, although the Legislature might possibly have provided for other cases had their attention been directed to them'); *R* v. *Barham* (1828) 8 B. & C. 99, 104 (*per* Lord Tenterden CJ); *Notley*

and some years into the twentieth, judges who professed to interpret the language of statutes strictly according to its plain meaning were still very much at large. 'If the words of an Act are clear, you must follow them', Lord Esher opined in 1892, 'even though they lead to a manifest absurdity.'[71] A fair number of his near contemporaries were similarly minded.[72]

Not that it takes much effort to unearth disparaging comments about the plain-meaning rule. That this should be so is hardly surprising, for the very notion of plain meaning has to be negotiated cautiously. What looks to be plain regularly turns out not to be: Wittgenstein famously and vividly illustrated the point with his example of *A*'s request that *B* '[s]hew the children a game' being met by *B* 'teach[ing] them gaming with dice'.[73] In a particular setting one might use the word 'parent' to mean biological parent, yet one's interpreter might assume the plain meaning of the word to include those who are not biological parents of, but who have de facto parental responsibility for, a child (and perhaps also to exclude biological parents who have no contact with the child).[74] Although discerning plain

---

v. *Buck* (1828) 8 B. & C. 160, 164 *per* Lord Tenterden CJ ('The intention certainly was to prevent voluntary preferences; the words may probably go beyond the intention; but if they do, it rests with the Legislature to make an alteration; the duty of the Court is only to construe and give effect to the provision'). From the United States around the same period, cf. *US* v. *Fisher*, 6 US (2 Cranch.) 358, 356 (1805) (Marshall CJ) (If 'the meaning of the legislature be plain ... it must be obeyed'); *Putnam* v. *Longley*, 28 Mass. (11 Pick.) 487, 499 (1831) (Shaw CJ) ('[W]here the language is clear, and where of course the intent is manifest, the Court is not at liberty to be governed by considerations of inconvenience').

[71] *R* v. *Judge of the City of London Court* [1892] 1 QB 273 (CA), 290. See also *Abley* v. *Dale* (1850) 20 LJCP 33, 35 (*per* Jervis CJ).

[72] See, e.g., *Vacher & Sons Ltd* v. *London Society of Compositors* [1913] AC 107 (HL), 121 *per* Lord Atkinson ('If the language of a statute be plain, admitting of only one meaning, the Legislature must be taken to have meant and intended what it has plainly expressed, and whatever it has in clear terms enacted must be enforced though it should lead to absurd or mischievous results'); also William Feilden Craies, *A Treatise on Statute Law*, 2nd edn (London: Stevens & Haynes, 1911), 73; and, in the United States, *Ragland* v. *The Justices of the Inferior Court*, 10 Ga. 65, 70 (1851) (Nisbet J) ('If the meaning was wholly free from doubt, no interpretation would be admissible, for any construction variant from the clear meaning of a Statute, would be judicial legislation'); *Bennett* v. *Worthington*, 24 Ark. 487, 494 (1866) (Compton J) ('The correct rule, as we apprehend, to be extracted from the authorities, is, that where the will of the legislature is clearly expressed, the courts should adhere to the literal expression of the enactment, without regard to consequences, and that every construction derived from a consideration of its reason and spirit should be discarded'); Theodore Sedgwick, *A Treatise on the Rules Which Govern the Interpretation and Application of Statutory and Constitutional Law* (New York: Voorhies, 1857), 231–2, 306–11.

[73] Ludwig Wittgenstein, *Philosophical Investigations*, trans. G. E. M. Anscombe (Oxford: Blackwell, 1978 [1945–9]), 33.

[74] See *Re C (Minors) (Adoption: Residence Order)* [1994] Fam. 1 (CA), 7 (*per* Butler-Sloss LJ).

meanings demands sensitivity to context (which includes an appreciation of the possibility of a word's meaning having changed, perhaps significantly, over time),[75] it does not follow that careful attention to context will always yield a plain meaning: a statutory provision requiring local authorities to provide public services 'economically', for instance, might – even accounting for context – be interpreted as meaning either that authorities must take account of commercial principles when providing services or that they must strive to avoid waste when providing services.[76] All of the Law Lords who decided *Ellerman Lines* v. *Murray* were agreed that the word 'wages' has a plain meaning in the context of the Merchant Shipping (International Labour Conventions) Act 1925. They simply could not agree on what that plain meaning was.[77] While an agreement as to the plain meaning of a term will sometimes be easy to reach, moreover, the

[75] Kent Greenawalt, 'The Nature of Rules and the Meaning of Meaning' (1997) 72 *Notre Dame L. Rev.* 1449, 1450–1.

[76] In *Bromley LBC* v. *Greater London Council* [1983] 1 AC 768, both the House of Lords and the Court of Appeal interpreted 'economic' in the Transport (London) Act 1969, s. 1 (requiring 'the Greater London Council ... to promote the provision of integrated, efficient and economic transport facilities') to mean 'not wasteful' rather than 'in the orthodox business way' (ibid. 778, *per* Oliver LJ), whereas the Divisional Court had been of the view that the word could accommodate either meaning and that the determination of which meaning is to prevail should be left to politicians (*R* v. *Greater London Council, ex p. Bromley London Borough*, in *The Times*, 4 November 1981, 21).

[77] See *Ellerman Lines* v. *Murray* [1931] AC 126; also Willis, 'Statute Interpretation in a Nutshell', 11. In *Newbury DC* v. *Secretary of State for the Environment* [1981] AC 578, the House of Lords accorded the word 'repository' a 'general meaning' (ibid. 605, *per* Lord Fraser) which, in the Court of Appeal, Lawton LJ had considered to be one which 'no literate person' would adopt: *Newbury DC* v. *Secretary of State for the Environment* [1978] 1 WLR 1241, 1253. In *Liversidge* v. *Anderson* [1942] AC 206, the majority of the House of Lords decided that a minister had the power to order detention without either a warrant or the judgment of a court if he had – to quote the words of regulation 18B of the Defence (General) Regulations 1939 – 'reasonable cause to believe any person to be of hostile origin or associations or to have been recently concerned in acts prejudicial to the public safety or the defence of the realm'. Lord Atkin alone dissented, arguing that 'reasonable cause' had to be construed objectively (i.e., that a court is entitled to look for evidence as to the reasonableness of the minister's belief) if it were to mean anything other than that a person should be detained because a minister believes he should be detained. As he famously observed: 'I view with apprehension the attitude of judges who on a mere question of construction when face to face with claims involving the liberty of the subject show themselves more executive minded than the executive ... In this case I have listened to arguments which might have been addressed acceptably to the Court of King's Bench in the time of Charles I ... The words [in regulation 18B] have only one meaning ... They have never been used in the sense now imputed to them ... I know of only one authority which might justify the suggested method of construction: "When I use a word," Humpty Dumpty said in a rather scornful tone, "it means what I choose it to mean, neither more nor less"' (ibid. 244–5).

surrounding language might be ambiguous: anyone interpreting the instruction to 'wear socks, shoes and gloves which are black' will probably have no difficulty understanding any of the words, for example, but will very likely question if the qualifying part of the statement connects to all three items or only to the last.

The standard criticisms of the plain-meaning rule are that it inhibits judicial creativity (which can impose additional law-making costs on the legislature),[78] that it generates interpretations which tend to be either inordinately narrow or downright absurd,[79] that it ignores the fact that the meaning of statutory language is often anything but plain[80] and that it offers an unrealistic account of how judges actually deal with statutes.[81] Any student of the rule quickly becomes aware of a veritable rogues' gallery of cases supporting these and other criticisms,[82] and judges themselves have hardly been impervious to the potential for plain-meaning interpretations to result in bad law. In *ex parte Francis & Francis*,[83] for example, the House of Lords recognized that a statutory provision excluding from lawyer–client privilege 'items held with the intention of furthering a criminal purpose' referred, on its plain meaning, only to

[78] See, e.g., Henry J. Friendly, *Benchmarks* (University of Chicago Press, 1967), 54 (an 'exceedingly wooden attitude … needlessly imposed'); Jaffe, *English and American Judges as Lawmakers*, 76 ('the literal, unimaginative reading of statutes by the courts makes the statute book more and more unwieldy, full of minutiae trying to do what the judges should be doing').

[79] See, e.g., Jerome Frank, 'Words and Music: Some Remarks on Statutory Interpretation' (1947) 47 *Columbia L. Rev.* 1259, 1262 ('Sometimes a literal interpretation of a piece of legislation … will yield a grotesque caricature of the legislature's purpose'); Carleton Kemp Allen, *Law in the Making*, 3rd edn (Oxford: Clarendon Press, 1939), 400–2.

[80] See, e.g., Anthony Lester, 'English Judges as Law Makers' [1993] *Public Law* 269, 272; also *Smith* v. *Smith* [2006] UKHL 35 at [81] (Lord Carswell) ('The phrase "total taxable profits" [in the Child Support (Maintenance Assessments and Special Cases) Regulations 1992, sch. 1, para. 2A] is not a term of art bearing a defined and ascertainable meaning in tax law or child support law. It is on its face ambiguous and its meaning cannot be determined by applying the plain meaning test of statutory interpretation').

[81] See, e.g., Richard A. Posner, 'Statutory Interpretation – in the Classroom and in the Courtroom' (1983) 50 *Univ. Chicago L. Rev.* 800, 807–8.

[82] See, e.g., *Tilling-Stevens Motors Ltd* v. *Kent CC* [1929] AC 354 (petrol–electric vehicle to be licensed as an electrically propelled vehicle); *Fisher* v. *Bell* [1961] 1 QB 394 (exhibiting a knife accompanied by a price ticket in a shop window is to make an invitation to treat rather than an offer for sale); *R* v. *Harris* (1836) 7 C. & P. 446 (impossible to wound someone by biting off the end of their nose when wounding is statutorily restricted to harms inflicted by use of an instrument); *Whiteley* v. *Chappell* (1868–9) LR 4 QB 147 (impossible to be guilty of impersonating a person entitled to vote if the person being impersonated is dead).

[83] *R* v. *Central Criminal Court, ex p. Francis & Francis* [1989] AC 346.

the intention of the holder of the items. By the time the relevant items were demanded, they were in the possession not of the perpetrator of the crime but of his solicitor, and so they were no longer being held with the intention of furthering a criminal objective. The plain-meaning rule – the application of which two of the Law Lords in *Francis* endorsed – supported the conclusion that the items were protected by legal privilege. But the majority of the House rejected this approach on the basis that it was clear that parliament's intention in passing the relevant statute was to confer powers on the police to enable them to detect the perpetrators of crime, and that a court would be making a mockery of that intention were it to place on the statute an interpretation which protected from inspection documentation that came into existence for the purpose of furthering crime.

One could easily go to town elaborating a catalogue of grievances about the plain-meaning rule. There are, however, at least two reasons for taking the rule seriously. First of all, for all that the rule is often presented as if it were nothing but the refuge of the slot-machine justice judge – consider, for example, Fuller's Justice Keen[84] – the interpretation of a statute on its plain meaning is sometimes the key to its creative application. Consider two illustrations. In *Solanke*, the Court of Appeal held that writing a letter threatening to murder someone comes within the statutory definition of acting 'maliciously', even if one sends that letter to someone other than the intended victim, since the maliciousness of the action – according 'the word "maliciously" … its ordinary meaning'[85] – has nothing to do with who receives the letter but only with the fact that the action is intentional and without lawful excuse. In *Attorney-General's Reference (No. 3 of 1999)*, Lord Steyn purported to adopt a plain-meaning approach to statutory interpretation so as to ensure that the possibility of determining the truth of an allegation of serious crime was not thwarted by a particular rule concerning admissibility of evidence. According to the Police and Criminal Evidence Act 1984, section 64(3B), '[w]here [DNA] samples are required to be destroyed' – because the provider was cleared of the offence – 'information derived from the sample of any person entitled to its destruction … shall not be used – (a) in evidence against the person so entitled; or (b) for the purposes of any investigation of an offence'. In this instance, the police were able to

---

[84] See Lon L. Fuller, 'The Case of the Speluncean Explorers' (1949) 62 *Harvard L. Rev.* 616, 631–7.

[85] *R v. Solanke* [1970] 1 WLR 1, 3 *per* Salmon LJ.

connect the defendant to a violent rape because there existed a DNA sample which had been taken in relation to an earlier burglary offence of which the defendant had been acquitted, and which should have been destroyed on his acquittal. The defendant was arrested for the rape, and a new DNA sample was obtained and used against him at trial. This second sample was not obtained in contravention of clause (a). But the police only obtained this sample because their use of the first sample fell foul of clause (b). The question for the House of Lords was whether, at trial, the new DNA evidence should have been excluded. The House of Lords held that it did not have to be excluded because, as Lord Steyn observed, 'the plain words of [clause (b) of] the statute'[86] do not state that DNA evidence should be deemed inadmissible when a sample is wrongly used to investigate an offence. This plain, indeed literal, reading of clause (b) was creative in much the same way as strained interpretations of statutory language are often creative: it avoided making the law endorse what is considered an injustice. But in terms of general principle the law was left, as Steyn duly acknowledged, 'in a distinctly unsatisfactory state',[87] for clause (a) was undermined: there is no point determining that an unlawfully retained DNA sample cannot be admitted in evidence if the police are allowed to obtain a new sample which can be admitted.

The fact that judges do not necessarily eschew creativity when they adopt the plain-meaning rule points to a second reason for taking the rule seriously: it can serve a variety of important functions. Enabling creativity is one (if an unlikely one) of these functions. The main functions of the plain-meaning rule fall into five broad, overlapping categories: what might be termed the supremacist, preservationist, signalling, co-ordinative and baseline accounts of plain meaning. On the supremacist account, courts abide by the plain-meaning rule out of regard for the principle of legislative supremacy: once the legislature has passed a law, the best way to ensure that it is this law that governs – that it is not turned into a law different from what was enacted – is for the courts to give the statute's words, assuming those words to be unambiguous, their ordinary and natural meaning.[88]

The second and third of the other functional accounts of the plain-meaning rule come in at least two forms. The first version of the preservationist account complements the supremacist account and will be

---

[86] A-G's Reference (No. 3 of 1999) [2001] 2 AC 91, 118.
[87] R v. Chief Constable of South Yorkshire, ex p. LS/Marper [2004] UKHL 39 at [33].
[88] See The Sussex Peerage (1844) 11 Cl. & F. 85, 86 (per Tindal CJ).

recognizable to American lawyers as a textualist article of faith:[89] the virtue of judges interpreting statutes according to the plain-meaning rule is that the likelihood of their altering what the legislature enacted is kept to a minimum – the plain-meaning interpretation, that is, is likely to confirm or clarify the law without supplanting it. The second version, which common lawyers generally will recognize as the presumption against alteration discussed in Chapter 2, concerns the preservation of the common law rather than the statute: judges who wish to interpret a statute so that it alters the law no further than it was supposed to alter the law are best advised to interpret the statutory language according to its ordinary and natural meaning.[90]

The first version of the signalling account concerns reliability and the expectations of citizens: an advantage of courts presuming to accord statutory language its plain meaning, assuming that language to be unambiguous, is that citizens can be confident as to how they ought to organize and plan their affairs (including decisions as to whether they should litigate) in light of what the law says – for what they understand the law to mean is what the courts are likely to take it to mean.[91] When courts adopt the plain-meaning rule, they also send a message to the legislature: that its drafting personnel, if they are to be confident that they are changing the law in the way it is supposed to be changed (as well as minimizing the likelihood of unnecessary litigation), do best to choose statutory language carefully and with regard for the ordinary meanings of words.[92]

The fourth of the functional accounts of the plain-meaning rule, the co-ordinative account, builds from the premise that a shared convention can operate as a labour-saving device. It might be objected that there is nothing in this premise that specifically commends the plain-meaning

---

[89] i.e., that if it is accepted as a matter of principle that statutory language is open to a limited range of reasonable interpretations, and that a statute must not be made to say something which cannot be squared with at least one of those interpretations, the law is afforded 'some protection' – albeit not 'ironclad protection' – against 'the judge who wishes to impose his will'. Scalia, 'Response', in *A Matter of Interpretation*, 129–49 at 132.

[90] See Max Rheinstein, 'Common Law and Civil Law: An Elementary Comparison' (1952–53) 22 *Revista Jurídica de la Universidad de Puerto Rico* 90, 98.

[91] See Munday, 'The Common Lawyer's Philosophy of Legislation', 194. Munday is describing this function, not commending it. His impression in 1983 was that judicial support for the plain-meaning approach was in decline (ibid. 202).

[92] Cf. J. A. Clarence Smith, 'Legislative Drafting: English and Continental' [1980] *Statute L. Rev.* 14, 19 ('The English legislative draftsman habitually excuses the contorted particularity of his style as being his only defence against the obstinate misinterpretation by the bench of clear drafting').

rule: the point looks simply to be that if judges are clear as to their conventions of interpretation, drafters of statutes may, over time, come to understand this and so write statutes with these conventions in mind, the overall consequence of which may be a reduction in the costs of legislating. But this objection misrepresents the co-ordinative account. If plain meaning has any distinctive labour-saving value as an interpretive convention, it is because it is shared among judges rather than between judges and legislators: on this argument, judges who abide by the principle that a statute is essentially the text as ordinarily understood by reasonable people reading it in context significantly constrain their range of disagreements as to how statutes might be interpreted. Schauer sets out the argument in relation to decision making by the United States Supreme Court: it is perhaps unremarkable that 'plain meaning appears now for all of the Justices to be a strong factor in their decisionmaking', he observed in 1990, for by adopting this approach they are 'cutting off access to' various interpretive choices (plain meaning refers, after all, not only to 'what is plainly in a statute, but also [to] what is plainly not in it') so that they might 'reach some methodological consensus', notwithstanding the probability of their having 'widely disparate political views and social experiences'.[93]

Schauer concedes that the plain-meaning rule is 'a blunt, frequently crude, and certainly narrowing device', a 'second-best coordinating solution' which 'incorporates numerous categorical choices, all of which are contingent and value-laden'.[94] But the core difficulty with this functional explanation of the plain-meaning rule – indeed, with any functional explanation of any rule of statutory interpretation – is essentially to do with history rather than with how a rule performs suboptimally. If we examine the Supreme Court's statutory construction cases from its 1989 Term, Schauer suggests, it seems reasonable to conclude that in those cases where the language of the relevant statute is clear (a significant number of cases had, of course, ended up in the Supreme Court precisely because the statutory language was not clear), a plain-meaning approach to interpretation was consistently 'at the very least a factor' – possibly 'a presumptive factor' – 'in the [Justices'] decisionmaking'.[95] Perhaps it is reasonable to reach this conclusion about any particular year in the Supreme Court's history. Yet there have been periods in that history – the period from the 1960s through to the mid-1980s stands out[96] – when the Court has

---

[93] Frederick Schauer, 'Statutory Construction and the Coordinating Function of Plain Meaning' [1990] *Supreme Court Rev.* 231 at 249, 252, 241, 232, 255.

[94] Ibid. 252, 232, 251.   [95] Ibid. 249.

[96] See Nelson, *Statutory Interpretation*, 256–7 ('members of the later Warren Court and the Burger Court seemed somewhat more willing than their predecessors to let legislative

seemed as much if not more disposed to the idea that the ordinary meaning of a statute will not always accurately reflect actual or probable legislative intentions and that Justices, if they are to be faithful agents of the legislature, sometimes do better to eschew the plain-meaning approach in favour of one which seeks out, and seeks to give effect to, the general purpose (or purposes) behind the text.[97] Textualism, as a judicial philosophy, seemed to emerge very much as an outcry against this disposition.[98]

While the plain-meaning rule may perform valuable functions, then, an account of the rule purely in terms of those functions leaves unanswered why, even in instances when the language of a statute yields a plain meaning, courts sometimes forsake the rule in favour of some other interpretive method. The last of our functional explanations, the baseline explanation, serves to reiterate this point. Since the nineteenth century, English judges, when negotiating statutes, have often assumed plain meaning to function not so much as a rule or even as a convention but rather as an interpretive baseline from which there will sometimes be good reason to depart. In 1888, Lord Halsbury endorsed 'the modern view – which is I think in accordance with reason and common sense – that, whatever the instrument, it must receive a construction according to the plain meaning of the words and sentences therein contained'.[99] This notion of strong fidelity

---

history persuade them that statutory language meant something other than what the face of the statute seemed to say'); also William N. Eskridge, Jr, 'The New Textualism' (1990) 37 *UCLA L. Rev.* 621, 626–7.

[97] See, e.g., *International Longshoremen's & Warehousemen's Union* v. *Juneau Spruce Corp.*, 342 US 237, 243 (1953) (Douglas J) ('[L]iteralness is no sure touchstone of legislative purpose. The purpose here is more closely approximated ... by giving the ... phrase ["district court of the United States"] a looser, more liberal meaning in the special context of [the Labor Management Relations Act 1947, s. 303(b)]'); *United Steelworkers* v. *Weber*, 443 US 193, 200–8 (1979) (Brennan J) (delivering the Court's opinion that on the basis of legislative history, Title VII of the Civil Rights Act 1964 does not forbid voluntary affirmative action plans given its general purpose of improving the economic status of racial minorities). For examples outside the Warren and Burger eras, see *Pickett* v. *United States*, 216 US 456, 461 (1910) (Lurton J) ('The reason of the law, as indicated by its general terms, should prevail over its letter, when the plain purpose of the act will be defeated by strict adherence to its verbiage'); *Ozawa* v. *United States*, 260 US 178, 194 (1922) (Sutherland J) ('We may ... look to the reason of the enactment and inquire into its antecedent history and give it effect in accordance with its design and purpose, sacrificing, if necessary, the literal meaning in order that the purpose may not fail'); *Keifer & Keifer* v. *Reconstruction Finance Corp.*, 306 US 381, 389 (1939) (Frankfurter J) ('The Congressional will must be divined ... by ... the ascertainment of policy immanent not merely in the single statute ... but in a series of statutes ... and drawing significance from dominant contemporaneous opinion').

[98] See Scalia, 'Common-Law Courts in a Civil-Law System', 16–25.

[99] *Leader* v. *Duffey* (1888) LR 13 App. Cas. 294, 301.

to the plain meaning of the text is not quite today's modern view: judges nowadays generally presume to rely upon the plain meaning of statutory language, but also know that it might be necessary to work to a different plan.[100]

We will see in the next section that this baseline approach to plain meaning was, as compared with the position espoused by Halsbury, probably a better approximation of the modern view even in the nineteenth century. But before we turn our attention to the questions of just when judges should adopt a different interpretive plan, and what sorts of plans they might adopt, it is worth highlighting two simple points of legal history. First, it is evident from Halsbury's observation that he appreciated, in 1888, that statutory interpretation according to the plain-meaning rule was a modern art. This point warrants reiteration. A law student today could be forgiven for forming the impression that the more modern approach to statutes is the purposive approach, and that plain-meaning interpretations are old school. But this, as will become clear, is to turn the history of statutory interpretation almost completely on its head. Suffice it to say for now that an English treatise on statute law dating from the 1830s cites no pre eighteenth-century authority for statutory interpretation according the plain-meaning rule;[101] indeed, there is nothing before 1700 to which one might point to support any functional justification of the rule, for the rule appears not to have existed before then.

Secondly, Halsbury, Robert Stevens has written, had a 'simplistic view of life and language' and 'was anxious to restate the formalistic theory … that English judges merely declared preexisting law'.[102] From this observation

---

[100] See, e.g., *Secretary of State for Work and Pensions* v. *Hourigan* [2003] 1 WLR 608 (CA), 616 (*per* Auld LJ); *R* v. *Oxfordshire CC, ex p. Sunningwell Parish Council* [2000] 1 AC 335 (HL), 343 *arguendo* ('As a matter of statutory interpretation, the literal meaning of an enactment is to be preferred wherever possible'); *Secretary of State for the Home Department* v. *British Union for the Abolition of Vivisection* [2008] EWHC 892 at [37] (Eady J) ('One should try to give words contained in a statute their ordinary English meaning unless the context is such as to make clear that some specialist interpretation is required').

[101] See F. W. L. Dwarris, *A General Treatise on Statutes*, 2 vols. (London: Saunders & Benning, 1830–1), II, 738–51. Dwarris's principal authorities are *R* v. *Ditcheat* (1829) 9 B. & C. 176, 186 *per* Parke J ('I think we ought to give effect to the words of the Act of Parliament in their plain, natural sense, unless we see clearly from the context that the intention of the Legislature was different'); and *Paddon* v. *Bartlett* (1835) 3 Ad. & El. 884, 896 *per* Lord Abinger ('It is true that, if the words of a statute are plain, they must be strictly followed; but, if they are ambiguous, the whole context must be looked to for the explanation').

[102] Robert Stevens, *Law and Politics: The House of Lords as a Judicial Body, 1800–1976* (Chapel Hill: University of North Carolina Press, 1978), 89–90.

it is no great leap to the surmise that Halsbury offered his observation of 1888 because he failed to appreciate that, even in the nineteenth century, judges who espoused plain meaning as an interpretive principle were in fact practising a form of conceptual ascent – stepping away from the baseline and altering their interpretive technique when a plain-meaning approach seemed unsuited to the problem before them. But this is a risky leap to take. Only two years later, in *Cox* v. *Hakes*, Halsbury professed his inclination – which was certainly not shared by other judges in the case – to interpret a particular statute according to its presumed purpose rather than with strict regard for 'the letter of the Act'.[103] By 1902, he was again prioritizing the plain meaning of statutory language.[104] Normal service had been resumed. He had, nevertheless, shown himself to be not quite fixed to the baseline, not quite so possessed of the simplistic view that Stevens attributes to him. The lesson is obvious enough: beware the temptation to stick a label on a judge.

4 The golden rule

It was observed in Chapter 2 that Maitland considered the distinguishing feature of eighteenth-century statutes to be 'extreme and verbose particularity' which would rarely 'rise to the dignity of a general proposition'.[105] Judges commonly took this approach to legislative drafting to be indicative of parliament's effort to express its intention precisely and unambiguously, and so they tended to assume that little, if anything, had been left to implication. Before the eighteenth century, however, statutes were generally drafted in comparatively less detail. Judges were relatively less inclined to read statutory language as if it yielded a plain meaning because they typically presumed that parliament preferred not to close off the possibility of their interpreting a statute according to its spirit rather than its letter so as to supply some of the detail themselves. Indeed, if these earlier judges had adopted plain meaning as their standard interpretive convention, their interpretations of statutory language would as often as not have been patently unsatisfactory. It would be inappropriate to interpret the

---

[103] *Cox* v. *Hakes* (1890) LR 15 App. Cas. 506, 518. Lords Herschell and Field adhered rigidly to what, in 1888, Halsbury had termed the modern view (see ibid. 528, 542).

[104] *Hilder* v. *Dexter* [1902] AC 474 (HL), 477–8. Halsbury declined to give a judgment in this case because he had been responsible for drafting the relevant statute.

[105] F. W. M[aitland], 'English Law', in *Encyclopædia Britannica*, 11th edn (New York: Cambridge University Press, 1910), IX, 600–7 at 605.

Statute of Westminster 1285 according to the principle of plain meaning, Lord Abinger observed in 1842, for

> the framers ... were not so prolific in words as the authors of modern acts of Parliament. In the present day, in framing a statute, the course is to employ all the rhetoric of conveyancers and special pleaders, and to provide for every case that suggests itself to the imagination of the person who draws the act. Formerly it was otherwise, and courts of law were left to interpret the meaning of the legislature.[106]

Two years earlier, in *Gwynne* v. *Burnell*, Lord Brougham expressed reluctance to depart from the plain-meaning rule but, in the process of doing so, noted why this rule tended not to be preferred when courts had to interpret ancient statutes:

> If we depart from the plain and obvious meaning ... we in truth do not construe the act, but alter it ... This becomes peculiarly improper in dealing with a modern statute, because the extreme conciseness of the ancient statutes was the only ground for the sort of legislative interpretation frequently put upon their words.[107]

The approaches preferred by the courts in interpreting pre eighteenth-century statutes will occupy us in the next chapter. But consider, first of all, another reason for departing from the baseline of plain meaning. In the seventeenth century, as we know from *Bonham's Case* (Chapter 2), there was at large the proposition that a court might legitimately control a statute by declaring it to be of no effect where it demanded something contrary to reason. In the eighteenth century, judges started to entertain another possibility: that if the language of a statute yields a plain meaning but generates an absurd or unjust outcome, a court might neither give effect to that plain meaning nor declare the statute to be of no effect but instead modify the wording of the statute so as to avoid an outcome which the legislature could never have intended.

This so-called 'golden rule' of statutory interpretation came into its own during the mid nineteenth century. But it should come as no surprise – given its resemblance to the argument which emerged in the sixteenth and seventeenth centuries in favour of controlling repugnant statutes – that illustrations of it can be found before this period.[108] 'In expounding acts of parliament, where words are express, plain and clear', Parker CB

---

[106] *Patrick* v. *Stubbs* (1842) 9 M. & W. 830, 836.
[107] *Gwynne* v. *Burnell* (1840) 6 Bing. N. C. 453, 561.
[108] Precisely when lawyers began to refer to this interpretive convention as the 'golden rule' is unclear. Jervis CJ refers to it thus in 1854, though it is obvious from his remarks that

observed in 1766, 'the words ought to be understood according to their genuine and natural signification and import, unless by such exposition a contradiction or inconsistency would arise in the act by reason of some subsequent clause, from whence it might be inferred the intent of the parliament was otherwise.'[109] It should be noted that Parker's proposal was that the plain-meaning interpretation of a statutory provision ought to be resisted only if that interpretation undermines another part of the statute which can reasonably be assumed to be indicative of the legislature's real intention. He was very clearly not suggesting that a judge might ignore the meaning of a plainly but inconveniently worded provision by purporting to locate the intention of the legislature outside the text of the statute; there must, he insisted, be within the statute itself something which indicates that the offending provision really is a mistake. '[I]n the first instance, the grammatical sense of the words is to be adhered to', Burton J of the Irish King's Bench concurred in 1829, but if this 'would involve any absurdity, repugnance, or inconsistency in [the statute's] different provisions, the grammatical sense must then be modified, extended, or abridged, so far as to avoid such an inconvenience, but no further'.[110]

In 1836, Parke B accepted Burton's statement almost verbatim as 'a very useful rule ... in the construction of a statute'.[111] The following year, he put the principle into his own words – and, perhaps unintentionally, relaxed its formulation slightly by omitting to include the express stipulation that whatever is read into or taken out of the statute must go 'no further' than resolving the absurdity or inconsistency.[112] During the 1840s, Parke

the term was already commonly used: see *Mattison v. Hart* (1854) 14 CB 357, 385 ('We must, therefore, in this case, have recourse to what is called the golden rule of construction, as applied to acts of parliament, *viz.* to give to the words used by the legislature their plain and natural meaning, unless it is manifest from the general scope and intention of the statute injustice and absurdity would result from so construing them'). Judges of the period often attributed the term to Lord Wensleydale.

[109] *Mitchell v. Torup* (1766) Park. 227, 233.

[110] *Warburton v. Loveland, d. Ivie* (1829) 1 Huds. & Bro. 623, 648. The Irish courts at this point were still very much a limb of the English courts: many of the judges of the King's Bench were English-born (as was Burton), English case law was treated as precedent (all of the cases on statutory construction cited in *Warburton v. Loveland* are English cases), and appeals could be taken to the House of Lords (as *Warburton v. Loveland* was: see (1832) 2 Dow. & Cl. 480).

[111] *Becke v. Smith* (1836) 2 M. & W. 191, 195.

[112] 'The rule by which we are to be guided in construing acts of Parliament is to look at the precise words, and to construe them in their ordinary sense, unless it would lead to any absurdity or manifest injustice; and if it should, so to vary and modify them as to avoid that which it certainly could not have been the intention of the legislature should be done.' *Perry v. Skinner* (1837) 2 M. & W. 471, 476.

regularly approved of the golden rule in this relaxed form,[113] as did other judges of the period.[114] The assessment offered by Herbert Broom in the first edition of his *Legal Maxims* (1845) – that the golden rule is 'an established rule of [statutory] construction'[115] – had become, by the following decade, a commonplace in English judicial opinions.[116]

That the golden rule should have been approved thus is only to be expected, for it is essentially a debugged version of the plain-meaning rule (though it is not quite correct to say that the two rules merge into one).[117] The common expression of the golden rule is that a statute should be interpreted according to its plain meaning apart from when the

---

[113] See, e.g., *Smith v. Bell* (1842) 10 M. & W. 378, 389; *Steward v. Greaves* (1842) 10 M. & W. 711, 719.

[114] See, e.g., *Wansey v. Perkins* (1845) 7 Man. & G. 127, 142–3 *per* Cresswell J ('It may be laid down as a safe rule, in the construction of acts of parliaments, that we are to look at the words of the act and to render them strictly, unless manifest absurdity or injustice should result from such a construction').

[115] Herbert Broom, *A Selection of Legal Maxims, Classified and Illustrated* (London: A. Maxwell & Son, 1845), 248.

[116] See, e.g., *Arnold v. Ridge* (1853) 13 CB 745, 763 (*per* Maule J); *Fell v. Burchett* (1857) 7 El. & Bl. 537, 539 (*per* Lord Campbell CJ); *Abbott v. Middleton* (1858) 7 HL Cas. 68, 114 (*per* Lord Wensleydale); *Thellusson v. Rendlesham* (1859) 7 HL Cas. 429, 519 (*per* Lord Wensleydale); *Eastern Counties and the London & Blackwall Railway Companies v. Marriage* (1860) 9 HL Cas. 32, 40 *per* Blackburn J ('I think it much better, in construing an Act, to follow what has been called the golden rule …'); *Birks v. Allison* (1862) 13 CB (NS) 12, 23 (*per* Byles J); *Christopherson v. Lotinga* (1864) 15 CB (NS) 809, 813 *per* Willes J ('I should have thought we might have arrived at a satisfactory conclusion by acting upon the rule laid down by Lord Wensleydale in *Becke v. Smith* … I subscribe to every word of that [statement], assuming the word "absurdity" to mean no more than "repugnance." With that modification, it seems to me that the rule thus laid down is perfectly consistent with good sense and law'); *Reed v. Braithwaite* (1870–1) LR 11 Eq. 514, 519–20 (*per* Malins VC); *Abel v. Lee* (1871) LR 6 CP 365, 371 (*per* Willes J); *Bradlaugh v. Clarke* (1882–3) LR 8 App. Cas. 354, 384 *per* Lord Fitzgerald ('I prefer to guide my judgment by the rule of construction laid down in *Warburton v. Loveland* …'); *Stone v. Yeovil Corporation* (1876) 1 CPD 691, 701 *per* Brett J ('It is a canon of construction that, if it be possible, effect must be given to every word of an Act of Parliament or other document; but that, if there be a word or phrase therein to which no sensible meaning can be given, it must be eliminated'); *River Wear Commissioners v. Adamson* (1877) LR 2 App. Cas. 743, 764 *per* Lord Blackburn ('I believe that it is not disputed that what Lord Wensleydale used to call the golden rule is right …'); *Vestry St John, Hampstead v. Cotton* (1887) LR 12 App. Cas. 1, 7–8 (*per* Lord Watson).

[117] Cf. E. A. Driedger, 'Statutes: The Mischievous Literal Golden Rule' (1981) 59 *Can. Bar Rev.* 780, who argues that golden-rule interpretations are not 'departures from the literal meaning' but 'steps taken to find the literal meaning' (781) – i.e., 'by giving the [relevant statutory] words a special, restricted or enlarged meaning or by adopting a less normal but permissible grammatical structure' so as to avoid 'some disharmony' (780) in the statute (or in statutes *in pari materia*). This argument trades on a weak version of the golden rule. When courts adopt a more aggressive form of the rule – i.e., avoiding an

statutory language directs a court to bring about a patently absurd state of affairs. But it is also clear that some formulations of the rule accommodate another interpretation: that a court might forgo interpreting a statute according to its plain meaning when the statutory language, while not necessarily requiring that the court reach an absurd decision, is obviously incompatible with the enacting legislature's intention. 'The sound rule of construction with respect to acts of Parliament is, that the words are to be read in their ordinary and usual grammatical sense', Parke observed in 1840, 'unless that mode of construction leads to manifest inconvenience, *or* is repugnant to the plain intention of the legislature.'[118] For Parke, like Parker and Burton before him, determining whether a plain-meaning interpretation of a statutory provision will produce an outcome incompatible with legislative intention means looking to the rest of the statute for evidence of what that intention must have been. But judges who make such determinations will not necessarily confine themselves to advancing intentions discernible from the text of the statute. Interpretations according the golden rule have been defended, for example, on the basis that not to depart from the plain meaning of a provision would support an unreasonable contravention of a tacit interpretive presumption regarding legislative intention – such as the presumption that citizens should not be able to rely on statutes to bring an action based on their own wrongs, or that police officers cannot rely on special statutory rights and privileges apart from in the course of duty.[119] In 1842, Alderson B purported to favour a version of the golden rule whereby statutes are construed 'according to the plain, literal, and grammatical meaning of the words in which they are expressed, unless that construction leads to a plain and clear contradiction of the apparent purpose of the act, or to some palpable and evident absurdity'.[120] On this reading of the rule, a court might depart from the plain meaning of a statutory provision if abiding by that meaning would

---

absurd outcome by reading words into or out of a statute – it is incorrect to say that the statute is being interpreted on the basis of a secondary but contextually plain meaning of its language.

[118] *Edmonds* v. *Lawley* (1840) 6 M. & W. 285, 289 (emphasis added). Likewise his observation in *Turner* v. *Sheffield & Rotherham Railway Co.* (1842) 10 M. & W. 425, 434: 'the ordinary grammatical construction ... ought to prevail, unless it leads to an absurdity, or be manifestly repugnant to the intention of the legislature, as collected from the context, in which case the language may be modified so as to obviate such absurdity, or cure such repugnance'.

[119] See, e.g., *Morris* v. *Beardmore* [1981] AC 446 (HL); *R* v. *Chief National Insurance Commissioner, ex p. O'Connor* [1981] 2 WLR 412 (QBD).

[120] *A-G* v. *Lockwood* (1842) 9 M. & W. 378, 398.

either perpetuate a legal absurdity or would ensure that a defect in the law which the enacting legislature apparently – but not necessarily obviously – sought to remedy remained unaddressed. Alderson looked to be opening the door to imputed legislative intention.

Whether Alderson meant to go quite this far is unclear. It seems doubtful that either he or any of the other early proponents of the golden rule would have read much, if anything, into the distinction between interpretations which generate absurdities and interpretations which yield outcomes at variance with legislative intent; their observations would probably have been delivered extempore, with little thought being given to the exact form of words used to express what was in all likelihood taken to be a straightforward principle. Nevertheless, some judges of the period were troubled by more expansive formulations of the golden rule. The principal worry was that acceptance of the rule – particularly a version of it which entertains the possibility of courts departing from the plain meaning of statutory language when it is judged to be at variance with an intention which a court *supposes* to be attributable to the enacting legislature – risks eliding the distinction between statutes being interpreted to give effect to what are known to be the legislature's enacting intentions and statutes being interpreted to give effect to what a court thinks those intentions ought to have been.

There was also concern that the golden rule could be invoked to override perfectly acceptable plain meanings. In 1842 Parke, in one of his articulations of the rule, gave cause for this concern when he suggested that even if there is no reason to suspect that interpreting statutory language on its plain meaning would generate a legal absurdity, a court might still legitimately decline to abide by that meaning if a different interpretation had already become settled as precedent: '[i]t is our duty to construe the statute according to the grammatical meaning of the words, unless some absurdity would ensue from so construing it, or an [*sic*] uniform series of decisions had already established a particular construction'.[121] Broom, in his *Legal Maxims*, considered this proposition authoritative.[122] It is certainly not difficult to understand why the proposition would have struck a chord: lawyers, after all, are perhaps as likely to treat as authority

---

[121] *Doe d. Ellis* v. *Owens* (1842) 10 M. & W. 514, 521.

[122] Broom, *A Selection of Legal Maxims*, 248 ('an act of Parliament shall be read according to the ordinary and grammatical sense of the words, unless, being so read, it would be absurd or inconsistent with the declared intention of the Legislature, to be collected from the rest of the act, or unless an uniform series of decisions has already established a particular construction').

an interpretation of a statute discernible through a line of precedents as they are to rely on the language of the statute itself. Yet, in the eyes of many nineteenth- and early twentieth-century judges, this was precisely the sort of legislature-defying proposition which support for the golden rule seemed to slide towards rather too easily. In 1930, an American legal realist, Max Radin, disparaged the rule on the basis that it most definitely does not allow for the purposive interpretation of statutes: the rule is essentially a dressed-up version of the plain-meaning rule, 'the golden rule of "plain" interpretation',[123] he argued, in that it ultimately confines the interpreter to the language of the enactment. Yet, in the eighty or so years before Radin offered this observation, most confessions to wariness about the rule emphasized the extent to which it allows judges to depart from the language of a statute and create laws which the legislature had never, and would never have, intended to create. It was observed at the outset of this section that in *Gwynne* v. *Burnell* in 1840, Lord Brougham showed himself to be reluctant to depart from the plain-meaning rule. This reluctance was shared by the majority of the court. One of the judges, Patteson J, was initially of the view that the relevant statute was best interpreted according to the golden rule. On reflection, however, he could not be sure that by utilizing this rule he was applying the law as the legislature would have wanted it applied as opposed to making the law as he wanted it made. And so he changed his mind:

> after further consideration of the act of parliament, I am not so sure of the intention of the legislature as to feel that I was warranted in entertaining that opinion [*sc.*, that words could reasonably be read into the relevant statute so as to 'effectuate the obvious intention of the legislature']: and, as it may be possible, that, by putting such a construction upon the act, I am altering or adding to it, instead of simply interpreting it, I feel myself bound to abide by the literal [*sc.*, plain] meaning of the words.[124]

Patteson was not the only nineteenth-century judge who struggled to embrace the golden rule. In 1857, Lord Wensleydale certainly did embrace it – but he very pointedly approved the formulation of the rule by Burton J, whereby a court must depart 'no farther' than is necessary from the plain meaning of a statute in order to avoid 'absurdity and inconsistency'.[125] Compton J had expressed the point more directly in 1853: 'I do not understand the [golden] rule of construction to go so far as to authorize us,

---

[123] Radin, 'Statutory Interpretation', 870 n 13; see also ibid. 872.
[124] *Gwynne* v. *Burnell*, 503–4.
[125] *Grey* v. *Pearson* (1857) 6 HL Cas. 61, 106.

where the legislature has enacted something which leads to an absurdity, to repeal that enactment and make another for them.'[126] In the previous year, the Court of Exchequer had considered a series of statutes, beginning with the Treason Act 1766, requiring members of both commons and lords to take an oath of abjuration 'on the true faith of a Christian'. What if someone of the Jewish faith seeking membership of either house were to refuse to take this oath? For Martin B, the golden rule might as well have been designed for the purpose of resolving this very dilemma: 'can a stronger instance of absurdity be given than to insist that a Jew, to whom the oath was administered, should swear it "upon the true faith of a Christian"?'[127] On 'the true construction of the statute', he contended, 'a Jew ought to take the oath of abjuration omitting the words in question: … a construction the other way … excludes Jews from sitting and voting in Parliament, not by a direct and intentional legislative Act, but by an unforeseen and unintended application of a few words'.[128]

But Martin spoke in dissent. The rest of the court was of the view that the meaning of the statutory language was clear, and that Jews therefore had to take the oath if they wanted to be members of parliament.[129] Alderson B, who a decade earlier had spoken in support of the golden rule, captured the view of the majority when he declared that the rule must only ever be used 'so far as is absolutely necessary to get rid of … absurdity',[130] and that if there is no absurdity but only injustice, it should not be deemed applicable:

> we must take good care, in applying the golden rule, not to confound injustice with absurdity. The reason of the rule is, that the absurdity induces us to conclude that the legislature did not so intend. I am afraid, if we say that in old times … the legislature must be held not to have intended what now we judge to be unjust, we shall ourselves be guilty of the grossest absurdity. I am afraid that I should, if that were the proper principle to be adopted, be obliged to hold that almost all the penal statutes had no operation at all, for I think that the most of them were grievously unjust. I can see nothing in this or the subsequent Acts containing the oath of abjuration, to induce me to believe that the legislature did not intend literally what they said expressly – *viz.* that these Acts, and this

---

[126] *Woodward* v. *Watts* (1853) 2 E. & B. 452, 458.
[127] *Miller* v. *Salomons* (1852) 7 Ex. 475, 529.
[128] Ibid. 530.
[129] Parliament eventually intervened to accord special dispensations under the Jewish Relief Acts of 1858 and 1860.
[130] *Miller* v. *Salomons*, 539.

oath, were to apply to, and be taken by, all the classes of persons therein named, of whatsoever form of religion.[131]

The golden rule may well have come into its own in the 1840s and 1850s, but case law from the later decades of the nineteenth century reveals that some judges were distinctly reluctant to accept it as a standard principle of statutory construction. In 1863, Pollock CB and Bramwell B vigorously defended the interpretation of statutes on their plain meaning[132] – as did the House of Lords in *Bradlaugh* v. *Clarke* in 1883[133] and again in *Salomon* v. *Salomon* in 1897.[134] By 1884, Bramwell's position had softened somewhat: 'I am now content to take it as a good rule … that you are to abide by the grammatical and ordinary sense of the words unless that would lead to some absurdity.'[135] But he remained suspicious, and indeed personally resisted utilizing the rule: it 'opens a very wide door. I should like to have a good definition of what is such an absurdity that you are to disregard the plain words of an Act of Parliament. It is to be remembered that what seems absurd to one man does not seem absurd to another.'[136]

This attitude of suspicion persisted into the twentieth century. Bramwell's worry that absurdity is very much in the eye of the beholder is echoed in a joint report on statutory interpretation issued in 1969 by the English and Scottish Law Commissions. '[T]he golden rule', the Commissioners concluded, 'sets a purely negative standard by reference to absurdity, inconsistency or inconvenience, but provides no clear means to test the existence of these characteristics or to measure their quality or extent. When a court decides that a particular construction is absurd, it

---

[131] Ibid. 539–40.

[132] *A-G* v. *Sillem* (1863) 2 Hurl. & C. 431, 514 *per* Pollock CB ('In construing the statute it is our duty to ascertain the true legal meaning of the words used by the legislature and to collect the intention from the language of the statute itself, either the preamble or the enactments, and not to make out the intention from some other sources of information and then construe the words of the statute so as to meet the assumed intention'), 530 *per* Bramwell B ('The law that governs this case is a written law, an act of parliament, which we must apply according to the true meaning of the words used in it. We must not extend it to anything not within the natural meaning of those words').

[133] See, in particular, *Bradlaugh* v. *Clarke*, 372 (*per* Lord Blackburn). In *Bradlaugh*, as noted already, Lord Fitzgerald spoke in favour of the golden rule (specifically, Burton J's version of the golden rule). He did not, however, consider the rule to be applicable to the case.

[134] See *Salomon* v. *Salomon* [1897] AC 22, 31 (*per* Lord Halsbury LC), 38 (*per* Lord Watson) and 54 (*per* Lord Davey).

[135] *Hill* v. *East & West India Dock Co.* (1883–4) LR 9 App. Cas. 448, 464.

[136] Ibid. 464–5. In a similar vein, see *Rhodes* v. *Rhodes* (1881–2) LR 7 App. Cas. 192 (PC), 205–6 (*per* Lord Blackburn).

implies, although often tacitly, that the construction is absurd because it is irreconcilable with the general policy of the legislature.'[137] Lawyers and judges who were wedded to the plain-meaning approach tended to eschew interpretation according to the golden rule not only because they regarded it as a method by which judges could deny the legislature's intentions and enact their own, but also because they considered the rule defeated by the reason that had brought plain meaning to prominence in the first place. As statutes became increasingly detailed and more precisely worded, that is, judges were ever more inclined to abide by the presumption that what an Act expressly refers to can be regarded by implication as excluding everything that it does not refer to (*expressio unius exclusio alterius est*), that parliament expresses its full meaning and leaves nothing to implication.[138] 'If the language of the statute be plain,' Lord Atkinson stated in 1913, 'the Legislature must be taken to have meant and intended what it has plainly expressed, and whatever it has in clear terms enacted must be enforced though it should lead to absurd ... results.'[139] The point was reinforced in 1930 by Lord Hewart: '[i]t ought to be the rule, and we are glad to think that it is the rule,' he professed, 'that words are used in an Act of Parliament correctly and exactly, and not loosely and inexactly. Upon those who assert that that rule has been broken the burden of establishing their proposition lies heavily. And they can discharge it only by pointing to something in the context which goes to show that the loose and inexact meaning must be preferred.'[140] In 1936, in *Altrincham Electric Supply* v. *Sale UDC*, a slender majority of the House of Lords pointedly rejected the Court of Appeal's resort to the golden rule to avoid the absurd consequence of ascribing to a statutory provision its plain meaning, precisely because there was nothing in the statute to which one could point which suggested that any other meaning might reasonably be inferred.[141]

Note that Hewart, unlike Atkinson, was issuing only a presumption, not a taboo, against departing from the plain meaning of a statute. The golden

---

[137] *The Interpretation of Statutes*, para. 32.
[138] See J. A. Corry, 'Administrative Law and the Interpretation of Statutes' (1936) 1 *Univ. Toronto L. J.* 286, 300.
[139] *Vacher & Sons Ltd* v. *London Society of Compositors* [1913] AC 107 (HL), 121–2.
[140] *Spillers Ltd* v. *Cardiff (Borough) Assessment Committee* [1931] 2 KB 21 (KBD), 43; approved by Lord Macmillan in *Borough of New Plymouth* v. *Taranaki Electric-Power Board* [1933] AC 680 (PC), 682.
[141] See *Altrincham Electric Supply Co. Ltd* v. *Sale UDC* (1936) 154 LT 379, esp. at 386 (*per* Lord Russell) and 388 (*per* Lord Macmillan); also E. Russell Hopkins, 'The Literal Canon and the Golden Rule' (1937) 15 *Can. Bar Rev.* 689, 693–5.

rule neither rose and rose nor rose and fell, but rose and plateaued. To this day it is recognized as a core principle of statutory interpretation[142] – though there are some who have urged that it be given a wide berth,[143] and those judges who do utilize it tend to do so circumspectly. Many modern decisions which appear to invoke the golden rule either do not invoke it, or invoke it only in a weak form, for courts often avoid an absurd application of a statute by attributing to its language a plain yet secondary meaning. It is always 'proper to look for some other possible meaning of the word or phrase' in a statute, Lord Reid remarked in 1969, when 'the natural or ordinary meaning of that word or phrase … leads to some result which cannot reasonably be supposed to have been the intention of the legislature'.[144] So it is that the House of Lords unanimously reversed the decision of the Court of Appeal in *Nottingham County Council* v. *Secretary of State for the Environment.* The Court of Appeal had interpreted the word 'applicable' as it appears in section 59 of the Local Government Finance Act 1982 as meaning 'capable of being applied'; as a consequence, the guidance the Act provided to the Secretary of State for the purpose of reducing local authority expenditure for the budgetary year 1984–5 was inapplicable, because local authority budgets for that year had been set by the time the guidance was issued. The House of Lords avoided this consequence by interpreting 'applicable' to mean 'to be applied'.[145] Lord Bridge, speaking for the House, reasoned that this interpretation was not inconsistent with 'the scheme and underlying purpose'[146] of the legislation, and

---

[142] See, e.g., *Dingmar* v. *Dingmar* [2007] Ch. 109 (CA), 119–20 (*per* Lloyd LJ); *Secretary of State for Defence* v. *Hopkins* [2004] EWHC 299 at [4] (Newman J).

[143] See, e.g., *Pinner* v. *Everett* [1969] 1 WLR 1266 (HL), 1273 *per* Lord Reid ('We have been warned again and again that it is wrong and dangerous to proceed by substituting some other words for the words of the statute').

[144] Ibid. English courts have long abided by the principle that where statutory language accommodates more than one plain meaning, preference should be given to the meaning which best comports with justice: see, e.g., *Simms* v. *Registrar of Probates* [1900] AC 323 (PC), 335 (*per* Lord Hobhouse); *Holmes* v. *Bradfield RDC* [1949] 2 KB 1 (Div. Ct.), 7–8 (*per* Finnemore J).

[145] See *Nottingham CC* v. *Secretary of State for the Environment* [1986] AC 240. In much the same vein, see *Royal College of Nursing* v. *DHSS* [1981] 1 All ER 545 (HL). See also Glanville Williams, 'The Meaning of Literal Interpretation' (1981) 131 *New LJ* 1128–9, 1149–51 at 1129 ('[recognition of] secondary meaning (a meaning that can be coaxed out of the words by argument) … is compelled by the rule that words are to be interpreted in their context'); Driedger, 'The Mischievous Literal Golden Rule', 780 ('the adoption of a secondary meaning is not a departure from the literal meaning; the secondary meaning is the literal meaning in the context in which the words are used').

[146] *Nottingham CC* v. *Secretary of State for the Environment*, 261.

that while the interpretation traded on a secondary rather than a primary meaning, it is unlikely that the drafter of the legislation would have had this distinction and its potential ramifications in mind.[147]

Quite often, nevertheless, modern judges will explicitly or implicitly modify the language of a statute rather than accord it a secondary meaning in order to avoid an absurd legal outcome. The stipulation in section 3 of the Official Secrets Act 1920 that '[n]o person in the vicinity of any prohibited place shall obstruct … any member of His Majesty's forces' must be read to mean 'no person in or in the vicinity of …', Lord Parker observed in *Adler* v. *George*, as 'it would be absurd, if an indictable offence was thereby created when the obstruction took place outside the precincts of the station [*sc.*, prohibited place], albeit in the vicinity, and no offence at all was created if the obstruction occurred on the station itself'.[148] The golden rule is certainly what the House of Lords had in mind in *Stock* v. *Jones* in 1978. The claimant, who had been sacked along with other striking employees, alleged unfair dismissal on the basis that employees who renounced strike action and returned to work before the date of the dismissals were not sacked. Her claim was supported, she contended, by schedule 1, paragraph 8(2)(a) of the Trade Unions and Labour Relations Act 1974, which provided that 'dismissal shall not be regarded as unfair unless it is shown … that one or more employees of the same employer … who also took part in that action, were not dismissed for taking part in it'. The meaning of the statutory language, and the conclusion to be reached in the light of that meaning, seemed plain: some employees had taken part in the industrial action yet had not been sacked, therefore the

---

[147] See ibid. ('It is contended for the respondents … that the phrase "principles applicable to all local authorities" conveys a crucially different meaning from the phrase "principles to be applied to all local authorities." … As we listened to the argument, I could not help feeling, in common I believe with others of your Lordships, that we were back among the medieval schoolmen debating nice theological differences about angels dancing on the head of a pin. I should be extremely reluctant to accept that the draftsman of the legislation by so small a difference of language intended to achieve so fundamental a difference in legislative effect').

[148] *Adler* v. *George* [1964] 2 QB 7 (QBD), 10. In a similar vein, see *Deria* v. *General Council of British Shipping* [1986] 1 WLR 1207, CA (statute made not to apply in race-discriminatory manner by reading the words 'the employee does his work wholly outside Great Britain' in s. 8(1) of the Race Relations Act 1976 as 'the employee does or is to do his work wholly outside Great Britain'). For an instance of reading words out rather than in, see *McMonagle* v. *Westminster CC* [1990] 2 AC 716 (HL).

claimant's dismissal had to be unfair. But the House of Lords rejected this conclusion, finding that it would be absurd to interpret paragraph 8(2)(a) as making no distinction between those who took part in and remained committed to strike action and those who took part in but abandoned strike action.[149] Nevertheless, in using the golden rule to avoid an anomalous result which would otherwise have been derived from a statute, various of the Law Lords sought to elaborate the argument, first set down by Burton J in 1829, that interpretations based on the rule must be disciplined. If the golden rule is to be invoked, it was explained in *Stock*, then it must be the case that to apply the plain meaning of the statute would generate a state of affairs that parliament would never have been willing to countenance – a state of affairs so absurd as to make it obvious that parliament had erred in its choice of words. The modification of the plain meaning, furthermore, must not only remove the absurdity but also be compatible with legislative intent.[150]

5   Interim reflections

The principal reason that Justinian's prohibition on the interpretation of the *Digest* was fated to failure is that once a standard regarding proper conduct – such as whether one should be permitted to interpret a code – is adopted as a legal standard, it becomes a matter of fact rather than of value.[151] A legal standard, as a matter of fact, has to be interpreted: legal rules and doctrines cannot decide for themselves if they have a bearing – and, if they do, how they have a bearing – on particular problems. Interpretations of statutes as legal standards – this could equally be said of interpretations of wills, trust instruments, contracts and other legal documents – tend to be judged good or bad depending on how well they dispel obscurity and ambiguities, and enable people to understand what the text means.[152] Competing statutory interpretations tend to be judged comparably better or worse rather than true or false, and two incompatible

---

[149]   *Stock v. Frank Jones (Tipton) Ltd* [1978] 1 WLR 231 (HL).

[150]   See ibid., 234–5 (*per* Viscount Dilhorne), 236–7 (*per* Lord Simon) and 238–9 (*per* Lord Scarman); similarly *Western Bank Ltd v. Schindler* [1977] Ch. 1 (CA), 18 (*per* Scarman LJ).

[151]   See Raz, *Between Authority and Interpretation*, 107–15.

[152]   Interpretations in other contexts might be judged good or bad according to criteria different from those which apply to the interpretations of statutes. An interpretation of a particular artefact (such as a painting or a piece of music) might be lauded, for example,

interpretations could each be considered good interpretations.[153] The fact that courts interpret statutes in the process of adjudicating competing claims means, however, that they cannot pronounce interpretations to be equally good, for the point of the interpretive exercise is not only to derive meaning from the statute but to establish a particular meaning as authoritative – to establish what the law *is*. The interpretation and the authority of a statute are intimately connected.

So far, we have been concerned with two 'simple' approaches to statutory interpretation. The first is that if a statute has a plain meaning, then that meaning should be treated as authoritative. The second is that if a statute has a plain meaning, then that meaning should be considered authoritative so long as treating it thus does not generate a ruling which is absurd or incompatible with the legislature's intention. The second approach grows out of, and so is quite often assumed to be superior to, the first; it is certainly true that few if any judges nowadays would abide by the principle that statutes should be interpreted on their plain meaning whatever the consequences. But both approaches have significant limitations, and each – as has been intimated already in this study – became popular only once statutory drafting evolved into something of a rigorous art. In the modern era, the idea that a court might somehow embark on a voyage of discovery beyond the surface text that the legislature has enacted has often been frowned upon.[154] Yet there was a time when English judges were comparatively relaxed about taking this voyage. To assume, furthermore, that rigorous drafting put an end to the voyage would be a mistake; indeed, it would be startling were it otherwise, for statutory drafting can

---

not because some people are convinced that it provides them with a better understanding of what the artefact means but because the interpretation inspires their imaginations or gives them a reason to pay attention to something about the artefact that they would otherwise have ignored or overlooked. Note also that other domains of legal interpretation sometimes rely on techniques which are not applied in relation to statutes. For example, a charitable trust which cannot be implemented because its terms, though genuinely charitable, are impossible to perform might be salvaged by interpretation according to the *cy-près* doctrine, which enables a court to direct the property under the trust to be held for a purpose similar to that specified by the settlor. (On the inapplicability of this particular doctrine to statutory interpretation problems, see Frederick J. de Sloovère, 'Preliminary Questions in Statutory Interpretation' (1932) 9 *New York Univ. Law Q. Rev.* 407, 419.)

[153] See Raz, *Between Authority and Interpretation*, 228, 270–1.

[154] See, e.g., *Magor and St. Mellons RDC* v. *Newport Corporation* [1952] AC 189 (HL), 191 (*per* Lord Simonds).

never be perfect, and the principles of interpretation considered so far cannot resolve every instance where statutory language turns out to be ambiguous. The account of statutory interpretation elaborated up to this point has yielded a story which can be traced back to the late eighteenth century. The next part of the story requires that we begin by returning to the sixteenth century.

6

Purposivism, past and present

Sometimes, a judge will interpret a statutory provision so that it yields a meaning which was never contemplated by the enacting legislature but which it can reasonably be assumed the legislature would, had it contemplated that meaning, have been happy to see the statute accommodate. But more often than not, statutory interpretation proceeds on the basis that a provision has a meaning which corresponds to the intention of the legislature in enacting it. Certainly English courts, as was explained at the outset of the last chapter, have traditionally demonstrated fidelity to statutory meaning rather than to actual or presumed legislative intent. When negotiating statutes, nevertheless, judges will usually opt for the convention of statutory interpretation which they believe best minimizes – which, ideally, eliminates – any gap between the meaning of the language the legislature has enacted and an intention it appears to have had.

This can be a difficult objective to pursue. The statutory language might be unclear, or clear but absurd. Ascertaining the intention of the legislature on every contested point of law will be impossible, even if a court is willing to look to legislative history and other external sources that form the background to a statute. Those judges who looked askance at the golden rule saw the core dilemma clearly enough: even fidelity to plain meaning is not a safeguard against judicial legislation; but when, for whatever reason, a statute is interpreted on the basis of something other than its plain meaning, there is an especial danger that a court will determine the law to be not what the legislature wanted, or even what the legislature would have wanted had it thought (or formulated its thoughts) about a matter more carefully, but rather what the court would have liked the legislature to want – even though the legislature appears never to have wanted anything of the sort.

It would be inordinately cynical, however, to conclude that whenever statutory interpretation departs from the plain meaning of the text, the likelihood is that the judiciary usurps the legislature's function. 'A court', one legal realist once claimed, 'chooses whichever of the rules [of statutory interpretation] produces a result that satisfies its sense of justice in the case before it'[1] – the implication being that judges simply pick and choose among interpretive principles so as to further their own law-making predilections. This claim is not easily reconciled with the history of statutory interpretation. In English law the standard judicial presumption, we have seen, is that statutes will be interpreted according to their plain meaning. When judges do not interpret statutes thus, they are rarely if ever discarding this presumption on a whim. Rather, they displace it by recourse to specific reasons, such as that fidelity to plain meaning generates an absurdity or that the statute has been drafted in such a way that it is impossible to discern any such meaning. It is tempting to respond – as a legal realist well might – that the process of displacing the presumption that statutory language be given its plain meaning is itself just part of the trick: that judges stick with plain meanings when it suits them, and find reasons for proceeding otherwise when it does not. But this, again, is simplistic. An interpretation of statutory language according to its plain meaning might contradict prevalent judicial instincts as to how a case should be decided, and yet judges may declare themselves committed – while professing that they would prefer not to be committed – to such an interpretation: the negotiation of the Game Act 1670 in *Jones* v. *Smart*, considered in the last chapter, illustrates the point particularly vividly.

What, in this sort of instance, is really going on? Perhaps judges are, in fact, deciding instinctively, but their fundamental instinct is respect for the principle of legislative supremacy. The difficulty with this answer is that it is not clear that it does justice to the thought processes of those judges – and we saw, in the last chapter, that there are such judges – who chop and change, who will be faithful to the plain meaning of the language that parliament enacted in one instance while departing from such meaning in another. A more precise formulation of the answer requires some unpacking.

Most conventions of statutory interpretation entail two complementary assumptions: that legislatures have particular intentions when they enact a statute, and that an interpretation which is faithful to the meaning of the statute's language will very likely give effect to those intentions. Particular intentions do not have to be explicit intentions: the reason for using an interpretive convention will sometimes be that a legislature cannot be expected to stipulate absolutely everything it specifically intends in enacting a statute, and that some legislative commitments – to enacting

---

[1] John Willis, 'Statute Interpretation in a Nutshell' (1938) 16 *Can. Bar Rev.* 1, 16.

non-retroactive statutes, for example – therefore ought to be taken for granted in the absence of statutory words clearly indicating otherwise.[2] It is certainly not always the case, moreover, that an interpreter chooses one interpretive convention over others because it seems to be the one which best reveals the relevant intention of the enacting legislature. Consider, for example, the principle of lenity: that if a court cannot be sure as to parliament's objective in enacting criminal legislation – if it is unclear how far a statute's prohibitions are supposed to stretch, for example, or how severely particular conduct ought to be punished – the legislation should be interpreted so as to give defendants the benefit of the doubt.[3] It is conceivable that a court could resort to this principle with possible *future* legislative intentions in mind: certainly one potential consequence of – though not necessarily a reason for – a court applying the principle is that parliament may resolve to be clearer as to its intentions in the future (most likely by seeking to legislate further so as to make the relevant law less weighted against prosecutors).[4] An interpretation of a criminal statute according to the principle of lenity is not, however, an attempt to give effect to the intentions of parliament at the time of enactment. A court which applies the principle seeks, rather, to avoid imposition of criminal liability that parliament may well have intended be imposed but which defendants, because of statutory ambiguity, were not fairly (clearly) warned about.[5] When judges resort to the principle of lenity in interpreting criminal

---

[2] This would appear to be the standard rationale for invoking the presumption against ousting the jurisdiction of the courts, though this presumption has to be approached cautiously given that in a landmark administrative law case it was relied on despite parliament having enacted statutory language (the Foreign Compensation Act 1950, s. 4(4): 'The determination by the commission of any application made to them under this Act shall not be called into question in any court of law') making clear that it intended to remove jurisdiction. See *Anisminic* v. *Foreign Compensation Commission* [1969] 2 AC 147 (HL).

[3] See, e.g., 1 Bl. Comm. 88; *R* v. *Bloxham* [1983] AC 109 (HL); *R* v. *Allen* [1985] AC 1029 (HL); *R* v. *Bristol Justices, ex p. E* [1999] 1 WLR 390 (QBD), 397 (*per* Simon Brown LJ); *Massey* v. *Boulden* [2003] 1 WLR 1792 (CA), 1797–8 (*per* Simon Brown LJ); also Andrew Ashworth, 'Interpreting Criminal Statutes: A Crisis of Legality?' (1991) 107 *LQR* 419 at 432, 438–45, where it is observed that the principle is only rarely used in English criminal law.

[4] See Einer Elhauge, 'Preference Eliciting Statutory Default Rules' (2002) 102 *Columbia L. Rev.* 2162, 2193–4. The explanation for balking at treating this as an explicit reason is pithily captured by Caleb Nelson: 'isn't it perverse for courts to try to goad legislatures into action by articulating rules of law that the legislatures are almost certain to hate?' Caleb Nelson, *Statutory Interpretation* (New York: Foundation Press, 2011), 25–6.

[5] See Henry J. Friendly, *Benchmarks* (University of Chicago Press, 1967), 209 ('[T]he "rule of lenity" … rest[s] … presumably [on] the instinctive distaste against men languishing in prison unless the lawmaker has clearly said they should'). Conventions such as that statutes should be presumed not to interfere with individual liberties or private property

legislation, in short, it is difficult to conceive that they might be trying to ensure (which is not to discount that, inadvertently, they might ensure) that the meaning of a statute matches what the legislature intended it to mean.

It is important, therefore, to keep in mind that some principles of interpretation are not supposed to connect the meaning of statutory language to the intentions of the enacting legislature. For the most part, nevertheless, principles of interpretation do facilitate this connection. Many interpretive presumptions – such as that the legislature does not intend its enactments to apply retroactively,[6] or that a statute is to be treated as always speaking,[7] or that the legislature intends obviously non-exhaustive lists of items within a statute (obvious because the list ends with words such as 'or any other like right') to be restricted to type or category[8] – are primarily presumptions as to probable legislative intent; it may well be, indeed, that drafters sometimes choose statutory language knowing that particular presumptions will be relied on by judges when they interpret it. Some special presumptions are employed by courts for the purpose of revealing intent which is actual rather than probable: for instance, the point of the presumption of rectifying construction – that judges, in interpreting statutes, will correct patent drafting errors[9] – is not simply to render statutory provisions intelligible, but to render them intelligible

---

rights if it is not clear that they are supposed to be applied to these ends similarly support general principles of legality rather than aim to uncover legislative intent.

[6] See, e.g., *Secretary of State for Social Security* v. *Tunnicliffe* [1991] 2 All ER 712 (CA), 724 (*per* Staughton LJ); *L'Office Cherifien des Phosphates* v. *Yamashita-Shinnihon Steamship Co. Ltd* [1994] 1 All ER 20 (HL), 29 (*per* Lord Mustill).

[7] See, e.g., *R* v. *Hammersmith & Fulham LBC, ex p. M* (1998) 30 HLR 10 (CA), 16 (*per* Lord Woolf MR); *Victor Chandler International Ltd* v. *Customs And Excise Commissioners* [1999] 1 WLR 2160 (Ch. D), 2167 (*per* Lightman J).

[8] See, e.g., *Tillmanns & Co.* v. *SS Knutsford Ltd* [1908] 2 KB 385 (CA); also Rupert Cross, *Statutory Interpretation*, 3rd edn J. Bell and G. Engle (Oxford University Press, 2005), 134–7; E. A. Driedger, 'A New Approach to Statutory Interpretation' (1951) 29 *Can. Bar Rev.* 838, 841.

[9] See, e.g., *R* v. *Ettridge* [1909] 2 KB 24 (CCA), 27–8 *per* Darling J ('Where no meaning can be given to certain words of a statute without rejecting some of those used in it, or where the statute would become a nullity were all the words retained, the Court has power to read a section as though the words which make it meaningless or nullify it were not there'); *R* v. *Moore* [1995] QB 353 (CA), 362 (*per* Sedley J); Kenneth Diplock, *The Courts as Legislators* (Birmingham: Holdsworth Club, 1965), 10 ('[I]f … the Courts can identify the target of Parliamentary legislation their proper function is to see that it is hit: not merely to record that it has been missed'). Drafting errors, to reiterate a point noted in the last chapter, are by no means always obvious.

and consistent with the legislature's discernible (which is not to say always easily discernible)[10] intentions.[11]

When judges use principles of statutory interpretation, then, there are reasons for thinking that they are not normally choosing the ones which simply produce the results they desire. A court which departs from the plain meaning of a statute should not be assumed to be seeking to put its own law-making intentions in the place of the legislature's. It is more likely, rather, to be relying on an interpretive principle because it believes that the principle will yield a statutory meaning which connects to legislative intent. Courts generally prioritize and opt for gap-reducing rather than gap-widening interpretive conventions, because those conventions are the ones which are likely to yield legal directives consistent with what the legislature has sought to establish.[12]

Conventions which widen and conventions which reduce the gap between legislative intent and a court's determination of the legal directive reside on a continuum rather than in opposing camps. Consider, as a simple illustration of this continuum, four different questions that a judge might ask when interpreting a statute:

1. What does the language of the statute mean?
2. What did the legislature intend the statute to mean?

---

[10] On the dangers, when second-guessing legislatures' intentions, of correcting what needs no correcting and not correcting what does need correcting, see Frederick Schauer, 'The Practice and Problems of Plain Meaning: A Response to Aleinikoff and Shaw' (1992) 45 *Vanderbilt L. Rev.* 715, 729–33.

[11] See, e.g., *Miller* v. *Salomons* (1852) 7 Ex. 475, 553 (*per* Parke B); *Sutherland Publishing Co. Ltd* v. *Caxton Publishing Co. Ltd* [1938] Ch. 174 (CA), 201 (*per* MacKinnon LJ); *Western Bank Ltd* v. *Schindler* [1977] Ch. 1 (CA), 18 *per* Scarman LJ ('Judicial legislation is not an option open to an English judge ... But our courts do have the duty of giving effect to the intention of Parliament, if it be possible, even though the process requires a strained construction of the language used or the insertion of some words in order to do so ... The line between judicial legislation, which our law does not permit, and judicial interpretation in a way best designed to give effect to the intention of Parliament is not an easy one to draw'); also Larry Alexander and Saikrishna Prakash, '"Is That English You're Speaking?" Why Intention Free Interpretation is an Impossibility' (2004) 41 *San Diego L. Rev.* 967, 980 ('To speak of [drafters'] errors ... is to have a baseline of legislative intent, for it is only against that baseline that it is possible to speak of legislative misspeaking').

[12] See Caleb Nelson, 'A Response to Professor Manning' (2005) 91 *Virginia L. Rev.* 451, 454. The notion of consistency with what the legislature has sought to establish fits somewhat uncomfortably with interpretive jurisprudence in the United Kingdom since the Human Rights Act 1998 came into effect, given that nowadays the issue for resolution will sometimes be whether the interpretation of statutory language yields legal directives which are compatible with parliament's intentions (i.e., what it sought to establish) in enacting the HRA. See further section 6, *infra*.

3. What was the legislature's purpose in enacting the statute?
4. What purposes (including ones which the enacting legislature did not, and might even have been unwilling to, entertain) could the statute conceivably be taken to serve?

The first two questions motivate the plain-meaning and golden rules which were considered in the last chapter. Both of these interpretive conventions are primarily gap-reducing. The most common argument in favour of the plain-meaning approach is that it is the one which is most likely to ensure that a statute is applied consistently with how the legislature intended it to be applied. Interpretations of statutes according to the golden rule are normally favoured by judges when the actual language of a statutory provision requires something that cannot conceivably have been the legislature's real intention, and when it is possible to draw inferences from the language and structure of the statute as a whole to determine how the provision might be subjected to a strained interpretation – or, if necessary, modified – so that it can be applied to bring into effect either what the legislature is known to have intended or what it can reasonably be presumed to have intended. Applications of the golden rule in an effort to establish what the legislature is presumed to have intended a statute to mean could be gap-widening or gap-reducing, depending on whether the revealed apparent intention bears any resemblance to the legislature's actual intention.

The fourth question invites an approach to statutory interpretation which will most likely prove gap-widening – an approach which, in English law, has traditionally been considered out of bounds. Courts become supreme legislators, so goes the objection to this approach, if they assume the capacity to marry statutes to purposes which the enacting legislature not only would not have contemplated but would have resisted supporting. In fact, this approach is not quite so frowned upon as it once was. Outside the context of English law, various modern theorists of statutory construction have developed sophisticated arguments to the effect that judicial interpretations of statutes might legitimately float free of the law-making expectations of an enacting legislature – because the meaning of statutes alters over time, for example,[13] or because, in a representative democracy, judges might be justified in trying to interpret statutes in accordance with the requirements of the community for which

---

[13] See, e.g., William N. Eskridge, Jr, *Dynamic Statutory Interpretation* (Cambridge, Mass.: Harvard University Press, 1994).

the statutes were enacted rather than the aims of the legislature in enacting them.[14] In the United Kingdom, furthermore, judicial interpretations
which are intended to ensure that statutes comply with the European
Convention on Human Rights – though they might accord with the
intention of parliament in enacting section 3 of the Human Rights Act
1988 – may derive from a particular statute a purpose which the enacting
parliament never had, and perhaps never would have had.

There will be more to say in due course about the impact of the Human
Rights Act on statutory interpretation. At this point, it is worth returning
to the four questions set out above, for nothing has been said so far about
approaches to statutory interpretation that can be identified with the
third question. But then one might reasonably ask whether that question
really ought to be posed, for it is not, strictly speaking, distinguishable
from the one which precedes it: if a legislature had a purpose in enacting
a statute, it had legislative intent, for one's purposes are an aspect of one's
intentions.[15] The common understanding of the notion of statutory purpose, indeed, is the defect in the existing law that the legislature *intended*
to remedy by enacting a statute.[16] Small wonder that judges often treat
purpose and intention as one and the same thing.

In the context of statutory interpretation, nevertheless, there is a distinction of sorts to be made, for 'purpose' is sometimes used to denote *general*
legislative intent.[17] A legislature might not only intend something specific
by enacting a statutory provision but might also be trying to achieve some
general aim by legislating so as to give effect to the specific intention. The
intention of parliament in enacting section 1(1) of the Law of Property Act
1925, for example, was clear enough: to determine that, from 1 January
1926 onwards, the only estates in land which could subsist or be created as
legal estates were the freehold and leasehold estates. But parliament also

---

[14] See, e.g, William S. Blatt, 'Interpretive Communities: The Missing Element in Statutory
Interpretation' (2001) 95 *Northwestern Univ. L. Rev.* 629; also Amartya Sen, 'Rights, Laws
and Language' (2011) 31 *OJLS* 437, 443–9.

[15] See Richard Ekins, 'The Intention of Parliament' [2010] *Public Law* 709, 725–6.

[16] See, e.g., *Black-Clawson International Ltd* v. *Papierwerke Waldhof-Aschaffenburg AG*
[1975] AC 591 (HL), 622 *per* Viscount Dilhorne ('The reason why one is entitled to consider what was the mischief at which the Act was aimed is surely that that will throw
a revealing light on the object and purpose of the Act, that is to say the intention of
Parliament').

[17] See, e.g., John M. Kernochan, 'Statutory Interpretation: An Outline of Method' (1976) 3
Dalhousie L. J. 333, 353 ('Legislation … is a purposive act and the effort must be to reconstruct the purpose that propelled the lawgivers … Even if evidence of a specific intention
is available, the legislative purpose is still vital as a check on that evidence and as a guide
to its use').

had a general objective in restricting the number of possible legal estates to these two: to rid English law of an inordinately complicated doctrine of estate holding which militated against free alienability (and thus marketability) of title.[18] Behind a specific legislative intention there may be a general legislative objective.

The fact that general objectives can accompany specific intentions does not support the conclusion that statutes can never be understood without reference to their purposes. Statutory provisions, like other prescriptive statements, are often intelligible without any reference to the purposes behind them. Nor is it clear that much turns on the difference between intention and purpose. If a court finds the language of a statute to be ambiguous, it might draw a conclusion as to the meaning of that language by considering the legislature's purpose – i.e., the defect in the law that it sought to remedy – in enacting the statute. But this is to treat purpose as tantamount to intention. In so far as the difference ever comes into its own, it is in those instances where a court argues in effect that a legislature's specific enacting intention does not warrant the inference that parliament wanted to further some aspect of a general purpose which the language of the statute supports. Parliament certainly intended, by enacting section 51 the Adoption Act 1976, that an adoptive person should, on reaching the age of 18, be entitled to obtain 'such information as is necessary to enable that person to obtain a certified copy of the record of his birth'. But it would not have been integral to parliament's general purpose, in enacting this provision, to ensure that such information is supplied to persons who are likely to use it to track down and harm their natural parents.[19]

The common objection to asking, 'What was the legislature's purpose in enacting the statute?' is not that this question is indistinguishable from the question about the legislature's intent, but that any answer to the question will be based on opinion. Those purporting to uncover the legislature's purpose in enacting a statute are likely to be pointing to one of a range of purposes that might have been contemplated, or to a purpose which the interpreter would like to think was contemplated, at the point of enactment. According to Aharon Barak, the former president

---

[18] See Avner Offer, 'The Origins of the Law of Property Acts 1910–25' (1977) 40 *MLR* 505, 514–5; Peter Birks, 'Before We Begin: Five Keys to Land Law', in *Land Law: Themes and Perspectives*, ed. S. Bright and J. Dewar (Oxford University Press, 1998), 457–86 at 462–7.

[19] See *R v. Registrar General, ex p. Smith* [1990] 2 All ER 170 (Div. Ct); affirmed by the CA at [1991] 2 All ER 88.

of the Israeli Supreme Court, '[t]he purpose of a statute is the interests, goals, values, aims, policies, and function that a statute is designed to accomplish'.[20] The 'uniqueness of purposive interpretation', properly undertaken, rests in the fact that 'it takes all purposes into account and tries to synthesize them' by relying on '[p]resumptions of purpose'.[21] But what are these presumptions? 'There is no exhaustive list', though it must include presumptions that statutes seek to 'guarantee security, certainty, consistency, and normative harmony ... reflect ethical values ... social objectives, proper forms of behavior ... human rights ... the rule of law', as well as presumptions that 'statutes do not conflict with the constitution, that implementing legislation does not conflict with primary statutes, that different provisions of a statute do not conflict with each other, and that a statute integrates into the general law'.[22] Yet even though these and other purposive presumptions might enable judges to rein in the number of 'interpretive possibilities',[23] the sheer range of conceivable statutory purposes and potentially applicable presumptions (which will themselves 'sometimes contradict each other')[24] means that there will always be instances when 'the scales remain balanced'[25] and the interpreter cannot point 'to a single, unique solution'.[26] For detractors from purposive interpretation, this is to understate the problem.[27] There will, as was observed in Chapter 4, be multiple background purposes to a statute. Some of these purposes – optimizing free alienability of land, for example, versus protecting disorganized proprietary rights – will come up against each other. Some of them (ensuring that all legal estates in England and Wales are, in time, recorded on a central land register) may belong to the specific legislative scheme, while others (ensuring legal stability, coherence, non-retroactivity and effective law enforcement) will be ascribable to most or even all legislative initiatives. The danger, according

---

[20] Aharon Barak, *Purposive Interpretation in Law*, Eng. trans. S. Bashi (Princeton University Press, 2005), 340.

[21] Ibid. 117, 172.   [22] Ibid. 173–4, 358.

[23] Ibid. 91.   [24] Ibid. 176.

[25] Ibid. 369.   [26] Ibid. 176.

[27] Though for a sympathetic assessment of Barak's position, see Kent Greenawalt, *Legal Interpretation: Perspectives from Other Disciplines and Private Texts* (Oxford University Press, 2010), 331–6 and esp. 335 ('He may have more confidence than I do about how judges should weigh various factors over a wide range of legal texts; but for him, as for me, matters come down to a weighing of various kinds of factors without any simple formula').

to the opponent of purposive interpretation, is that one determines relevant purpose, and chooses purposive presumptions, so as to fill the gaps of a statute in the way one wants them filled.[28]

Note, none the less, that Barak's defence of purposive interpretation, with its emphasis on the use of presumptions, does not amount to an endorsement of fitting a statute to whatever purpose(s) one likes. This reflects an important general point. It is, indeed, tempting to assume that purposivism is the approach of those who prefer the holes in a statute to the statute itself, and who turn to purpose so as to interpolate rather than interpret.[29] No doubt purposive interpretation sometimes does manifest itself thus. But the history of this approach to statutory interpretation suggests something else: that interpretations according to purpose are usually, or at least are usually intended to be, methodologically constrained – that purposive interpretation is supposed to be a disciplined form of interpretation. Much of the rest of this chapter constitutes an attempt to substantiate this proposition.

1   Is law nuts?

It would be a mistake to categorize the purposive approach to statutory interpretation as the one to which judges turn when the plain-meaning and golden rules prove unsuited to the task. Certainly modern common-law judges are inclined to assert the primacy of the plain meaning of the text, and to rely on an interpretive approach which departs from that meaning only if they see compelling reasons for making such a departure. But the history of English case law, as was spelled out in the last chapter, shows that purposivism precedes plain meaning as a standard approach to statutory interpretation.

One of the most famous modern accounts of medieval political philosophy, Ernst Kantorowicz's *The King's Two Bodies*, begins with the argument that the notion of the king having both a 'body natural' and a 'body politic' finds its first clear elaboration in the *Commentaries* of the

---

[28] See, e.g., Antonin Scalia, 'Common-Law Courts in a Civil-Law System: The Role of United States Federal Courts in Interpreting the Constitution and Laws', in *A Matter of Interpretation: Federal Courts and the Law*, ed. A. Gutmann (Princeton University Press, 1997), 3–47 at 46 ('at the end of the day an evolving [*sc.*, purposively constructed] constitution will evolve the way the majority [of the US Supreme Court] wishes').

[29] See Lon L. Fuller, 'The Case of the Speluncean Explorers' (1949) 62 *Harvard L. Rev.* 616, 634.

Elizabethan lawyer, Edmund Plowden.[30] The *Commentaries* are, first and foremost, a collection of cases, decided between the 1550s and the 1570s, which raised significant points of law. But Plowden did not simply report these cases; rather, like his early seventeenth-century protégé, Sir Edward Coke, he treated cases as an occasion to provide a learned gloss on legal doctrine.[31] The gloss that especially intrigues Kantorowicz concerns the relationship between the body politic and the body natural. The former, according to Plowden, can be seen to be superior to – in the sense that it can eradicate the imperfections of – the latter.[32] More significant still, the fact that the king's body politic is corporate but not material, that it can neither be seen nor touched, means that it cannot, and therefore that the king cannot, be subject to death. When the king's body natural dies, his corporate body politic instantly migrates to the body natural of the next king;[33] 'in this capacity', as Coke would elaborate in 1608, 'the King is esteemed to be immortal, invisible, not subject to death, infirmity, infancy, nonage etc'.[34]

Plowden's principal point in distinguishing the king's two bodies was to explain how the head of the realm reigns in uninterrupted, infinite perpetuity. Unsurprisingly, he did not offer an analogous argument to the effect that statutes likewise retain their legal validity *in saecula saeculorum*. But he did think that statutes, like kings, have their material and immaterial dimensions. '[I]t is not the words of the law, but the internal sense of it that makes the law,' he observed in a note on a Common Bench judgment which he reported in 1573, 'and our law (like all others) consists of two parts, *viz.* of body and soul, the letter of the law is the body of the law, and the sense and reason of the law is the soul of the law.'[35] The general idea that a judge might be justified in trying to look beyond the text of the statute was hardly new to the mid sixteenth century;[36] and it is worth

---

[30] See Ernst H. Kantorowicz, *The King's Two Bodies: A Study in Medieval Political Theology* (Princeton University Press, 1997 [1957]), 7–23.

[31] Coke was, as compared with Plowden, more inclined to rewrite rather than report doctrine: see Peter M. Tiersma, 'The Textualization of Precedent' (2007) 82 *Notre Dame L. Rev.* 1187, 1199–200.

[32] See Kantorowicz, *The King's Two Bodies*, 11.

[33] See ibid. 13.

[34] *Calvin's Case* (1608) 7 Co. Rep. 1, 10a.

[35] *Eyston* v. *Studd* (1573) 2 Plowd. 459, 465.

[36] In a Year Book case from the early fourteenth century, for example, Bereford CJ concluded that the drafters of the Statute *De Donis* (1285) had negligently omitted certain words and that it was necessary for him to supply those words so as to give effect to what parliament had meant: *Belyng* v. *Anon.* YB 5 Edw II, i. 176; (1312) B & M 52. This is not the only instance in which Bereford engaged in statutory interpolation: see Theodore

spelling out now that the two specific ideas which are at the centre of the discussion which follows – that statutes ought to be interpreted according to 'equity', and that they ought to be interpreted by reference to the 'mischief' they are intended to suppress – crystallized but by no means originated in the late Tudor and early Stuart periods. This is not to claim, however, that Plowden was merely repeating established mantras. Rather, he was, in the process of reporting decisions, endeavouring to explain the feasibility – as he would have it, the desirability – of adopting a methodological approach to the interpretation of statutes which does not necessarily prioritize the text. His formulation of the basic proposition is one of the more memorable passages of old English law:

> the law may be resembled to a nut, which has a shell and a kernel within, the letter of the law represents the shell, and the sense of it the kernel ... [Y]ou will be no better for the nut if you make use only of the shell ... as the fruit and profit of the nut lies in the kernel ... in the sense more than in the letter. And it often happens that when you know the letter, you know not the sense, for sometimes the sense is more confined and contracted than the letter, and sometimes it is more large and extensive. And equity ... enlarges or diminishes the letter.[37]

Note that Plowden appreciated that an equitable interpretation of a statute will not necessarily be an expansive interpretation. By rooting out the purpose or kernel of a statute, a judge will sometimes determine that it applies to a more limited range of circumstances than would have been the case had it been interpreted by reference to its language or shell. Nor

---

F. T. Plucknett, *Statutes & Their Interpretation in the First Half of the Fourteenth Century* (Cambridge University Press, 1922), 53; also, more generally, W. H. Loyd, 'The Equity of a Statute' (1909) 58 *Univ. Pennsylvania L. Rev.* 76, 77–8 ('an inspection of the year book cases reveals that ... the phrase *"per l'equite de le statut"* is frequently on the tongue of counsel and judge'); and S. E. Thorne, 'The Equity of a Statute and Heydon's Case' (1936) 31 *Illinois L. Rev.* 202, 207–11.

[37] *Eyston* v. *Studd*, 465. Plowden's reasoning was adopted in other late Tudor discourses on equity: see Edward Hake, *Epieikeia: A Dialogue on Equity in Three Parts*, ed. D. E. C. Yale (New Haven: Yale University Press, 1953 [*c*.1600]), 16; Thomas Ashe, *Epieikeia: Et Table generall a les Annales del Ley, per quel facilment troueres touts les cases contenus in yceux; queux concerne le exposition des Statutes per Equitie* (London: printed for the Societie of the Stationers, 1609), 2–6. Curiously, John Cowell's legal dictionary of this period contained no entry for Equity. The definition of the term, when it was eventually added, emphasized Plowden's observation that equity can either expand or contract the letter of the law: see John Cowell, *Nomothetes, the Interpreter, Containing the Genuine Signification of such obscure words and terms used either in the Common or Statute Lawes of this Realm*, 4th edn (London: printed by J. Streater for H. Twyford et al., 1672; 1st edn publ. 1607), f. 104 ('Equity ... [i]s of two sorts ... [T]he one doth abridge, and take from the letter of the Law, the other doth inlarge, and add thereto').

would it be correct to read Plowden as claiming that the letter of the statute counts for nothing. The search for statutory meaning must always, he observed in 1552, begin with the language of the text (and, with penal statutes, it usually ought to end there).[38] '[W]ords', however, 'do not constitute the statute, but are only the image of it … [T]he life of the statute rests in the minds of the expositors of the words … And if they are dispersed, so that their minds cannot be known, then those who may approach nearest to their minds shall construe the words, and these are the sages of the law whose talents are exercised in the study of such matters.'[39]

This last observation – encountered already in Chapter 4 – might be read as an admission that statutory interpretation has to be an exercise in deriving meaning from words. Plowden, however, meant it differently. Yet to what else, other than statutory language, were these sages of the law supposed to apply their talents if they were to discern the purpose or life of a statute? Plowden's answer forms one of the most influential passages in the history of statutory interpretation:

> in order to form a right judgment when the letter of a statute is restrained, and when enlarged, by equity, it is a good way, when you peruse a statute, to suppose that the law-maker is present, and that you have asked him the question you want to know touching the equity, then you must give yourself such an answer as you imagine he would have done, if he had been present.[40]

Plowden here anticipates what, in the eighteenth century, would commonly be referred to as the *verum factum* principle, as elaborated by Giambattista Vico in his critical analyses of Cartesian method.[41] But the

---

[38] *Partridge* v. *Strange and Croker* (1552) 1 Plowd. 77, 86; though cf. *Buckley* v. *Rice Thomas* (1554) 1 Plowd. 118, 127 ('yet it is taken by equity of the statute … notwithstanding it is a penal statute …'); and *Platt* v. *Lock* (1550) 1 Plowd. 35, 36. For a modern extension of the argument that penal statutes should be interpreted on their plain meaning rather than equitably, see *W. T. Ramsay Ltd* v. *IRC* [1982] AC 300 (HL), 323 *per* Lord Wilberforce ('A subject is only to be taxed upon clear words, not upon "intendment" or upon the "equity" of an Act. Any taxing Act of Parliament is to be construed in accordance with this principle').

[39] *Partridge* v. *Strange*, 82.

[40] *Eyston* v. *Studd*, 467. The manoeuvre supporting Plowden's answer – ask what would be the response of an imagined reasonable person who has a capacity to speak to the matter for resolution – is one with which modern English lawyers are familiar. Cf., e.g., the early twentieth-century 'officious bystander' test for determining implied contractual terms: *Shirlaw* v. *Southern Foundries (1926) Ltd* [1939] 2 KB 206 (CA), 227 (*per* MacKinnon LJ).

[41] The principle, that is, that historians produce knowledge through the imaginative reconstruction of past deeds: see R. G. Collingwood, *The Idea of History* (Oxford University Press, 1946), 64–5; also Jeremy Bentham, *Of Laws in General*, ed. H. L. A. Hart (London:

more obvious comparison is with Aristotle, on whom Plowden relied explicitly. '[T]he equitable is just', Aristotle claimed; it is 'not the legally just', however, 'but a correction of legal justice'.[42] Legal justice inevitably requires some equitable correction, for, while laws are laid down in general terms, there are some matters about which we cannot correctly speak in such terms. Where 'it is necessary to speak generally, but not possible to do so correctly, the legislator lays down that which holds good for the majority of cases, though is not ignorant of the possibility of error. And that legislation is none the less correct; for the error is not in the law nor in the legislator but in the nature of the thing'.[43] Legislators are 'unable to define [such] things exactly', that is, and so 'are obliged to legislate as if that held good always which in fact only holds good usually'.[44] Aristotle's conclusion to this argument (which we considered briefly in Chapter 2) is as Plowden's: 'it is right', when a specific problem is not covered by the general language of the statute, 'to correct the omission – to say what the legislator himself would have said had he been present, and would have put into his law if he had known'.[45]

Athlone Press, 1970 [1782]), 162 ("Interpretation ... may be styled liberal where the will you attribute to him [*sc.*, 'the legislator'] is not that which you suppose he really entertained, but ... which ... you suppose[,] ... had the individual case which calls for interpretation been present to his view, he would have entertained ... as if it had been his reality').

[42] *Nicomachean Ethics*, V. 10. 1137ᵇ.

[43] Ibid.

[44] *Rhetoric*, I. 13. 1374ᵃ. Much the same argument is to be found in Plato, the *Digest*, Aquinas, Bentham, Hart and (as we saw in the last chapter) Montaigne: see Plato, *Statesman,* 294ᵇ ('law does not perfectly comprehend what is noblest and most just for all and therefore cannot enforce what is best. The differences of men and actions, and the endless irregular movements of human things, do not admit of any universal and simple rule. And no art whatsoever can lay down a rule which will last for all time'); D 1. 3. 12 ('It is not possible for every point to be specifically dealt with either in statutes or in *senatus consulta* ...'); Aquinas, *Summa Theologiae*, I-II, q. 96, a. 6 ('the lawgiver cannot have in view every single case ...'); Bentham, *Of Laws in General*, 164–5; H. L. A. Hart, *The Concept of Law*, 2nd edn (Oxford: Clarendon Press, 1994), 128–9. See also Raymond B. Marcin, '*Epieikeia*; Equitable Lawmaking in the Construction of Statutes' (1978) 10 *Connecticut L. Rev.* 377 at 381–2, 391; A. Arthur Schiller, 'Roman *Interpretatio* and Anglo-American Interpretation and Construction' (1941) 27 *Virginia L. Rev.* 733, 756–9; Eric G. Zahnd, 'The Application of Universal Laws to Particular Cases: A Defense of Equity in Aristotelianism and Anglo-American Law' (1996) 59 *Law & Contemporary Problems* 263, 271.

[45] *Nicomachean Ethics*, V. 10. 1137ᵇ. For a detailed analysis of the argument, see Jim Evans, 'Aristotle's Theory of Equity', in *Prescriptive Formality and Normative Rationality in Modern Legal Systems: Festschrift for Robert S. Summers*, ed. W. Krawietz, N. MacCormick and G. H. von Wright (Berlin: Duncker & Humblot, 1994), 225–43.

Plowden referred to the importance of interpreters seeking out the sense (or life, or kernel) of a statute when the enacted language leaves some crucial matter within the remit of the statute unresolved. Yet the Aristotelian method that he advocated – the requirement that one imagines how or if the legislator, were he present, would have the statute deal with that matter – seems to be calling on judges to accomplish something more specific: to impute legislative intent. Note that Plowden considered the determination of unspecified legislative intention through conjectural reconstruction to be not an end itself, but 'a good way' of determining the equity of a statute.[46] Two centuries after Plowden, Lord Mansfield would claim that 'the equity of an Act can be carried no further than to what was within the view and intention of the Legislature'.[47] But neither Plowden nor the majority of his contemporaries appeared to understand equity in quite this way. 'Equity is a righteousness which considers all of the particular circumstances of the deed', St German had observed in 1530:

> to follow the words of the law is in some cases both against justice and the common wealth: wherefore in some cases it is *good and even* necessary to leave the words of the law, and to follow that [which] reason and justice require, and to that intent equity is ordained, that is to say to temper and mitigate the rigour of the law.[48]

St German's words do not lend themselves to an obvious reading, but his point seems to be that when there is a divergence between the known or likely intentions of the legislature and what would be intended according to the requirements of 'reason and justice', a statute should be interpreted by

---

[46] See Warren Lehman, 'How to Interpret a Difficult Statute' (1979) *Wisconsin L. Rev.* 489, 497 ('He suggests that we try it … that we see if it works for us').

[47] *R v. Williams* (1757) 1 Burr. 402, 407. See also Frederick J. de Sloovère, 'The Equity and Reason of a Statute' (1936) 21 *Cornell L. Q.* 591, 593–5 (attributing this conception of the equity of the statute to sixteenth-century lawyers as well as to Mansfield).

[48] Christopher St German, *Doctor and Student*, ed. T. F. T. Plucknett and J. L. Barton (London: Selden Society, 1974 [1530]), 95, 97 ('Equytye is a ryghtwysenes that consideryth all the pertyculer cyrcumstaunces of the dede … [T]o folowe the wordes of the lawe were in some case both against Iustyce & the common welth: wherefore in some cases it is *good and even* necessary to leue the wordis of the lawe & to folowe that reason and Justyce requyreth & to that intent equytie is ordeyned, that is to say to tempre and myttygate the rygoure of the lawe'). Cf. Christopher St German, *Doctor and Student*, ed. W. Muchall (Cincinnati: Clarke, 1874 [1530]), 44–5 ('Equity is a right wiseness that considereth all the particular circumstances of the deed … [T]o follow the words of the law were in some case both against justice and the commonwealth. Wherefore in some cases it is necessary to love [*sic*] the words of the law, and to follow that [which] reason and justice requireth, and to that intent equity is ordained; that is to say, to temper and mitigate the rigour of the law').

reference to the latter. Various jurists of the period were similarly minded – and could be similarly obtuse. 'Sometimes Statutes are expounded by Equities', Christopher Hatton observed in 1570, 'because Law and Reason repugn to the open sense of the words, and therefore they are reformed to consonance of Law and Reason.'[49] Nobody articulated this sentiment more regularly than did Plowden himself. '[T]he sages of the law' have not only sometimes 'construed statutes quite contrary to the letter', he remarked in 1559, but have 'always' interpreted 'the intent of the Legislature … according to that which is consonant to reason and good discretion'.[50] Counsel for the defendant, he commented on the case of *Stowel* v. *Zouch*, 'sought help from the intent of the makers of the act, which intent is not found in the express letter … but is gathered from reason'.[51]

The implication to be drawn from these passages is that the judges invariably assumed the legislature's intention in enacting a statute and the equitable interpretation of that statute to be complementary. Perhaps judges always did make this assumption. But occasionally one finds Plowden implicitly acknowledging that the intention of an enacting parliament might not have been commensurate with the motivations of an equitable interpreter, and that the equitable construction of a statute demands that a court impute to the legislative assembly a concern for reasonableness or fairness which it cannot be said to have displayed. '[I]t is reasonable that a man may lease his land, to which he comes lawfully, although he has not been in possession for the space of a year', Plowden commented in 1552, '[a]nd to say that the intent of the statute was to restrain such leases, would be too hard an exposition, and contrary to all reason and equity'.[52] His point seems to be that equity precludes, rather than that parliament could not have intended, the hard exposition of the statute. An Act concerning the validity of leases not exceeding 21 years did not apply to perpetually renewable tenancies of periods shorter than that term, he observed apropos of *Fulmerston* v. *Steward*, 'for it cannot be reasonably taken that such was the intent of the makers of the statute,

---

[49] Christopher Hatton, *A Treatise Concerning Statutes, or Acts of Parliament: And the Exposition thereof* (London: printed for Richard Tonson, 1677 [*c*.1570]), 44–5 (punctuation modified).

[50] *Stradling* v. *Morgan* (1559) 1 Plowd. 199, 205. This case serves as an illustration of restrictive equitable interpretation: a statute of Edward VI's reign, which referred to receivers and treasurers without any qualifying words, was held on an equitable construction to refer only to officials appointed by the king and not to officials acting for private persons.

[51] *Stowel* v. *Zouch* (1563) 1 Plowd. 353, 362.

[52] *Partridge* v. *Strange & Croker*, 87–8.

for it would be against all reason and equity'.[53] Again, the claim appears to be not that parliament could not have intended the statute to apply strictly (to leases running beyond 21 years because of renewal), but only that equity cannot support such a reading. It seems that the sixteenth-century argument that judges do well to discover the equity of the stat-ute equates only up to a point with the claim that judges should try to ascertain, and should interpret statutes in accordance with, the known or apparent intentions of the enacting legislature.[54] To satisfy equity, it was probably enough that a court could settle on an enacting intention that equity itself would supply.

2   Lingering mischief

From the proposition that ambiguous statutes ought to be interpreted according to the dictates of reason and equity it is, perhaps, no great distance to the contention that a statute which confounds any common sense of right or reason ought to be controlled and, if necessary, adjudged void. But the Aristotelian idea of the equity of the statute is not, it has to be emphasized, the idea that Coke was to set out in 1610. Plowden was intrigued by how the sages of the law had interpreted statutes so as to make them applicable without offence to equity, whereas Coke, in *Bonham's Case*, was asserting that there were instances when the consequence of a particular judicial interpretation having been placed on a statute was that the statute was rendered ineffective.

Both ideas were to run their course. During the seventeenth and eight-eenth centuries, we saw in Chapter 2, Coke's was challenged and rejected. The idea of the equity of the statute was to endure a similar fate. Sir William Jones, a judge of the King's Bench, remarked in 1638 that 'equity … is too general a ground' for statutory interpretation.[55] Between the seventeenth and eighteenth centuries, according to C. K. Allen, the doctrine gradually

---

[53] *Fulmerston v. Steward* (1554) 1 Plowd. 101, 109.
[54] See further Hans W. Baade, 'The *Casus Omissus*: A Pre-history of Statutory Analogy' (1994) 20 *Syracuse Jnl of International Law & Commerce* 45, 77–9; and cf. Frank E. Horack, Jr, 'Statutory Interpretation – Light from Plowden's Reports' (1931) 19 *Kentucky L. J.* 211, 218–9, who errs in treating 'the discovery of intention by "reason" … known as interpretation according to the "equity of the Statute"' as a method by which judges would justify passing off as 'real legislative intent' a 'legislative intention subjectively determined according to the judicial conception of justice'.
[55] *James v. Tintney* (1638) Jones W. 421, 422.

receded from view.[56] Now and again, it would re-emerge: although no mention of it is to be found in the first edition of Matthew Bacon's *A New Abridgement of the Law*,[57] for example, later editions discuss at length 'in what cases a statute ought to have an equitable construction'.[58] Certainly by the nineteenth century, none the less, judges and treatise writers alike were declaring the idea discredited. 'I cannot forbear observing', Lord Tenterden remarked in 1827, 'that I think there is always danger in giving effect to what is called the equity of a statute, and that it is much safer and better to rely on and abide by the plain words'.[59] A quarter of a century later, we find Pollock CB declaring how he could 'not believe' that the idea of equitable 'construction of a statute would be tolerated in modern times'.[60]

But something of the idea – something we have not yet touched upon – survived. During the Tudor and early Stuart periods, drafters of statutes began to realize that if some judges were indeed inclined to construct statutes as Plowden described – in accordance with what reason required, and not necessarily in accordance with what the enacting legislature can be said to have intended – then one way to minimize the likelihood of parliament's intentions being usurped by the predilections of an equity-minded judge would be to include in a statute a preamble setting out parliament's reasons for enacting it. '[T]he lawyers of this realm are wont always to take light' of the preamble, Sir Francis Bacon observed in the first major case he ever argued, 'but our preambles are annexed for exposition; and this gives aim to the body of the statute'.[61] Within the half century before

---

[56] Carleton Kemp Allen, *Law in the Making*, 3rd edn (Oxford: Clarendon Press, 1939), 377. It certainly did not disappear overnight. We find it relied on, for example, in *Pemble* v. *Stern* (1666) 2 Keb. 230, 232–3.

[57] [Matthew Bacon,] *A New Abridgement of the Law by a Gentleman of the Inner Temple*, 5 vols. (London: printed for D. Lintor, 1736). Only the first two volumes appeared in 1736. Volume 3 first appeared in 1740, volume 4 in 1759 and volume 5 in 1766 (Bacon died *c.* 1757).

[58] Matthew Bacon, *A New Abridgement of the Law*, 3rd edn, 5 vols. (London: printed for J. Worrall, 1768), IV, 649. Though, as we will see in a moment, the observations on equitable statutory interpretation as set out in this and later editions need to be treated with caution.

[59] *Brandling* v. *Barrington* (1827) 6 B. & C. 467, 475. See also *Guthrie* v. *Fisk* (1824) 3 B. & C. 178, 182 (*per* Bayley J).

[60] *Miller* v. *Salomons* (1852) 7 Ex. 475, 559. See also Fortunatus Dwarris, *A General Treatise on Statutes: Their Rules of Construction, and the Proper Boundaries of Legislation and of Judicial Interpretation*, 2nd edn (London: Benning & Co., 1848), 616–17.

[61] *Chudleigh's Case* (1594), in *The Works of Francis Bacon*, 15 vols., ed. J. Spedding, R. L. Ellis and D. D. Heath (Boston: Houghton Mifflin, 1900), XV, 155–87 at 170.

Bacon made this observation, Thomas Egerton had written of how 'the duetye of the preamble ... is no more but to shewe the cause whye the statute was made & what was the mischief at the commen lawe'.[62] Egerton himself echoed Sir James Dyer, whom Plowden had reported as considering 'the preamble ... to be ... a key to open the minds of the makers of the Act, and the mischiefs which they intended to redress'.[63] Reasonable conjecture as to how, or if, a legislature would have wanted a statute applied to facts to which it does not obviously apply, or to which it applies only to generate an injustice, might prove somewhat easier if the interpreter can determine from the statute's preamble that it was enacted for the purpose of eradicating some defect in the law which, until the enactment, had not been (or had not been effectively) addressed. The basic point – that 'the cause of making the statute'[64] might be equated with 'the mischief ... that the Parliament intended to redress'[65] – can be found in English case law dating as far back as the mid fourteenth century,[66] and surfaces regularly throughout Plowden's case reports.[67] It is notable, nevertheless, that Egerton had a slightly different point in mind: preambles do not always identify the mischief,[68] and so, even in the age of the preamble, the sages of the law will still, sometimes, have to do the identifying themselves.

The doctrine of the equity of a statute was not reducible to this idea of locating the mischief that the statute was intended to suppress. Rather, that idea is present in the doctrine. Plowden generally referred to 'equity' in relation to statutes to draw attention to the possibility of judges recognizing as a matter of right judgment that an exception should be read into a broadly worded provision, say, or that a situation which lies outside a statute's express terms ought (given reasonable conjecture as to what the actual legislator would have said if present) to be deemed within its reach. The point of the method he extolled – and it certainly is a method – is to

---

[62] [Thomas Egerton,] *A Discourse upon the Exposicion & Understanding of Statutes, With Sir Thomas Egerton's Additions*, ed. S. E. Thorne (San Marino, Calif.: Huntington Library, 1942 [c. 1565]), 114.

[63] *Stowel v. Zouch*, 369.

[64] *Hill v. Grange* (1555) 1 Plowd. 164, 173.

[65] *Stradling v. Morgan*, 203.

[66] See *Tornerghe v. Abbot of Furness* (1341) YB 15 Edw. III, 126 ('law ought to be in accordance with reason and to take away mischief unless the contrary practice has been in use as law').

[67] See, e.g., *Wimbish v. Tailbois* (1550) 1 Plowd. 38, 55; *Reniger v. Fogossa* (1550) 1 Plowd. 1, 13–14; *Dive v. Maningham* (1550) 1 Plowd. 60, 63; *Willion v. Berkley* (1560) 1 Plowd. 223, 235.

[68] See *A Discourse upon the Exposicion & Understanding of Statutes*, 115–17.

show that the most apposite interpretations of statutes need be committed neither to the meaning of enacted language nor to the legislature's intentions at the point of enactment. Plowden clearly appreciated, as a good Aristotelian, that 'equity' has other associations. When a statute is enacted to remedy a defect in the law, he observed on more than one occasion, the expectation is that it will 'aid things in like degree'[69] – that the statute will be applied so as to try to ensure that 'the same equality will exist between the persons and between the things concerned'.[70] But it is also clear that equity as equality is not what he primarily had in mind when he wrote of subjecting a statute to an equitable interpretation. To interpret a statute thus is to form the correct judgment about how it is to be applied, he maintained, and to form this judgment one does well – certainly when familiarity neither with the enacted language nor with the intentions of the legislature at the point of enactment brings into focus the statute's true 'sense' or purpose – to try to imagine what the legislature would say it wanted that statute to achieve were the legislature reassembled for the purpose of advising on the problem before a court today.

Plowden was not the last English lawyer to conceive of equitable interpretation as an attempt to reach a correct judgment about statutory applicability which is not necessarily faithful to enacted language or to parliament's known or probable enacting intentions. Henry Hobart, the successor to Edward Coke as Chief Justice of Common Pleas, observed in 1615 that determining the 'equity and meaning of the statute' means trusting to 'that liberty and authority that Judges have over laws, especially over statute laws, according to reason and best convenience, to mould them to the truest and best use'.[71] In the Court of Chancery at the beginning of that year, one of Coke's nemeses, Thomas Egerton (by now Ellesmere, LC), remarked even more forthrightly on how 'the Judges themselves do play the Chancellors' Parts ... upon Statutes, making Construction of them according to Equity, varying from the Rules and Grounds of Law, and enlarging them *pro bono publico*, against the Letter and Intent of the Maker'.[72] But these observations are not representative of

---

[69] *Buckley v. Rice Thomas*, 127; *Hill v. Grange*, 178; and see also James McCauley Landis, 'Statutes and the Sources of Law', in *Harvard Legal Essays Written in Honor of and Presented to Joseph Henry Beale and Samuel Williston* (Cambridge, Mass.: Harvard University Press, 1934), 213–46 at 215–16.

[70] *Nicomachean Ethics*, V. 3. 1131ᵃ.

[71] *Sheffeild v. Ratcliffe* (1615) Hob. 334 at 337, 346. Equitable interpretation is also endorsed around this time in *Cross v. Westwood* (1611) 2 Brownl. 108; and *Folliett v. Saunders* (1625) 2 Roll. 500.

[72] *Earl of Oxford's Case* (1615) 1 Rep. Ch. 1, 12.

the jurisprudence of statutory interpretation which was emerging in the late sixteenth and early seventeenth centuries. Whereas Plowden's observations on statutory construction make little of equity as equality, this emerging jurisprudence was grounded in the idea that equitable interpretation is, first and foremost, an exercise in formal justice, or ensuring that the same laws are applied to what are materially the same cases. Interpreting a statute according to equity requires, on this approach, that it be fitted to a mischief, and that cases not covered by the language of the statute might still be resolved by it if they fall under that mischief. After Plowden, courts are regularly reported as ruling on whether an action not explicitly covered by a statute is nevertheless within its terms because it is 'in equal mischief' to actions which the statute explicitly does cover.[73] To borrow the terse language of one early seventeenth-century headnote, remedial statutes were to be construed so as to suppress the mischief and extend the remedy.[74]

This was, by the second half of the seventeenth century, an established principle of statutory interpretation. That it had become so was neither wholly nor even mainly attributable to Plowden. Edward Coke, in the first part of his *Institutes of the Laws of England* (1628), refers to a passage from Thomas Littleton's mid fifteenth-century treatise on tenures which suggests that certain entails, though not being within the 'express words' (*expresse parols*) of the Statute of Westminster II, were nevertheless 'caught by the equity of said statute' (*prise par le equite del dit Statute*). The Year Books offer instances dating back to around 1428 of lawyers and judges taking just this approach to statutory construction.[75] In his commentary on the passage from Littleton, Coke connects the idea of equity as extending statutes to disputes which fall within their mischief yet outside their

---

[73] See, e.g., *Earl of Westmerland's Case* (1575) 3 Leo. 59; *Wiseman's Case* (1581) 2 Leo. 148; *Slywright v. Page* (1587) Gould. 101; *Smith v. Vanger Colgay* (1594) Cro. Eliz. 384; *Nevil's Case* (1604) 7 Co. Rep. 33; *The Duke of Lenox* (1609) 2 Brownl. 301; *Colt & Glover v. Bishop of Coventry & Lichfield* (1612) Hob. 140. Most of the cases in this line come after Plowden's reports, though before and contemporaneous with Plowden there are some brief reports by Brownlow & Goldesborough and by Jenkins – *Lynche v. Porter* (1531) 2 Brownl. 1; *Anon.* (1527) Jenk. 192; *Anon.* (1559) Jenk. 221; *Anon.* (1561) Jenk. 226 – as well as the equally terse version of *Hill v. Grange* as reported by Dyer (*Hill v. Grange* (1555) 2 Dyer 130).

[74] *Parker v. Sanders* (1616) Cro. Jac. 418.

[75] See, e.g. (1428) YB 7 Hen. VI 5, 9 *per* Paston ('Et comment que le statut ne donne action par express parols, uncore il est plus que ouel mischief, et sera pris par l'equite'), cited after Norman Doe, *Fundamental Authority in Late Medieval English Law* (Cambridge University Press, 1990), 105, where other fifteenth-century examples are set out.

language with Aristotle's observation that it is unrealistic to expect that the language of a statute will capture the mischief in full:

> Equitie is a construction made by the Judges, that cases out of the letter of a stat[ute] yet being within the same mischiefe, or cause of the making of the same, shall be within the same remedie that the Statute provideth: And the reason hereof is, that for the lawmakers could not possibly set downe all cases in expresse termes.[76]

Coke had delivered a more formulaic statement on this matter over three decades earlier. *Heydon's Case* concerned land over which *W* held a copyhold estate for life, subject to the will of the landlord and the custom particular to the manor. The landlord subsequently granted an eighty-year lease of the land to *H*. Soon after this lease was granted, the landlord's business was dissolved. By virtue of a statute of Henry VIII, the crown thereby became entitled to the landlord's freehold. But this statute also affirmed (31 H. 8. c. 13) the continuation of 'any estate or interest for life' over the land other than that to which the Crown had become entitled. Once the landlord was stripped of his freehold, what happened to the estates held by *W* and by *H*? The Court of Exchequer found that the grant to *H*, being an estate for a term of years rather than for life, was void. The crucial question was 'whether the copyhold estate of Ware and Ware [*sc.*, *W*] for their lives, at the will of the Lords, according to the custom of the said manor, should, in judgment of law be called an estate and interest for lives, within the said general words and meaning of the said Act'.[77] The Barons of the Exchequer found that even though the copyhold was technically revocable at the will of the landlord, it 'was an estate for life, within the words and meaning of' 31 H. 8. c. 13,[78] and therefore was protected after the landlord was denuded of his freehold estate. That the language of the statute did not specifically extend to copyhold estates was, Coke reported, of no consequence.

> And it was resolved … that for the sure and true interpretation of all statutes in general (be they penal or beneficial, restrictive or enlarging of the common law,) four things are to be discerned and considered: –
>
> 1st. What was the common law before the making of the Act.
> 2nd. What was the mischief and defect for which the common law did not provide.

---

[76] 1 Co. Inst. 21, 24b.
[77] *Heydon's Case* (1584) 3 Co. Rep. 7a, 7b.
[78] Ibid.

> 3rd What remedy the Parliament hath resolved and appointed to cure the
> disease of the commonwealth.
>
> And, 4th. The true reason of the remedy; and then the office of all the
> Judges is always to make such construction as shall suppress the mischief,
> and advance the remedy, and to suppress subtle inventions and evasions
> for continuance of the mischief ... and to add force and life to the cure
> and remedy, according to the true intent of the makers of the Act.[79]

The basic principle set out in this passage – the so-called 'mischief rule'
of interpretation – came to be accepted as a standard convention of statutory construction in the seventeenth century.[80] *Heydon's Case* was still
cited regularly by counsel and judges during the eighteenth century, when
the plain-meaning rule started to come into its own. When Blackstone, in
the first volume of his *Commentaries* (1765), set out the main 'rules to be
observed with regard to the construction of statutes', the mischief rule
was the first one on his list.[81] Yet, during the eighteenth century, *Heydon's
Case* tended to be referred to in court as authority for the principle that
copyhold estates ought to be protected against the Crown; only rarely was
the case associated with the mischief rule,[82] and when judges were referring to this rule they certainly did not always endorse it.[83] Though the rule
was not without its detractors in the nineteenth century,[84] it gradually

---

[79] Ibid.

[80] See, e.g., *Lee* v. *Brown* (1617) Pop. 128; *Fawkeners* v. *Bellingham* (1624) Cro. Car. 80; *James* v. *Tutney* (1638) Cro. Car. 532; *Read* v. *Palmer* (1647) Sty. 106; *Harrington* v. *Smith* (1657) 2 Sid. 41; *Burges* v. *Pierce* (1659) 1 Sid. 16; *Vere* v. *Sampson* (1672) Hardr. 205; *Glover* v. *Cope* (1691) Skin. 305; *R* v. *Waters* (1694) 2 Show. KB 319.

[81] 1 Bl. Comm. 87; see also ibid. 61 ('[T]he most universal and effectual way of discovering the true meaning of a law, when the words are dubious, is by considering the reason and spirit of it; or the cause which moved the legislator to enact it'). For the dating of the pub-lication of the first volume, see Wilfrid Prest, *William Blackstone: Law and Letters in the Eighteenth Century* (Oxford University Press, 2008), 216–19.

[82] For instances when it was associated with this rule, see in particular *Arminer* (1773) Lofft 114; *Jackson's Case* (1773) Lofft 249; and *Hickey* v. *Hayter* (1795) 6 Term Rep. 384.

[83] See, e.g., *Bradley* v. *Clark* (1793) 5 Term Rep. 197, 201–2 *per* Buller J ('With regard to the construction of statutes according to the intention of the Legislature; we must remember that there is an essential difference between the expounding of modern and ancient Acts of Parliament. In early times the Legislature used (and I believe it was a wise course to take) to pass laws in general and in few terms; they were left to the Courts of Law to be construed so as to reach all the cases within the mischief to be remedied. But in modern times great care has been taken to mention the particular cases in the contemplation of the Legislature, and therefore the Courts are not permitted to take the same liberty in construing them as they did in expounding the ancient statutes').

[84] See *R* v. *St Lawrence in Appleby* (1845) 6 QB 842, 844–5 (Denman CJ to counsel: 'What do you say is the mischief to be remedied by this Act? ... The framers of the statute have

came back into vogue,[85] and was championed particularly by Lord Justice Kay[86] and Lord Blackburn.[87] The rule was regularly relied on in the twentieth century; likewise, to this point, in the twenty-first.[88]

Though the mischief rule has been part of the common-law tapestry for quite a long time, judges and academic lawyers have not subjected it to much analysis. Perhaps this is because the clarity and detail of Coke's account of it has made further elaboration seem for the most part unnecessary. But the rule and its reception warrant careful examination if we are to understand the history and evolution of purposive statutory interpretation. It is often assumed that Coke, by devising the

---

studiously avoided saying what you would make them say'); and *Lord Bruce (A Child) v. Marquess of Ailesbury* [1892] AC 356 (HL), 361–2 (*per* Lord Halsbury LC); though cf. Halsbury's less reserved assessment of the rule in *Eastman Photographic Materials Co. Ltd v. Comptroller-General of Patents, Designs and Trade Marks* [1898] AC 571 (HL), 573.

[85] *R v. Ivie M'Knight* (1830) 10 B. & C. 734; *Warburton v. Loveland* (1832) 2 Dow. & Cl. 480, 496–7 (*per* Tindal LCJ); *R v. Justices of Suffolk* (1841) 2 QB 85; *A-G v. Walker* (1849) 3 Ex. 242, 258 (*per* Pollock CB); *Coe v. Platt* (1851) 6 Ex. 752, 755 (*arguendo*) ('The well-known rule in the construction of statutes …'); *McKinnon v. Penson* (1853) 8 Ex. 319; *Hawkins v. Gathercole* (1855) 6 De G.M. & G. 1; *Blackwell v. England* (1857) 8 El. & Bl. 541, 549 *per* Erle J (citing *Heydon's Case* for the proposition that '[w]e are to look at the object, and to construe ambiguous phrases in the sense that will further that object, not in the sense that will frustrate it'); *McManus v. Lancashire & Yorkshire Railway* (1859) 4 Hurl. & N. 327; *A-G v. Sillem* (1863) 2 Hurl. & C. 431; *Re Keane* (1871) LR 12 Eq. 115; *R v. Holbrook* (1878–9) LR 4 QBD 42, 46 (*per* Lush J); *Re Mayfair Property Co* [1898] 2 Ch. 28, 35 (*per* Lord Lindley MR).

[86] See *Re Leavesley* [1891] 2 Ch. 1, 8–9; *Pelton Bros v. Harrison (No 1)* [1891] 2 QB 422, 424.

[87] See *Peek v. North Staffordshire Railway* (1863) 10 HL Cas. 473, 492 ('Independently of the high authority of Lord Coke, I think there is much reason in this'); *Easton v. Richmond Highway Board* (1871–2) LR 7 QB 69, 76; *R v. Castro* (1873–4) LR 9 QB 350, 360–1; *River Wear Commissioners v. Adamson* (1876–7) LR 2 App. Cas. 743, 764; *Bradlaugh v. Clarke* (1882–3) LR 8 App. Cas. 354, 372–3.

[88] See, e.g., *Lennox v. Stoddart* [1902] 2 KB 21 (CA); *Kirkwood v. Gadd* [1910] AC 422 (HL), 423–4 (*per* Lord Loreburn LC); *Re Samuel* [1913] AC 514 (PC), 518 (*arguendo*); *Cornelius v. Phillips* [1918] AC 199 (HL), 213 (*per* Lord Dunedin); *Whitley v. Stumbles* [1930] 1 KB 393 (CA), 398–9 (*per* Scruton LJ); *Potts v. Hickman* [1941] AC 212 (HL), 235–6 (*per* Viscount Maugham); *Asher v. Seaford Court Estates* [1950] AC 508 (HL), 524 (*per* Lord Normand); *A-G v. Parsons* [1956] AC 421 (HL), 456–7 (*per* Lord Cohen); *Re Harpur's WT* [1962] Ch. 78 (CA); *Coutts & Co v. IRC* [1964] AC 1393 (HL); *Gartside v. IRC* [1968] AC 553 (HL), 612 (*per* Lord Reid); *Schaefer v. Schuhmann* [1972] AC 572 (PC), 595–6 (*per* Lord Cross); *Applin v. Race Relations Board* [1975] AC 259 (HL); *Maclaine Watson & Co Ltd v. DTI* [1989] Ch. 72 (CA), 225 (*per* Ralph Gibson LJ); *J. H. Rayner Ltd v. DTI* [1989] Ch. 72 (CA); *Sheldon v. RHM Outhwaite (Underwriting Agencies) Ltd* [1996] AC 102 (HL), 153 (*per* Lord Nicholls); *Yaxley v. Gotts* [2000] Ch. 162 (CA), 182 (*per* Clarke LJ); *Donoghue v. Folkestone Properties* [2003] 2 WLR 1138 (CA), 1159 (*per* Brooke LJ); *Avonridge Property Co. Ltd v. Mashru* [2005] UKHL 70; *Flora v. Wakom* [2006] EWCA Civ 1103 at [16] (Brooke LJ); *R v. T* [2009] UKHL 20; *British Pregnancy Advisory Service v. Secretary of State for Health* [2011] EWHC 235 at 15 (Supperstone J).

mischief rule, expressed in canonical form the equitable approach to the construction of statutes which had been advocated by Plowden – that the approaches which each of them took to statutory interpretation were not distinguishable in any significant way.[89] Modern commentators who make this assumption sometimes point to a passage in the third edition of Matthew Bacon's *A New Abridgement of the Law* (1768), in which the two approaches are treated as one:

> An Equitable construction is a Construction by which a Case not within the Letter of a Statute is holden to be within the meaning thereof, because it is within the Mischief for which a Remedy is thereby provided. The Reason for such Construction is, that the Law-maker could not possibly set down every Case in express Terms. In order to form a right Judgment whether a Case be within the Equity of a Statute, it is a good way to suppose the Law-maker present; and that you have asked him this Question, did you intend to comprehend this Case? Then you must give yourself such Answer as you imagine he being an upright and reasonable Man would have given. If this be that it is within the Equity you may safely hold it to be so. For while you do no more than he would have done, you do not act contrary to the Statute but in Conformity thereto.[90]

But this passage, which is unlikely to have been written by Bacon himself,[91] merges Plowden and Coke rather too readily. It is certainly true that neither Plowden nor Coke thought that judges should exalt statutory language. And it is true that both formulated methodologies with the aim of enabling judges to justify their interpreting a statute on the basis of a purpose which could reasonably (albeit hypothetically) be ascribed to the legislature which enacted it. But their actual methodologies were quite different. For Plowden, to interpret a statute according to its equity is not to be enslaved to its language but to be faithful to its spirit, which means making the statute accord with the requirements of reason and justice; one way to do this is to imagine that the enacting legislature is present and is asked how, or if, it would apply the statute to the problem for resolution. For Coke, the discovery of the 'true intention' of the makers of an

---

[89] See, e.g., John F. Manning, 'Textualism and the Equity of the Statute' (2001) 101 *Columbia L. Rev.* 1, 31–3; J. A. Corry, 'Administrative Law and the Interpretation of Statutes' (1936) 1 *Univ. Toronto L. J.* 286, 294; Ruth Sullivan, *Sullivan and Driedger on the Construction of Statutes*, 4th edn (Vancouver: Butterworths, 2002), 196; Cross, *Statutory Interpretation*, 19.

[90] Bacon, *A New Abridgement of the Law*, 3rd edn, IV, 649.

[91] After Bacon's death, the fourth and fifth volumes of the *Abridgement* were substantially rewritten by Owen Ruffhead, a barrister of the Middle Temple, and by Joseph Sayer, a serjeant at law and the author of *The Law of Costs* (Dublin: printed for J. Milliken, 1768).

Act requires a judge to enquire into the state of the common law before the Act was passed, how the legislature considered the common law to be defective and what the legislature determined the statutory remedy for the defect (or defects) should be; having made these enquiries, the judge must then decide if the problem before the court falls within the mischief that the statute was designed to remedy and, if it does, interpret the statute in a manner sympathetic to the legislature's objective ('suppress the mischief, and advance the remedy').[92] Each jurist was endeavouring to justify his own disciplined version of purpose-oriented statutory construction: to devise an approach to interpretation which would enable judges to identify statutory purposes not as general political or legal objectives, but as reasonably hypothesized or even (in the case of Coke's method) actual intentions of enacting legislatures. But their approaches were hardly indistinguishable.

While Coke's perspective on statutory interpretation was, in the long term, more favourably received than was Plowden's, it was sometimes misunderstood. Judges would occasionally run the golden and mischief rules together, for example, as if no distinction is to be drawn between them.[93] Even judges who demonstrate a sound grasp of the mischief rule are unlikely, certainly today, to conceive of it as Coke did: for while Coke presumed that the defect to be remedied by the statute being interpreted must be one which the common law has not suppressed, it is taken for granted nowadays that the rule applies to 'existing law',[94] whatever its form. The relevant defect in the existing law will, as often as not, be statutory: section 8(1) of the Administration of Justice Act 1973, to take but one example, remedies the mischief not suppressed by section 36 of the Administration of Justice Act 1970.[95] (Often, moreover, the point

---

[92] See further L. H. LaRue, 'Statutory Interpretation: Lord Coke Revisited' (1987) 48 *Univ. Pittsburgh L. Rev.* 733 at 748–9, 753.

[93] See, e.g., *Salkeld* v. *Johnson* (1848) 2 Ex. 256, 273 *per* Pollock CB ('the words of the statute … we are to … modify or alter so far as it may be necessary to avoid some manifest absurdity or incongruity, but no further. It is proper also to consider the state of the law which it proposes or purports to alter, the mischiefs which existed, and which it was intended to remedy, and the nature of the remedy provided … These are the proper modes of ascertaining the intention of the legislature'). Consider also Alderson B's explanation of the golden rule (considered in the last chapter) in *A-G* v. *Lockwood* (1842) 9 M. & W. 378, 398.

[94] *Ealing LBC* v. *Race Relations Board* [1972] AC 342 (HL), 368 (*per* Lord Kilbrandon).

[95] The 1970 Act accorded courts a discretion to postpone an order for possession of property on which a mortgagor had defaulted if he or she was likely to be able to pay 'any sums due' within a reasonable period. Since mortgage default clauses at that time usually stated that failure to repay two successive instalments made the mortgagor liable to repay the

of enacting legislation is not to remedy any sort of legal mischief but to create a regulatory platform that previously did not exist – a Welsh Assembly Government,[96] say, or a Serious Organized Crime Agency,[97] or a new Supreme Court.[98])

In 1969, the English and Scottish Law Commissions contended that the term 'mischief' is archaic and that courts would do better to refer instead to 'general legislative purpose'.[99] But a statutory purpose equates not with a mischief but with a remedy for a mischief.[100] This is not to claim that the concept of mischief, as used in the context of statutory interpretation, is unproblematic. The main difficulty with mischief-oriented statutory construction concerns not the identification of the mischief to be remedied – though this certainly can be a difficulty given, first, that statutory provisions do not always aim at just one mischief and, secondly, that statutes do not normally refer explicitly to the law that they overturn[101] – but the application of a statute to a mischief which the enacting legislature never had any intention of remedying. Appeals have regularly been upheld in recent years, to take but one example, against decisions supporting senior police officers' reliance on sections 12 and 14 of the Public Order Act 1986. The appeals have tended to be successful where the statutory provisions have been relied on to deal with purported mischiefs which they do not address: section 14(1)(a), for instance, allows for the imposition of conditions on, or dispersal of, not *any* public assembly, but only those at which there is reason to believe that there may be 'serious public disorder, serious damage to property or serious disruption to the life of the community'.[102] The general interpretive difficulty is easily exaggerated. Certainly

---

entire loan, the Act provided scant protection on default. So parliament determined in the 1973 Act that 'any sums due' applies to the mortgage arrears rather than to the entire loan.

[96] Government of Wales Act 1998.

[97] Serious Organized Crime and Police Act 2005, s. 1.

[98] Constitutional Reform Act 2005, part 3.

[99] The Law Commission and the Scottish Law Commission, *The Interpretation of Statutes*, Law Com. No. 21; Scot. Law Com. No. 11 (London: HMSO, 1969), para. 32 n. 78 and para. 81 n. 177.

[100] See F. A. R. Bennion, *Statutory Interpretation: A Code*, 5th edn (London: Butterworths, 2008), 922–3.

[101] Though it may be perfectly clear what the offending law is. The primary purpose of the Housing Repairs and Rents Act 1954, s. 41, was 'no doubt … to reverse the decision in *Cow* v. *Casey* [1949] 1 KB 474', Lord Reid observed in *Maunsell* v. *Olins* [1975] AC 373 (HL), 382. Nevertheless, s. 41 (now repealed) made no explicit reference to *Cow* v. *Casey*.

[102] See, e.g., *R (on the application of Moos)* v. *Commissioner of Police of the Metropolis* [2011] EWHC 957 (Admin); *Austin* v. *Commissioner of Police of the Metropolis* [2007] EWCA

there is the danger that an interpreter determines that a mischief to which a statute is to be applied is one to which the enacting legislature would not have wanted it applied. But this possibility does not warrant the conclusion that the mischief rule must undercut the intentions of an enacting legislature more readily than do the other main conventions of statutory construction. Judicial legislation might be the outcome when a court purports to remedy the mischief, or revive the legislature, or remove absurdity from the text – or even, occasionally, when its effort to give statutory language its plain meaning misfires.

3   Modern equity

Contemporary jurists have quite often assumed that the mischief rule is to be used specifically when the language of a statute is ambiguous.[103] This assumption is certainly understandable. It would be unusual for a judge in the modern era – because of the rise, from the eighteenth century onwards, of the plain-meaning approach to interpretation – to seek out the mischief which is to be remedied by a statute before determining if the language of the text carries a meaning which any reasonable person would ascribe to it. '[T]here is no rule of construction which authorises a Judge, when the remedy is complete, and the enactment is distinct and clear ... to limit its operation to the particular mischief', Pollock CB observed in 1852. 'This is in truth to legislate, not to construe.'[104] But this could not be described as Coke's view. He was concerned with 'the sure and true interpretation of all statutes'; the statutory provision at the centre of *Heydon's Case*, moreover, was not ambiguous – the Barons of the Exchequer could easily have interpreted 'any estate or interest for life' on its plain meaning and declared that the language did not extend to a copyhold revocable at will.

But then why might anyone have reason to resort to the mischief rule where the meaning of statutory language is clear? Sometimes, a court will consider that the language of a statute yields a plain meaning but that to give the statute that meaning, or only that meaning, will result in it failing to suppress the mischief as the enacting legislature must have

---

Civ. 989; *R (on the application of Laporte)* v. *Chief Constable of Gloucestershire* [2006] UKHL 55.

[103] See, e.g., J. H. Baker, *An Introduction to English Legal History*, 4th edn (London: Butterworths, 2002), 212; D. J. Gifford and John Salter, *How to Understand an Act of Parliament* (London: Cavendish, 1996), 79.

[104] *Miller* v. *Salomons*, 552.

wanted it suppressed. So it is that cases in which the mischief rule takes effect are quite often ones where the meaning of the statutory language is not ambiguous, but the court – recognizing that a complex and changing world can outmanoeuvre any enacted text – considers the language to be unsuited to making a determination in accordance with what might reasonably be regarded as legislative intent.[105] The mischief principle also occasionally functions so as to tease out the fact that the legislature really did mean what it plainly enacted. The Misuse of Drugs Act 1971, section 5(1), is hardly ambiguous: 'it shall not be lawful for a person to have a controlled drug in his possession'. In *Boyesen*, the respondent was charged with unlawful possession of five milligrams of cannabis resin – an amount so minute as to be unusable as a controlled drug. Did the statute make it unlawful to possess any quantity of a controlled drug, or a usable quantity? Counsel for the respondent argued that if the statute were interpreted according to the mischief it was designed to remedy, possession of a controlled drug had to mean possession of a usable quantity. But the House of Lords applied the statute on its plain meaning, so determining that it prohibited the possession of a controlled drug in any quantity, on the basis that to exempt the possession of miniscule quantities would have left outside the scope of the statute at least one instance of the mischief it was intended to suppress: the case in which a defendant accumulated quantities of a controlled substance but sought to avoid prosecution by transporting the substance only in minute amounts.[106]

It is not inconceivable that a statute's language could be garbled, or incomplete, thus making it impossible for the interpreter to be confident that any meaning attributed to the statute would correspond with the legislature's intentions in enacting it. But such instances are highly unusual. Even when judges do declare their exasperation with egregious drafting, they still usually settle on some method by which to apply the

---

[105] See, e.g., *Nokes* v. *Doncaster Amalgamated Collieries* [1940] AC 1014 (HL), 1051 (*per* Lord Porter); the entire opinion of Lord Evershed in *Baker* v. *Sims* [1959] 1 QB 114 (CA), 118–30; and, more generally, Jim Evans, 'Reading Down Statutes', in *The Statute: Making and Meaning*, ed. R. Bigwood (Wellington: LexisNexis, 2004), 123–52 at 132–5, 151–2 (on 'outweighing exceptions' cases).

[106] See *R* v. *Boyesen* [1982] AC 768 (HL), 777 *per* Lord Scarman ('the view that possession is only serious enough, as a matter of legal policy, to rank as an offence if the quantity possessed is itself capable of being misused is a highly dubious one. Small quantities can be accumulated. It is a perfectly sensible view that the possession of any quantity, which is visible, tangible, measurable, and "capable of manipulation" … is a serious matter to be prohibited if the law is to be effective against trafficking in dangerous drugs and their misuse').

statute – drawing inferences as to the mischief, relying on an established interpretive presumption, according words secondary meanings, reading words into or out of the text and so on – rather than admit defeat and put it to one side.[107] The mischief rule would, in fact, be of no use in the case of the genuinely meaningless statute, because it would be impossible to interpret the statute by reference to the mischief it was meant to suppress. When judges resort to the mischief rule, it is usually either because the statutory language, though admitting of a plain meaning, does not satisfactorily represent the intentions of the legislature or, more commonly, because the ambiguity of the language makes it impossible to state with confidence what the legislature's specific enacting intentions were. As we saw in Chapter 5, even when judges are convinced that a statute yields a plain meaning they may discover that other judges believe it offers up a very different plain meaning. It is, typically, in these instances, when judges seek out plain statutory meaning in vain, that the interpretive conventions associated with Coke – and with Plowden – rise to the surface.

Precisely how have these conventions endured? Before enquiring into their fate in English law, it is worth looking to the United States, where the conventions – though they have proved influential – have been received rather differently. During the nineteenth and twentieth centuries, Coke's reasoning in *Heydon's Case* was cited approvingly in American courtrooms on a fairly regular basis.[108] In 1942, Max Radin 'recast' the mischief rule in the terminology of general legislative purpose 'to serve a modern need' (though he did not spell out what that need was).[109] Henry Hart and Albert Sacks, in their famous *Legal Process* teaching materials, also considered the rule to be the epitome of purposive statutory construction.[110]

---

[107] See Cross, *Statutory Interpretation*, 48–105.

[108] See, e.g., *SEC v. Brennan* 230 F.3d 65, 79 (2d Cir. 2000); *Elliot Coal Mining Co. v. Office of Workers' Compensation Programs*, 17 F.2d 616, 631 (3d Cir. 1994); *Keystone Insurance Co. v. Houghton*, 863 F.2d 1125, 1128 (3d Cir. 1988); *Pittston Stevedoring Corp. v. Dellaventura*, 544 F.2d 35, 51 (2d Cir. 1976); *Pierson v. Ray*, 386 US 547, 561 (1967) (Douglas J, dissenting); *Hamilton v. Rathbone*, 175 US 414, 419 (1899); *Smith v. Townsend*, 148 US 490, 494 (1893); *Winder v. Caldwell*, 55 US 434, 437 (1852); *Bank of US v. Lee*, 38 US 107, 118 (1839).

[109] See Max Radin, 'A Short Way With Statutes' (1942) 56 *Harvard L. Rev.* 388, 421–2. Similarly James Willard Hurst, *Dealing with Statutes* (New York: Columbia University Press, 1982), 41 ('the general approach in *Heydon's case* (1584) is still timely … [b]ut to grasp the full reality of its impact we should see it as part of a flow of policy-making activity').

[110] See Henry M. Hart, Jr and Albert M. Sacks, *The Legal Process: Basic Problems in the Making and Application of Law* (1958), ed. W. N. Eskridge and P. P. Frickey (Westbury, NY: Foundation Press, 1994), 1111, also 1125.

Modern American lawyers and judges have, as it were, seen attraction in mischief much as have their English counterparts. But the legacy of equitable statutory interpretation in the United States is different, for it is not Coke's method but Plowden's which has met with more enthusiasm.

It was suggested earlier that Plowden's proposal that we imagine the legislator to be on hand to take questions when interpreting an ambiguous statute invites a comparison with Aristotle. But American lawyers might be inclined to draw a more immediate comparison with Learned Hand,[111] or Richard Posner,[112] or Hart and Sacks,[113] or even John Chipman Gray.[114] Indeed, many American lawyers will simply associate the proposal with 'imaginative reconstruction', one of the main interpretive approaches utilized by twentieth-century US courts and agencies in instances when the interpretation of a statutory text according to its plain meaning proves impossible or undesirable. The approach is illustrated in the well-known early twentieth-century case of *Riggs* v. *Palmer*, in which a legatee under a will, to ensure his inheritance, murdered the testator. The relevant statute on testamentary dispositions suggested that,

---

[111] See *Guiseppi* v. *Walling*, 144 F.2d 608, 624 (2d Cir. 1944) (Hand J, concurring) ('As nearly as we can, we must put ourselves in the place of those who uttered the words, and try to define how they would have dealt with the unforseen situation; and, although their words are by far the most decisive evidence of what they would have done, they are by no means final'); *Lehigh Valley Coal Co.* v. *Yensavage*, 218 F. 547, 553 (2d Cir. 1914) (Hand J.); *NLRB* v. *National Maritime Union*, 175 F.2d 686, 690 nn. 4 & 7 (2d Cir. 1949); *Usatorre* v. *The Victoria*, 172 F.2d 434, 439–41 (2d Cir. 1949); *Commissioner* v. *Beck's Estate*, 129 F.2d 243, 245 n. 4 (2d Cir. 1942); *Slifka* v. *Johnson*, 161 F.2d 467, 470 (2d Cir. 1947); Learned Hand, *The Spirit of Liberty: Papers and Addresses of Learned Hand*, 2nd edn I. Dillard (New York: Knopf, 1953), 106; also *Schwartz* v. *Mills*, 192 F.2d 727, 732–3 (2d Cir. 1951) (Frank J, dissenting); and William D. Popkin, *Statutes in Court: The History and Theory of Statutory Interpretation* (Durham, NC: Duke University Press, 1999), 138–9.

[112] See Richard A. Posner, 'Statutory Interpretation – in the Classroom and in the Courtroom' (1983) 50 *Univ. Chicago L. Rev.* 800, 817 ('The judge should try to think his way as best he can into the minds of the enacting legislators and imagine how they would have wanted the statute applied to the case at bar').

[113] See Hart and Sacks, *The Legal Process*, 1378 ('In determining the more immediate purpose which ought to be attributed to a statute … a court should try to put itself in imagination in the position of the legislature which enacted the measure'); also John Manning, 'What Divides Textualists and Purposivists?' (2006) 106 *Columbia L. Rev.* 70, 78 ('Hart-and-Sacks-style purposivists recognize that a judge's task, properly conceived, is not to seek actual legislative intent; rather, their method of interpretation poses the objective question of how a hypothetical "reasonable legislator" (as opposed to a real one) would have resolved the problem addressed by the statute').

[114] See John Chipman Gray, *The Nature and Sources of the Law*, 2nd edn (New York: Macmillan, 1921), 173 ('when the Legislature has had no meaning at all … what the judges have to do is … guess what it would have intended on a point not present to its mind, if the point had been present').

however the criminal law might apply to the legatee, the will would not be declared invalid, for '[n]o will in writing … shall be revoked … otherwise than by some other will in writing, or some other writing of the testator'.[115] Earl J, delivering the opinion of the majority of the New York Court of Appeals, explicitly drew on the Aristotelian notion of equitable construction to avoid according the statutory language its plain meaning and thereby allowing the legatee to inherit:

> The equitable construction which restrains the letter of a statute is defined by Aristotle as … *Aequitas est correctio legis generaliter latoe qua parte deficit* [Equity is the correction of that part of the law where it is deficient by reason of its generality]. If the law-makers could, as to this case, be consulted, would they say that they intended by their general language that the property of a testator or of an ancestor should pass to one who had taken his life for the express purpose of getting his property? … What could be more unreasonable than to suppose that it was the legislative intention in the general laws passed for the orderly, peaceable, and just devolution of property that they should have operation in favor of one who murdered his ancestor that he might speedily come into the possession of his estate? Such an intention is inconceivable.[116]

Imaginative reconstruction looks to be well suited to a case like *Riggs* v. *Palmer*, in which the relevant statute law is incomplete in the sense that it does not speak to the issue before the court – whether murderous legatees should be allowed to benefit from the principle that donative intentions should be honoured – yet it seems reasonable to infer that the legislature, were it now present, would prefer that the sense of the statute, to use Plowden's language, be more confined than the letter. Note, nevertheless, that the New York Court of Appeals was not united on this issue: 'the matter does not lie within the domain of conscience', Gray J reasoned in dissent, for '[w]e are bound by the rigid rules of law, which have been established by the legislature, and within the limits of which the determination of this question is confined … I think that a valid will must continue as a will always, unless revoked in the manner provided by the statutes'.[117] To allow the argument for the appellants to prevail,

---

[115] *Revised Statutes of the State of New York*, 3 vols., 7th edn (Albany: Banks & Bros, 1882), III, 2286.

[116] *Riggs* v. *Palmer*, 22 NE 188, 189–90 (NY 1889). In the nearest-comparable English case – *Re Sigsworth* [1935] Ch. 89 (in which a son killed his mother so as to take advantage of a statutory provision on intestacy which did not exempt murderous next-of-kin from survivorship) – Clauson J simply declared the relevant provision inapplicable on grounds of public policy (ibid. 92–3).

[117] *Riggs* v. *Palmer*, 191–2.

Woodworth J added, 'would involve the diversion by the court of the testator's estate into the hands of persons whom, possibly enough, for all we know, the testator might not have chosen or desired as its recipients'.[118] Soon after the decision in *Riggs*, much the same problem arose again in *Shellenberger* v. *Ransom*, in which the Supreme Court of Nebraska on first hearing followed Earl J's reasoning: 'had it been in the mind of the framers of our statute of descent that a case like this would arise under it', Cobb CJ remarked, 'they would have so framed the law that its letter would have left no hope for the obtaining of an inheritance by such means'.[119] But on rehearing, the Court had a change of heart: 'the horror and repulsion with which it may justly be supposed the framers of our statute would have viewed the crime and its consequences … is no justification … for assuming to supply legislation … which did not occur to the minds of those legislators by whom our statute of descent was framed. Neither the limitations of the civil law nor the promptings of humanity can be read into a statute from which, without question, they are absent, no matter how desirable the result to be attained may be.'[120] Imaginative reconstruction is unwarranted, according to this line of reasoning, because, whatever the motives of the judge might be, it is interpolation: the point of the imaginative exercise is not to discover meaning within the statute but to read into it a meaning which its language does not carry.

It might still be argued that if statutory enactment is understood to be a method by which the legislature communicates with judges, and if the legislature sometimes fails to communicate clearly (and can no longer be asked what it meant by its communication), judges may consider imaginative reconstruction to be the most sensible interpretive option. Richard Posner draws an analogy with a platoon commander who, in the course of an attack, finds his path blocked by an unexpected enemy pillbox. 'He has two choices: go straight ahead at the pillbox, or try to bypass it to the left. He radios the company commander for instructions. The commander replies, "Go – "; but the rest of the message is garbled. When

---

[118] Ibid. 192.

[119] *Shellenberger* v. *Ransom*, 47 NW 700, 704 (Neb. 1891).

[120] *Shellenberger* v. *Ransom*, 59 NW 935, 939 (Neb. 1894). Within a decade of its decision in *Riggs*, the New York Court of Appeals modified its ruling, holding that murderous heirs can indeed inherit by will or intestate succession, but that it is still possible to prevent their unjust enrichment by determining that they hold the inherited property for beneficiaries under a constructive trust. See *Ellerson* v. *Westcott*, 42 NE 540 (NY 1896); also James Barr Ames, 'Can a Murderer Acquire Title by His Crime and Keep it?' (1897) *American Law Register & Review* 225, 226–7.

the platoon commander radios back for clarification, he is unable to get through.'[121] It would be wrong for the platoon commander to do nothing, Posner reasons, since the part of the message that was received makes it clear that he was to get by the enemy pillbox, either by attacking it or bypassing it; whatever we imagine the company commander's instruction to be, we can be sure that it would have been one of these two options, and that he would have preferred the commander to take either rather than to let the attack fail. A court, like a platoon commander, has an obligation to interpret: it would be irresponsible to treat ambiguity as a reason not to decide – 'when the orders ... are unclear, this does not absolve them [*sc.*, judges or platoon commanders] from the responsibility for helping to make the enterprise succeed'.[122]

Were this a book about statutory interpretation in the United States, it would make sense to say much more about how judges and law professors there have both defended and attacked the concept of imaginative reconstruction. To defend the concept by drawing an analogy between military commands and statutory directives seems to invite the charge of oversimplification. Judges seeking to decode the intention behind a legislature's ambiguous order are likely to be guessing as to the preferred course of action not of a specific individual of whom they most likely have personal knowledge but of a large, diverse assembly, possibly from many years past. An ambiguous statutory communication, furthermore, could accommodate a range of possible options, some of which the legislature, were it available to be asked, might well consider less preferable than the court declining to apply the statute and deciding the case instead according to, say, established common-law principles; even the platoon commander might wonder if his superior wanted him neither to attack nor to bypass the pillbox but, perhaps so as not to risk endangering another field manoeuvre, to wait ('Go nowhere yet'). But to emphasize these criticisms would be to risk underestimating Posner's central, and important, point: that imaginative reconstruction – in the courtroom as on the battlefield – will sometimes simply be the best, though by no means the ideal, way of dealing with irreparably poor communications.

The judge imagining what the legislator would say were he available to clarify his position is – as Posner appreciates[123] – really imagining what

[121] Richard A. Posner, 'Legal Formalism, Legal Realism, and the Interpretation of Statutes and the Constitution' (1986) 37 *Case Western Reserve L. Rev.* 179, 189.
[122] Ibid. 190.
[123] See Richard A. Posner, *The Problems of Jurisprudence* (Cambridge, Mass.: Harvard University Press, 1990), 275–6.

he, the judge, would say were he that legislator. Convincingly distinguishing between what a judge genuinely assumes the legislator would have
wanted and what a judge would have wanted were he that legislator is
likely to prove difficult if not impossible, for 'the basic intellectual operation in such interpersonal comparisons is imaginative empathy. We
imagine ourselves to be in the shoes of another person, and ask ourselves
the question, "If I were now really in *his* position, and had *his* taste, *his* education, *his* social background, *his* cultural values, and *his* psychological
make-up, then what would now be *my* preferences between various alternatives …?"'[124] The central argument against imaginative reconstruction,
however, is not that it glides over the philosophical difficulty of imagining oneself as another, or even – recalling one of the standard objections
to the idea of legislative intent – that it really requires the interpreter to
imagine the likely intention not of a single legislator but of a large, polyphonous assembly. The argument, rather, is that imaginative reconstruction
is the interpretive approach preferred by judges who regard statutes as
base metals awaiting alchemy: that judges sometimes adopt the technique
not so as to render an unworkable statute workable, but, as in *Riggs* v.
Palmer, so as to make a workable but inconvenient statute work as they
want it to work. Even proponents of imaginative reconstruction tend to
appreciate the danger.[125]

When the term 'imaginative reconstruction' is used in modern English
courts, it usually denotes an unreliable account given in the witness box,
or an inappropriate method for working out how a patentee would have
defined her invention;[126] barely ever, certainly since the beginning of the
twentieth century, has a judge explicitly made of use of the method set
out by Aristotle and Plowden.[127] But this does not mean that the tradition of equitable statutory interpretation became irrelevant to English
law. It has been observed already that the mischief rule lives on to this
day, though it has undergone various alterations. One notable change has

---

[124] John C. Harsanyi, 'Morality and the Theory of Rational Behavior' (1977) 44 *Social Research* 623, 638. (Emphases in original.)

[125] See, e.g., Hand, *The Spirit of Liberty*, 106 ('When a judge tries to find out what the government would have intended which it did not say, he puts into its mouth things which he
thinks it ought to have said, and that is very close to substituting what he himself thinks
right. Let him beware, however, or he will usurp the office of government, even though
in a small way he must do so in order to execute its real commands at all').

[126] See, e.g., *Hewlett Packard GmbH* v. *Waters Corp.* [2002] IP & T 5 at [32] (Ch. D.); *Kuwait
Airways Corp.* v. *Iraqi Airways Co. (No. 11)* [2003] EWHC 31 (Comm) at [126].

[127] See, for a rare sighting, *Seaford Court Estates* v. *Asher* [1949] 2 KB 481 (CA), 499 (*per*
Denning LJ).

been that, in the second half of the twentieth century, the word 'mischief' came increasingly to be treated as synonymous with 'purpose'.[128] 'If one looks back to the actual decisions of th[e] House [of Lords] on questions of statutory construction over the past 30 years', Lord Diplock remarked in 1975, 'one cannot fail to be struck by the evidence of a trend away from the purely literal towards the purposive construction of statutory provisions.'[129] Three years later, he attempted, like Plowden and Coke before him, to invest this style of construction with some discipline and methodology. In doing so, he blended together the language of Coke and the modern language of purpose:

> I am not reluctant to adopt a purposive construction where to apply the literal meaning of the legislative language used would lead to results which would clearly defeat the purposes of the Act. But ... three conditions ... must be fulfilled in order to justify this course ... First, it was possible to determine from a consideration of the provisions of the Act read as a whole precisely what the mischief was that it was the purpose of the Act to remedy; secondly, it was apparent that the draftsman and Parliament had by inadvertence overlooked, and so omitted to deal with, an eventuality that required to be dealt with if the purpose of the Act was to be achieved; and thirdly, it was possible to state with certainty what were the additional words that would have been inserted by the draftsman and approved by Parliament had their attention been drawn to the omission before the Bill passed into law. Unless this third condition is fulfilled any attempt by a court of justice to repair the omission in the Act cannot be justified as an exercise of its jurisdiction to determine what is the meaning of a written law which Parliament has passed. Such an attempt crosses the boundary between construction and legislation.[130]

Diplock, it should be observed, takes the point of purposive construction to be not the resolution of statutory ambiguity, but the remedial modification of the text where the drafter has omitted something that

---

[128] See, e.g., *Kahn v. Newberry* [1959] 2 QB 1 (QBD), 9 (*per* Donovan J); *Shaw v. DPP* [1962] AC 220 (HL), 257 (*arguendo*); *Warner v. Metropolitan Police Commissioner* [1969] 2 AC 256 (HL), 266 (*arguendo*); *IRC v. Joiner* [1975] 1 WLR 1701 (HL), 1707 (*per* Lord Diplock); *Cartlidge v. Chief Adjudication Officer* [1986] QB 360 (CA), 376 (*per* Ralph Gibson LJ); *BBC Enterprises Ltd v. Hi-Tech Xtravision Ltd* [1990] Ch. 609 (CA), 619 (*per* Beldam LJ); *Horton v. Sadler* [2007] 1 AC 307 (HL), 322 (*per* Lord Bingham); *R (on the application of Al-Skeini) v. Secretary of State for Defence* [2008] 1 AC 153 (HL), 178 (*per* Lord Bingham).

[129] *Carter v. Bradbeer* [1975] 1 WLR 1204 (HL), 1206–7.

[130] *Jones v. Wrotham Park Settled Estates* [1980] AC 74 (HL), 105 (decided Dec. 1978).

clearly should have been included in it. Whether it must be possible to state with certainty what the words missing from the text are is debatable.[131] Since Diplock enumerated these three conditions, furthermore, at least one other appears to have been added: 'that before our courts can imply words into a statute the statutory intention must be plain and the insertion not too big, or too much at variance with the language in fact used by the legislature'.[132] Perhaps the most interesting question to consider about the conditions Diplock set out, however, is not whether they are all genuine conditions, or whether the list is exhaustive, but what is required if the conditions are to be satisfied. The judge confronted with the incompletely drafted text must identify the mischief that the statute is supposed to remedy, determine whether there has been a drafting omission and, if there has been an omission, be satisfied as to how the legislature would have proceeded had the omission not gone unnoticed. This information may well not be discoverable simply by reading the statute. But what else is a judge to do? Note, first, what Diplock would not have a judge do: imaginatively reconstruct legislative intention. It must be possible to 'determine' the mischief that the statute was supposed to remedy, the drafting omission must at least be 'apparent' and any judicial attempt to rectify that omission must be based not on conjecture but on what we can 'state with certainty' about what the legislature would have done had the omission been spotted at the time of enactment. Modern English purposivism certainly owes a debt to Coke, but, unlike American purposivism, it owes little to the tradition of Aristotle and Plowden. Rather than meet legislative gaps (or, for that matter, ambiguous statutory language) with imaginative reconstruction, English judges amenable to purposivism typically confine themselves to trying to *work out* what the legislature would have wanted – by looking to the entirety of the statute and, occasionally, to certain sources of information relevant but external to it.

---

[131] See *Inco Europe Ltd* v. *First Choice Distribution* [2000] 1 WLR 586 (HL), 592 *per* Lord Nicholls ('the court must be abundantly sure of three matters: (1) the intended purpose of the statute or provision in question; (2) that by inadvertence the draftsman and Parliament failed to give effect to that purpose in the provision in question; and (3) the substance of the provision Parliament would have made, although not necessarily the precise words Parliament would have used').

[132] *Western Bank Ltd* v. *Schindler*, 18 (*per* Scarman LJ). The reasoning is echoed in judicial observations on the interpretive obligation imposed by s. 3 of the Human Rights Act 1998: see section 6, below.

4   Il n'y a pas de hors-texte?

What are the sources to which judges might look? Consider, first of all, the preamble. We know already that, in the sixteenth century, parliament began to use preambles to signal the mischief that a statute was intended to suppress. Yet preambles, for all that contemporary judges sometimes wax wistfully about them,[133] are to be found only rarely in modern English statutes.[134] It is not obvious why this should be so. One possible explanation for the demise of the preamble is interpretive culture. A legislature which puts a premium on precise drafting is likely to accord less significance to preambles than one which expects its statutes to be interpreted by reference to their purposes. An example of the latter type of enactment is European Community legislation, in which preambles are a standard feature, and to which the European Court of Justice takes a 'teleological' approach irrespective of whether the text of the statute is incomplete or ambiguous. We saw in Chapter 2 that, in the 1950s, Lord Denning urged judges to adopt something close to this approach (though he did not advocate the purposive interpretation of even plainly worded enactments) and was duly rebuked by the House of Lords.[135] To English lawyers, he noted around the time that the United Kingdom joined the Common Market, the European approach to statutory drafting and interpretation was simply alien:

> How different is this Treaty [*sc.*, the Treaty of Rome]! It lays down general principles. It expresses its aims and purposes … But it lacks precision. It uses words and phrases without defining what they mean. An English lawyer would look for an interpretation clause, but he would look in vain. There is none. All the way through the Treaty there are gaps and lacunae.

[133] See, e.g., Lord Oliver, 'A Judicial View of Modern Legislation' (1993) 14 *Statute L. Rev.* 1, 10 ('I think that there is much to be said for statutes to be preceded by some statement of what Parliament is seeking to achieve … in the form of perhaps a return to the days of the preamble containing recitals'). Cf. *Making the Law: The Report of the Hansard Society Commission on the Legislative Process* (chair: Lord Rippon) (London: Hansard Society, 1993), para. 250 (recommending inclusion in statutes of notes on sections so as to aid purposive interpretation); also Cross, *Statutory Interpretation*, 201–3.

[134] Preambles tend to be used nowadays only 1) in private statutes, where parliament's intervention in what is by definition a private matter requires explanation, and 2) to recite the purpose of a treaty in statutes implementing treaty obligations. See Ian McLeod, *Principles of Legislative and Regulatory Drafting* (Oxford: Hart, 2009), 91.

[135] Cf. also Denning's eschewal of plain meaning in favour of purposive interpretation in *Nothman* v. *London Borough of Barnet* [1978] 1 All ER 1243 (CA), 1246 with Lord Russell's repudiation of his comments as 'sweeping' when the case was heard in the House of Lords: [1979] 1 All ER 142, 151.

These have to be filled in by the judges, or by Regulations or directives. It is the European way ... In case of difficulty, recourse is had to the preambles. These are useful to show the purpose and intent behind it all. But ... [t]he details are to be filled in by the judges ... English courts ... must follow the European pattern. No longer must they examine the words in meticulous detail. No longer must they argue about the precise grammatical sense. They must look to the purpose or intent ... They must divine the spirit of the Treaty and gain inspiration from it. If they find a gap, they must fill it as best they can.[136]

Common lawyers of this period may well have been surprised by 'the European way' with statutes, but they would have understood why preambles are not exceptional in EC legislation. Preambles, after all, were prevalent in English law in an era when parliament was similarly in the habit of enacting loosely drafted statutes which courts would often interpret, and which parliament knew courts would often interpret, according to their apparent purpose or 'spirit'. When, in the eighteenth century, legislative drafting became more granular, the value of the preamble waned.

But this is not the only possible explanation for the demise of the preamble in English statute law. Preambles in statutes are not worth the legislature's effort if courts stop placing any store in them. It appears that no modern judge has publicly declared the preamble otiose – though perhaps some judges have been concerned that courts might be less committed to determining the plain meaning of enacting provisions if there is a mischief-revealing preamble at hand.[137] Judicial estimation of the

---

[136] *Bulmer* v. *Bollinger* [1974] Ch. 401 (CA), 425–6. That statutory interpretation in European law should never have been wedded to the plain-meaning approach makes perfect sense when one considers that European Community obligations are implemented in multiple official languages: see *CILFIT Srl* v. *Ministero della Sanita (case 283/81)* [1983] 1 CMLR 472, 490 paras 18–19 ('[I]t must be borne in mind that Community legislation is drafted in several languages and that the different language versions are all equally authentic ... It must also be borne in mind, even where the different language versions are entirely in accord with one another, that Community law uses terminology which is peculiar to it. Furthermore, it must be emphasised that legal concepts do not necessarily have the same meaning in Community law and in the law of the various member-States').

[137] See *Powell* v. *Kempton Park Racecourse Co. Ltd* [1899] AC 143 (HL), 185 *per* Lord Davey ('[T]he preamble is a key to the statute, and affords a clue to the scope of the statute when the words construed by themselves without the aid of the preamble are fairly capable of more than one meaning. There is, however, another rule or warning which cannot be too often repeated, that you must not create or imagine an ambiguity in order to bring in the aid of the preamble or recital'); though cf. *A-G* v. *Prince Ernest Augustus of Hanover* [1957] AC 436 (HL), 463 *per* Viscount Simonds ('To say ... that you may not call in aid the preamble in order to create an ambiguity in effect means very little ... [T]his rule ... is better stated by saying that the context of the preamble is not to influence the meaning otherwise ascribable to the enacting part unless there is a compelling reason for it').

preamble has, nevertheless, diminished somewhat: the predominant modern view – the formation of which can be traced back at least to the early eighteenth century[138] – is that since preambles belong to the descriptive rather than to the operative or law-making portion of a statute,[139] they cannot have the same weight as enacting provisions and so are at best aids to construction when those provisions are ambiguous.[140] Perhaps parliament has gradually formed the conclusion that drafting a preamble for a statute rarely warrants the effort required.

Statutes have, in any event, other integral features – the long title or the recital with which a statute opens, the schedules and even the basic interpretive provisions – which will sometimes help, much as a preamble might help, those seeking to identify a mischief. Not that any of these features is of value to only one type of interpreter. As we have seen already, the judge who is intent on giving statutory language its plain meaning is likely, and certainly ought, to interpret that language in context, and so is in principle no different from the purpose-oriented judge in considering titles, preambles, schedules, interpretive clauses and other elements of statutes besides their enacting provisions to be potentially relevant to how they are interpreted.[141] Nor would it be correct to claim that plain-meaning advocates and purposivists are divided over whether sources outside the statute can be consulted for guidance, for there are some such sources – statutes *in pari materia* and interpretations of statutes established by judicial precedent are examples – which judges of all interpretive persuasions tend to regard as legitimate aids to construction. Furthermore, since the late nineteenth century (it was not always thus)[142] the courts have been

---

[138] See *Mills* v. *Wilkins* (1706) 6 Mod. 62, 62 *per* Holt CJ ('[T]he preamble of a statute is no part thereof, but contains generally the motives or inducements thereof'); also John R. Rood, 'Interpretation of Statutes' (1921) 13 *Modern American Law* 1, 7–8.

[139] See *A-G* v. *Prince Ernest Augustus of Hanover*, 475 (*per* Lord Somervell).

[140] See, e.g., *Powell* v. *Kempton Park Racecourse Co. Ltd* [1897] 2 QB 242 (CA), 285 (*per* Rigby LJ); *The Cairnbahn* [1914] P 25 (CA), 29–30 (*per* Sir Samuel Evans); *The Norwhale* [1975] QB 589 (QBD), 594–5 (*per* Brandon J); though cf. *A-G* v. *Prince Ernest Augustus of Hanover*, 460–1 *per* Viscount Simonds ('[T]he bald general proposition that where the enacting part of a statute is clear and unambiguous, it cannot be cut down by the preamble … I wish … to … dissent from … if it means that I cannot obtain assistance from the preamble in ascertaining the meaning of the relevant enacting part').

[141] See *A-G* v. *Prince Ernest Augustus of Hanover*, 461 (*per* Viscount Simonds); though cf. *Ellerman Lines* v. *Murray* [1931] AC 126, where, because the language of the applicable provision was unambiguous, the House of Lords refused to refer to either the statute's preamble or to its schedule.

[142] See *Re Dean of York* (1841) 2 QB 1, 34 (*per* Lord Denman CJ); *Salkeld* v. *Johnson* (1848) 2 Exch. 256, 273 (*per* Pollock CB).

willing to consult law commission reports, green papers, white papers and other official documents prepared as background to a statute under interpretation in order to ascertain the mischief the statute was intended to cure[143] – though, until quite recently, the tendency was to balk at using such materials to establish what parliament meant by the language it used to put the cure into effect.[144] It is tempting to assume that an interpretation of a statute according to the meaning of its language (allowing for a presumption against absurdity) must be confined to the four corners of the text, and that what distinguishes those who consider themselves constrained to take this approach and those who are prepared to construe a statute by reference to the mischief it was intended to remedy is a willingness to take account of information relating but extraneous to the statute when interpreting it. But this is simplistic. It is difficult to see how anyone could genuinely believe that everything outside a statute must be considered irrelevant to its interpretation.

There is, nevertheless, one source of information which many judges, certainly English judges, have traditionally preferred not to take into account when interpreting statutes: legislative history. In 1919, François Gény, a civilian jurist who opposed judicial efforts at statutory updating

---

[143] See, e.g., *Eastman Photographic Materials* v. *Comptroller-General of Patents, Designs and Trademarks* [1898], 575 (*per* Lord Halsbury LC); *Assam Railways & Trading Co. Ltd* v. *IRC* [1935] AC 445 (HL), 456–7 *per* Lord Wright ('[O]n principle no such evidence [*sc.*, 'certain recommendations from a Report of a Royal Commission on Income Tax in 1920'] for the purpose of showing the intention, that is the purpose or object, of an Act is admissible; the intention of the Legislature must be ascertained from the words of the statute with such extraneous assistance as is legitimate'); *Pillai* v. *Mudanayake* [1953] AC 514 (PC), 528 (*per* Lord Oaksey).

[144] This step appears first to have been taken in *R* v. *Secretary of State for Transport, ex p. Factortame Ltd (No. 1)* [1990] 2 AC 85, where a Law Commission report, or rather parliament's having pointedly not implemented one of the recommendations in the report, was relied on by the House of Lords to draw an inference regarding specific legislative intention. See in particular ibid. 149–50 (*per* Lord Bridge). Cf. *Letang* v. *Cooper* [1965] 1 QB 232 (CA), 240 (*per* Lord Denning MR); *Black-Clawson* v. *Papierwerke Waldhof-Aschaffenburg*, 629 *per* Lord Wilberforce ('[I]t is not proper or desirable to make use of such a document as a committee or commission report, or for that matter of anything reported as said in Parliament, or any official notes on clauses, for a direct statement of what a proposed enactment is to mean or of what the committee or commission thought it means'), 637 *per* Lord Diplock ('It is for the court and no one else to decide what words in a statute mean. What the committee thought they meant is, in itself, irrelevant. Oral evidence by members of the committee as to their opinion of what the section meant would plainly be inadmissible. It does not become admissible by being reduced to writing').

and imaginative reconstruction,[145] suggested that 'the record preliminary to a statute should not be received as an authoritative illustration of the text … unless the ideas one discovers in it have been expressed without notable contradiction, under conditions making it possible to attribute them to the best remembered collective will which created the statute, and with the additional proviso that the text of the statute does not repudiate these complementary explanations'.[146] English judges, on the very rare occasions when they made use of legislative history between the mid seventeenth and late twentieth centuries, tended to be similarly judicious. Lord Westbury interpreted the Bankruptcy Act 1861 by drawing attention to words removed from the bill during its amendment: the alterations, he contended, supported the conclusion that the statute did not extend to bankruptcy commissioners a wide discretionary power to refuse bankrupts an order of discharge, but rather permitted such orders only where one of the offences set out in section 159 of the Act had been committed.[147] In the Court of Chancery in 1678, Lord Nottingham seemed to be taking English law back to the era of Hengham CJ (see Chapter 1) when he determined that a fraud statute was not to be interpreted as applying retrospectively because 'I had some reason to know the meaning of this law; for it had its first rise from me, who brought in the bill into the Lords' House'.[148]

Instances of legislative history being put to cautious use in English courts between the mid seventeenth and late twentieth centuries are exceptional. What was to become the standard, and strict, convention concerning reliance on such history was established the year after Lord Nottingham had sought to revive the interpretive casualness of the early fourteenth century.

---

[145] See François Gény, *Méthode d'interprétation et sources in droit privé positif: Essai Critique*, 2nd edn, 2 vols. (Paris: LGDJ, 1954 [1919]), I, 269 ('Without taking account of modifications which have come about unexpectedly within general conceptions or the facts of social life, [the legislator] should always interpret … by referring to the very origin or the statute'), 301 ('… I think the first thing to banish from the legitimate sphere of statutory interpretation is any search with the intention of discovering not the expressed and effective intent of the legislator, but what he *would have* decided had he directed his thoughts to this object').

[146] Ibid. 295.

[147] *Re Mew and Thorne* (1862) 31 LJ Bk 87.

[148] *Asll* v. *Abdy* (1678) 3 Swans. 664, 664. The fact that the Court of King's Bench had very recently reached the same conclusion about the statute 'I was glad to hear of', Lord Nottingham added, 'but … if they had adjudged it otherwise, I should not have altered my opinion' (ibid. 665).

'The sense and meaning of an Act of Parliament must be collected from what it says when passed into a law', Willes J stated in 1769, 'and not from the history of changes it underwent in the house where it took its rise.'[149] Over the next two centuries, this convention – which came to be known as the exclusionary rule – was judicially affirmed on a fairly regular basis.[150]

Only late in the twentieth century did court practice begin to change. In 1978, Lord Denning rather cheekily subverted the exclusionary rule by relying on academic commentary informed by legislative history: 'I hope ... that our teachers will go on quoting *Hansard*', he remarked, 'so that a judge may in this way have the same help as others have in interpreting a statute.'[151] Although statements in parliament cannot be relied on to determine legislative intent, Widgery LJ had opined in the Court of Appeal a year earlier, it is legitimate to consult them for evidence of government policy.[152] This position was supported in 1980 by a House of Commons resolution that parliamentary proceedings might be referred to in court for the purpose of ascertaining policy, without the need for a formal petition to the House seeking leave to refer.[153] The House of Lords (in its judicial role) began to hint at a retreat from the exclusionary rule in the late 1980s, first of all by determining that, when interpreting statutory instruments 'not subject to the Parliamentary process of consideration and amendment in Committee', it is 'entirely legitimate for the purpose of ascertaining the intention of Parliament to take into account the terms in which the draft was presented by the responsible Minister and which formed the basis of its acceptance'.[154] Goff LJ had already concluded in the Court of Appeal that reliance on *Hansard* to interpret statutory instruments is permissible if the information to be found therein makes their purpose 'absolutely plain'.[155] In 1990, Hoffman J extended the reasoning

---

[149] *Millar* v. *Taylor* (1769) 4 Burr. 2303, 2332.

[150] See, e.g., *R* v. *Hertford College* (1878) LR 3 QBD 693 (CA), 707 *per* Lord Coleridge CJ ('The statute is clear, and the parliamentary history of a statute is wisely inadmissible to explain it').

[151] *R* v. *Local Commissioner for Administration for the N & E Area of England, ex p. Bradford CC* [1979] QB 287 (CA), 311.

[152] See *R* v. *Secretary of State for the Home Department, ex p. Hosenball* [1977] 1 WLR 766, 775.

[153] See HC Debs, 5th ser., vol. 975, cols. 167–97 (3 December 1979); HC Debs, 5th ser., vol. 991, cols. 879–916 (31 October 1980). See also David Miers, 'Citing Hansard as an Aid to Interpretation' (1983) 4 *Statute L. Rev.* 98; and, for examples of this type of referral, *Re Findlay* [1985] AC 318 (HL); *R* v. *Secretary of State for the Home Department, ex p. Cheblak* [1991] 1 WLR 890 (CA).

[154] *Pickstone* v. *Freemans plc* [1989] AC 66, 112 (*per* Lord Keith).

[155] *Conerney* v. *Jacklin* (CA), 25 January 1985, reported in *The Times*, 2 February 1985, 8.

to primary legislation: legislative history, he remarked, could be consulted for the purpose of affirming the mischief that a statute (in this case, the Shops Act 1950) was supposed to remedy much as could white papers and other pre-enactment committee reports.[156] Soon afterwards, in *ex parte Brind*, the House of Lords relied on clarifying statements in parliamentary debates to determine that the Secretary of State had not exceeded the limits of his discretion under section 29 of the Broadcasting Act 1981.[157]

The statements referred to in *Brind* were only considered relevant to the application for judicial review of ministerial action; they were not used to determine the meaning of the statutory language. But this final, decisive step away from the exclusionary rule was not long coming. The tale of what was to happen next has been thoroughly documented by legal commentators, and for the purposes of this study the complicated facts might be simplified. A schoolmaster at an expensive private college was entitled, as an employee, to take the benefit of a concessionary fee scheme, meaning that his son could be educated at the college at just one fifth of the cost charged to regular parents. Under section 61 of the Finance Act 1976, the schoolmaster was liable to pay tax on the 'cash equivalent' of the benefit provided by his employer. The Inland Revenue calculated the cash equivalent of the benefit to be a proportion of the total cost of running the school, whereas the schoolmaster objected that the cash equivalent should be calculated in line with the marginal cost of providing additional places under the concessionary fee scheme. Which was it to be?

The Court of Appeal decided the schoolmaster should be taxed on a proportion of the total cost, as, in November 1991, did the House of Lords. But in February the following year, four of the five Law Lords who had heard the appeal indicated that they wanted the case re-argued before a panel of seven lords so as to determine if the precedent should be overruled. Those who called for the re-hearing did so because their attention had since been

---

[156] See *Stoke-on-Trent CC* v. *B & Q plc* [1991] Ch. 48 (Ch. Div.), 66 ('[I]n the exceptional case in which the court is concerned with the purpose of the legislation rather than its construction, consultation of Hansard is permitted'). The possibility was entertained hypothetically by Lord Simon in *Dockers' Labour Club and Institute Ltd* v. *Race Relations Board* [1976] AC 285 (HL), 299 (decided 1974), though it was explicitly rejected the following year by the Renton Committee: *The Preparation of Legislation: Report of a Committee Appointed by the Lord President of the Council* (Chair: Sir David Renton, MP) (Cmnd 6053, London: HMSO, 1975), para. 19.19. See also *Owens Bank Ltd* v. *Bracco* [1992] 2 AC 443, 488 (*per* Lord Bridge), although in this instance the legislative history was referred to because it left 'no room for doubt' (ibid.) about the interpretation on which the House of Lords had already settled.

[157] *R* v. *Secretary of State for the Home Department, ex p. Brind* [1991] 1 AC 696.

drawn to a passage in *Hansard* which showed that the Financial Secretary
to the Treasury Committee intended, at the time that the Finance Bill was
going through parliament, that someone in the schoolmaster's circumstances should be taxed on the marginal cost created by admitting extra
pupils under the concessionary fee scheme. The enlarged panel attached
considerable importance to what the Financial Secretary had said, revers-
ing its first decision and interpreting the statutory provision in favour of
the taxpayer. In 1892, the United States Supreme Court determined that
it could consult legislative history to ascertain the meaning of ambiguous
statutory language.[158] One century later, in *Pepper* v. *Hart*, the House of
Lords had determined the same.[159]

5   Negotiating legislative history

We have seen already how Plowden and Coke set out interpretive conventions which entail no commitment to deriving legislative intent from
statutory language but which – perhaps precisely because they do not fix
on statutory language – emphasize specific constraining methods and
criteria (imaginative reconstruction, identification of the mischief to be
remedied) that, if taken seriously, might lessen the likelihood of statutes
being made to mean what an interpreter would like them to mean. The
majority in *Pepper* v. *Hart* was similarly of the view that the construction
of a statute on the basis of a source other than the enacted text – a source
which might amount to nothing more than an off-the-cuff ministerial
statement in a parliamentary debate – has to be disciplined.

Indeed, the case marked the relaxation of the exclusionary rule, but it
by no means put an end to it. References to parliamentary material (cop-
ies of which, it was confirmed soon after the decision, counsel would have
to supply to the court and the other parties in advance)[160] were held to be
permissible only in instances:

(a) 'where the expression of the legislative intention is genuinely ambiguous or obscure or where a literal or *prima facie* construction leads to a

---

[158] *Holy Trinity Church* v. *United States*, 143 US 457 (1892). 'Legislative history' meaning, at
this point, legislative committee reports. It would be another thirty years or so before US
courts began to look at floor statements made by individual legislators: for a summary of
how the practice of consulting legislative history developed, see *Wright* v. *Vinton Branch
of the Mountain Trust Bank of Roanoke*, 300 US 440, 463 n. 8 (1937).

[159] *Pepper (Inspector of Taxes)* v. *Hart* [1993] AC 593 (decided November 1992).

[160] See *Practice Note (Procedures: reference to Hansard)* [1995] 1 All ER 234.

manifest absurdity and where the difficulty can be resolved by a clear statement directed to the matter in issue';[161] and

(b) 'where the very issue of interpretation which the courts are called on to resolve has been addressed in Parliamentary debate and where the promoter of the legislation has made a clear statement directed to that very issue';[162] and

(c) 'where ... the material relied upon consists of one or more statements by a Minister or other promoter of the Bill together if necessary with such other Parliamentary material as is necessary to understand such statements and their effect'.[163]

Although the House of Lords made it clear in *Pepper* v. *Hart* that legislative history had to be used sparingly and cautiously, it seemed somewhat uncomfortable with its precedent and gradually reined it in.[164] 'The ... ruling is sound in principle, removing as it did a self-created judicial anomaly', Lord Nicholls observed in 2006, and so 'it would be unfortunate if ... [it] were now to be sidelined'; nevertheless, he added, the ruling 'is currently under something of a judicial cloud'.[165]

That cloud was partly of his making,[166] though his reservations had been compounded principally by what Lord Steyn had to say about *Pepper* v. *Hart* in his H. L. A. Hart Memorial Lecture of May 2000.[167] Steyn had originally welcomed the decision, but had come to the conclusion that there was really only one situation in which the use of legislative history to determine the meaning of ambiguous statutory language was justified: that in which a court ought to be estopped from interpreting a statute in favour of one party because clear statements on the parliamentary record led the other party reasonably to believe, and detrimentally to act on the assumption, that the statute yielded a contrary interpretation. 'That is

---

[161] *Pepper* v. *Hart*, 620 (*per* Lord Oliver).

[162] Ibid. 617 (*per* Lord Bridge).

[163] Ibid. 640 (*per* Lord Browne-Wilkinson). See also his comment at ibid. 634: 'I cannot foresee that any statement other than the statement of the Minister or other promoter of the Bill is likely to meet these criteria.'

[164] See Stefan Vogenauer, 'A Retreat from *Pepper* v. *Hart*? A Reply to Lord Steyn' (2005) 25 *OJLS* 629, 639–51; also *Bocardo SA* v. *Star Energy UK Onshore Ltd* [2010] UKSC 35 at [43] (Lord Hope). Vogenauer makes the interesting point that the lower courts took to the precedent with comparative ease: see 'A Retreat from *Pepper* v *Hart*?', 641, 648.

[165] *R (on the application of Jackson)* v. *A-G* [2006] 1 AC 262 (HL), 291–2.

[166] See *R* v. *Secretary of State for the Environment, Transport and the Regions, ex p. Spath Holme* [2001] 2 AC 349 (HL), 399–400; *Wilson* v. *First County Trust Ltd (No. 2)* [2004] 1 AC 816 (HL), 840–1.

[167] Johan Steyn, '*Pepper* v *Hart*; A Re-examination' (2001) 21 *OJLS* 59.

what happened in *Pepper* v. *Hart*', Steyn observed, though 'that is not how the reasoning of the House ... was formulated.'[168] Today, *Pepper* v. *Hart* is very much confined to the estoppel scenario. Legislative history tends to be relied on in court for the purpose of statutory interpretation only when (a) the language of the enactment is ambiguous and is amenable to resolution by no other interpretive technique; (b) some statement by the minister or promoter of the bill clearly removes the ambiguity; (c) a citizen reasonably relies on what was stated; and (d) the statute is interpreted as meaning something contrary to what was stated, so that the citizen is disadvantaged.[169]

It might be argued that the House of Lords, by reining in its own carefully reasoned and confined departure from the exclusionary rule, was unduly timid. Yet it is not particularly surprising that the decision to relax the rule should have provoked considerable judicial agonizing, for, over many years, all sorts of arguments had been advanced for treating the rule as sacrosanct. One of these arguments – that it is a mistake to equate ministerial statements about a legislative proposal with what parliament intended in enacting the text which stemmed from the proposal – has been examined already in Chapter 4. In early opinions extolling the exclusionary rule, the records relating to parliamentary debates over old statutes – between 1803 and 1909, *Hansard* contained only summaries rather than comprehensive accounts of proceedings – are often considered about as reliable an historical testimony as the average French salon painting.[170]

---

[168] Ibid. 67. The analogy to estoppel is rough-and-ready. With estoppel, a defendant is prevented from taking some benefit owing to fact that he has made a (not necessarily precise or detailed) representation to the claimant which the claimant has reasonably relied on to her detriment, or because he allows the claimant to invest in his property and then changes his plans regarding that property in such a way as to diminish or defeat her reasonable expectations about the investment. In the case of ministerial statements, it is unlikely that there will exist the relationship or nexus as between claimant and defendant that exists in the typical estoppel scenario; for, unlike the instances of explicit and tacit representation that can give rise to estoppel claims, such statements are unlikely to be directed towards somebody specific.

[169] See *McDonnell* v. *Congregation of Christian Brothers Trustees* [2004] 1 AC 1101 (HL), 1116–7 (*per* Lord Steyn); also *R* v. *A (No. 2)* [2002] 1 AC 45 (HL), 79 *per* Lord Hope ('[T]his exercise is available for the purpose only of preventing the executive from placing a different meaning on words used in legislation from that which they attributed to those words when promoting the legislation in Parliament'); Vogenauer, 'A Retreat from *Pepper v Hart*?', 652–3.

[170] See, e.g., *Millar* v. *Taylor*, 2332–3; *A-G* v. *West Riding of Yorkshire CC* [1906] 2 KB 676 (CA), 716 *per* Farwell LJ ('we have only to deal with the construction of the Act as printed and published. That is the final word of the Legislature as a whole, and the antecedent

Whether or not the records are reliable, they are, like statutes, texts to be interpreted. Since a ministerial statement, even when expressed clearly, may be technical, ill considered, subsequently withdrawn or varied, or at odds with other statements to be found in the parliamentary debates, interpretations of the text could quite easily go awry.[171] A common modern objection to the relaxation of the rule – one which appears to have been voiced first by Lord Reid in 1967 – is that the likely costs to litigants and to the court system outweigh the possible benefits.[172] Others have worried that relaxation puts courts which decline to consider legislative history in the position of appearing to prejudge the case;[173] that judges who do countenance the history but question the reliability of a minister's or sponsor's statement may find themselves to be in breach of article 9 of the Bill of Rights;[174] that, in the absence of the rule, ministers and others might seek strategically to make statements in parliament so as to influence how a statute is interpreted;[175] that judges and counsel will try to render statutory language ambiguous if the legislative history points to the possibility of an interpretation which they prefer and which otherwise would not be feasible;[176] that courts which consider legislative history to be relevant to the interpretation of statutes could become 'merely a reflecting mirror' of what government has to say about legislative proposals;[177] that the meaning of a statute might be deemed inseparable from the predispositions

---

debates and subsequent statements of opinion or belief are not admissible. But they would be quite untrustworthy in any case'); also *The Interpretation of Statutes*, para. 56.

[171] See *Davis* v. *Johnson* [1979] AC 264 (HL), 349–50 (*per* Lord Scarman). This is particularly well illustrated, in relation to legislative history in the United States, by Adrian Vermeule, 'Legislative History and the Limits of Judicial Competence: The Untold Story of *Holy Trinity Church*' (1998) 50 *Stanford L. Rev.* 1833.

[172] *Beswick* v. *Beswick* [1968] AC 58 (HL), 74 (decided June 1967) ('For purely practical reasons we do not permit debates in either House to be cited: it would add greatly to the time and expense involved in preparing cases involving the construction of a statute if counsel were expected to read all the debates in *Hansard*, and it would often be impracticable for counsel to get access to at least the older reports of debates in Select Committees of the House of Commons; moreover, in a very large proportion of cases such a search, even if practicable, would throw no light on the question before the court').

[173] See Steyn, '*Pepper* v *Hart*', 66.

[174] i.e., that 'freedom of speech and debates or proceedings in Parliament ... not ... be impeached or questioned in any court or place out of Parliament'. This argument was comprehensively rejected in *Pepper* v. *Hart*.

[175] See, e.g., *Chartbrook Ltd* v. *Persimmon Homes Ltd* [2009] UKHL 38 at [38] (Lord Hoffmann).

[176] See Jim Evans, 'Controlling the Use of Parliamentary History' (1998) 18 *NZ Univ. L. Rev.* 1, 26–45.

[177] *Black-Clawson* v. *Papierwerke Waldhof-Aschaffenburg*, 629 (*per* Lord Wilberforce).

and values of those responsible for ensuring it was passed into law;[178] that drafters might, if only unconsciously, get into the habit of choosing their words less carefully than was the case when legislative history could not be relied on to interpret statutory language;[179] and that courts are relying on information which, by virtue of the circumstances of its production, is very likely untrustworthy.[180] Possibly the strongest argument in favour of the exclusionary rule is that to interpret statutes by reference to legislative history is to risk determining that past action incurred, at the time it was taken, a legal consequence which the actor could not have discovered. '[T]he need for legal certainty demands that the rules by which the citizen is to be bound ... be ascertainable ... by reference to identifiable sources that are publicly accessible', Lord Diplock remarked in *Fothergill* v. *Monarch Airlines* (1980).

> The source to which Parliament must have intended the citizen to refer is the language of the Act itself. These are the words which Parliament has itself approved as accurately expressing its intentions. If the meaning of those words is clear and unambiguous and does not lead to a result that is manifestly absurd or unreasonable, it would be a confidence trick by Parliament and destructive of all legal certainty if the private citizen could not rely upon that meaning but was required to search through all that had happened before and in the course of the legislative process in order to see whether there was anything to be found from which it could be inferred that Parliament's real intention had not been accurately expressed by the actual words that Parliament had adopted to communicate it to those affected by the legislation.[181]

While some of the arguments against the relaxation of the exclusionary rule were easily dispensed with in *Pepper* v. *Hart*, it ought to be kept in mind just how widespread, and how committed, support for the rule had been. In 1969 and 1975, official reports on statutes and statutory interpretation recommended that the rule be retained.[182] Five months before

---

[178] See, e.g., Johan Steyn, 'The Intractable Problem of the Interpretation of Legal Texts' (2003) 25 *Sydney L. Rev.* 5, 12–13.

[179] See Steyn, '*Pepper* v *Hart*', 66.

[180] See, e.g., J. A. Corry, 'The Use of Legislative History in the Interpretation of Statutes' (1954) 32 *Can. Bar Rev.* 624, 633 ('It is always sensible to appeal from Philip drunk to Philip sober. But to appeal from the carefully pondered terms of the statute to the hurly-burly of parliamentary debate is more like appealing from Philip sober to Philip drunk'); also Hurst, *Dealing with Statutes*, 54–5.

[181] *Fothergill* v. *Monarch Airlines* [1981] AC 251 (HL), 279–80 (decided July 1980).

[182] See *The Interpretation of Statutes*, paras 53–62; *The Preparation of Legislation*, paras 19.19 and 19.26.

Lord Diplock spoke up for the exclusionary rule in *Fothergill* v. *Monarch Airlines*, an interpretation bill aimed at (among other things) modifying the rule had been introduced into the lords unsuccessfully.[183] A second bill, put before the commons the following summer and devised with much the same objective, likewise fell on stony ground.[184] The use of external aids to construction in instances of statutory ambiguity was hardly unheard of in English courts in the early 1990s, it has been argued, and so *Pepper* v. *Hart* 'in some respects does not represent a radical departure from what ha[d] gone before'.[185] Yet that there was any sort of departure was quite remarkable, considering the accumulated common-law wisdom favouring the *status quo ante*.

Though certainly one might ask, with the benefit of hindsight, why the exclusionary rule should have endured as it did. Even before *Pepper* v. *Hart*, references to relevant extracts from parliamentary debates were provided at the head of the general notes to acts in the *Current Law Statutes* and elsewhere[186] (though, perhaps somewhat ironically, the 1976 *Current Law Statutes* carry no such references for the Finance Act). It was not unknown, furthermore, for judges to confess to looking at *Hansard* on the sly when statutory language confounded them.[187] That they should have done so is not surprising. After all, the prima facie case for looking to legislative history for the purposes of statutory interpretation is obvious enough: if it is accepted that legislative supremacy demands that courts try to establish as accurately as they can what is meant by the language that the legislature enacted, and if it is acknowledged that what is meant

---

[183] See HL Debs, 5th ser., vol. 405, col. 306 (13 February 1980).

[184] See HC Debs, 6th ser., vol. 6, col. 704 (12 June 1981); also F. A. R. Bennion, 'Another Reverse for the Law Commission's Interpretation Bill' (1981) 131 *New LJ* 840; Alec Samuels, 'The Interpretation of Statutes: No Change', *Law Soc. Gaz.*, 7 October 1982, 1252.

[185] Cross, *Statutory Interpretation*, 156.

[186] See Lord Lester, '*Pepper* v *Hart* Revisited' (1994) 15 *Statute L. Rev.* 10, 17.

[187] See, e.g., *Hadmor Productions* v. *Hamilton* [1983] 1 AC 191 (HL), 201 (*per* Lord Denning MR); also *Pepper* v. *Hart*, 618 (*per* Lord Griffiths); Lord Oliver, 'A Judicial View of Modern Legislation', 7; and HL Debs, 5th ser., vol. 418, col. 1346 (26 March 1981) (Lord Hailsham) ('It really is very difficult to understand what [the Parliamentary draftsmen] mean sometimes. I always look at *Hansard*, I always look at the Blue Books. I always look at everything I can in order to see what is meant and as I was a member of the House of Commons for a long time of course I never let on for an instant that I had read the stuff. I produced it as an argument of my own, as if I had thought of it myself. I only took the trouble because I could not do the work in any other way. As a matter of fact, I should like to let your Lordships into a secret. If you were to go upstairs and you were a fly on the wall in one of those judicial committees that we have up there, where distinguished members of the Bar … come to address us, you would be quite surprised how much we read … The idea that we do not read these things is quite rubbish').

by the language that the legislature enacted is ambiguous, then it makes sense at least to look to the statements of those responsible for promoting the bill to see if any of those statements clarify the mischief at which the legislative proposal was aimed and so stand as probative evidence of the statute's meaning. That clarifying legislative history is considered a valid source of information in instances where the meaning of the statutory language is ambiguous does not mean that it has to be a decisive source of information. The reason there is 'no constitutional impropriety' in counsel and judges having '[r]ecourse ... to white papers and official reports', Lord Browne-Wilkinson observed in *Pepper* v. *Hart*, is that they do not 'determine the meaning of the statutory words' but rather 'assist the court to make its own determination'.[188] Clear statements on the legislative record are likewise but an aid to construction.

> They are part of the legislative background, *but they are no more than this* ... Government statements, however they are made and however explicit they may be, cannot control the meaning of an Act of Parliament. As with other extraneous material, it is for the court, when determining what was the intention of Parliament in using the words in question, to decide how much importance, or weight, if any, should be attached to a Government statement. The weight will depend on all the circumstances.[189]

It is difficult to assess how much genuine support exists nowadays for the proposition that legislative history should never be allowed to have a bearing on the interpretation of a statute. Lord Mackay came close to this position in his dissent in *Pepper* v. *Hart*, though he stopped short of saying that he considered the relaxation of the exclusionary rule to be inconceivable under any circumstances.[190] Other senior judges have, since Lord Mackay's retirement from judicial service in 1997, reflected that his dissent may have been the voice of wisdom, given particularly that time spent by counsel sifting through legislative history seems so often to bring

---

[188] *Pepper* v. *Hart*, 640.
[189] *R* v. *Secretary of State for the Environment, ex p. Spath Holme*, 400 *per* Lord Nicholls (emphasis in original). He makes the point again in *Wilson* v. *First County Trust*, 843 ('[T]he courts must be careful not to ... give a ministerial statement, whether made inside or outside Parliament, determinative weight'). For a formulation of the argument in relation to statutory interpretation in the United States, see Adrian Vermeule, *Judging under Uncertainty: An Institutional Theory of Legal Interpretation* (Cambridge, Mass.: Harvard University Press, 2006), 30.
[190] 'I would certainly be prepared to agree the rule should no longer be adhered to', he observed, were it possible to guarantee that parties' legal advisers do not thereby become obligated 'to study *Hansard* in practically every ... case to see whether or not there is any help to be gained from it.' *Pepper* v. *Hart*, 615.

their clients little or no benefit at considerable expense.[191] But the core point of those voicing this concern has been that legislative history needs to be used only rarely, and always extremely carefully, rather than completely avoided; as in the United States, even judges who are especially sceptical about the use of legislative history recognize that it is probably best never to say never.[192]

So it is that the debate over the exclusionary rule appears now to have run its course. Today's standard wisdom has it that '[r]eference to *Hansard* does not often help the courts with issues of statutory interpretation, but ... that it does so occasionally'.[193] Disagreements regarding the use of legislative history are normally differences of opinion over how sparingly – rather than over whether – it ought to be used. But this does not mean that the topic no longer poses any intellectual challenges. One obvious peculiarity is why it should have taken the House of Lords a century

[191] See, e.g., *Robinson* v. *Secretary of State for Northern Ireland* [2002] UKHL 32 at [39]-[40] (Lord Hoffmann), [65] (Lord Hobhouse) and [97] (Lord Millett); also *Chartbrook Ltd* v. *Persimmon Homes,* at [38] (Lord Hoffmann). Given that most parliamentary debates since the early nineteenth century are now digitized, and are as easy to access and search as the statutes on which they have a bearing, it could be that the expense to clients of counsel looking at legislative history is not as considerable as it once would have been. But it is impossible to know. Reductions in search costs will not necessarily be passed on as a financial benefit to clients, and in any event we cannot discover what the comparable costs would have been before *Pepper* v. *Hart* as there was generally no point in counsel taking the trouble to look at legislative history.

[192] Neither Antonin Scalia nor Frank Easterbrook, the two American judges best known for their resistance to the use of legislative history, have been completely resistant to its use in the context of statutory interpretation. Justice Scalia has opined that if statutory language requires an absurd outcome and if the legislature cannot possibly have intended what the statutory language suggests it intended, resort to legislative history is warranted not to furnish the statute with an alternative meaning but 'to verify that what seems ... an unthinkable disposition ... was indeed unthought of'. *Green* v. *Bock Laundry Machine Co.,* 490 US 504, 527–8 (1989). Judge Easterbrook's position is yet more relaxed: see, e.g., *Board of Trade* v. *SEC,* 187 F.3d 713, 720 (7th Cir. 1999) (Easterbrook J noting that reliable legislative history might be used 'when there is a genuine ambiguity in the statute'); Frank H. Easterbrook, 'Text, History, and Structure in Statutory Interpretation' (1994) 17 *Harvard Jnl of Law & Public Policy* 61, 64; 'What Does Legislative History Tell Us?' (1990) 66 *Chicago-Kent L. Rev.* 441, 448 ('Intelligent, modest use of the background of American laws can do much to bring the execution into line with the plan'); 'Statutes' Domains' (1983) 50 *Univ. Chicago L. Rev.* 533, 550.

[193] *R* v. *Secretary of State for the Environment, ex p. Spath Holme,* 403 (*per* Lord Cooke). Australia abolished the exclusionary rule by amending legislation in 1984: Acts Interpretation Amendment Act 1984 (Cth), s. 7. In New Zealand the rule has never been clearly established or rejected, while Canada still supposedly retains it – *A-G of Canada* v. *The Reader's Digest Association (Canada) Ltd* [1961] SCR 775 – though there are indications there of the rule being relaxed. See, generally, Francis Bennion, 'Hansard – Help or Hindrance? A Draftsman's View of *Pepper v Hart*' (1993) 14 *Statute L. Rev.* 149, 156–9.

longer than it took the United States Supreme Court to permit recourse to legislative history for the purposes of statutory construction.

On this there is, perhaps, nothing that can be offered but speculation. The answer is certainly not that English courts had no reason to look at such history, nor is it that *Hansard* has been markedly less accessible than the *Congressional Record* and other US legislative history documents.[194] The difference might be attributable to the fact that congressional deliberations are, generally speaking, more comprehensively reported than are those of parliament.[195] But one would expect the significance of this difference to be offset by the tendency of Congress to speak with a less unified voice than parliament, and by the fact that ministerial explanations of proposed legislation in the United Kingdom are more likely – not least because there is no long history of their being considered relevant to statutory construction – to be accepted at face value as compared with statements by sponsors and other participants in congressional debates and committees.[196] Since English statute law has traditionally been almost exclusively the product of professional drafters who generally understand the interpretive methods and predilections of barristers and judges, the call to seek out clarifying statements on the legislative record has perhaps

[194] Though, in other jurisdictions, attitudes to the use of legislative history do sometimes seem to be at least partly shaped by whether or not the history is easily obtainable: see, e.g., Stig Strömholm, 'Legislative Material and the Construction of Statutes: Notes on the Continental Approach' (1966) 10 *Scandinavian Studies in Law* 173, where it is argued that, certainly until the 1960s, the French courts derived less assistance from legislative history than the German and Swedish courts because in Germany and Sweden not only was the history reported more extensively than it was in France, but it was normally made available to all courts and lawyers' offices as well as to public and university libraries and similar institutions (see ibid. 198, 216–17). As regards making legislative history available to courts and lawyers' offices, England was somewhat behind the game as compared with the United States, where movements in this direction began in the early 1940s: see Richard A. Danner, 'Justice Jackson's Lament: Historical and Comparative Perspectives on the Availability of Legislative History' (2003) 13 *Duke J. of Comparative & Int'l Law* 151, 190–1. But the lag does not explain why the United States Supreme Court should have sanctioned the use of legislative history as an aid to statutory construction a century earlier than the House of Lords did. Over half a century after the Supreme Court's *Holy Trinity* decision, one of its Justices lamented that legislative history still remained largely inaccessible to ordinary citizens and their legal advisers: see Robert H. Jackson, 'The Meaning of Statutes: What Congress Says or What the Court Says' (1948) 34 *ABAJ* 535.

[195] See Robert G. Vaughn, 'A Comparative Analysis of the Influence of Legislative History on Judicial Decision-Making and Legislation' (1996) 7 *Indiana Int'l & Comparative L. Rev.* 1, 7–8.

[196] The point being that participants in the US legislative process are more likely, given the historical absence of an exclusionary rule, to put on the legislative record statements

not been as pressing as it has been in the United States, where many bills are produced not by the Congressional Legislative Drafting Service but by interest groups, congressional aides and other parties whose principal job is not law writing.[197] Possibly American judges have been more willing to entertain legislative history in the courtroom and in their opinions because, unlike in the United Kingdom where the appeal courts have been making use of judicial assistants for little over a decade, there is a long tradition of judicial reliance on law clerks for help with research, fact checking and analysis. It is also possible that the judiciary in the United States was far quicker to allow legislative history to play a part in statutory interpretation because the statutes which Congress enacts, as compared with those enacted by parliament, tend to be worded to accommodate extensive compromise: American judges struggling to determine the meaning of statutory language are perhaps more likely to suspect that in the details of deals which were struck in committees and on the floor of Congress rests the clue to the legislature's real enacting intention.[198] The standard attitude of English judges towards such suspicions was well summarized by Lord Browne-Wilkinson in *Pepper* v. *Hart*: very rarely

---

which purport to clarify the language of a bill – and which might therefore influence the interpretation of what is passed into law – but which never had a realistic chance of surviving the rigours of bicameralism and making it into the text of the statute. See Scalia, 'Common-Law Courts in a Civil-Law System', 34 ('Ironically, but quite understandably, the more courts have relied upon legislative history, the less worthy of reliance it has become. In earlier days, it was at least genuine, and not contrived – a real part of the legislation's *history*, in the sense that it was part of the *development* of the bill, part of the attempt to persuade those who voted. Nowadays, however, when it is universally known and expected that judges will resort to floor debates and (especially) committee reports as authoritative expressions of "legislative intent," affecting courts rather than informing Congress has become the primary purpose of the exercise. It is less that the courts refer to legislative history because it exists than that legislative history exists because the courts refer to it.' Emphases in original.)

[197] See Stephen Breyer, 'On the Uses of Legislative History in Interpreting Statutes' (1992) 65 *Southern California L. Rev.* 845, 868 ('… unlike our country, they have developed other institutions to bring about and maintain necessary interpretive consistency and coherence. In England … the office of [the] Parliamentary Counsel … drafts almost all legislation. Because the drafters understand how the English judiciary (a relatively homogeneous group) tends to interpret statutes, their drafting reinforces those interpretive tendencies'). On parliament's preference for professional legislative drafters, see Stephen Laws, 'Drawing the Line', in *Drafting Legislation: A Modern Approach*, ed. C. Stefanou and H. Xanthaki (Aldershot: Ashgate, 2008), 19–34.

[198] See William S. Jordan, III, 'Legislative History and Statutory Interpretation: The Relevance of English Practice' (1994) 29 *Univ. San Francisco L. Rev.* 1, 23–4; also Elhauge, 'Preference Eliciting Statutory Default Rules', 2223–4.

will there be a 'crock of gold'.[199] None of these possibilities seems obviously discountable for the purpose of trying to understand why UK courts should traditionally have been less amenable to the use of legislative history than US courts have been. But it is equally the case that none of them solves the basic puzzle.

6   Intention against (meta-)intention

Legislative intention does not control statutory interpretation. English judges, as has been emphasized at various points throughout this study, have been inclined to ask what statutory language actually means, rather than what the legislature would have intended by enacting that language. Nevertheless, the only intentions that count for the purpose of statutory interpretation – as opposed to interpolation – are intentions attributable to the legislature. The primary reason most judges favour interpreting a statute according to the plain meaning of its language is that the ruling which such an interpretation yields is the one most likely to conform with the legislature's enacting intentions. When a court abandons the plain-meaning approach in favour of the golden rule, its reason for doing so is normally that a statute is worded in such a way that to abide by its plain meaning would be to produce an absurd outcome that the legislature would not have countenanced. To enquire as to the mischief to be remedied by a statute is to try to ascertain the legislature's law-changing intention in enacting that statute. To adopt the approach to statutory construction favoured by Aristotle and Plowden is to try to imagine what the legislature's intention would have been had it contemplated the case before the court today. Statutory interpretation might not be controlled by, but it certainly relies heavily on, conceptions of legislative intention.

When, however, might a court interpret a statute so that it yields a meaning independent of any which the legislature either actually or could be imagined to have wanted it to yield? Recall the four questions, posed early in this chapter, which it was suggested a judge might ask when interpreting a statute. It was argued that the second and third questions, although often treated as separate in the context of statutory interpretation, do not mark out a genuine analytical distinction. To ask what a legislature intends a statute to mean is to enquire as to legislative intention; but then the same goes for asking what the legislature's purpose is in enacting a statute. But consider the fourth question: judges who ask what

---

[199] *Pepper* v. *Hart*, 637.

purposes a statute could conceivably be taken to serve – including purposes which the legislature did not and would not have entertained – are no longer necessarily concerned with legislative intention.

The possibility of judges ascribing to statutes purposes which the legislature never would have countenanced is not inconceivable. Indeed, it is not unknown for American law professors in particular to urge courts to explore this possibility more ambitiously. But is a court which pursues this possibility not simply abandoning interpretation in favour of legislation? Can one be interpreting a statute when one makes it mean something that the enacting legislature did not intend it, and would never have intended it, to mean?

Non-legal texts are often treated thus in the name of interpretation; there are, in fact, literary theorists who would have it that authorial intent is irrelevant to textual meaning, that such meaning is determined by the consumer rather than the producer. The proposition that statutory interpretation is likewise essentially about reader response has not been without its defenders,[200] and it is certainly not impossible to conceive of the reader of a statute determining, Humpty Dumpty-style, that the text means only what he wants it to mean. But this reader would be, to use Roscoe Pound's language, producing a spurious interpretation of the statute.[201] Why so? Because as a general principle – and leaving aside statutorily imposed obligations to interpret other statutes in line with treaty obligations – the consequences of investing a statute with meanings which its creators would never have, and would never have wished to have, entertained risks generating certain undesirable states of affairs which are unlikely to arise when one imports unintended meanings into other types of text.

This is not to imply that contra-intentionalist interpretations of non-statutory texts never produce undesirable states of affairs. To

---

[200] See, e.g., Stanley Fish, *There's No Such Thing as Free Speech and it's a Good Thing, Too* (Oxford University Press, 1994), 144–8 (on the Uniform Commercial Code); also Walter Benn Michaels, 'Against Formalism: The Autonomous Text in Legal and Literary Interpretation' (1979) 1 *Poetics Today* 23, 25–8.

[201] See Roscoe Pound, 'Spurious Interpretation' (1907) 7 *Columbia L. Rev.* 379, 382 ('[T]he object of spurious interpretation is to make, unmake, or remake, and not merely to discover. It puts a meaning into the text as a juggler puts coins, or what not, into a dummy's hair, to be pulled forth presently with an air of discovery. It is essentially a legislative, not a judicial process ...'); and cf. Editor [Arthur W. Spencer], 'Genuine and Spurious Interpretation' (1913) 25 *Green Bag* 504, 507 ('The spectre of judicial usurpation ... will never vanish ... But one cannot jump to the conclusion that the legislative powers of the judiciary are unlimited').

interpret legal texts other than statutes without regard for authorial intent is, more often than not, to interpret poorly. Placing one's trust in out-landish, intention-ignoring interpretations of certain types of non-legal text – one might imagine a surrealist negotiation of an operating manual for a device with, say, sharp blades or a mains connection – could prove disastrous. And even though the intentions of the creator of, say, a literary text or a musical score are usually unimportant for the purpose of inter-preting the work's meaning, there are instances when those intentions might be significant: playwrights and other literary authors might cite their intentions, for example, when seeking to establish that an interpret-ation of their work infringes copyright.[202] Nevertheless, interpretations of statutes deliberately in defiance of all possible renderings of legislative intention beget unique hazards. The most obvious is that the authority of a legislative assembly to make directives which are binding on the citi-zenry is undermined if its intentions to change the law in specific ways can be overridden by courts in receipt of its statutes.[203] But it is not only the authority of the legislature that is undermined; so, too, is the principle that statutes are enacted for the sake of persons. An interpretation which hijacks the meaning of a statute, that is, militates against the primary rea-son for enactment: to provide directives sufficiently precise to enable citi-zens (and lawyers and judges) confidently to make determinations about what is lawful and what is not.[204]

Statutory construction by reference to a purpose attributable to some person or body other than the legislature is certainly interpolative rather than interpretive. But knowing which type of construction we are dealing with is sometimes difficult, for we cannot always tell if the intentions of a court in applying a statute are distinct from the intentions of a legisla-ture in enacting it. We know already that although the point of courts relying on interpretive presumptions is commonly to give effect to the actual or likely intentions of the legislature, the use of some presump-tions does not straightforwardly correlate with such an explanation. For

---

[202] See, e.g., *Hubbard* v. *Vosper* [1972] 2 QB 84 (CA). In this case, interpretation took the form of selective reproduction of excerpts from a text, and the intentions of the text's author were found to be irrelevant to the question of whether there had been copyright infringement: see ibid. 94 (*per* Lord Denning MR).

[203] See Joseph Raz, *Between Authority and Interpretation: On the Theory of Law and Practical Reason* (Oxford University Press, 2009), 248.

[204] See John Finnis, 'Legal Reasoning as Practical Reason' (1992), in his *Reason in Action. Collected Essays: Volume I* (Oxford University Press, 2011), 212–30 at 220.

example, in the (rare) event that a court makes use of the lenity presumption – that ambiguous penal statutes be interpreted so as to impose the lowest possible penalty on the allegedly criminal act – its interpretation is likely to be at odds with a legislature's intentions; indeed, a parliament whose legislative record shows it to be tough on crime and its causes might more realistically be presumed to prefer that courts deal with ambiguous penal statutes by opting for a severe rather than a lenient interpretation.[205] Likewise, judicial efforts to update statutes may or may not connect to hypothesized legislative intent. An updated reading might be justified on the basis that it reflects what it can reasonably be presumed the legislature would have intended the statute to mean were the assembly reconstituted and able to advise on the case before the court today. But a case for statutory updating might sometimes be made on non-intentionalist grounds. The United States Congress of 1964 is unlikely to have intended the Civil Rights Act to allow affirmative action, and there is no reason to assume that, if its members could be reassembled today, it would recommend that Title VII of the Act should be interpreted as supporting that objective. Under the Johnson and Nixon administrations, however, executive orders were implemented and enforced in an effort to ensure that minorities and women were adequately represented in all areas of employment where they were then under-represented; gradually, the United States accepted affirmative action as necessary to the enforcement of its civil rights laws.[206] Courts, some American legal theorists have argued, ought to treat important social changes such as the normalization of affirmative action as reason enough to update a statute by interpretation, notwithstanding that there may be no evidence that the legislature would have

---

[205] See Elhauge, 'Preference Eliciting Statutory Default Rules', 2193. Note that the notion of 'penal statutes' needs to be approached with care, as some statutes will contain a mixture of civil and criminal provisions. Examples would be statutes setting out civil preventive orders (anti-social behaviour orders, non-molestation orders, restraining orders, travel restriction orders and the like) which are enforceable through a court with civil jurisdiction but which, in the event that a defendant breaches an order without reasonable excuse, impose a penalty for a criminal offence: see, e.g., the Crime and Disorder Act 1998, section 1 (as amended). In the case of ambiguity, one might assume that the principle of lenity should apply only to the interpretation of those parts of a hybrid statute that are subject to purely penal enforcement. But in some instances, the civil and criminal elements of a statute might not be straightforwardly extricated, or the tenor of the statute may be (say) very obviously civil rather than criminal: for an exploration of these and other nuances, and attendant interpretive problems, see Jonathan Marx, 'How to Construe a Hybrid Statute' (2007) 93 *Virginia L. Rev.* 235.

[206] See Eskridge, *Dynamic Statutory Interpretation*, 24–5.

approved, and possibly even evidence that it would have disapproved, of the modernizing construction.[207]

This form of argument is not without jurisprudential pedigree. The ideal judge, when 'decid[ing] how to read statutes whose meaning is uncertain', would, according to Ronald Dworkin, treat the legislature 'as an author earlier than himself in the chain of the law ... and he will see his own role as fundamentally the creative one of a partner continuing to develop, in what he sees is the best way, the statutory scheme [which the legislature] began'.[208] While this manner of interpretation 'will in part depend on' legislative history, it 'will also depend on the best answer to political questions' such as whether the scheme originally devised by the legislature should now be revised in deference to 'public opinion'.[209] A judge might on occasions legitimately ignore legislative history altogether, Alexander Aleinikoff has argued, and simply take responsibility for bringing a statute into the present: if '[l]aw is a tool for arranging today's social relations and expressing today's social values', and if 'we fully expect our laws, no matter when enacted, to speak to us today', then the proper way to read a statute is to treat it 'as if it had been enacted yesterday and try ... to weave it into today's legal system, to make it responsive to today's conditions'.[210]

Jurisprudential arguments in favour of courts updating statutes are not matched by judicial endorsements. One American law professor who devised a fairly elaborate argument supporting the judicial updating of statutes has spoken about it with markedly less enthusiasm since his appointment to the bench,[211] and judges generally – on both sides of

---

[207] See, e.g., William N. Eskridge, Jr, 'Dynamic Statutory Interpretation' (1987) 135 *Univ. Pennsylvania L. Rev.* 1479, 1494 ('when societal conditions change in ways not anticipated by Congress and, especially, when the legal and constitutional context of the statute decisively shifts as well, this current perspective should, and will, affect the statute's interpretation, notwithstanding contrary inferences from the historical evidence'); also Guido Calabresi, *A Common Law for the Age of Statutes* (Cambridge, Mass.: Harvard University Press, 1982), 88–9. Although Calabresi emphasizes the importance of candour in statutory interpretation (ibid. 178–81), he does not explicitly set out his case for the judicial updating of statutes in terms of overriding legislative intent, though it seems reasonable to infer that he considers overriding intent to be unavoidable if judicial updating is to become an accepted practice (see ibid. 215–16).

[208] Ronald Dworkin, *Law's Empire* (London: Fontana, 1986), 313.

[209] Ibid.

[210] T. Alexander Aleinikoff, 'Updating Statutory Interpretation' (1988) 87 *Michigan L. Rev.* 20 at 58, 49–50. (Emphasis omitted.)

[211] See *Hayden v. Pataki*, 449 F.3d 305, 367 n 6 (2d Cir. 2006) (Calabresi J, dissenting): 'some scholars, myself included, have suggested that it might be a good idea if, as a starting point, in certain circumstances, courts were permitted to read the law according to what

the Atlantic – have given the idea a wide berth.[212] That the idea should have met with a cool reception from judges is not at all surprising. The obvious disadvantage of 'present-oriented' interpretations is that they 'cut the tie between the legislative intent … and the statute itself';[213] if courts deliberately construe statutes so as to disconnect the meanings of the text from the intention of the enacting legislature, there cannot be legislative supremacy. Such interpretations also have the potential to frustrate reliance interests. To say that judges should interpret a statute as if it had been enacted yesterday is to say that they should ascribe to it a meaning which was undisclosed, at which citizens could only guess, before a case came to court. The attribution of an updated meaning to statutory language, furthermore, is unlikely to bring an end to the problem. For updating, one would assume, has to be an open-ended process: judges would have to update not only statutes but also outdated updates of statutes. Basically, updating militates against efforts to provide sound legal advice: one can never be sure, at the point when one wants to know, what a statute actually means.

Given that updating interpretations of statutes seem potentially perilous, one might expect that they are never countenanced in English law. But this is not the case. In certain circumstances, legislation incorporating international treaty obligations into national law specifically directs courts to try to update statutes. The significance of this for statutory interpretation requires careful attention. Before we head in that direction, however, it is worth observing that even absent a specific instruction from parliament, judges will still sometimes update statutory language – though it is certainly true that when they have taken it upon themselves to try to bring a statute into the present, they have been careful not to appear dismissive of legislative intent.[214] The boldest illustration of this form of updating is to be found in a case decided by the UK Supreme Court early in 2011. '[I]t is common place for courts to have to consider

they perceived to be the will of the current Congress, rather than that of a long-gone-by one … [W]hatever the merits of such an arrangement in the abstract, it is simply not a part of our legal system … [T]he only justification for such statutory updating, even in theory, is that the legislature may be stalled by inertia, with the result that an outmoded and antimajoritarian statutory scheme becomes fixed in stone.'
[212] On the position in the US, see Nelson, *Statutory Interpretation*, 972.
[213] Steven D. Smith, 'Law Without Mind' (1989) 88 *Michigan L. Rev.* 104, 117.
[214] See, e.g., *Dyson Holdings* v. *Fox* [1976] QB 503 (CA), 511 (*per* James LJ); *Helby* v. *Rafferty* [1979] 1 WLR 13 (CA), 16–17 (*per* Stamp LJ); *Williams & Glyn's Bank Ltd* v. *Boland* [1981] AC 487 (HL), 502 (*per* Lord Wilberforce); *Fitzpatrick* v. *Sterling Housing Association Ltd* [1998] Ch. 304 (CA), 325 (*per* Roch LJ).

whether circumstances, beyond those at the forefront of Parliament's consideration, may properly be held to be within the scope of a provision, having regard to its purpose', Lord Rodger observed in *Yemshaw v. London Borough of Hounslow*.[215] His specific point was that 'violence' in the context of section 177(1) of the Housing Act 1996 should be interpreted as including any deliberate conduct, or threat of such conduct, that may cause psychological harm.[216] In arguing as much, he was concurring with Baroness Hale, who reasoned that since modern dictionaries attribute 'violence' with a secondary meaning of 'strength or intensity of emotion; fervour, passion',[217] the term ought not to be confined to physical action but should also be taken to include threatening or intimidating behaviour and any other form of abuse which, directly or indirectly, may give rise to the risk of harm.[218] Law Commission reports and other official documents from the early to mid 1990s – including a report containing recommendations which eventually formed Part IV of the Family Law Act 1996 – show that family and anti-discrimination lawyers at this time were using the word 'violence' to include non-physical abuse.[219] The fact, furthermore, that the definition of an 'associated person' under section 178 of the Housing Act bore 'a very close resemblance to' the definition of the same under section 62 of the Family Law Act seemed to 'indicate[] a consciousness in 1996 of the need to align housing, homelessness and family law remedies for victims of domestic violence'.[220] Baroness Hale's conclusion was that even though the official documents from the 1990s did not relate directly to the Housing Act, and even though it was the language of section 178 rather than 177 of the Housing Act that bore resemblance to section 62 of the Family Law Act, it seemed reasonable to infer in relation to both the family and the housing legislation that 'violence' was not to be narrowly construed: 'by the time of the 1996 [Housing] Act the understanding of domestic violence had moved on from a narrow focus upon battered wives and physical contact. But if I am wrong about that, there is no doubt that it has moved on now.'[221]

That last sentence seems especially revealing. Lord Hope was unconvinced by Baroness Hale's reasoning: 'I cannot hide my profound doubt as to whether at any stage of their legislative history the "domestic violence" provisions with which we are here concerned … were intended to extend

---

[215] *Yemshaw v. London Borough of Hounslow* [2011] UKSC 3 at [45].
[216] Ibid. at [46].   [217] Ibid. at [19].
[218] Ibid. at [28].   [219] Ibid. at [20]–[21].
[220] Ibid. at [22]–[23].   [221] Ibid. at [24].

beyond the limits of physical violence … I do not say that psychological abuse is … incapable of being described as "violence" … I do say, however, that Parliament is unlikely to have contemplated or intended th[is].'[222] But that objection does not speak to Baroness Hale's argument in its entirety: even if one is not convinced that parliament, in enacting the Housing Act 1996, intended 'violence' to extend to threatening or intimidating behaviour, she is claiming, it would surely intend this if it were enacting the legislation today. This is perhaps the closest any English judge has ever come to entertaining the possibility of dynamic statutory interpretation without regard for the real or hypothesized intentions of the enacting legislature.

We have seen already in this study that judges might sometimes insert new material into, or take existing material out of, statutes and yet – because they are simply making corrections to drafting errors which currently obscure legislative intent – be deemed to be engaging in genuine statutory interpretation. There is a temptation to extend this claim by observing that one ought to categorize as spurious interpretation any rendering of a statute that cannot be squared with the intentions of the legislature which enacted it. But this observation would be incorrect. Sometimes, a court will be understood to be interpreting a statute even though statutory meaning is determined by reference to some purpose, or purposes, which cannot, even if one resorts to imaginative reconstruction, be attributed to the legislature as composed, or even to any members of the legislature as composed, at the time of enactment. These sorts of instances typically arise when enacted legislation has to be read in the light of the legislature's incorporation of international treaty obligations into domestic law.

Parliament's enactment of the European Communities Act 1972 is one such instance. Where there is a conflict between domestic legislation and a European statute which takes direct effect (i.e., which needs no implementing legislation) in the United Kingdom, the European law takes precedence – because parliament has legislated (and, if it wished to do so, could legislate away from) this conclusion.[223] Article 189 of the EC Treaty requires the courts of member states, when confronted with a clear conflict between national law and a directly applicable European directive, to give priority to an interpretation of the domestic statute which achieves the objectives of the European law and to avoid, so far as is

---

[222] Ibid. at [48], [51].
[223] See European Union Act 2011, s. 18.

possible, applying domestic statutes which conflict with these objectives. In 1990, the European Court of Justice held that a national law had to be interpreted, 'as far as possible, in the light of the wording and the purpose of' a European directive 'in order to comply with art. 189 of the treaty' even though the relevant directive did not have direct effect (indeed, had not yet been implemented in the relevant member state).[224] The House of Lords took a clear view that the ECJ's decision was not to be read as either requiring or inviting UK courts to distort the meaning of national statutes in order to enforce indirectly applicable European directives.[225]

But what if the UK courts were to find it impossible to apply national legislation without that application directly conflicting with EC law? In such an instance, the House of Lords resolved in *Factortame (No. 2)*, a court must treat the national law as automatically inapplicable and enforce European law instead: 'there is nothing in any way novel in according supremacy to rules of Community law in those areas to which they apply', Lord Bridge maintained. '[T]o insist that, in the protection of rights under Community law, national courts must not be inhibited by rules of national law from granting interim relief in appropriate cases is', he added, 'no more than a logical recognition of that supremacy.'[226] This decision does not mark the end of parliamentary sovereignty. Not only is sovereignty retained owing to the fact that parliament still has the right to withdraw from its obligations under European law, but a court which applies European law instead of national law in a case of direct conflict between the two is neither removing national law from the statute book nor doing anything contrary to parliament's own enacting intentions in passing the European Communities Act. Clearly, nevertheless, the introduction of EC law into UK law placed on the courts new interpretive obligations: courts must, so far as is possible, interpret national legal rules so as to make them compliant with European legal rules and, if rendering the two sets of rules compliant proves impossible, give precedence to the European rules and treat the national rules as inapplicable.

A similar scheme of obligation arises with the incorporation of the European Convention on Human Rights into UK law. The two schemes of obligation are not quite identical because whereas, in the case of European

---

[224] *Marleasing SA* v. *La Comercial Internacional de Alimentación SA* (C-106/89) [1993] BCC 421 para. 8.

[225] See *Duke* v. *GEC Reliance Ltd* [1988] AC 618 (HL), 639–40 (*per* Lord Templeman); *Webb* v. *Emo Air Cargo (UK) Ltd* [1993] 1 WLR 49 (HL), 59 (*per* Lord Keith); *White* v. *White* [2001] 1 WLR 481 (HL), 489 (*per* Lord Cooke).

[226] *R* v. *Secretary of State for Transport, ex p. Factortame Ltd (No. 2)* [1991] 1 AC 603, 659.

Union law, the courts are negotiating apparent conflicts between national and supra-national rules, human rights law poses the possibility of conflict not between two sets of rules but between national rules and basic human rights. So far as is possible, the UK courts are required to interpret national legal rules so as to make them compliant with the human rights norms enumerated in the European Convention. If achieving compliance turns out not to be possible, the courts must still apply the national legal rules, but also draw parliament's attention to the fact that those rules appear not to comply with Convention norms.

When a court seeks to demonstrate compliance, the national legislation applicable to the case for decision is interpreted in accordance with the intentions of parliament not in passing that legislation, but in enacting the Human Rights Act 1998. Section 3 of the HRA, the interpretation section, requires that UK courts, so far as is possible, interpret and apply primary and subordinate legislation in a manner compatible with Convention rights – so that domestic statutes might accord, in other words, with parliament's intention (in passing the HRA) to incorporate the ECHR into domestic law. This means that a court might justifiably ascribe to a statute a meaning which the legislature, as composed at the point of enactment, never intended the statute to yield; the interpretation is justifiable because it is faithful to parliament's intentions in enacting governing legislation in the form of the HRA. 'The traditional doctrine of statutory interpretation was, of course, to … start with the ordinary meaning of the words' in the statute so as to try 'to divine the intention of Parliament in the legislative measure before them', Laws LJ observed in 2004. 'Section 3 of the HRA', however, 'enjoins the Judges to adopt a radically different view of intention.'

> Now, the *prevailing* legislative intention will be that contained in the HRA. Another statute … might be entirely clear as to the policy and objects that are intended … If, however, the fulfilment of the Act's purpose through the section or sections in question would in the Court's view involve a violation of a Convention right, then the Court is to *prefer* the legislative intention of the HRA over the legislative intention of the other Act.[227]

---

[227] Lord Justice Laws, 'The Impact of the Human Rights Act 1998 on the Interpretation of Enactments in the UK', in *The Statute: Making and Meaning*, 241–50 at 248. (Emphasis in original.) Note that the point of s. 3 is not to do away with established interpretive conventions, but to enable courts to construe statutes remedially, should this be necessary, *after* they have been interpreted in accordance with those conventions.

A vivid illustration of the impact of section 3 can be found in a case decided around the time that Laws offered this observation. Schedule 1, paragraph 2(2) of the Rent Act 1977 stipulates that someone living with a tenant 'as his or her wife or husband' is entitled to succeed the tenancy on the tenant's death. The legislation was amended in the 1980s so that it accorded the same survivorship right to unmarried heterosexual couples. Since it had not been amended to extend the right to same-sex partners, however, it was, on a plain-meaning interpretation, incompatible with article 14 (read in conjunction with article 8) of the European Convention. In *Ghaidan* v. *Godin-Mendoza*, the House of Lords, upholding a decision of the Court of Appeal, interpreted 'as his or her wife or husband' to mean '*as if they were* his wife or husband', so as to extend the entitlement accorded under schedule 1, paragraph 2(2) to surviving partners in same-sex relationships.[228]

This was not an attempt at imaginative reconstruction: Lord Millett, though he dissented from the majority, is unlikely to have provoked any quarrel when he observed that in 1988, the point at which the Rent Act provision had last been amended, the extension of the entitlement to '[c]ouples of the same sex ... would have been highly controversial' and, in any event, 'was not then required by the Convention'.[229] Nor was the language of either the original or the amending legislation ambiguous. The point was simply that section 3 of the HRA – the application of which, '[i]t is ... generally accepted ... does not depend upon the presence of ambiguity in the legislation being interpreted' – requires judges to construe statutes so as to make them Convention-compatible, even if this means that judges will sometimes 'depart from ... the intention of the Parliament which enacted the legislation'.[230] Lord Reid's Holmesian observation of 1975 – that to interpret a statute is to determine not the enacting legislature's intention but the meaning of the language it enacted[231] – no longer rang true. An enacting legislature's intention

---

[228] *Ghaidan* v. *Godin-Mendoza* [2004] 2 AC 557.

[229] Ibid. 592.

[230] Ibid. 571 (*per* Lord Nicholls), also 585 *per* Lord Steyn ('[E]ven if, construed in accordance with ordinary principles of construction, the meaning of the legislation admits of no doubt, section 3 may require it to be given a different meaning'). See also *R* v. *A (No. 2)*, 67 *per* Lord Steyn ('[T]he interpretative obligation under section 3 ... applies even if there is no ambiguity in the language in the sense of the language being capable of two different meanings').

[231] *Black-Clawson* v. *Papierwerke Waldhof-Aschaffenburg*, 613. Cf. O. W. Holmes, Jr, 'The Theory of Legal Interpretation' (1899) 12 *Harvard L. Rev.* 417, 419 ('We do not enquire

might be sidestepped, *and* the language it enacted altered, in the pursuit of compatibility.[232]

'If a statute is to make sense', Karl Llewellyn claimed in 1950, 'it must be read in the light of some assumed purpose' – be it purpose in the form 'of the policy of the statute' or the interpreting court's 'own version of such policy'.[233] Section 3 requires a form of interpretation which need not be either of these things. Judges cannot make whatever policy they like, for they must have regard for the Human Rights Act.[234] While section 3 permits courts to give statutory provisions broader or narrower meanings than those provisions could ordinarily be said to accommodate, and even 'to read in words which change the meaning of' a statutory provision, it would be 'cross[ing] the constitutional boundary' if the court were to 'adopt a meaning inconsistent with a fundamental feature of' a statute.[235] Nevertheless, when a court actually alters statutory language so as to

what the legislature meant; we ask only what the statute means'); also Felix Frankfurter, 'Some Reflections on the Reading of Statutes' (1947) 47 *Columbia L. Rev.* 527, 538. For striking applications of this principle in American law – determining that statutory language means what it says even when it is obvious that the language does not capture what the legislature intended – see *United States* v. *Locke*, 471 US 84 (1985) and *Spivey* v. *Vertrue Inc.*, 528 F.3d 982 (7th Cir. 2008). Both cases concern statutes containing badly drafted deadlines.

[232] Cf. Roger Masterman, *The Separation of Powers in the Contemporary Constitution: Judicial Competence and Independence in the United Kingdom* (Cambridge University Press, 2011), 162, who claims that, since *Ghaidan*, '[p]arliamentary intent clearly continues to play a role ... but is certainly no longer the courts' sole concern'. Intent indeed still is potentially relevant for the purposes of statutory interpretation – though the relevant intention might not be that of parliament at the time that it enacted the statute which is to be interpreted. It is misleading, however, to claim that legislative intent is no longer the sole concern of the courts when interpreting statutes, for it is not clear that it has ever been the courts' sole concern. Certainly since the eighteenth century – to repeat a point emphasized already in this study – courts have been more likely to try first to ascertain the meaning of the text to be interpreted rather than parliament's intentions in enacting it.

[233] Karl N. Llewellyn, 'Remarks on the Theory of Appellate Decision and the Rules or Canons about How Statutes are to be Construed' (1950) 3 *Vanderbilt L. Rev.* 395, 400.

[234] Although the emphasis here is on the interpretive obligation under s. 3, it should be borne in mind that judges also have to take into account the rulings of various European decision-making bodies (in particular, the jurisprudence of the European Court of Human Rights): Human Rights Act 1998, s. 2(1). Taking into account has tended to mean treating as more than merely persuasive authority: see, e.g., *R (Alconbury Developments Ltd)* v. *Secretary of State for the Environment, Transport and the Regions* [2001] UKHL 23 at [26] (Lord Slynn); *R* v. *Special Adjudicator, ex p. Ullah* [2004] UKHL 26 at [20] (Lord Bingham); also Tom Bingham, *Lives of the Law: Selected Essays and Speeches 2000–2010* (Oxford University Press, 2011), 185–7.

[235] *Ghaidan* v. *Godin-Mendoza*, 571–2 (*per* Lord Nicholls). See also *Doherty* v. *Birmingham CC* [2009] 1 AC 367 (HL), 410 *per* Lord Hope ('section 3(1) provides the court with a

make it compatible with Convention norms, it adopts what Lord Millett termed a 'quasi-legislative' as opposed to a 'purely interpretative' function.[236] It is 'by no means easy to decide in the abstract' what constitutes an abuse of this function.[237] The determining factor, Lord Rodger remarked in *Ghaidan*, is certainly not the number of words that are imported into the statute;[238] it has to do, rather, with whether the imported words 'are consistent with the scheme' – whether they 'go with the grain' – of the statute which is being interpreted.[239] To recall a distinction elaborated in Chapter 1, a court which goes against the grain of a statutory rule is laying down new rather than developing already existing law: not modifying a legal rule while remaining faithful to the underlying scheme of the legislation, that is, but abrogating the rule and putting a different one – one which is attributable to judicial, and not in any genuine sense to parliamentary, initiative – in its place.

We know that Plowden – who considered the statute to be more like an acorn than an oak – advocated Aristotle's notion of imaginative reconstruction as a reliable means by which to get to the kernel behind the shell. But how might one know if an interpretation of a statute goes with, or against, its grain? In *Ghaidan*, the most carefully elaborated answer to this question is to be found in the dissenting speech. Lord Millett sought to explain the idea of consistency with the essence of a statutory scheme by developing an argument which, though not explicitly Aristotelian like Plowden's, bears some resemblance to Aristotle's analysis of the role of predicates in relation to subjects when assessing contradictory propositions.[240] Words mean what they mean and not something else, but whether a word can be taken to include something else – whether, for example, 'it may be possible to read "black" as meaning "black or white"' – depends upon whether that word 'is the essential feature of the statutory

---

    powerful tool to enable it to interpret legislation and give effect to it. But it does not enable the court to change the substance of a provision from one where it says one thing into one that says the opposite').

[236] *Ghaidan* v. *Godin-Mendoza*, 585.

[237] Ibid. 597 (*per* Lord Rodger).

[238] For examples of HRA cases in which judges have significantly altered the wording of statutory provisions while claiming to be giving effect to the presumed intentions of parliament, see *R (Baia)* v. *Secretary of State for the Home Department* [2008] UKHL 53; *Principal Reporter* v. *K* [2010] UKSC 56.

[239] *Ghaidan* v. *Godin-Mendoza*, 601. See also ibid. 572 *per* Lord Nicholls ('The meaning imported by application of section 3 must be compatible with the underlying thrust of the legislation being construed').

[240] See Aristotle, *On Interpretation* IX–XII, 18ᵇ–22ᵇ.

scheme'.[241] The easiest way to make a particular word, or form of words, essential to a statutory scheme is to use unequivocally exclusionary language: by stipulating in an interpretation section, for example, that 'red, blue and green' means only those three primary colours and no other colour. Inferences as to exclusivity might also be drawn on the basis of established linguistic or interpretive conventions, as, for example, when judges use as an aid to construction the maxim, *expressio unius est exclusio alterius* – meaning, as was observed in the last chapter, that mention in a statute of one or more things in a particular class implies (absent evidence of an error in drafting) the exclusion of other things within that class.[242] Furthermore, predicates and other forms of qualifying language sometimes operate so as to preclude the extension of a subject to a more general class: 'cats' could include 'dogs', and 'oranges' could include 'apples', if we take it that the essential concepts in each instance are domestic pets and fruit. But one cannot make these extensions if the statute stipulates 'Siamese cats' or 'Seville oranges'.[243]

To determine if a modification of statutory language would offend against the fundamental legislative scheme, then, a court, in resorting to the interpretation section of the Human Rights Act, must ask not 'what was the intention of the legislature which enacted the statute that is being interpreted?', or even 'what do we imagine the intention of the enacting legislature would be were it available to advise the court today?', but instead: 'would a section 3 interpretation offend against what the language and, if relevant, the history of the statute show the enacting legislature to have treated as non-negotiable (such as that it specifically meant those three primary colours, that species of cat or that type of orange)?' A section 3 interpretation of a statute may invest it with meanings which were never entertained, even with some meanings which would never have been accepted, by the parliament which enacted that statute: the distinction, drawn at the outset of this book, between enacted legislation and judge-made law – between laying down law and developing the law laid down – is less straightforward than it once was. It would be wrong to conclude, however, that the distinction is no more. For the court which accords a statute a meaning which the enacting parliament can be

---

[241] *Ghaidan* v. *Godin-Mendoza*, 586.

[242] See ibid.; also John Mark Keyes, 'Expressio Unius: The Expression that Proves the Rule' (1989) 10 *Statute L. Rev.* 1.

[243] See *Ghaidan* v. *Godin-Mendoza*, 586. Of course, many predicates and other forms of qualifying language – e.g., 'married women' – do not preclude extensions to more general (and sometimes a variety of more general), classes.

understood to have positively excluded from its legislating objective – a meaning which the statute fundamentally rejects rather than fails naturally to accommodate – is still overstepping the mark and legislating in what Austin called the 'improper' sense.

Lord Millett had 'the misfortune to be unable to agree with th[e] conclusion' of the majority in *Ghaidan*.[244] He thought that the gender-specific formulation of the relevant tenancy legislation was a fundamental feature of the statutory scheme – that parliament, in using 'as his or her wife or husband', must have intended to exclude couples of the same sex. But his analysis captured a point with which none of those in the majority disagreed, and with which English courts have struggled at least since the fifteenth century: that interpretations of statutes which do not prioritize the text – which instead purport to unearth some mischief, sense, purpose or kernel within or even outside the statutory language – are still modes of technical reasoning which, when treated seriously, normally constrain interpreters from ignoring the identifiable or reasonably presumed intentions of the enacting parliament (including, nowadays, the intentions of parliament in legislating to bring treaty obligations into national law). Methodology and discipline remain the watchwords of purposive interpretation. It is important to keep in mind that a statute is to be interpreted to conform with Convention rights only so far as it is possible to do so, Lord Bingham cautioned in 2004, and that sometimes a declaration of incompatibility will be unavoidable because there will be no Convention-compliant interpretation of the statute which would not run contrary to its underlying thrust.[245] The reasoning resembles, though it is certainly not identical to, the interpretive reasoning that emerged in the sixteenth and seventeenth centuries: interpret the statute as consonant (compatible) with reason and justice, unless the statute simply defies such an interpretation, in which case it should be controlled (which, in the case of HRA interpretations, certainly does not mean 'adjudged void').

This last paragraph – connecting purposivism past and present – makes for a tidy conclusion, but it is not the right place at which to draw this long chapter to a close. The equitable statutory interpretation doctrines of Plowden and, especially, Coke are supported by a steady accretion of judicial wisdom over the centuries. Anyone who studies those

---

[244] Ibid. 583.

[245] *Attorney-General's Reference (No. 4 of 2002)* [2005] 1 AC 264, 303–4 (delivered October 2004). For instances where the House of Lords was unable to come up with Convention-compliant interpretations, see *R (Anderson)* v. *Secretary of State for the Home Department* [2002] UKHL 46; and *Bellinger* v. *Bellinger* [2003] UKHL 21.

doctrines discovers easily enough what they entail, and where and how they are applied today. But what of statutory interpretation governed by the Human Rights Act? Nobody could seriously say that there has been scant juristic reaction to the interpretation section of the Act, and there is already evidence of an interpretive jurisprudence – centring on the idea of legitimate section 3 interpretations being consistent with the fundamental features of impugned statutes – coalescing in the courts.[246] But it is early days, and already concern has been expressed at the highest level of the judiciary that the interpretive approach endorsed since *Ghaidan* is not disciplined enough – that it enables no clear distinction between a section 3 interpretation and judicial legislation.[247]

What does seem obvious is that the story of modern purposivism will not, in the future, be recounted as one of continuity with the past. The main evidence of discontinuity is the fact that alterations to statutory language – alterations beyond corrections of patent drafting errors and emendations to save statutes from absurdity – can now be made in the name of statutory interpretation. But this is not all of the evidence. There is also the fact that the role of courts as faithful agents of parliament has altered. Legislatures, it was observed in Chapter 3, tend to be large assemblies whose many members hold diverse viewpoints and speak for a range of constituencies. Deliberation and decision making depend not only on

---

[246] See, e.g., *Principal Reporter* v. *K*, at [61], [66], [69] (Lord Hope & Baroness Hale); *AS (Somalia)* v. *Secretary of State for the Home Department* [2009] UKHL 32 at [19] (Lord Hope); *R (Wilkinson)* v. *IRC* [2005] 1 WLR 1718 (HL), 1723–4 (*per* Lord Hoffmann); *R* v. *Z* [2005] 2 AC 467 (HL), 505 (*per* Lord Steyn); *Cadogan* v. *Pitts* [2010] 1 AC 226 (HL), 265 (*arguendo*). Cf. the reception of this jurisprudence in Australia: in *R* v. *Momcilovic* [2010] 25 VR 436, the Court of Appeal of the Supreme Court of Victoria declined to apply *Ghaidan* jurisprudence to the Charter of Human Rights and Responsibilities Act 2006, s. 32(1). The High Court, while allowing Momcilovic's appeal and quashing her conviction, was equally unenthusiastic about resorting to *Ghaidan*: see *Momcilovic* v. *The Queen* [2011] HCA 34, esp. *per* Gummow J at paras 155 ('Australian courts must approach the questions presented by the Charter with a clear recognition of … the fact that … both the structure and the text of other human rights systems reflect the different constitutional frameworks within which they operate. In particular, in considering decisions made by the House of Lords about the UK [Human Rights] Act, or decisions of the Privy Council about human rights charters in force in nations that were once British colonies, there are important differences of both context and text that must not be ignored') and 160 (*Ghaidan* jurisprudence has 'exercised a fascination to the point of obsession in the preparation and presentation of much of the submissions in the present appeal. That proved unfortunate …'), and, in a similar vein, French CJ at para. 49, Heydon J at paras 447–51, and Crennan and Keifel JJ at para. 546.

[247] See Lord Phillips, 'The Art of the Possible: Statutory Interpretation and Human Rights' (Weedon lecture, Brick Court Chambers, April 2010), at www.brickcourt.co.uk/uploads/lecture- - -the-art-of-the-possible-by-lord-phillips.pdf (visited 13 September 2012), 38–44.

rules of parliamentary procedure – determining how debates are initiated and concluded, how bills are proposed and voted on, how agenda are
settled and the like – but also on the production of a text to be debated
and amended and ultimately accepted or rejected. Since that text is, as
it were, bargained for, and since its point is to change the law in some
specific way, the language used to compose it is chosen carefully and is
commonly taken to mean what it says. Perhaps there is little room for
complaint if statutes enacted since the Human Rights Act came into force
are significantly reinterpreted to ensure their Convention-compliance.
Parliament, after all, ought to know the score by now,[248] and, so long as
the HRA remains in force, should choose statutory language which minimizes the possibility (though it could never eradicate the possibility)[249]
of judges revising what it enacts on the basis that section 3 obliges them
to do so. But pre-HRA statutes were for the most part enacted on a different basis: on the assumption that courts respect the principle of legislative authority by interpreting enacted language on its plain meaning,
or, where the language yields no such meaning, by opting for interpretive conventions which – leaving aside exceptional instances warranting
resort to specialized presumptions – enable judges, so far as is possible,
to connect the language of the statute to the discernible or reasonably
hypothesized intentions of the legislature responsible for its enactment.
The operation of section 3 can result in the courts placing on a statute an
interpretation which would certainly 'have come as a surprise'[250] to members of the parliament which enacted it. This is not to suggest that pre-
HRA statutes should not be subject to the obligation imposed by section
3, but simply to note that the actual or presumed intentions of parliament
in enacting those statutes are, for the purposes of statutory interpretation,
no longer quite as significant or valuable as they once were.

---

[248] Particularly as s. 19 of the HRA requires that ministers in charge of bills make a statement regarding Convention compatibility (or incompatibility) before second reading.

[249] Consider, for example, the House of Lords' interpretation of s. 11(2) of the Terrorism
Act 2000 in *Attorney-General's Reference (No. 4 of 2002)*, esp. at 314 *per* Lord Bingham
(discussed in Chapter 5).

[250] *R (Wilkinson)* v. *IRC*, 1724 (*per* Lord Hoffmann).

INDEX